ST

TRANSPORT

SC

S

STARS
of
STEAM

Classic Locomotives and their Engineers

Geoffrey Williams

Atlantic

STARS
of
STEAM

Classic Locomotives and their Engineers

Geoffrey Williams

Atlantic

Published by Atlantic Transport Publishers, Trevithick House,
West End, Penryn, Cornwall, TR10 8HE

© Geoffrey Williams 2000

ISBN: 0 906899 84 2

Design and Layout by Barry C. Lane, Sutton-in-Craven
Reproduction and printing by The Amadeus Press
Bradford, West Yorkshire

British Cataloguing in Publication Data
A catalogue record for this book is available from the
British Library

ABBREVIATIONS

ARLE	Association of Railway Locomotive Engineers	LCDR	London Chatham & Dover Railway
BR	British Railways	LMS	London Midland & Scottish Railway
CR	Caledonian Railway	LNER	London & North Eastern Railway
CLC	Cheshire Lines Committee	LNWR	London & North Western Railway
CME	Chief Mechanical Engineer	LSWR	London & South Western Railway
DMU	Diesel multiple unit	LTSR	London Tilbury & Southend Railway
ECML	East Coast Main Line	LYR	Lancashire & Yorkshire Railway
EGR	Edinburgh & Glasgow Railway	Loco. Supt.	Locomotive Superintendent
GSWR	Glasgow & South Western Railway	MBR	Manchester & Birmingham Railway
GCR	Great Central Railway	MGNJR	Midland & Great Northern Joint Railway
GER	Great Eastern Railway	MR	Midland Railway
GNR	Great Northern Railway	MSLR	Manchester Sheffield & Lincolnshire Railway
GtSWR	Great Southern & Western Railway (Ireland)	NBR	North British Railway
GWR	Great Western Railway	NER	North Eastern Railway
HBR	Hull & Barnsley Railway	NLR	North London Railway
HR	Highland Railway	SDJR	Somerset & Dorset Joint Railway
ICE	Institute of Civil Engineers	SECR	South Eastern & Chatham Railway
ILE	Institute of Locomotive Engineers	SER	South Eastern Railway
IME	Institute of Mechanical Engineers	SR	Southern Railway
LBSCR	London Brighton & South Coast Railway	WCML	West Coast Main Line

CONTENTS

To
George Robert and Eva
Thank you for everything

INTRODUCTION

What's in a name? Well, quite a lot actually. Take 'Star', for example. Obviously, the locomotive engineers featured in this book are not of the shining brightly in the night sky variety. On the other hand, not one of these featured locomotive engineers possessed what we today might recognise as being star quality. No, our stars were responsible for some of the finest steam locomotives to run in Britain: they were the stars of their profession. Then again, even that assertion is tempered by the fact that, in the vast majority of cases, their practical detail work towards any specific locomotive design was usually minimal and, very often, non-existent.

So, why are they stars? Ultimately, it is down to human nature. It seems to be something of a human trait to credit, or to hold one person responsible for all manner of things. Thus, we have William the Conqueror putting one over Harold Godwinson, at the Battle of Hastings; never mind the 10,000 or so extras who did all the fighting. In my rock group (very appropriately called Losing Track), I write the words and music, and undertake the arrangements for our original songs. The keyboard player, drummer and bass guitarists then use this as a basis to evolve their parts within the general plan, the singer interprets the words, I add the guitar and there you have it. Only the copyright is G.R. Williams, not Losing Track. With different musicians, the song would have a different interpretation; with another leader, the songs would be something else entirely.

As far as new locomotive designs go, that musical scenario is not entirely dissimilar to the situation on a railway. The board, or possibly the General Manager, tells the locomotive engineer that an improved heavy goods locomotive has been requested by the operating authorities. The engineer consults his production managers — Chief Draughtsman and so forth and, aside from saying it must be an outside 2-cylinder 2-8-0 using as many standard components as possible, leaves the whole shebang to his underlings. A year later, the first engine emerges, and the railway announces that it was designed by Mr. A.B. Sea, the company CME.

Now, Mr. Sea's direct involvement might have been no more than saying, "we need a larger boiler than anything used so far, so go and design one; oh, and don't forget to use a superheater". Or he might approve various design aspects but, most important, he takes full responsibility for the new design. If it works, fine; if not, he might blame Tomkins — the nincompoop in the Drawing Office, but the board will most surely blame the CME. That is one reason why they were paid such vast salaries. On the other hand, new design was only a small, if most visual, part of a CME's job.

All of which brings us to the job title. Locomotive Superintendent; Locomotive Engineer; Locomotive, Carriage & Wagon Engineer; Chief Mechanical Engineer or Chief Mechanical and Electrical Engineer: take your pick. The duties of, say, a Locomotive Superintendent or a CME might be identical, or could be quite different. Some 19th century Locomotive Superintendents, for example, held almost absolute power — and with it ultimate responsibility, for the design, building, maintenance, repair and running of all locomotives, carriages and wagons. Added to that some, such as F.W. Webb, were responsible for all manner of other items, from steel production to soap; Dean, on the GWR, was responsible for the pumping equipment for the Severn Tunnel. On other railways, and the LNER was a prime example, the CME had no responsibility whatsoever for locomotive running. Each position, while superficially similar, could be entirely different.

More than simply engineers, our Stars of Steam — and this includes many of similar rank not featured in this book — were managers of men and resources: often astoundingly vast resources. Webb, once again, was responsible for one of the largest manufactories in Britain, possibly the largest railway works in the world. Collett, in the 1920s, was responsible for the work of about 15,000 men at Swindon alone, and nearly 50,000 throughout the GWR. Read that figure again and put it into a modern perspective: small wonder that he found little time to become involved in the niceties of detail locomotive design and was a stranger in the Drawing Office.

Nowadays, such men (or even women) would obviously have a university degree or two — engineering would, no doubt, be optional. They would have survived the company graduate training scheme, attended numerous management courses and hold a professional qualification — most likely as an accountant, but a lawyer would be a good alternative. Like most things in our modern world, it was not always thus. Almost to a man, our Stars of Steam served either a pupil (premium) or ordinary apprenticeship, usually with a railway, and then did the rounds to gain experience. Many moved to another railway to seek promotion — in more ways than one, Churchward was exceptional. It was a rustic and unsophisticated ladder, but it worked and, as our various Stars of Steam show, worked surprisingly well.

Mind you, there was a time when even that pretty basic training was not obligatory. J. Ramsbottom (LNWR), for example, did not formally train as an engineer. He was not alone. Gooch gained experience in several engineering works throughout Britain, before joining up with Brunel and the GWR. Even then, despite being responsible for the outstanding 'Firefly' class, he not only had to work through the night to keep those earliest GWR engines running the next day, but even had to drive them. This was not usually the case for our Stars of Steam but, then again, no others were a Locomotive Superintendent at the age of 21!

The steam engine took a long time to evolve from a stationary machine to a locomotive. Progress thereafter, not unlike that of the motor car, went in fits and starts, with periods of rapid advancement followed by a decade or more of little development. The Frenchman Denis Papin built the first steam atmospheric engine towards the end of the 17th century and, in 1698, Cornishman Thomas Savery built the first to be commercially viable. This was intended to prevent the flooding of local tin mines and Thomas Newcomen built the first successful atmospheric steam engine, in 1705.

By the second half of the 18th century, British manufacturing industry was making rapid progress towards and was the catalyst behind the world's first industrial revolution. Water was an essential source of power for the new mills where, for the first time, industrial capital — as opposed to merchant capital — was changing not only the economy, but a way of life. Steam power was an attractive alternative to water and wind power, but no more. Then, the advent of the sun and

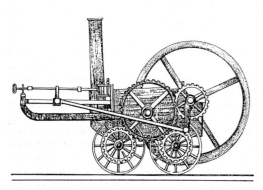

Richard Trevithick's 'Catch Me Who Can' was an almost fairground attempt at attracting public interest towards the newest form of motive power. Almost unbelievably, it had very little impact in promoting the use of the steam locomotive.
(C. Sieniawska)

G. Stephenson's 'Locomotion' was something of a flop insofar as being a working locomotive was concerned, for the fledgling Stockton & Darlington Railway. That did not prevent it being regarded as one of the most important steam engines in the history of world railways though.
(C. Sieniawska)

planet gears, probably developed by William Murdoch, in 1871, allowed James Watt — backed by Matthew Boulton, to further advance the new fangled engines. Suddenly, driven rotary motion was possible, offering who knew what opportunities.

In 1884, Murdoch built the first moving steam locomotive, albeit a model, and while Watt still favoured its use only as a stationary power source, another Cornishman broke a most important barrier. In 1804, Richard Trevithick built the world's first full-size working steam locomotive, for the Penydarren Iron Works. Even this was not his first locomotive to run, but it was the first to do so commercially. However, at 4 tons, it was too heavy for the rails and, despite obvious interest — which included the 'Catch Me Who Can' exhibition in London, progress almost stopped dead in its tracks.

Cue the move to the opposite end of the country. To County Durham, in fact, and the dark, dank and harsh unyielding coal fields. During the second and third decades of the 19th century, the north-east mines were the forcing ground for a completely new form of world transport: the equivalent to NASA in the 1960s, or the Thames Valley to Grand Prix racing today. Despite an aborted attempt by John Blenkinsop and Matthew Murray to run the latter's Middleton Colliery Railway with cog-wheeled locomotives which, nevertheless, were the first to run commercially, it was to Durham that the advance-

ment of the steam locomotive shifted — emphatically.

George Stephenson, the man of legend, myth and even the odd reliable fact, had his first engine, 'Blucher', up and running by 1814 — not terribly well, admittedly, but it was a start. The same year saw William Hedley working with Timothy Hackworth — effectively the first Locomotive Superintendent of the Stockton and Darlington Railway — to build three locomotives: 'Puffing Billy' and 'Wylam Dilly' have both survived to this day. Jonathon Forster was also involved with Hackworth and, in the 1820s, he linked up with John Rastrick to build the locomotive 'Agenoria', also preserved, and the first locomotive to run in America.

Between the Stockton and Darlington Railway opening in 1825, mostly using horse power, and the Liverpool and Manchester Railway, only five years later, Robert Stephenson — the great man's inventive offspring — had returned to England from South America and was beginning to make waves.. His 'Planet' engine, of 1830, was the first with inside cylinders and, while such locomotives were still crude machines, the second wave of engineers was coming through by 1840. Edward Bury, Thomas Crampton, Charles Beyer, Robert Hawthorn and many others, of which Gooch was one, were to carry the advance of the steam locomotive to the point where it became relatively reliable, could exceed speeds of 50 mph and was the catalyst for the building of many new

It all went wrong for Hackworth at the Rainhill Trials. Minor mechanical problems, followed by infringements of the regulations and, finally, cylinder failure ensured that 'Sans Pareil' was anything but the expected match for Stephenson's engine. *(C. Sieniawska)*

One of the most famous steam engines of all times. The performance of 'Rocket' at the Rainhill Trials secured the future of the steam engine, ensured that both George and Robert Stephenson would play a major role in the development of Britain's railways, and gained itself an indelible place in the history of the world. Do you know any adult who has not heard of this engine? *(C. Sieniawska)*

railways. By 1850, the rout of the roads was complete and the crushing of the canals well in hand.

At which point, our first Stars of Steam make their appearance in the world of railways. Gooch dazzled very brightly indeed, while Adams, Stirling and Ramsbottom were each to gain their first senior position. Steam engine design was never an exact science, but even by then Gooch was ensuring that different manufacturers all followed his requirements to the letter. Yes, there was still a very long way to go, but as the pioneers gave way to the first professionals, so the lines of future development were clearly laid out.

Quite naturally, Locomotive Superintendents were merely railway company employees — servants, but damned important ones. Without the successful organisation of their increasingly vast departments, there were no locomotives, carriages or wagons to earn revenue. In any case, passengers care little for the civil engineering, still less for booking offices and the like. As for the locomotives, well, even hardened commuters occasionally glanced at what was hauling their daily trains. No wonder then that the designer, or the man responsible for such work, seemed to be very important: to the enthusiast, he may well become a god-like figure.

Our Stars of Steam were most certainly not gods, but talented and lucky mortals. The wages they received were occasionally staggering — there is nothing new with very fat

cats in industry. Perhaps what is most surprising of all, is that they nearly all led relatively ordinary, even apparently dull, orthodox and mundane lives. Of course, they enjoyed successful careers, while some made the odd useful invention, but none of them did anything of particular note or notoriety outside their main career, such as mountaineering, anything sporting or even something of an artistic nature. True, Gooch became a wealthy businessman and successfully bridged the gap between bourgeoisie and Establishment, but he was the exception. That, more than anything, shows that these were very ordinary men.

Still, this book is aimed at celebrating the work of the chosen Stars of Steam, not to denigrate or criticise them: they, after all, did it, we can only read about their work. While most of our Stars were not generally flamboyant characters, and still less did most lead particularly varied lives, the results of their professional work demands our attention and recognition. Of course, it is their locomotive designs that are really the attraction, and all of our Stars of Steam, plus many others not featured here, have produced outstanding examples. It is these that dominate each chapter and which really made their reputations, so enjoy them in their multitudinous forms. They and their like will never be seen again in the ever-more competitive, increasingly standardised world in which we live.

DANIEL GOOCH
The First Star of Steam

Though not quite a rags to riches story — for the Gooch family was hardly poor, the latter part is most certainly true. No other British locomotive engineer attained the heady cocktail of industrial power, political influence and establishment honours achieved and bestowed on Daniel Gooch. Of more relevance was the widespread respect in which he was held during his life and, even today, he is one of the few steam locomotive engineers whose name is still recognised by the world at large.

Active sportsmen, like railway enthusiasts, can often be somewhat obsessive about their favourite pastime, occasionally to the exclusion of all else: not all anoraks stand on platform ends! Recently, after a hockey match, I asked several players which Stars of Steam they recognised. For any steam enthusiast who thinks railways the be-all and end-all of life, the results would be just a little disappointing. Gresley, Stanier, Churchward, who are they? Stirling? A town in Scotland, surely, and so on. Of course, everyone knew of Stephenson and Trevithick, but only Gooch of the company Locomotive Superintendents gained even the barest recognition. As a sadistic act of revenge though, apart from the Olympian Sean Kerly, how many hockey players can you name?

If a person makes his mark in a new field at an early stage of development, as did W.O. Bentley — whose cars won five Le Mans 24 hours' races, one's reputation is more likely to be remembered, even venerated. Gooch was not one of the first steam locomotive designers, but his engines were hauling the world's fastest train service before he reached his 30th birthday. Indeed, at that time, and for a decade afterwards, nothing else even approached the magnificent daily work his engines performed.

That, by itself, would not necessarily gain Gooch such an exalted position in railway history though. There was another important factor: one of a decisive nature. Most people know of the engineering genius called Isambard Kingdom Brunel; a name once heard, surely never forgotten. Among many outstanding successes, and a fair sprinkling of disasters, Brunel was responsible for the GWR's first and finest main lines. Brunel built the railway, Gooch provided the engines: a civil and mechanical engineering partnership without parallel in Britain. When GWR trains ran at over 60 mph on the superbly aligned road from London-Bristol, and averaged 50 mph to Swindon — while all other railways stuttered along at little more than half those speeds, is there any wonder that Gooch and Brunel hit the headlines? Theirs was one of the wonders of the world. After all, little more than a decade before, 'Rocket' had barely touched 30 mph at the Rainhill Trials.

There is also another important factor in all this. Whereas the northern railways used Stephenson's gauge of 4 ft. 8½ in. — the standard gauge, Brunel had much grander ideas. He opted for a gauge of 7 ft. 0¼ in. — the Broad Gauge, and this helped Gooch immensely. Soon Gooch was building locomotives with a capacity far greater than anything running on the standard gauge railways. His 'Iron Duke' class, for example, had a 4 ft. 9 in. diameter boiler — not equalled by the standard gauge for nearly 50 years; a huge grate of 25 sq. ft.; and a combined heating surface of almost 2,000 sq. ft. — about the size of Stanier's 'Black 5s'. Little wonder that they were the fastest express engines in the world; they were massive.

By the late-1840s, as much of Europe plunged into popular uprising and the railway mania climaxed and then exploded at home, GWR expresses dashed from London-Bristol along the world's finest main line, hauled by the fastest, most powerful engines. Brunel's Broad Gauge might have appeared an outcast, after the Gauges Commission ruled that new lines had to be built to the standard gauge, but it still continued to venture ever-outwards. From London, the Broad Gauge reached Wolverhampton, Cheltenham, Neyland, Weymouth, Falmouth and finally, in 1867, Penzance. By that time, however, the Broad Gauge was on the retreat, the GWR had reached its nadir, Brunel was dead, and Gooch was no longer the Locomotive Superintendent. Instead, he was the company's Chairman and, reluctantly accepting that the glorious Broad Gauge was done for, set about restoring the once-proud world leader back to its allotted pedestal.

That, though was some way off from Gooch's more humble beginnings in the Northumberland village of Bedlington. His father was a cashier at the local ironworks, and G. Stephenson and Joseph Locke were both occasional visitors to the Gooch household. Needless to say, their occasional presence did not pass unnoticed, and their influence was considerable. Gooch's elder brother, John Viret, went on to become the Locomotive Superintendent of the LSWR and later the Eastern Counties Railway; Thomas Longridge became a renown railway civil engineer; and younger brother William Frederick was appointed Swindon Works Manager, under Daniel. All right, so there was a bit of nepotism here and there, but these achievements by a generation of a single family are quite phenomenal.

Young Daniel was educated at the village school — remember, there was no state education at that time — and started work at the Tredegar Iron Works in Monmouthshire, following Dad's footsteps. Within two years, his father had died and the family uprooted. Gooch spent the next 3½ years gaining a broad engineering experience and honing his capacity for hard work. Thus, he tried his hand at R. Stephenson's Vulcan Foundry, in Newton le Willows, before assisting his brother, T.L., surveying the London and Birmingham Rly. In 1835, he spent a year working on marine engines at the Dundee Foundry Co., that belonged to an uncle of P. Stirling, and then moved to Newcastle, and back to R. Stephenson & Co. again. Within a few months, Gooch was involved in an unsuccessful engine-building venture with Robert Hawks, in Gateshead. Then, kicking his heels while again helping brother T.L., this time on the Manchester and Leeds Rly. in mid-1837, he had the temerity to write to Brunel regarding the position of locomotive engineer on the GWR.

Can you imagine that happening today? Of course, Gooch had some modest experience in steam locomotive design and building, but he was no sort of expert. Fortune certainly favoured the brave, or naive, and Brunel travelled north to see Gooch, recognised his great potential and promptly appointed him at fully £300 p.a. Gooch was not even 21 years old.

At that time, the London-Bristol line was still under construction, but the sheer potential of the Broad Gauge certainly appealed to Gooch. Brunel had already ordered about 20 steam locomotives from several builders who, by and large, had been given the barest of guidelines and allowed the luxury of doing the rest. When these weird and wonderful contraptions began to arrive, and not work, Gooch realised that he might have bitten off a bit more than he could expect to chew. Fortunately, as the railway was not due to begin operating from London-Maidenhead until June 1838, Gooch had a vital breathing-space to not only to organise the building of engine houses at both these places but, somehow, to prepare Brunel's engines for service.

Whatever Brunel's many engineering abilities, steam locomotives were clearly not his forte. The most adventurous of these engines that, much to Gooch's dismay, continued to arrive over the next year, was an articulated affair with a 10 ft. — yes, ten feet diameter — driving wheel. Incredibly, this was part of a 2-2-2 leading truck, with the boiler mounted on an 0-6-0 trailing chassis. Gooch was not entirely surprised when he found such contraptions could hardly move themselves, let alone propel a train. It was an awkward situation: Gooch was responsible to Brunel and this period was not exactly one of unbridled harmony between them. The youngster was hardly living in awe of the maestro.

Among our Stars of Steam, Gooch is unique in having an abridged version of his diaries published ('Sir Daniel Gooch: Memoirs and Diary' ed. R.B. Wilson) that records the main events of his life. Gooch notes his feelings and criticisms of Brunel, although he undoubtedly held him in the highest respect. The watershed in their relationship came soon after the London-Maidenhead service had begun in 1838. Only 6 of Brunel's 19 engines were able to run to any effective extent and, were it not for a 2-2-2 locomotive named 'North Star', offered by R. Stephenson & Co. — part of a cancelled order by the New Orleans Rly., disaster would have struck. The two men were called before the board to explain the dire situation, and Gooch bravely spoke out and, effectively, criticised his, even then, illustrious boss. At least this gave Gooch greater autonomy in locomotive matters, and the hatchet was soon buried.

So, Gooch was left to get on and run the train service with plainly inadequate locomotives. Day and night, his life was devoted to getting the engines in service for the next day. 'North Star' was the mainstay of the locomotive flotilla — one could hardly call it a fleet — and even this had its not irregular failures. Soon, it was joined by a sister engine. 'Morning Star' had 6 ft. 6 in. driving wheels and Gooch claimed a hand in the design of both these locomotives, from his brief time at Stephenson's. This may, or may not be true, for the engines Gooch was involved with were sent to Russia. Still, it seems that the two 'Stars' might have been similar to the earlier engines. Authorisation was given for the purchase of a further ten 'Stars' and, although Gooch still had much work to do in keeping the show on the road, the GWR was assuredly in business.

The service was extended to Twyford by mid-1839 and,

Whatever doubts about the extent to which the 'Star' class were really Gooch engines, there is no question about the provenance of the 'Fireflys'. This picture of 'Argus' shows how brightly the haystack-type firebox was polished, as it is nearly invisible, while the iron coffin — a rather uncomfortable perch for the unlucky incumbent — is at the back of the tender. The complete absence of weather protection was the norm for engine crews, and they regarded the later introduction of cabs as being somewhat effeminate. *(NRM)*

given due notice of Gooch's locomotive predicament, the board instructed that he design and purchase some suitable locomotives. Not un-surprisingly, Gooch opted for something very similar to the 'Stars', the most obvious difference being an enlarged haystack firebox. Thus, many soon-to-be-familiar Broad Gauge features took their bow on Gooch's first design, such as outside sandwich frames — with a thick layer of oak as the meat, a domeless boiler clothed in highly polished wood, and inside cylinders. Gooch also took several precautions to ensure that the ensuing 'Fireflys' were not going to bring the GWR to its knees. Copies of the drawings and templates were sent to the seven manufacturers, to ensure standards were maintained: no chances were taken this time. Finally, and very sensibly, he insisted on a 1,000 mile operational guarantee from all the builders. There was to be no repeat of Brunel's nigh-disaster.

Gooch had appointed T.R. Crampton as Chief Draughtsman by that time, and he probably undertook most of the detail work for the new design. That should not detract from Gooch though: it was the same with all our Stars of Steam. All 62 'Fireflys' were built in only two years — the first large-scale production class of steam locomotive, and they soon showed their prowess. The GWR reached Reading by 1840, and the route was opened to Bristol by mid-1841. The 'Stars' were regarded as the main express locomotives, but the 'Fireflys' were every bit their equal. These two classes worked east of the junction with the Cheltenham branch, where engines were changed; a pretty nondescript place near Swindon.

Naturally, speeds were modest by modern standards, but were sensational for the time. In the Gauge Trials of 1845/6, the 'Firefly' locomotive 'Ixion' exceeded 60 mph and was able to run from London-Didcot, hauling 71 tons, at almost 55 mph. This was far superior to anything on the standard gauge, while the reliability of the new engines was without equal in the country.

Gooch's responsibilities widened as the GWR grew, and new engine sheds, and carriage and wagon stock all fell on him. Most important of all, the GWR decided to have its own locomotive building and repair facilities, and Brunel and

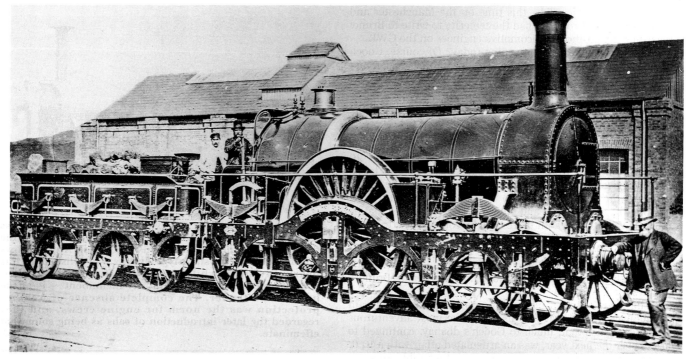

Pride of the line and of Britain's railways. 'Great Britain' belonged the 'Iron Duke' class, the most powerful and fastest express passenger engines in the world. It was built in 1847 and not withdrawn until 1880. This was probably the first really great class of steam engines, and their daily performances, regularly running at average speeds up to 60 mph, were not bettered for nearly 50 years. A spectacle plate is a small measure of protection for the otherwise exposed crew. *(NRM)*

Gooch chose a suitable site at Swindon, in 1840. Within three years the works was open, with over 400 employees — this multiplying to over 1,800 within 5 years, and Gooch's assistant, A. Sturrock — later Locomotive Superintendent of the GNR — become the first Works Manager.

In the meantime, Gooch had driven the first Royal Train, a task he was to undertake regularly for many years, while producing an intermediate passenger and two goods designs. These were all built to the same exacting requirements as the 'Fireflys', and proved to be equally successful in their own spheres. The 'Sun' class was, in effect, a smaller 'Firefly', being designed for the Swindon-Bristol line and other branch lines. One engine, 'Hesperus', was fitted with return boiler tubes. These endowed it with a greater heating surface that improved its economy and performance, but as it remained a singleton, one might assume that other difficulties and costs were encountered. Within a few years, the poor adhesion of the 'Sun' class resulted in many engines being rebuilt as saddle tanks, in which form the last was not withdrawn until 1879.

Gooch produced the 'Leo' class, a 2-4-0 version of the 'Sun' class, for goods trains: these were also rebuilt as saddle tanks. Then in 1842, four 0-6-0 goods engines were ordered for comparative purposes; the appropriately named 'Hercules' class being effectively 'Fireflys' above the frames, matched with 5 ft. wheels from the 'Leos'. Thus, four of the five main engine classes that ran all GWR services until after the Gauge Trials, shared many common components and design features: an unprecedented level of standardisation not seen again until Churchward got to work.

In 1844, the Bristol and Exeter Railway opened throughout and Gooch drove the first train from London-Exeter, 194 miles in only 5 hours, and then returned in 4 hours 40 mins. At a stroke, a journey time that took days by stage coach, was slashed. That Gooch drove this train, plus the Royal Trains, shows how far his duties extended beyond that of simply providing locomotives and rolling stock for the railway. He then advocated an express service between the two cities to run in only 4½ hours, and thereafter claimed to be the father of the express train.

Despite his admiration for Brunel, even Gooch could not hide the utter disbelief with which he greeted the former's Atmospheric propulsion scheme for the South Devon Railway, beyond Exeter. Not in the least surprised at its failure, Gooch did not gloat, but simply got on with providing locomotives to work the line, just as he privately expected in the first place.

Despite all this success, Gooch was not yet 30 years old. He was constantly trying new ideas to effect improvements. A corrugated firebox was fitted to two engines, without any obvious benefit but, in 1843, he introduced his stationary-link valve gear — probably designed in conjunction with J.V. Gooch. This allowed the use of expansive steam, which enhanced economy and was used on GWR locomotives until the end of Gooch's reign. Not surprisingly, Stephenson's link-motion — that came out a few months beforehand, was widely used on standard gauge railways and became a British standard. But Gooch's valve gear found widespread use in Europe, possibly following Crampton's success with his Patent engines.

The Gauge Trials kept Gooch fully occupied during the mid-1840s, and in 1846 Swindon Works built its first complete engine, the 'Great Western': initiation to completion in only 13 weeks. This was a much enlarged design, though visually similar to the 'Fireflys'. If the latter class was far too good for the standard gauge contenders, 'Great Western' simply trounced them. Gooch had already built the first-ever dynamometer car and was soon actively involved in taking indicator diagrams, perched quite unprotected on the front of the locomotives, to scientifically demonstrate their prowess.

'Great Western' was put to task, and in May 1846 hauled 150 tons from Didcot-London at 55 mph, and then a train of 60 tons, over the same route, at an astonishing 67 mph average speed. These magnificent performances were not trumpeted to a world somewhat sceptical of speed at the time, but a round-trip to Exeter — out in 3 hrs. 28 mins. and back in 3 hrs. 31 mins — fairly astounded a wary public. Soon though, the engine itself ran into problems.

The weight of the locomotive broke the leading axle and 'Great Western' was rebuilt as a 4-2-2, the two leading axles being mounted rigidly in the frames. As such, it became a forerunner of the great 'Iron Duke' class that achieved immortality as being the finest passenger engines in the world and, as rebuilt or renewed, ran the principal Broad Gauge expresses until its demise in 1892.

Thanks to Gooch's work, after 'Great Western' had made her outstanding runs, the GWR was able to schedule its fastest trains to Bristol in 2½ hours and Exeter in 4 hrs. 25 mins. These West Country expresses soon became the sole domain of the renown 'Iron Duke' class. Although similar to the 'Great Western', the 'Iron Dukes' had a raised round-top firebox, with a mid-feather to increase the heating surface area: this also gave additional strengthening. They were by far and away the most powerful engines of their day, hauling expresses to Bristol and Wolverhampton until withdrawn, in the 1880s. So good was the basic design, that their replacements were virtually, identical, and worked as far west as Newton Abbot.

The 'Iron Dukes' were magnificent and distinctive engines, probably the first truly great steam locomotive design. One could hardly call them elegant, bereft of any weather protection — and they looked somewhat better when renewed with a modest cab, but there is no doubt, they were the kings of the road. In 1848, 'Great Britain' ran from London-Didcot at an average speed of 67 mph, hauling over 80 tons, while even service trains were habitually covering that journey at speeds of almost 60 mph. These were phenomenal performances, the more so considering the rolling resistance of the coaches. Let's face it, such spirited running was hardly the norm even in the heyday of British steam. There is no doubt that while the GWR owed Brunel dearly for his outstanding main lines, it was

solely thanks to Gooch that their potential was exploited far beyond the capacity of any other British railway.

So began Gooch's second phase of locomotive design. From 1846-52, three successive classes of goods engine were built at Swindon. The 'Premier' class was Gooch's last design with a Coppernob-type firebox, and the 'Pyracmon' and 'Caesar' classes were essentially improvements on the 'Premiers'. While all were withdrawn in the 1870s, they served the GWR well during its most difficult years.

Gooch's last goods design emerged after the 'Caesar' class was complete: the 'Standard Goods' or 'Ariadne' class. Over the next ten years, 102 of these powerful 0-6-0s were built, the first 66 using the 'Waverley' class boiler, with later engines receiving further modest improvements. Like many locomotive engineers, Gooch considered the boiler the heart of a steam engine and lavished great care on its design. He was a big boiler man, just like Ivatt, Gresley, Stanier and Bulleid of our Stars of Steam. The 'Standard Goods' saw out the Broad Gauge itself, and the locomotive 'Europe' hauled the final Broad Gauge goods train, from Plymouth-Swindon on the 21st May 1892. After that train passed, the lines were converted to standard gauge.

As the GWR expanded, so there was a need for still more locomotives and the 'Prince' class 2-2-2 was designed to work non-express passenger trains. This differed to Gooch's earlier designs by having inside frames, but shared many other common components. They worked in the West Midlands, and were later relegated to various branches all round the system.

All was not well in the West Country though, for while the BER used its own locomotives from 1849, the SDR needed something with a bit of oomph to overcome the notorious

---

Gooch's standard goods, the 'Ariadne' class, became numerically the largest on the Broad Gauge. These were very competent engines, typical Gooch in all respects: well engineered, reliable and entirely satisfactory for all their required duties. 'Liffey' was built in 1857, but only had a short life, being scrapped in 1872 as the Broad gauge began to be cut back.   (NRM)

banks between Newton Abbot and Plymouth. Gooch produced two 4-4-0STs of the 'Corsair' class, having a leading bogie. This was a genuine bogie — unlike the fixed axles of the 'Iron Duke' class, but that was not the only innovation. With inside frames that only extended to the leading coupled wheels, the boiler was a load-bearing component. This arrangement is not unlike that of a traction engine and bears comparison with the engine being a stressed-member of a racing car: something considered revolutionary in the 1960s, but over 100 years behind Gooch.

While these were quite successful locomotives, 'Corsair' itself had a distinctly novel form of braking. Gooch only fitted brakes to a locomotive's tender, but for 'Corsair' he evolved something quite uncharacteristically bad: sledge brakes. These comprised levers that were forced down onto the rails in front of the driving wheels and, not surprisingly, it did not take long before major problems were encountered. For a start, they did little for the rail surface, while they also jacked-up the engine off the rails! If applied at points and junctions, the chances of the engine staying on the rails was not high: an unorthodox way of bringing a train to a halt. It was an experiment that was, not surprisingly, quickly terminated. Once the SDR had its own locomotives the 'Corsair' class was moved on, though some survived until the end of the Broad Gauge.

The mid-1850s saw another frenzy of design activity for Gooch. He produced the 'Banbury' class, for banking; the 'Victoria' class 2-4-0s, for secondary duties — although they often worked expresses to Weymouth; and the 'Waverley' class 4-4-0s, with two leading axles just like the 'Iron Dukes'. All three designs had inside sandwich frames. The 'Waverleys' were intended to work the South Wales expresses west of Swindon, via Gloucester, but were not entirely successful and eventually found their niche on heavy expresses elsewhere.

This period also saw the GWR amalgamate with several standard gauge railways within, or bordering, its northern division. Facts had to be faced and, in the long-term, the Broad Gauge was doomed. Gooch, a passionate adherent of the grand system at the Gauge Trials, simply had to get on and design suitable standard gauge locomotives. Various types emerged, including passenger 2-2-2s, goods 0-6-0s and mixed-traffic and passenger 2-4-0s. Many of these were built by outside manufacturers and, once again, plans and templates were provided to ensure standards were maintained, while they shared common components whenever possible.

More standard gauge designs emerged in the early 1860s, though by that time they bore some design traits of Joseph Armstrong, in charge at the Wolverhampton Works. Then, in 1862, Gooch produced his final Broad Gauge design, a rather unsuccessful 2-4-0T with outside cylinders and a well tank for London's new underground lines. These were the first steam engines to be fitted with condensing apparatus, but the arrangement with the Metropolitan Railway did not last and some were rebuilt with tenders. The class as a whole was the shortest-lived of all Gooch's designs.

As a locomotive engineer then, Gooch more than had his moments, but the running of the GWR had deteriorated along with its finances throughout the 1850s. What had once been the world's leading railway for speed, had been toppled off its pinnacle and was even sliding down the national ladder. The standard gauge companies, meanwhile, had advanced and, though GWR services were not entirely overhauled until the 1870s, the pioneering and glorious days of Brunel and Gooch seemed far behind it.

Gooch finally resigned in 1864, a few years after Brunel died. His interests had begun to diversify during the 1850s, first by becoming an active and enthusiastic Freemason in 1850, and then getting heavily involved in other commercial ventures, including buying into coal mines. In 1859, Gooch bought Clewer Park, at Windsor, the final — and essential — step to entering the ranks of the gentry. By that time, his private income somewhat dwarfed his not inconsiderable GWR salary of £1,500 p.a.

The GWR had its fine infrastructure and locomotives but, it could be considered, had contrived to squander these advantages during the 1860s, when Gooch found himself increasingly out of step with the much-changed board. He was involved with the laying of the first trans-Atlantic telegraph cable, using Brunel's ship the 'Great Eastern'. This was not immediately successful but, in 1865, he was elected MP for Cricklade, Swindon's constituency. Then, on his return from the failed cable-laying voyage, Gooch was requested to become the Chairman of the stricken and divided GWR: what a turn round. He accepted, and the march towards financial health was soon underway.

The following two years saw Gooch reach his greatest personal heights. In 1866, he was aboard the 'Great Eastern' as it laid the first working trans-Atlantic telegraph cable, and then succeeded in recovering and completing the cable lost from the year before. For his role at the heart of this, Gooch was created Baronet of Clewer, while the following year he became a Deputy Lord Lieutenant of Berkshire. He had successfully made the transition from new rich bourgeoisie to the Establishment, a feat desired by many, yet achieved by few.

Thereafter, Gooch's interests ranged far and wide. He was directly involved in the laying of another trans-Atlantic telegraph cable in 1873, again using the 'Great Eastern', and he continued to work in other business spheres. As far as being a Star of Steam is concerned, his locomotive work was long-since over, but not his duties as Chairman of the GWR. Undoubtedly, Gooch was a locomotive engineer of rare adventurous talent, while he excelled at organisation, both of the GWR locomotive department and laying the telegraph cables, but as Chairman he demonstrated his strict and exacting fiscal prowess.

The GWR had been bleeding to death financially until, by the mid-1860s, it could no longer meet its liabilities. Gooch virtually halted all unnecessary expenditure on the path to restoring financial stability and health. Never again did the company face disaster, but there was to be no transformation of services. Eventually, he approved a modest degree of capital expenditure, while cash instead of stock dividends were restored and the GWR became a steady above-average payer. The Severn Tunnel was finally authorised, at great subsequent and unforeseen cost and, quite fittingly, the 68 year old Gooch was the first man to crawl through the hole that linked both tunnel bores, in 1884. The following year, he was on board the first special train to go through: in earlier years he would, no doubt, have driven it.

These are only some of the many achievements and honours bestowed on this initially unprepossessing Northumbrian. No wonder his name is so widely known when other, perhaps more deserving, Stars of Steam are a mystery to the non-specialist. Gooch produced the world's finest engines of his day, and then provided a means to test their performances. There must have been some innovative sparks flying when Gooch and Brunel got together, particularly in the 1840s. Unlike most Stars of Steam, Gooch was far more than just an engineer. Of course, he undertook the usual civic duties, such as being a magistrate, but he rather hated the social whirl in which Brunel thrived. Yet, he was fully accepted into the Establishment's fold.

As Chairman of the GWR, Gooch was no mere figurehead either. An inspired choice, he was a highly respected leader and it was thanks to his insistence on financial probity that the company recovered from its deepening low. Gooch was not always a thoughtful and easy man to work with, though by no means so opinionated and self-certain as Brunel, but few really successful people are. Toes have to be trodden on and tough decisions made if one is to progress. His family and its future welfare was of great importance to him, and the GWR formed part of that extended family. It certainly benefited in the long term, and the impetus and financial clout later allowed the Great Way Round to become God's Wonderful Railway. Subsequent Stars of Steam — Dean, Churchward and Collett — were able to effect their improvements to the locomotive stock due to the strengthened financial position, to say nothing of the legacy of Gooch's Swindon Works.

Gooch, then, took the basic Stephenson locomotive formula and enlarged, developed and embellished it with some original ideas to produce the finest locomotives of his day. He was able to go still further for another decade, but then the impetus ran out. Of course, he was caught and then surpassed, though his attention and energies had been diverted elsewhere. Even so, Gooch is undoubtedly a Star of Steam of the highest order. Then he moved on to be a great success in other fields and to finally return and rejuvenate the ailing giant: his beloved GWR That might just have been his greatest achievement: Northumbrian lad to Baronet notwithstanding.

GOOCH IN BRIEF

BORN:	24th August 1816, Bedlington, Northumb.
EMPLOYED:	1831, Tredegar Iron Works.
	1834, Vulcan Foundry, Newton le Willows.
	1835, Dundee Foundry Co.
	1836, Robert Stephenson & Co., Newcastle.
	1836, Robert Hawks, Gateshead.
SENIOR POSITIONS:	1837-64, Locomotive Superintendent GWR.
	1865-89, Chairman GWR.
	1867-89, Chairman, Telegraph Construction and Maintenance Co.
HONOURS:	1865-85, Conservative MP for Cricklade.
	1866, Baronet of Clewer.
	1867, Deputy Lord Lieutenant of Berkshire.
	JP in Berkshire.
DIED:	24th August 1889, Clewer Park, Berks.

Gooch's Locomotive Designs

YEAR	CLASS	WHEEL ARRANGEMENT	CYLINDERS (INCHES)	BOILER PRESSURE	DRIVING-WHEEL DIAMETER	WEIGHT	No. IN CLASS
1837	Star	2-2-2	16 x 16	60 psi	7 ft.	23 tons	12
1840	Firefly	2-2-2	15 x 18	50 psi	7 ft.	24¼ tons	62
1840	Sun	2-2-2	14 x 18	50 psi	6 ft.		21
1841	Leo	2-4-0	15 x 18	50 psi	5 ft.		18
1842	Hercules	0-6-0	15 x 18	50 psi	5 ft.		4
1946	Premier	0-6-0	16 x 24	80 psi	5 ft.	28 tons	12
1846	Gt. Western	2-2-2	18 x 24	100 psi	8 ft.	29 tons	1
1846	Prince	2-2-2	16 x 24	80 psi	7 ft.	26 tons	6
1847	Iron Duke	4-2-2	18 x 24	100 psi	8 ft.	38T 5 cwt	29
1847	Pyracmon	0-6-0	16 x 24	80 psi	5 ft.	27¼ tons	6
1849	Bacchus	0-6-0	16 x 24	80 psi	5 ft.		1
1849	Corsair	4-4-0ST	17 x 24	100 psi	5' 9"/6 ft.	35T 15 cwt	15
1851	Caesar	0-6-0	17 x 24	100 psi	5 ft.	32T 10 cwt	8
1852	Ariadne	0-6-0	17 x 24	120 psi	5 ft.	31 tons	102
1852	Banbury	0-6-0ST	17 x 24	120 psi	5 ft.	38 tons	4
1855	Waverley	4-4-0	17 x 24	120 psi	7 ft.	36½ tons	100
1856	Victoria	2-4-0	16 x 24	120 psi	6' 6"	30 tons	18
1862	Metro Tank	2-4-0T	(o)16 x 24	120 psi	6 ft.		22

Standard Gauge

YEAR	CLASS	WHEEL ARRANGEMENT	CYLINDERS (INCHES)	BOILER PRESSURE	DRIVING-WHEEL DIAMETER	WEIGHT	No. IN CLASS
1855	69 class	2-2-2	15½ x 22	120 psi	6' 6"	30¼ tons	8
1855	57	0-6-0	15½ x 22	120 psi	5 ft.	31 tons	12
1857	77	0-6-0	16 x 24	140 psi	5 ft.	27T 10 cwt	12
1860	93/94	0-6-0T	15 x 22		4' 2"	27T 10 cwt	2
1862	157	2-2-2	16 x 24	130 psi	7 ft.	29T 10 cwt	10
1862	Chancellor	2-4-0	16 x 24	130 psi	6' 6"	31 tons	8

GOOCH'S PRESERVED LOCOMOTIVES

YEAR	CLASS	NAME	TOTAL
1837	Star	North Star	1 *
1847	Iron Duke	Iron Duke	1 *

* Both of these are replicas

GEORGE JACKSON CHURCHWARD
God's Wonderful Railway's Anointed Son

It was easy for Muhammed Ali, the boxer. Even before he first became World Champion he declared, "I am The Greatest" and, to be frank, there were not too many who dared argue the point with him. Ali, of course, did not simply mean that he was the greatest heavyweight at the time and, by obvious implication the best boxer in the world, but that he was the greatest of all time.

Old stagers shook their heads in disbelief. Johnson would have out-danced Ali, Dempsey cut him in half, Louis out-foxed him and, why, one blow from Marciano would have Ali seeing more stars than any astronaut. Surely, the many sceptics thought, even reigning champion Liston would batter the young big-mouth into submission. Those who were a little less biased and could put down their rose-tinted spectacles, had an inkling that Ali, or Clay as he then was, might upset more than a few apple-carts. In time, Ali's achievements totally eclipsed those of any other boxer — the most gruelling of sports, and all and sundry soon agreed that he was indeed The Greatest.

Ali had it easy, being the first sporting showman with instant world-wide recognition. As his publicity machine whirled into frenzied life, few people thought he was anything other than The Greatest: the doubting-Thomas's became either new Ali evangelists, or remained isolated voices of dissent. In many other areas on life's great canvas, such matters are nowhere near so clear-cut and, far from declaring a person as the greatest of all time, it is safer to say that so-and-so was the greatest of his era. Even that notion has its draw-backs.

Many readers may consider Einstein the greatest mathematician this century, at least; perhaps the greatest physicist was none other than Newton, though how either would have fared in the minutiae of modern research is anybody's guess. Most cricket fans consider Bradman the greatest batsman of all, but he rarely faced an un-ending onslaught of lightning-fast, short-pitched bowling; and how about Churchill as our greatest 20th century Prime Minister? Surely you don't think Thatcher his equal, do you? Then, was Lindberg the greatest aviator, or Mortimer Wheeler the greatest archaeologist? We could go on forever with such matters and, unlike Ali with his universal publicity machine, these would all be simply matters for debate, and not conclusions.

Ultimately, so it is with steam locomotive engineers. None of our Stars of Steam was really a self-publicist, at least so far as the wider public were concerned, and while all the above-mentioned people achieved truly great deeds, it was these, rather than the publicity, that drove them forward.

So, who was the greatest British steam locomotive engineer? For most people interested in railways, Churchward was the foremost GWR locomotive engineer of the 20th century. For many, he was the greatest GWR engineer of all, while some consider him the best British engineer this

century. A somewhat smaller number — one assumes — almost worship Churchward as the best British steam locomotive engineer, and fewer still — who view the world through dark green, copper-rimmed spectacles — the greatest steam locomotive engineer of all time. Is any, or all of this really true and, if so, does it really matter in a world for which the steam locomotive is a long-since eclipsed form of motive power?

As with all things, most people who know anything about the subject hold an opinion. Steam locomotive engineers were a rather conservative, narrow-minded and inward-looking bunch, as are many engineers in general, and probably never considered themselves to be in direct competition with those of other railways. For a Locomotive Superintendent, it might be personally and professionally pleasing if one's engines were regarded as superior to those on another railway, but it was not the aim to design the best engine in its class every time a new proposal was mapped out. Few Stars of Steam were lucky enough to be given an open budget to simply build the best engine possible, even in its class. They were all servants of intended profit-making businesses.

Yet, human nature being what it is, we can never resist a pop at trying to establish just who was the greatest of all time, however irrelevant. Churchward has many supporters, yet it would be hard to formulate a consensus of the criteria by which a locomotive engineer should be judged, let alone agree a final pecking-order. For a start, can an engineer be considered as a great if he did not patent one single important invention of his own? Churchward didn't. Then again, Chapelon, often regarded as the greatest of all steam locomotive engineers, did not even have a single design wholly to his name. Like the maddest of dogs, we could easily end up chasing our own tails: all we can do is assess Churchward's stature in his own time.

A surprising number of authors have come out boldly and stated that Churchward was, at least, the greatest British steam locomotive engineer. If that is the case, one might well query just how far his influence went beyond our shores: certainly to nothing like the extent of Bury, Crampton, Ramsbottom, Beyer and W. Adams, to name but a few. In fact, Churchward was an importer of ideas, but part of his nigh-genius — if that be the correct description, was to select and adapt for his own use: the ensuing cocktail was usually so clearly Churchward's own, and could not otherwise be mistaken.

If Churchward was not a great engineer, in terms of invention, then he was certainly one of the greatest engineering organisers. He must have had great prescience as well, for his eventual equipping of the GWR was good enough to last a generation and more. Finally, he may not have been copied overseas, but no other Star of Steam could match his influence within Britain. Thanks to Stanier and then Riddles, many of Churchward's main design principles lasted until the end of British steam, while he influenced both Gresley and Bulleid and, of course, the GWR almost slavishly followed his designs until 1948. The effect of his work was enormous and passes almost without criticism. If Dean, with Churchward's help, had systematically dragged GWR locomotive design from the 19th into the 20th century, Churchward proceeded to take British locomotive engineering onwards a further 30 years: it took that long for his locomotives to be surpassed.

It was, in many ways, as if the GWR had been sticking rigidly to some grand plan. From the dark days of the 1860s, when it became clear that the Broad Gauge was the past rather than the future and financial constraints were crippling the great company, the GWR began an inexorable recovery that, over the next 50 years, saw it rise to become one of the very best British railways. D. Gooch became Chairman and immediately began to strengthen and improve the company's financial position.

First came stability, then the extension of the standard gauge, and the finances recovered to the extent that the absorption of four Broad Gauge railways, in 1876, caused barely a hiccough in the overall pattern of steady progress. The GWR hardly gained a crock full of gold with these railways, but the South Devon Railway had its own works, at Newton Abbot, and there worked a promising apprentice: G.J. Churchward. He finished his apprenticeship at Swindon and, like other Stars of Steam before him, was seemingly marked out for greater responsibility and higher things from an early age.

As Churchward first graduated to the Drawing Office, then helped 'Young' Joe Armstrong devise Swindon's continuous vacuum brake, before becoming the Assistant Manager of the Carriage & Wagon works — under J. Holden, so the GWR sought ways of justifying its epithet Great. The first of several eventual route improvements was begun with the daring, adventurous and financially draining Severn Tunnel. Meanwhile, the forward-thinking Dean consolidated the company's locomotive position and endeavoured to keep the old Broad Gauge ticking-over until its inevitable demise. Dean also encouraged the use of standard locomotive parts, seemed a keen — though often unsuccessful — builder of prototype locomotives and, most important of all, established scientific research departments and specialist teams of skilled craftsmen at Swindon.

The 1890s saw the GWR's seeming grand plan gallop ahead. The finances remained strong, and not only did the Broad Gauge finally disappear in 1892, but the old baulk road was gradually replaced. In particular, Dean's new engines — singles and four-coupled — allowed the company to run better services, including Britain's first all-corridor train, of which Churchward had a fair old say in the design. Swindon Works was constantly improved, while teams of top-quality staff worked on long-term projects. Still later, water troughs allowed long distance, non-stop running and further plans were laid to shorten circuitous routes and to effect line improvements.

During that momentous decade, Dean had advanced Churchward's cause until, by 1897, he was his designated successor. With increasing influence, yet by no stretch of the imagination taking overall control, the young-blood was allowed to experiment with new ideas on boilers and fireboxes. Progress was measured and steady, beginning with the slab-sided Belpaire firebox on the 'Badminton' class, extending to the later 'Dukes', and then gathering pace with the 'Camel' and 'Atbara' classes. These latter included new parallel domeless boilers — with a central safety valve, and flat-topped, outside frames. These various joint-designed locomotives, with the

utilitarian 'Aberdares' for heavy freight and Dean's glorious singles still well to the fore, not only gave the GWR some of the finest locomotives in Britain at the dawning of the 20th century, but gave Churchward a valuable breathing-space and important design experience.

Within 18 months of the new century, Churchward had succeeded Dean and began to implement the most far-reaching plan yet devised towards a long-term standardisation of locomotives in Britain. Concurrently, the board had continued its planning and financing of new routes that was to transform the Great Way Round into God's Wonderful Railway.

By 1910, several important cut-off lines had been opened as the GWR drove inexorably onwards towards its goal of becoming Britain's finest railway, once again. In 1903, the Badminton line was opened, which markedly reduced timings and, more important, mileage and costs to South Wales. By 1906, a series of new lines and other improvements created a shorter route to Exeter, via Westbury: this effectively ended competition from the LSWR, and gave double track all the way into Cornwall. The Stratford-Cheltenham and Cheltenham-Banbury lines opened useful cross-country routes while, in 1910, the Bicester cut-off enabled the GWR to, at last, compete with the LNWR's lucrative 2 hour Birmingham expresses. Of contemporary British railways, only the GCR could equal such commitment to new fixed capital expenditure, and the board expected to see a worthwhile return.

For Churchward, this was a golden opportunity. Money was not exactly thrown at his department, but there was certainly no point in having improved routes without the engines to take advantage of them. In 1901, Churchward produced a list of standard locomotives that, he envisaged, would cover most needs for well into the future. These would make full use of many standard components such as outside cylinders, long-travel piston valves — combined with a steam chest and smokebox saddle casting, standard axle-boxes and motion, and large bearings. The planned engines were an express passenger 4-6-0; a mixed-traffic 4-6-0 with 5 ft. 8 in. driving wheels; a 4-4-0; a passenger 4-4-2T; a 2-6-2T for mixed-traffic and banking duties; and a heavy freight 2-8-0. The designs on this far-sighted document eventually came to fruition except that the mixed-traffic 4-6-0 emerged as the '4300' class mogul.

With this, Churchward convinced the board that they had just the man for the future, insofar as locomotive matters were concerned. The last 7 years of Dean's reign had fully equipped the GWR for the present and, just to make sure, Churchward added a new Standard No. 4 taper boiler with sloping Belpaire firebox to an 'Atbara' chassis and created the 'City' class. It did not take long for these powerful engines to demonstrate that they were the fastest in Britain, and they were soon found on all the principal expresses of the line. Thus, Churchward gave himself all the time he could possibly need to plan, develop and build his proposed standard classes in quantity production.

It was not simply the far-sightedness of Churchward's grand plan that makes him a great locomotive engineer, nor even the intended degree of standard components to be used. No, it was the method with which he carried out his plan. He did not simply launch his department into building new engines the day after Dean retired, but began to plan and test on a scale then unknown in Britain. In other words, he used the cushion that the current motive power gave him to develop and fine-tune ideas into practical working prototypes, and to further develop and assess these in the light of everyday performance. Dean not only encouraged Churchward to

It might not have been everybody's cup of tea in Edwardian days, but many regard the lines of Churchward's 'Stars' as classic; if nothing else, they looked pure 20th century locomotives. No. 4022 'King William', built in 1909, stands at Plymouth Millbay when new. The long-taper boiler, long smokebox and the rearward slope of the Belpaire firebox can be seen to good effect. This engine was renamed 'The Belgian Monarch', in 1927, and was withdrawn in 1952. These really were the stars of pre-Grouping express passenger locomotives.

develop new boilers, but their joint designs removed all pressure from Churchward to produce the goods before he was ready. In fact, it was to be three years before Churchward's first designs were built in series production.

The first, assumed, Churchward design emerged just before Dean retired. No. 100, later named 'Dean' and still later 'William Dean', was a 2-cylinder 4-6-0 with a parallel boiler of 200 psi. Its performance was as revolutionary as was its distinctly ungraceful appearance, at least to Edwardian eyes. It proceeded to play with passenger trains in the West Country until beginning work on the new non-stop Cornish Riviera Limited, from London-Plymouth, all of 247 miles in only 265 minutes. No. 100 soon received a taper boiler and bigger valves, and eventually became a member of the 'Saint' class, but in 1903 it was joined by four further prototypes, two of which were also 4-6-0s.

No. 98 had a taper boiler and was modified, in the light of operating experience with No. 100, to become the true forerunner of the 'Saint' class. This engine positively toyed with the express trains and by the end of the year No. 171 'Albion' was built with a taper boiler of 225 psi: the new express design was developing nicely. That same year, No. 97 emerged as a heavy freight 2-8-0, being very similar to No. 98, except for its small driving wheels. This was the initial member of the '2800' class, while No. 99 was a 2-6-2T, the first member of the '3100' class. Finally, before that momentous year was out, Churchward accepted delivery of reputedly the finest express passenger design in the world: the du Bousquet/de Glehn 4-cylinder compound 'La France'.

The following years saw extensive tests involving 'La France' and 'Albion', the latter being rebuilt as an Atlantic to make these even more comparative. In 1905, Churchward built 13 more Atlantics and six 4-6-0s. The 2-cylinder simples were scarcely inferior to the complex 'La France' and so, to draw further comparisons, Churchward built No. 40, 'North Star', in

1906, as a 4-cylinder simple Atlantic. Again, the compound showed no effective advantage, while Churchward opted for the greater adhesion of the 4-6-0s over the Atlantics for all future main line express passenger locomotives.

While this was all a long way from the end of his testing, by 1906 Churchward had reached many firm conclusions and production of his standard designs was underway. His unique cocktail contained design elements that emanated from the world over: Belgium, France, USA., Britain and even those previously discarded by the GWR It was not simply a case of, "let's try a Belpaire firebox", fitting one and leaving it at that. If Churchward was a great borrower of ideas, it was his subsequent adaptation and development that gave him a unique distinction.

The Belpaire firebox was a case in point. Initially, it was an inelegant slab-sided affair, not without its demerits. Churchward rounded its corners, tapered its sides and sloped its top from front to rear. In this way, it was both strengthened and had greater circulation and heating capacity just where it was needed, next to the boiler. This was but one such adaptation. Others included a high boiler pressure, divided drive and large bearing surfaces, from France; horizontal outside cylinders, 10 in. long-travel piston valves — with a long steam lap and large exhaust ports, the single casting of smokebox saddle and cylinder steam-chests, deep and narrow piston rings and a taper boiler, from America. From closer to home, Churchward was impressed by Ivatt's wide firebox; and reverted to Gooch's domeless boiler — eventually with top-feed, and devised his own jumper-top blastpipe. It was Churchward's ultimate adaptation and assemblage that gave his locomotives such distinguished performance, economy and standardisation over the ensuing decades.

Thus, Churchward's designs were almost all highly successful from the outset. The 'Saints', built from 1906, had long taper boilers, rather than merely a tapered rear ring, a longer smokebox and were, undoubtedly, the finest express engines in Britain. Indeed, before Grouping, they were only comprehensively superseded by Churchward's 'Stars'. The '2800' class heavy freight locomotives were also equalled, but never bettered in series production, until Riddles' 2-10-0 came on stream in the Second World War, fully 40 years later. As for his various prairie tanks, a few others eventually matched them, though not in pre-Grouping days, but they were good enough to work until the end of steam, on duties for which they were originally designed. All in all, by the mid-point of the Edwardian period, Churchward conclusively led the field in British steam locomotive matters.

There were moments when all was not so well, as with the outside cylinder 'County' class 4-4-0s: not every engineman's friend. Built to work in the Welsh Marches, where the LNWR prohibited the use of the 4-6-0s, these were often regarded as Churchward's least effective design, while the 'County Tanks' were little better received. Though both of these designs were included in his 1901 plan, neither might have emerged had a couple more years elapsed. The 'Counties', though, were built until 1912 and worked extensively north of Wolverhampton, so their somewhat poor reputation is probably un-warranted, and was due more to being compared with the finest locomotives then running in Britain. Any other contemporary locomotive would have suffered likewise.

Although Churchward was, thus far, undoubtedly a worthy Star of Steam, it is the ability of any locomotive engineer to design an express passenger engine that ultimately determines his reputation, like it or not. Of our Stars of Steam, only T.W. Worsdell failed to produce a particularly successful express engine and for Churchward to be considered a great, such success was essential. There can be little doubt about it that the production 'Saints' were just about the finest such locomotives in Britain. They were, in every respect, thoroughly modern engines with no carry-over from Victorian days: in that, they were unique in 1906.

Churchward was certainly not one to sit on his laurels though, and 'North Star' displayed some distinct advantages over its 2-cylinder counterparts. This was especially applicable in the working of long-distance, high speed expresses that the GWR intended to develop further. The opportunity arose and Churchward made the most of it. Now there is little doubt that the 'Saints' would have been more than capable of dealing with express trains for the foreseeable future, as intended in the 1901 plan, but times had changed and Churchward was most impressed by the French 4-cylinder locomotives.

The main problem with the 'Star' class was how to operate 4-cylinders. The scissors valve-gear on 'North Star' was both complex and might have involved royalty payments to the MR, so the problem was overcome by using inside Walschaert's valve-gear, and divided drive. Not the easiest solution, by a long way, and it resulted in a of resistance at speed. Whatever the drawbacks, all subsequent GWR 4-cylinder locomotives adopted this arrangement.

It was soon apparent that Churchward, far from being caught, was moving way ahead of the pack. Let us make no bones about it, the 'Stars' were Britain's outstanding pre-Grouping express locomotive. It may be that an LNWR 'George the Fifth' would have given a 'Star' more than a good run for its money. Perhaps, but those brilliant 4-4-0s were advanced late-Victorian engines, not state-of-the-art Edwardian. Bowen Cooke's 'Claughtons' soon showed they were second-best to nothing, and were equally modern to boot. Unfortunately, they were under-boilered, thanks to the Civil Engineer, and were never fully developed before the First World War. Of course, Gresley's 'A1s' eventually eclipsed the 'Stars', at least in 'A3' guise, but this was fully 20 years after the first 'Stars' were built. Yes, the 'Stars' were that far ahead.

Even then, he was not finished. The potential of the wide firebox impressed Churchward, but he had been unable to test one: no matter how advanced his designs were, Churchward was duly conservative when it came to making unnecessary leaps into the dark. Still, he was authorised to construct Britain's first Pacific locomotive in 1908: 'The Great Bear' was born. In many respects this was an enlarged 'Star', having a massive 23 ft. long No. 6 boiler with the new No. 1 superheater, and a wide Belpaire firebox. In all other respects, 15 in. cylinders apart, it was a conventional 'Star', though its weight restricted it solely to the London-Bristol route.

'The Great Bear' was extensively tested over many years, and was given the No. 3 superheater in 1913. In all honesty, it hardly distinguished itself, though it easily worked express passenger, fast freight and even slow heavy goods trains: then again, it never needed to perform outlandishly. It was an occasional poor steamer and it might just have been a bit of a dud: a Friday's child. As a testbed though, it was more than useful and, should the need have ever arisen, Churchward and his team could have met any future requirements head-on.

In other respects, Churchward was more than capable of looking backwards to fulfil the needs of the present. He was quite happy and successful at rebuilding and modernising older designs, especially by fitting a Belpaire firebox with, or without, a domeless boiler. So, many former saddle-tanks reappeared with a pannier tank and a Belpaire firebox, while even some of Dean's singles gained the latter: Churchward was certainly not one to respect tradition for its own sake. Then, once the Stratford-Cheltenham line opened, he placed a standard No. 2 boiler on a 'City' chassis and replaced Dean's leading bogie with de Glehn's to produce the 'Flower' class. If that was something of a strange hybrid, albeit one using thoroughly standard parts, the 'Bird' class was nothing more than a 'Camel' with the de Glehn bogie. Indeed, in reality, they were classed as 'Camels', or 'Bulldogs' as they became known.

In 1910, Churchward created a tank engine version of the outstanding 2-8-0, the '4200' class, and the following year issued instructions for the design of a mixed-traffic engine utilising as many standard parts as possible. The '4300' class moguls were the first of their kind: true all-rounders. Both of these were built in prodigious numbers and were, once again, distinguished performers. That the moguls were virtually left to subordinates to complete showed just how far Churchward had taken the GWR for, apart from his own brilliant work and meticulous leadership, he had established a design and drawing team without peer in Britain. Thus, as the Edwardian era drew to its close, Churchward had just about completed a design for every conceivable need.

Thereafter, new design slowed as there was no requirement for anything else. Churchward's engines were not cheap to build — by Crewe's standards they were frightfully expensive, but they were economical to run, reliable and were more than adequate for several decades hence. Churchward's talented design team began to break up, and some found a stimulating new home at the SECR under Maunsell. The experimental 4-4-2T of the '4600' class came to nothing, and Churchward's last design, the '4700' class 2-8-0 for fast heavy goods, did not go into series production until after his retirement. Churchward set off at such a blistering pace throughout his first decade in charge that there was no real need to push on still further. The GWR clearly led the field insofar as British locomotive design was concerned, although it was the LNWR that undertook the most spirited running in the years before the First World War.

Such an array of advanced, highly standardised and eminently successful locomotive designs clearly mark Churchward out as being a great locomotive engineer. If he did nothing else, he would rank as one of the very best British exponents, but there was rather more to him than that. As Works Manager under Dean, he was responsible for the re-equipping of Swindon, and this continued apace when he became Locomotive Superintendent His method of working closely with his design team, and especially analysing test results, left many subordinates in reverential awe of him. It is doubtful if such a productive, forward-looking design team was ever assembled before or since in Britain. Stanier led a formidable team 30 years later, that produced many high quality designs but somehow, the 'Duchess' pacifics apart, there was none of the spark of brilliance and genius that occasionally radiated from rival the LNER camp.

Perhaps Churchward's non-locomotive crowning glory was the establishment of Swindon's stationary test plant. Then again, it could also have been his biggest white elephant for it was, by all accounts, grossly under-used. This was certainly not the case with road-testing, and a new dynamometer car was built and used extensively. Detail planning and exhaustive testing were the key factors in Churchward's seemingly endless supply of outstanding locomotives.

Nobody is perfect though, and while it is not easy to criticise Churchward professionally, his adoption of low-degree superheat can justifiably be cited as being less than progressive. On the other hand, while Churchward was probably not a brilliant engineer in his own right, he was an eminently pragmatic one. In 1906, he fitted a Schmidt superheater to a new 'Saint' class engine, one of the first in Britain. He was impressed by its attributes, but considered maintenance and lubrication problems as drawbacks that imposed too great a handicap in ordinary service. There was also the matter of royalty payments as well, but Churchward was bitten and decided to try another means.

The following year, an American Cole superheater was fitted to a 'Star', and proved even less satisfactory in ordinary use. Churchward then designed his own and 'The Great Bear' carried a Swindon No. 1 superheater, similar to the Cole version. A No. 2 superheater was produced for trials, and in 1909 the Swindon No. 3 superheater — with two rows and 14 elements that gave 245 sq. ft. of heating surface, became the standard production version. This raised steam temperatures to, about 550 degrees F., about 100 degrees below that of the Schmidt superheater. As such, Churchward has been criticised for adopting low-degree superheat, but there were sound reasons for this.

Inadequate lubricants for the cylinders was a continual source of problems: superheated steam was effectively dry and did not lubricate as did saturated steam. Superheated locomotives on other railways suffered with carbonisation and

seizure problems as the lubricants were not then up to the task. On the other hand, Churchward found that his superheated engines recovered the capital cost in fuel savings within a year, and by the First World War about 800 GWR locomotives were so fitted, far more than on any other British railway: bread today as against the promise of jam tomorrow. In any case, GWR engines had a much higher boiler pressure than other British locomotives, while many engineers who adopted superheaters further reduced the boiler pressure, all in the name of economy.

Churchward trod a pragmatic path. His superheater provided both a modestly improved performance and enhanced economy: in short, it worked. If Churchward is to be criticised, it ought to be for his continued application of relatively small, low-degree superheaters after the First World War when lubricants had improved immeasurably. Then, he failed to take a truly pragmatic approach, but he knew his days were numbered. In any case, there were other pressing needs and his engine designs — though more than a decade old — still comfortably led the field. Was it not Churchward's successors, including Stanier, who failed to read the way the superheater wind was blowing and slavishly followed Churchward's path, a route about which he would not have been so dogmatic? True enough, but Collett — with his 'Castles' and 'Kings' — could easily claim that his engines were unsurpassed. Even later, when Gresley and then Stanier usurped the GWR, these superheated engines were still more than capable of undertaking anything management ever asked of them.

Churchward has also been criticised for not further improving his designs. This argument ignores the onset of the First World War, and the growing concern about the burden of capital expenditure — and a less than commensurate rate of return — of shareholders in the years before the great conflagration. Despite his unrivalled stature in British steam circles, Churchward was a company servant, not vice versa. By the outbreak of war, the GWR had vastly improved its express passenger services, and running and maintenance economies were effected in all operations. These were due to Churchward's work over the previous decade. He had set the lead, it was for others to catch up.

Locomotives, though, were not the sole object of Churchward's work, and some noteworthy advances were made in coaches, particularly the introduction of the top-light stock, rail-motors and, in 1905, the legendary auto-trains. He was also responsible for wagon developments including,

In 1905, Churchward built 13 Atlantics for comparison with the French compounds. No. 180, stands at Plymouth Laira before it was named 'Coeur de Lion' and re-numbered No. 2981, in 1907. This was the last of the 'Saint' class Atlantics to be converted to a 4-6-0, in January 1913, and it was also the second last of the 1905 'Saints' to be withdrawn, in 1951.

Few locomotive engineers made such an brilliant start with their first production design. The 'City' class was magnificent express locomotives from the moment they turned a wheel, and on other railways they might have expected a long-run on front-line expresses. It was not to be on the GWR, for as the Churchward revolution gained momentum these fine engines became virtual second class citizens. No. 3441 'City of Winchester' is at Exeter St. David's in its early days. It was the first to be withdrawn, in 1927, after only 24 years.

before he became the Locomotive Superintendent, axle-box lubrication with oil. It was, indeed, his re-organisation of Swindon Works for war production that earned him a CBE, and while the morals of awarding such honours to those who stayed at home are repulsive — especially when Tommy Atkins and his ilk risked their all for far less, Churchward was a more deserving case than career civil servants and other such hangers-on.

Outside his professional life, Churchward undertook the usual public duties of one in his position. He never married but was keen on country sports, had a home workshop and enjoyed gardening. In short, he was a pretty ordinary person, not a demi-god as some would have us believe.

Evidence suggests that he was a highly competent, but far from great, engineer: at least in the manner of, say, Barnes Wallis. His work in modernising a large works, establishing

While attention is quite rightly lavished on Churchward's express passenger engines, he produced no better design than the magnificent '2800' class 2-8-0s. As this picture of No. 2851 shows, they bore a handsome, simple, yet thorough family look; every inch a classic. Though just about equalled by several heavy freight designs, they were not surpassed for over 30 years.

and motivating a design team, and devising and adhering to a standardised motive-power plan have all been emulated before and since Churchward's time. No, what made Churchward a brilliant Star of Steam was his accurate foresight of future needs, his ability to seek out and develop suitable design features, and to meld these into highly standardised designs that brought the future into the present.

Churchward was certainly lucky. Dean had undertaken much outstanding work at Swindon. He encouraged Churchward to experiment and the pair then combined to give the GWR an enviable locomotive fleet. That gave Churchward the time to develop his plans at his own pace. Churchward took over just when the company was at its most expansive for 60 years. Money was forthcoming but, as we all know, it needs to be spent wisely. Finally, the Edwardian age was one of re-born optimism: out with the old, in with the new. Despite all this in his favour, it is quite probable that no other British locomotive engineer could have succeeded to the extent Churchward did. Many had their standardisation plans, from Ramsbottom to Riddles, but none were as advanced as was Churchward's. Ultimately, of course, no steam locomotive engineer had such a widespread effect in Britain, apart from George Stephenson. Thereafter, to varying degrees, wherever Churchward led, others followed.

Looking back with hindsight on GWR locomotive events 90-odd years ago, it is easy to take it for granted. After all, Churchward's designs seem so logical and relatively obvious. For those who remember the last years of British steam, these are the types of locomotives with which one was familiar: outside cylinders, taper boilers, many standard parts and with a distinct family resemblance. It is only when we compare the work of Churchward with that of his contemporaries that we can appreciate just how advanced he was. Oh yes, several of these equalled or even exceeded Churchward with an odd design or two, but nobody did so over a range of locomotives: remember, six Stars of Steam held office for a number of years during Churchward's reign. These all did good work during that time, some did very good work, but only Churchward did truly great work during the fabled Golden Age of British railways.

If one accepts that argument, then Churchward could have done no more. Whether his work was superior to that of the pragmatic inventiveness of Gresley, the sound plans and designs of Stanier, or even the gallant intentions of the mercurial Bulleid, of the 20th century locomotive engineers, is purely debating matter. Time passes and advances are made and render such comparisons meaningless. A Manchester

was even hostile to his subordinates taking an active role in them. Some stories concocted about this remind one of the Hoover conspiracies in America: more fanciful lies than truth. Following his wife's death, Collett just about withdrew from what little public activities he had.

So, Collett was not the high profile, dynamic CME his General Manager — and formative spin-doctor — Sir Felix Pole desired, but what Collett lacked in charisma, he was about to make-up for in reality. After the Grouping of 1923, major changes and upheavals were underway at all four new companies. In many respects though, the GWR had it easy, as it absorbed several smaller railways which, collectively, made little impression on the new master. For Collett though, all was not plain sailing, as each of these railways had its own ramshackle — and often run-down — locomotive fleet, plus a works and other stock. All this capital equipment needed assimilating into the enlarged GWR, or disposing of, and Collett was the ideal person to ensure that this mundane task was undertaken thoroughly, quickly and as painlessly as possible. One potential headache was soon dispensed with.

On the other hand Churchward had bequeathed a locomotive legacy the envy of any railway in Britain. He had not only achieved a unique level of standardisation for that time but, almost without exception, his locomotives were thorough masters of their work, economical to run and maintain and, class for class, were about the best in the country. Only Gresley, on the LNER, showed any equal sign of innovation. All was not rosy in the GWR garden though for, with few exceptions, Churchward's designs had not materially advanced since the first superheated 'Stars' appeared in 1910. Yes, Churchward was then 15 years ahead of everyone else but, by 1923, others were catching up, and the 'Stars' were sometimes being pushed to the limit. Something new in the express line would be needed to maintain the GWR's position of pre-eminence.

Collett could have gone his own way and designed a nightmare — let's face it, many engineers did. Fortunately for the GWR, Collett's team enlarged Churchward's 'Stars' by fitting a new No. 8 boiler with outside steam pipes and a modern cab, tweaked minor bits here and there, and promptly produced the most powerful British express engine of its day. A true classic — both then and now — was born and immediately hit the headlines and, later, put its opposition to the sword. Yet, curiously, the design gave Collett's latter-day critics still more ammunition. Pole might have preferred a more gregarious CME, but Collett certainly delivered the goods. Naming this design the 'Castle' class was simply the cherry on the icing of the cake, for the GWR.

And the critics? Well obviously it would have been better had Collett produced, say, a 4-8-4 that was faster than an 'A4', stronger than a 'Duchess', more economical than a Mini and as cheap to build as a modern house — nothing to it really. Yes, the 'Castle' was little more than an enlarged 'Star' but, as in all aspects of life — and especially steam locomotive design — making something bigger hardly guarantees an improvement.

What, then, about developments in superheating? Collett either ignored, or dismissed this option, and stuck with the tried and tested: innovation or development is useful, change for change's sake is most decidedly not. Stanier, who has a reputation of being more adventurous than Collett, also used low-degree superheat on his original 'Princess' class pacifics, despite advice to the contrary from his talented design team.

Magnificent locomotives that they are, the 'Castles' are certainly not beyond criticism. Without a doubt, something more adventurous could have been done regards superheating, even if in future developments, as amply demonstrated in the

1950s. Then, initially at any rate, they appeared with a 'Star' type tender, and did not receive the high-sided, 4,000gal one until 1926: a case of economy taken too far?. Another criticism is that the 'Castles' were not as attractive as the 'Stars'. That is, surely, a matter of personal opinion. The outside steam pipes and new boiler certainly gave it a larger and more modern look but, once they received the larger tender, they were a far better proportioned engine than their somewhat quaint-looking predecessors.

A more serious criticism is that, in the opinion of the great railway author O.S. Nock, the 'Castles' varied from locomotive to locomotive to a greater extent than any other class he was familiar with — rather like British Leyland cars of the 1970s! That may well be down to build quality, although it did not apparently afflict other GWR engines. On the other hand, the GWR used hand-picked coal for its top duties, and 'Castles' employed on lesser trains might have had to endure a fair bit of slack, with all the attendant problems; a bit like running a car set-up for 5-star petrol, on 4-star.

Then again, the 'Castles' hauled the 'Cheltenham Spa Express', the legendary fastest train in the world. From 1932, this was timed to cover the 77.3 miles from Swindon-Paddington in 65 mins., an average speed of 71.4 mph. Apparently, it was a bit of a doddle, pulling a light-weight train on the gently falling grades of the finest aligned main line in Britain, at just over 80 mph. Still, it had to be done day in, day out.

The 'Castles' were obviously faced with much more onerous tasks, and 400+ ton expresses to Devon and Cornwall over the undulating, twisting Berks. & Hants. route into the teeth of a fierce south-westerly gale, were anything but a piece of cake. Such duties would tax both locomotive and crew to the limit, yet the 'Castles' carried out these tasks, both economically and reliably, for nigh-on 40 years. One can easily argue that such work, and their general versatility, rank the 'Castles' in serious contention for the accolade as the finest British express locomotive of all time, steam or not.

As far as Collett was concerned though, he could not sit back and accept all the plaudits. There was much work to be done. Of the many absorbed railways, those in the Welsh valleys were by far the busiest and most important, if not the biggest. Although these were rivals, to each other and the GWR, the 0-6-2T was almost universally used by the small South Wales railways, for all traffic duties.

Despite that, the GWR inherited a diverse bunch of locomotives, many of which had been severely run-down once the Grouping arrangements became known. Collett had to create a standardised order out of the disparate chaos, and he ordered the fitting of modified Swindon boilers, cylinders and so forth, in a rolling programme of renewal, along with much scrapping of obsolescent engines. Then, in 1924, Collett authorised the '5600' class of 0-6-2Ts. This was Swindon's version of the South Wales railways' favourite son.

Though versatile, economical and long-lived, Collett's critics willingly cite this class as being his only true design. Mind you, there usually follows the story of how the first one ground to a halt — amidst screeching metallic sounds — as it emerged from Swindon Works: a classic in how Collett got his calculations completely wrong. So, how did he do that? I thought it was usually claimed that Collett was never seen in the Drawing Office? If this story were true — and there is some doubt about its validity — it was far from being the first time such a scenario occurred, even at Swindon. In any case, the offending valve spindles were soon given the necessary support, and all ended well. The '5600' class became another member of the thoroughly successful, almost anonymous, all-

Not only was the 'King' class the best British express locomotive of its day, but it was probably the finest 4-6-0 to run in the country. The exquisite lines of No. 6011 'King James I' display not only the quality of the design, but an outstandingly high finish as well. Pride oozes from every joint.

rounder type of engine common to most British railways.

That same year, Collett submitted the only engineering paper to bear his name: 'The Testing of Locomotives on the GWR', this was delivered to the modestly titled World Power Conference, in London. Naturally, it was the 'Castles' that provided much of the data, and the published records of their economy were far ahead of anything running in Britain at that time: perhaps, it has been suggested, even being unbelievable.

Such results were ultimately borne out the following year, in trials with Gresley's 'A1' pacifics, and again in 1926 with a tour de force demonstration of power and economy on the LMS This latter, incidentally, led to a request being made for Swindon to build 50 'Castles' for the LMS — not 'Stars' by the way. Not un-naturally, this request was refused.

Back in 1924, Collett also authorised the conversion of the unique pacific 'The Great Bear', to a 'Castle'. Pole summoned him for an explanation. It has been claimed that this act was no more than the spiteful, jealous destruction of Churchward's masterpiece! Far from being a masterpiece though, the 'Bear' was ready for a major overhaul and was costly to maintain. Being restricted to the London-Bristol line, it was grossly under-utilised, had steaming problems and was more a liability than an asset. No, far from being envious of this engine, Collett took a sound, commercial decision: Pole had no answer. Of course, Collett could have been more adventurous and used the 'Bear' as a test-bed for a new design, but the opportunity went begging.

Finally, in 1924, one of Churchward's 'Saints' was rebuilt with 6 ft. driving wheels and a lowered boiler and cylinders. Fitted with a 'Castle' cab, No. 4900 gave the 'Saint' class a real 'St. Martin's' summer, as this became the first of a new standard mixed-traffic class when, in 1928, the 'Halls' went into production.

Once again, Collett's critics have railed about the 'Halls' being nothing more than a modest development of

Churchward's 'Saints'. Perhaps, but they were the first true all-purpose mixed-traffic 4-6-0. In time, they became the most numerous GWR tender locomotive, were considered by many enginemen to be the GWR's most versatile engine — working everything from slow goods to fast passenger trains, and were an excellent replacement for Churchward's '4300' moguls. Similarly, the 'Halls' have been claimed to be inferior to Stanier's 'Black Fives', but that was a later design, which was possibly better than the, still later, LNER equivalent, the 'B1' class. Such a comparison is invidious to all these fine engines. The 'Halls' were an outstanding success, were relatively cheap to build, run and maintain and, by developing an existing design, required little new capital equipment. Any business would welcome such a useful and versatile tool.

Ultimately, the 'Hall' theme was further developed with the 'Grange' class. These 4-6-0s, in true want-not, waste-not fashion, used wheels and motion from withdrawn '4300s' and were, to all intents and purposes, a 5 ft. 8 in. version of the 'Halls. As a result, the 'Granges' had all the attributes of their soul-mates, a wider route availability, and were equally successful and popular. That, though, did not satisfy Collett's critics whose comments, in true school report fashion, could be distilled as 'could do much better, must try harder'.

Finally, the last all-rounder design for which Collett held responsibility was virtually a lightweight 'Grange', intended for working secondary lines and the lines of the former Cambrian Railways. Despite having reduced cylinders, a new Swindon No. 14 boiler and altered draughting arrangements, all was expected to go well. However, whereas the 'Halls' and 'Granges' had delivered everything required of them, the 'Manors' were indifferent steamers and persistent under-performers. So they remained until BR tests, in the 1950s, led to a small reduction in the blastpipe jumper ring that promptly doubled their steaming capacity! The 'Manors' were transformed, along with their reputation and, belatedly, another Collett design was a success.

Some of the most stinging criticism of Collett has been levelled at his numerous workhorse designs, especially his adoption and development of older, even ancient designs. As with nearly all his locomotive work though, and somewhat ironically, there was not a dud amongst them. True, they were based on past successes, and innovation was about as rare as a

How can a locomotive engineer be criticised for being responsible for such a useful, yet outstanding design as the 'Halls'? Collett managed it. No. 4923 'Evenley Hall' has obviously seen better days, as it arrives at Reading in 1950. These were true all-rounders, Jacks-of-all-trades and masters of many of them. In the long history of the GWR, these were possibly the most useful of all the many fine designs from Swindon. *(W. Gilburt collection; K. Robertson)*

politician telling the truth, but they were ideal for their respective jobs.

Starting in 1928, Collett made some minor modifications to Churchward's 2-6-2T theme and, over the next decade, proceeded to build both large and small-wheeled versions, and to update some of Churchward's engines. The changes were minimal, but all these engines achieved the usual GWR tenets of build, maintenance and on-road performance, so major changes were quite unnecessary.

The following year, Collett dipped still deeper into the GWR archives and revived the 0-6-0 pannier tank. A variety of designs emerged, beginning with the '5700' class, that were little more than modestly updated versions of Dean's engines, themselves developed from Armstrong's saddle tanks. Others followed, over the next decade, to suit all kinds of tasks, and the cylinders, wheels, boilers and much else varied depending on the intended use of the engines, but the only obvious visual improvement was the fully enclosed cab. Pannier tanks were, of course, built by BR so let that be comment enough on their value and versatility.

Warming to the historic theme, by 1930 Dean's versatile 0-6-0 'Goods' were getting a bit geriatric. Heralding from 1883, these were war veterans of inestimable value and so, economical as ever, Collett merely added a standard, superheated No. 10 boiler onto a virtual Dean chassis and the '2251' class was born. It seems so simple, that you can almost hear Collett's critics crying out in despair. Well, simple it might have been, but successful as well, for 120 were built by 1948.

One might well have begun to wonder just when Collett would re-introduce a single-driver locomotive into the fold, for in 1932 he burrowed deeper into the archives than ever before, and produced an updated version of Armstrong's '517' class 0-4-2T, of 1870 vintage. I say updated, but not by much. The '4800' class, and its non push-pull fitted variant — the '5800', were little more than copies that came to embody all that was enchanting about the lonely, timeless branch line we all lament, but never used. Dismiss these locomotives at your peril though. Yes, I am quite sure the design could have been modified, or a totally new design been forthcoming had the will and drive had been there, but why?

As with the other railways of the Grouping era, older designs were either updated, or new engines built to the original patterns. The reasons for following this retrospective path is that such engines can be built easily and economically, while their performance is almost guaranteed. Such a scenario can never be the case for an entirely new design, as the

'Manors' displayed. Thus further, occasionally modified, versions of Churchward's '2800' and '4700' class 2-8-0s, '4300' class 2-6-0s and, especially, the conversion of the '4200' class 2-8-0Ts from short to medium-distance heavy freight 2-8-2Ts — of the '7200' class, were turned out. While this conservative approach perhaps lacked flair and invention, on Collett's retirement, the GWR had the most modern and standardised locomotive fleet in Britain.

All of this work clearly shows Collett to be a pragmatic and practical Star of Steam, if not necessarily one to stir the engineering student's blood. Of course, there has been one important omission: a design that was both Collett's masterpiece, and the key evidence of those aiming to illuminate his deficiencies. No one can seriously deny that the 'King' class was the ultimate in Swindon design. Powerful, elegant — even more finely proportioned than the 'Castles' — and relatively economical to build, maintain and run, Collett was responsible for producing Britain's finest express locomotive, in 1927. It was probably the most controversial as well.

Critics and supporters of Collett, and railway historians, have all argued the merits, defects, chronology and inspiration for the 'Kings', until well after the cows have returned to their byres. "The 'Kings' are merely enlarged 'Castles'", one might hear — which are, of course, enlarged 'Stars'... Or perhaps; "The 'Kings' featured an entirely new boiler, cylinders and motion, frames, wheels, leading bogie and so forth", so were an entirely new design. Or even, "Yes, the 'Kings' were magnificent locomotives, but what if...(insert Stanier, Gresley or Churchward) had been in charge?" Mind you, Collett was a merely Star of Steam, whereas those three were, let us be honest, great steam locomotive engineers. The distinction was more than subtle.

The 'Kings' originated through a combination of events. For a start, the Running Department was considering the need for a more powerful locomotive, and Sir Felix Pole wanted to regain the title of 'Britain's Most Powerful Express Locomotive', lost to the SR's 'Lord Nelsons' superior tractive effort. Meanwhile, Collett had been giving departmental time to a new express design and, most important, after discovering that most of the main line to Plymouth could accept locomotives with a 22 ton axle-load, the former 20 ton limit was to be raised. Thus, in 1926, Collett received what was effectively a clean sheet to design an express locomotive capable of blowing the socks off anything else then running, with the proviso that it needed to be ready for the following summer.

While most of Collett's critics admire the undoubted qualities of the 'Kings', it was not the socks that they consider Collett blew away, just the opportunity. True, there is no doubt that the 'Kings' were the most powerful express locomotives of their day. Also without question is the fact that they could have been better. This was amply demonstrated when BR fitted a double blastpipe and chimney and, in particular, a 4-row superheater. The advent of high-degree superheating was something that even Churchward failed to utilise, and Collett — possibly too close a Churchward disciple — did likewise. Not Gresley though, nor did he fail to learn from the harsh lessons meted out by Collett's 'Castles', in 1925. Within a year of the 'Kings' appearing, Gresley's 'A3' pacifics had emerged that, in all but tractive effort, were every bit as powerful, economical and even fleeter of foot than the 'Kings'. The writing was clearly on the wall.

The 'Kings' were a resounding success from the outset, though had severe route restrictions imposed on them. Still, Collett's detractors claimed that 'Castles' were the more reliable, or faster, or simply better locomotives. As both the GWR and BR used 'Kings' on the fastest and heaviest expresses until the end of steam, it may be true to say,

'anything a 'Castle' can do, a 'King' can do even better', and leave it at that.

Then again, it has been claimed that the 'King' class was not the ultimate development of GWR express design, the LMS 'Duchesses' deserve that accolade. Pathetic! Stanier's original 'Princess' pacifics may be — spurious — contenders, though they were far from successful until given larger superheaters, but the 'Duchesses' incorporated much that was not developed from Churchward's ideals and principals. The 'Kings', on the other hand — a quick modification of the leading bogie notwithstanding, were almost trouble-free from the start, and stole the railway shows on both sides of the Atlantic. Such a dramatic debut had became the accepted norm from the GWR, but the 'Kings' introduction was like nothing that had gone before.

Eventually, the 'Kings' were further improved by innovations first effectively applied, in Britain, on Gresley's locomotives. The reverse was also true when the Swindon method of optical alignment of cylinders, frames and motion was introduced to Doncaster. The moral of the story is, that there is always room for improvement: whether an advance is deemed either necessary, or economic, is management's decision. Collett and his staff were aware of superheater developments and chose to pursue their own path, whether through arrogance, ignorance, lack of foresight or a considered time/economy calculation. Incidentally, Collett also rejected out of hand, Hawksworth's and Stanier's proposals for a compound 4-6-0 or a pacific. Perhaps he really did believe that Wiltshire's hills were not suited to a 4-6-2!

A final matter that arose in the 1930s, and with which even most of Collett's detractors agreed, was his less-than-enthusiastic approach to streamlining. That was the decade

---

A missed opportunity. Many designs that were still running into the 1960s slipped the preservation net and vanished forever. Few former GWR types did so. The 'Counties' missed out and Collett's 'Granges' did likewise. Not all that different to the 'Halls', they more than adequately fulfilled the tasks formerly undertaken by the various pre-Grouping 4-4-0s: cross-country trains, semi-fasts, excursions and the like. No. 6833 'Calcot Grange' departs from Gloucester on a cross-country train in 1956 (*W. Gilburt collection; K. Robertson*)

when one could even buy a streamlined toaster — more aerodynamic for throwing at husbands, no doubt. Collett was asked to investigate the matter of locomotive streamlining, and he responded with a hastily and clumsily clad 'King' and 'Castle' pair of engines. Within months, the fairings began to be removed. They added nothing to the performance, so far as is known, and looked quite hideous.

On the other hand, for those who commend Collett for not following the blind alley of streamlining, tests showed that Gresley's 'A4s' enjoyed a significant reduction in air resistance at speeds above 70 mph, over his 'A3s'. One-off high speed demonstrations apart, which they won hands-down in any case, the 'A4s' were undoubtedly the fastest British steam locomotives, as demonstrated over decades of service: streamlining certainly made a difference. Collett's response to the challenge was mean-spirited, but the right one given that the requirement for such locomotives did not exist on the GWR. Had Collett been given a clean sheet to design a streamlined locomotive, now that might have been a quite different matter.

It would appear that Collett was not a great participator when it came to experimenting with new, often costly and un-reliable, innovations. True, a 'Saint' locomotive was fitted with rotary-cam poppet valve-gear, but nothing came of it. Nevertheless, Collett and his department fully utilised the dynamometer car to undertake numerous road trials, almost inevitably aimed at improving locomotive fuel economy.

Then, in 1935, Collett had Churchward's stationary locomotive testing plant modernised to be capable of absorbing 2,000 horsepower, up from the 500 h.p. of earlier days. This was a really useful asset and proved invaluable in measuring the constant boiler evaporation rates of engines. The main benefits of this plant were seen more in the 1950s, but it was thanks to Collett's foresight that this facility became of such use.

More than anything though, Collett was a workshop man, as might be expected from the nigh-20 years he spent as Swindon's Assistant or Works Manager. His work to improve the precision of boiler manufacture, during that period, was invaluable. Soon after he became CME, Collett rationalised the rolling stock and repair facilities of the absorbed railways. With a minimum of fuss, the former Rhymney Railway works, at Caerphilly, was thoroughly modernised to become the maintenance centre for the Welsh valley's. Five years later, in 1932, the Stafford Road Works, at Wolverhampton, was similarly improved to undertake maintenance work on all locomotives in the northern area.

Meanwhile, Swindon Works was updated and expanded to become the finest locomotive manufacturing and repair base in Britain. In 1924, his department employed 45,000 people, of whom 14,000 worked at Swindon alone. Those figures are staggering. No wonder CME's did not have time to sit at a drawing board all day, doodling out the minutiae of a new pet project.

Apart from the stationary locomotive testing plant, Collett introduced a Zeiss optical alignment system for cylinders, frames and motion, to Swindon. This assisted assembly to finer tolerances than hitherto, showing improvements in wear and performance, and a reduction in maintenance and running costs. Hand in glove with this was the purchase of suitable machine tools. It was the use of such equipment in manufacture and repair, from 1933 onwards, that led to the saying that Swindon scrapped equipment that was worn to the tolerances to which some other works manufactured. Arrogant and apocryphal that story might be, but when introduced to Doncaster, in the 1950s, the familiar clanking Gresley knock

became almost a thing of the past. Such work, though not in the public eye, was vital to a railway company and helped make the repair and maintenance costs of GWR engines the lowest in Britain, in 1938. While the LNER and LMS were dominating the public's attention with their virtuoso high-speed exploits, it was the GWR that really led the way.

Other aspects of a CME's work were not overlooked by Collett either. Coaches were constantly improved, though without undue flamboyance, and vast numbers were built in the 1920s. He tried articulated suburban stock, in 1925 — and not a resounding success, but some of his special-build stock, in particular the 1931 Super Saloons and the Centenary coaches of 1935, were very impressive. Of more relevance to the GWR as a whole, Collett introduced the Laycock buckeye coupler and re-introduced the chocolate and cream livery soon after taking charge. He also introduced the streamlined railcars, though not designed by the company, from 1933 onwards. Collett was very interested in carriages and wagons — more evidence that he was not a locomotive man? The ordinary GWR carriage stock was generally pleasant enough, with little in the way of ostentation or embellishment: not unlike Collett himself.

Collett retired in 1941 and, unlike Churchward who regularly popped into Swindon Works until his death, virtually severed all links with the company. This hints at a certain animosity, a claim that lacks evidence, and in this he was not alone. The death of Collett's wife gave him an interest in esoteric medicine and dietary remedies, and he claimed to have cured his own cancerous illnesses through such means, not long after.

Whether Collett was insular and dull or not, that should not cloud his massive achievements as CME of the GWR, for almost 20 years. Like most CME's, he did not personally design the locomotives that carry his name, though he bore full responsibility for all the products of his department. His rejection of a pacific or compound design for the orthodoxy of the 'King' 4-6-0's, shows that he had his own ideas and set the parameters within which others worked. During his tenure, quite apart from rebuilt locomotives, over 2,000 engines were built by the GWR: that is about twice as many Gresley built for the LNER which, in any case, had nearly twice as many engines.

To be frank, the level of criticism heaped on Collett from self-proclaimed GWR enthusiasts is bewildering. True, he was no Churchward, but Collett had the sense to successfully develop and build-on his mentor's massive foundations: one doubts many locomotive engineers would have done anywhere near so well. There is no question that innovation in any of life's activities is necessary, but constant change is doomed to failure: one has to take stock and to build on what is shown to work. Collett did that to almost the ultimate degree in locomotive circles, and in so doing produced two truly great locomotive designs, many that were very good indeed — even outstanding, and not a single flop. Alex Ferguson's successor, whoever he might be, will almost certainly settle for such an equivalent footballing record.

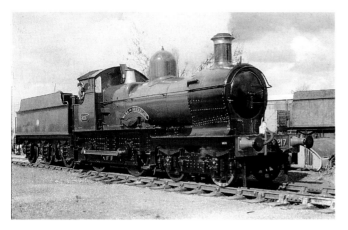

COLLETT IN BRIEF

BORN:	10th September 1871.
EDUCATED:	Merchant Taylors' School, London, and City and Guilds College.
TRAINED:	1887, Maudsley, Sons & Field Ltd. Engineering pupil.
EMPLOYED:	1893, Junior Draughtsman, Swindon Works, G.W.R.
	1898, Ass. to Chief Draughtsman.
SENIOR POSITIONS:	1900, Technical Inspector, Swindon Works.
	1901, Ass. Works Manager, Swindon.
	1912, Works Manager, Swindon.
	1919, Deputy C.M.E., G.W.R.
	1922, C.M.E. of G.W.R.
RETIRED:	1941, To Wimbledon.
HONOURS:	1919, O.B.E.
	1921-28, Swindon J.P.
DIED:	5th April 1952, London.

Collett's Locomotive Designs

YEAR	CLASS	WHEEL ARRANGEMENT	CYLINDERS (INCHES)	BOILER PRESSURE	DRIVING-WHEEL DIAMETER	WEIGHT	No. in CLASS
1923	Castle	4-6-0	(4)16 x 26	225 psi	6' 8½"	79T 15 cwt	180
1924	5600	0-6-2T	18 x 26	200 psi	4' 7½"	69 tons	200
1924	Hall	4-6-0	(o)18½ x 30	225 psi	6 ft.	72½-75 tons	258
1927	King	4-6-0	(4)16¼ x 28	250 psi	6' 6"	89 tons	30
1928	5100	2-6-2T	(o)18 x 30	200/225 psi	5' 8"	75½-78¼T	240
1929	5700	0-6-0PT	17½ x 24	200 psi	4' 7½"	40-50 tons	863
1930	2251	0-6-0	17½ x 24	200 psi	5' 2"	43T 8 cwt	120
1931	5400	0-6-0PT	16½ x 24	165 psi	5' 2"	46T 12 cwt	25
1932	6400	0-6-0PT	16½ x 24	180 psi	4' 7½"	45½ tons	90
1932	4800	0-4-2T	16 x 24	165 psi	5' 2"	41T 6 cwt	95
1934	1366	0-6-0PT	(o)16 x 20	165 psi	3' 8"	35T 15 cwt	6
1934	7200	2-8-2T	(o)19 x 30	200 psi	4' 7½"	92T 2 cwt	54
1936	Grange	4-6-0	(o)18½ x 30	225 psi	5' 8"	74 tons	80
1938	Manor	4-6-0	(o)18 x 30	225 psi	5' 8"	69 tons	30
1939	2181	0-6-0PT	16½ x 24	165 psi	4' 1½"	39T 15 cwt	10

Collett's Principal Re-builds, or Additions to Other Designs

YEAR	NEW CLASS	WHEEL ARRANGEMENT	OLD CLASS	ORIGINAL YEAR	No. in CLASS
1923	4700	2-8-0	4700	1919	9
1923	5205	2-8-0T	4200	1910	46
1925	4300	2-6-0	4300	1911	25
1927	4575	2-6-2T	4500	1906	100
1936	Dukedog	4-4-0	Duke/Bulldog	1895	30
1938	3100	2-6-2T	3150	1906	5
1938	8100	2-6-2T	3100	1906	10
1938	2800	2-8-0	2800	1903	83

COLLETT's PRESERVED LOCOMOTIVES

YEAR	CLASS	RUNNING NUMBERS	TOTAL
1923	Castle	4073/79, 5029/43/51//80, 7027/29	8
1924	5600	5619/37/43/68, 6619/34/86/95/97	9
1924	Hall	4920/30/36/42/53/79/83, 5900/52/67/72	11
1927	King	6000/23/24	3
1927	4575	4588, 5521/26/32/38/39/41/42/52/53/72	11
1928	5100	4110/15/21/41/44/50/60, 5164/93/99	10
1929	5700	5764/73/86, 7714/15/52/54/60	8
1930	2251	3205	1
1931	6100/5100	6106	1
1932	6400	6412/30/35	3
1932	1400/4800	1420/42/50/66	4
1933	5700/3600	3612/50, 3738, 4612, 9600/29/42/81/82	9
1934	1366	1363	1
1934	7200	7200/02/29	3
1936	Dukedog	9017	1
1938	2800	2885, 3802/3/14/22/45/50/55/62	9
1938	Manor	7802/08/12/19/20/21/22/27/28	9

SAMUEL WAITE JOHNSON
The Artistic Engineer

The late-19th century was a halcyon time for British steam locomotive engineers. Just look at those who held the highest offices in the final decade of that century: Webb ruled supremely and absolutely at Crewe; Drummond left his native Scotland behind to breath fire, brimstone and much else into the genteel counties of southern England; Jones blazed the trail in northern Scotland; McIntosh took a second-rank railway to the forefront of British steam traction; Adams, ah, now there was an artist and an innovator; Dean prepared the ground for a revolution at Swindon; and P. Stirling, the grand old man of them all, well, his engines still hauled the fastest train service in the world. What was it that propelled these engineers to the very summit of their profession, far ahead of their peers, yet each being quite distinct from the other?

As with any highly successful person, it is a combination of factors, with luck being one of the most important. Mind you, even the luckiest person in the world cannot be highly successful without talent — politicians and leading bureaucrats excepted, ambition, determination and by using personal contacts to the full. Somehow, one cannot imagine, say, Drummond opening his Victorian equivalent of the filofax and coming out with, "Hello there, is that Ritchie Moon? It's Dougie Drummond here. I just wondered if you fancied giving Franny the old heave-ho and breathing some real fire into Crewe?" Perhaps not, but each of all the aforementioned engineers added something to the development of the steam locomotive; their respective paths to the top seemingly pre-ordained.

It was not quite the same for Johnson. Bearing the same name as that irritatingly pompous, 18th century high-society snob, S.W. was anything but. While each of the above engineers was renowned for at least one design being, for example, the finest of its kind in Britain, or some other engineering accolade, Johnson was held in equal engineering esteem by the 1890s. Yet none of his locomotives held such an honour.

Johnson was neither an innovator, nor an inspired leader — if anything he was pretty anonymous, and whereas some railways hankered after, say, a Stirling 8 ft. single, few would swap their locomotives for a dainty, slight, MR Johnson 4-4-0. Yet, for all that, Johnson's designs were aptly suited to their tasks and all, passenger and goods alike, were outstandingly stylish and exquisitely turned out. Of course, Dean and Stirling built magnificent singles, Adams produced several masterpieces, McIntosh had his 'Dunalastairs' and so forth, but no contemporary engineer built such an homogeneous locomotive fleet as did Johnson.

In that respect, Johnson had much in common with Sir William Lyons, of Swallow Sidecars, S.S. Cars and finally Jaguar. Lyons' genius came to the fore in his styling work, culminating in the Jaguar XJ saloon. 'Grace, space and pace' was Jaguar's slogan of the 1950s and 1960s: that would have applied to the MR in Johnson's day. Grace, with Johnson's engines; space, MR carriages were the finest in Britain; and

pace, MR expresses were not the fastest, but they were little slower than the GNR's in terms of average speeds.

Being capable of pretty, detail design was hardly a great attribute in the harsh, empirical world of railway engineering though, so just how did Johnson rise to the top? He was not a prodigy, as was Webb, yet he became the Locomotive Superintendent of three companies and was a temporary incumbent at a fourth. Johnson's path was one more familiar to our own times: he used his personal contacts to the full. Why not, one might ask? Well, for a start, it's a bit of a problem bluffing your way along and then being caught out at regular intervals. Johnson need not have worried on that count, but he did not really find his niche until he joined the MR.

He got off to a fortunate start. Born into an engineering family, his father was later employed by the GNR, and once young Samuel left school he too undertook an engineering apprenticeship, at E.B. Wilson & Co., in Leeds. It was there that Johnson got lucky, for he reputedly assisted David Joy — of valve-gear fame — with drawings for their popular 'Jenny Lind' locomotives. As the first engine was built in 1847, Johnson cannot have added much, if anything, to the design but, no doubt, he made little of that triviality.

Using contacts through his father, Johnson then gained employment on the GNR, at Peterborough, eventually becoming the Works Manager, under C.R. Sacre — Stroudley was a fellow employee at that time. Both of these engineers were to feature in Johnson's career, over the next decade: Sacre became the Locomotive Superintendent of the MSLR, and Johnson followed him to Gorton, as Carriage and Wagon Works Manager, in 1859. Meanwhile, Stroudley moved north to become the Cowlairs Works Manager, for the Edinburgh and Glasgow Railway, and in 1864 Johnson became that company's Locomotive Superintendent.

As things transpired, just as our modern railway companies are selling-out or amalgamating with alarming rapidity, so it often was with the early railways. Johnson had not long got his feet comfortably under the chief's table at Cowlairs, when the EGR became part of the new NBR, in 1865. He had already purchased some 2-4-0 locomotives to his predecessor's design, and then designed some 0-4-2s, based on Beyer-Peacock locomotives already in service. These had double-frames and domeless boilers, but were otherwise undistinguished. Too much ought not to be expected too soon, but Johnson did not benefit from the amalgamation, becoming merely the Western Division Locomotive Superintendent of the N.B.R.

Having whetted his appetite for power, Johnson wanted more, and in 1866 he moved to Stratford, as the Locomotive Superintendent of the ambitious, yet penurious, GER. This railway had only been formed in 1862 and had soon outgrown its financial boots. Traffic was growing and the network needed to expand, but the financial wherewithal was distinctly lacking. As for its locomotive engineers, the GER was almost a Locomotive Superintendents finishing-school for, apart from

Johnson's GER 'No.1' class was designed for light passenger duties, in 1867. Adams added a dome and a stovepipe chimney, while Holden rebuilt the whole class from 1889-91. No. 34 is seen at Lowestoft, at the turn of the century. Fourteen were later given 160 psi boilers, but all were withdrawn by 1913.

Johnson, Adams and T.W. Worsdell also cut their despotic teeth at Stratford. Each produced some good work for the luckless railway, before moving on to greater things elsewhere. All this, eventually, left the GER with an increasingly disparate stock of incompatible locomotives.

That was in the future though, and it was while at the GER that Johnson developed ideas that came to fruition on the MR. In particular, his ability to match the engines to there intended tasks was an important feature of Johnson's later work, and equally his almost flawless styling. While these ideas germinated, the GER, desperately needed locomotives: so desperately in fact, that five 2-4-0s built by Neilson, Reid & Co. for the NBR were diverted south and delivered to Stratford, in 1867.

These double-framed engines went straight into service, and Johnson virtually copied them for his inaugural GER design, the 'No.1' class, or 'Little Sharpies'. He merely added a dome to the boiler and reduced the driving wheels from 6 ft. to 5 ft. 7 in. They were intended for light passenger trains and 40 were built over 5 years, as a measure of their ability. Of course, they were never going to blaze an innovative trail, but were invaluable. Although modified by Adams and then thoroughly rebuilt by Holden — some twice, the last 'Little Sharpie' was not withdrawn until 1913, still undertaking work for which they were originally designed.

Johnson's was a necessarily cautious start: the GER could hardly afford any extravagant failures. Agricultural traffic was building-up and to cater for this, also in 1867, Johnson produced the entirely orthodox '417' class 0-6-0. These diminutive engines were just what the doctor ordered: simple, cheap and reliable. So thoroughly typical were they that Johnson did not provide any worthwhile weather protection for the crews. In 1871, Johnson improved on this with the slightly larger '477' class goods engines. The last of these just saw in the new century, and formed the basis for his later freight designs.

Slowly but surely, Johnson ensured that the current locomotive needs of the GER were being fulfilled, producing the 'T7' class 0-4-2T for light branch work, in 1871. Once again, weather protection was given a miss, probably the only fault in yet another efficient design. This was fast becoming a Johnson trademark. Unfortunately, these were a bit too small for their intended tasks, and had relatively short lives, the first being withdrawn after only 20 years' service, the last by 1894.

Of much greater success, both for longevity and in setting a pattern for the future, was the '133' class 0-4-4T. Once again, Johnson omitted to protect his crews from the elements, but this design was to be a standard-bearer for the future. On the whole, Johnson is noted for his outstanding locomotive styling and their magnificent finish: he is not usually thought of as an innovator. That is as maybe, but this was Britain's first inside-frame 0-4-4 side-tank locomotive, a configuration multiplied not only by Johnson on the MR, but by railways throughout the land.

The '133' class was Johnson's answer to the need for powerful, yet fast accelerating locomotives to cope with London's ever-expanding suburban traffic. These were, if not an outright revelation, a major step forward in tank-engine design: simple, straight-forward, efficient and very capable performers on the new lines of north-east London. Johnson's successor, Adams, preferred outside cylinders, but he based his first design on the successful '133' class. Adams soon added cabs to Johnson's engines, as well, and not before time.

This was the last of Johnson's designs to be built while he held office at Stratford, but his final effort for the GER also broke new ground. Sinclair's singles hauled what main line traffic there was, but their days were increasingly numbered. Johnson grasped the nettle and, probably influenced by his sojourn in Scotland, produced the first English 4-4-0. The two engines of the 'C8' class were completed in 1874, having inside frames and cylinders, and an Adams bogie — no doubt Johnson's successor was pleased to see that. The engines also appeared with a cab, although that might have been Adams' work, and were soon placed on express work.

Adams was certainly influenced by the design and attempted to emulate it. Inside cylinder 4-4-0s eventually became not only the standard GER express locomotives, but the classic British express locomotive. Holden rebuilt both 'C8s' and they were withdrawn by 1898. Not, perhaps, a long life, but they were certainly the forerunners of great things to come, culminating in the outstanding 'Claud Hamilton' class.

Johnson's groundwork on the GER was vital to his developing career, to setting the locomotive pattern for the company and, of course, reached its zenith on the MR. His move from Stratford to Derby, in 1873, was to be the making of the man. Though he had done good work on the GER, the financial constraints were always keenly present, and Adams spent much of his first two years thoroughly re-organising Stratford Works. From that, we might assume, Johnson had not been an altogether outstanding success.

At Derby, though, the locomotive works was in much better shape: it was, after all, one of the finest in Britain even then.

Derby certainly expanded during Johnson's nigh 31 years in charge, but his predecessor, M. Kirtley, had left a first-rate outfit for the lucky successor. I was exactly the same for the locomotive fleet as well, while the board took the opportunity to split the locomotive and carriage building operations: Johnson was only responsible for the former.

Although the MR was a far bigger railway than the GER and, by opening the Settle & Carlisle line, was to aptly demonstrate its ambition, a tight rein on the purse-strings was the board's chief method of exerting control. Thus, the axle load of the main line to St. Pancras was only 12½ tons. Not only did this encourage the development of four-coupled engines at a time when coupling-rods were thought to restrict speed — and in reality did, but it imposed cost-constraints on new locomotives. Yes, the railway had a monopoly on its main lines south and south-west of Derby, but the GNR also served Nottingham, Sheffield, Leeds and Bradford. In addition, the lucrative Manchester traffic faced intense competition from the LNWR, while the East and West Coast companies were not going to sit back and allow the MR to pinch their Anglo-Scottish patronage.

So, the MR had to compete to survive on most of its main routes, and therefore had to develop a successful strategy. By the time Johnson arrived at Derby, the GNR expresses were already noted for their speed. Despite sharing a longer route with the MSLR, the GNR competed gallantly for Sheffield and Manchester traffic: this appealed to the brash, go-getting, empire-building mentality so prevalent at that time.

The LNWR was, on the other hand, the railway of bourgeois middle-England. Steady, dependable, comfortable: the self-styled Premier Line. Regular as clockwork, running on the finest permanent-way in the land, though at modest speeds; service with civility. Somehow, the MR had to compete. The board, not un-surprisingly, chose an appropriate course: the middle ground. Thanks to rather feeble permanent-way, loads had to be light and locomotives relatively small. There was no chance of the MR having a Stirling 8 ft. single equivalent at the head of an express: coupled engines were essential to stay within the low axle loading. So, the MR was unlikely to compete on speed, but that still left comfort, ambience and service.

As the MR permanent-way fell far short of the L.N.W.R's, so it was likely to lag behind in ride quality. However, with fine bogie coaches and Pullman cars, the MR then pulled the real ace from up its sleeve: abolition of second class travel and upgrading third class. Hence, the MR's tradition of fast, frequent and light trains was born: slowly at first, but gathering momentum throughout Johnson's tenure and beyond.

As far as passenger services were concerned, Johnson only had to produce engines of modest power, yet with a turn of speed capable of meeting the demands of the board's strategy. The ever expanding London bound goods services faced similar weight restrictions, so the same parameters pretty much applied there: light and yet powerful. It was soon apparent that, in Johnson, the MR had found exactly the man.

The long list of Johnson's locomotive classes suggests that he was something of an inveterate designer: no other locomotive engineer has penned so many. However, in reality, there were six basic main line types — plus the small yard shunters, each with only minor differences. Take the 4-4-0s, for instance. There are 13 separate classes, yet the first 11, built over a period of 25 years, had only detail differences. Early ones had smaller boilers and fireboxes, while steel boilers were introduced from 1885, and piston valves a decade later. It was, though, only the much bigger 'Belpaires' and finally the 'Compounds' that were major new designs. The same applied to all Johnson's engines. He analysed and filled the needs with a suitable design, and improved things as time went on: Johnson was never happy simply turning out more of the same.

This degree of standardisation had originated in Johnson's work on the GER, and he introduced four of his six basic MR types while at Stratford. For express passenger work, and in particular the opening of the Settle & Carlisle line, he developed the 'No. 1' class 2-4-0, that had much in common with Kirtley's designs. It was not an auspicious start. These engines were swiftly moved away from their intended main line tasks to work lowly local passenger trains in the East Midlands. They soon found a niche though as, despite being the first of Johnson's 2-4-0s to be withdrawn, in 1912, the last survived until 1950, and was then fully 74 years old.

Even before this class's limitations were apparent, a larger wheeled version, the '1282' class was being built for the southern main lines. As with Kirtley's designs, these were eventually used all over the MR, proving to be versatile, economical and dependable and soon predominated on the Settle & Carlisle line. Up until 1881, two more similar classes emerged with 6 ft. 9 in. and 7 ft. wheels respectively. The former also found themselves out in the bleak north, while the '101' class took their place on the main London expresses.

Johnson's 2-4-0s were steady-riding, useful engines that survived long after their notional sell-by date, because of the MR passenger train policy. Some even acted as main-line pilots into LMS days, on the odd occasion. They worked from London-Carlisle and York-Bristol and were, in truth, reasonably powerful for their time. Johnson eventually rebuilt many of Kirtley's 2-4-0s to give the MR a fleet that was, if not one of envy, at least adaptable, dependable and long-lasting.

Engineering reputations were not going to be made with such engines, though. Johnson's 4-4-0 for the GER indicated where his thoughts lay and, in 1876, he introduced his first MR design, the '1312' class. Initially intended to work the Peak District main line, this was, to all intents and purposes, a '1282' class 2-4-0 with a leading bogie. The following year, the '1327' class emerged with 7 ft. driving wheels: effectively a bogie version of the express '101' class 2-4-0s. These were also intended for the Peak line, but often worked to London. So, why was Johnson building almost identical engines, for similar duties, as both 2-4-0s and 4-4-0s?

The main reason seems to have concerned their riding qualities. The long, rigid wheelbase of the 2-4-0 did not cause undue wheel flange wear on corners, while the locomotives were steady at speed. The Adams bogie, used by Johnson on his 4-4-0s, ultimately caused even less wear and tear on the track, but the shorter, rigid wheelbase caused the engines to sway at speed. It took Johnson several years to make his mind up, but from 1881 he built no more 2-4-0s.

The early 4-4-0s looked rather puny alongside the 2-4-0s: the extra chassis length seemingly shortening the boiler. This did not worry Johnson though, and from 1882 he produced a whole series of almost identical 4-4-0s with either 6 ft. 9 in. or 7 ft. driving wheels. Like P. Stirling, Johnson did not want crews flogging his engines, so they were always under-boilered and over-cylindered. Indeed, as with his later singles, the boiler capacity was even reduced with the passing years, although the working pressure was gradually increased, at the expense of a larger firebox. Such a philosophy was, of course, contrary to the ideals of later locomotive engineers, but it ensured that the engines were worked as lightly and economically as possible.

Compare, if you will, respective Manchester expresses of

Johnson's first MR 2-4-0s were no better than those of his predecessor, M. Kirtley, but he got his sums right by the time the '1400' class emerged in 1878. Initially used on London-Leeds expresses, they worked as express pilots into LMS days. No. 1461 rests at Kettering early this century, with many years' work ahead of it, despite its already ageing looks.

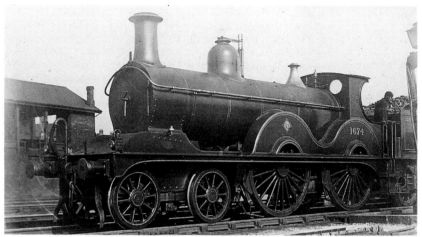

The fine lines of Johnson's earlier 4-4-0s can be appreciated in this picture of '1667' class No. 1674, at Kettering. This was built at Derby in 1884, and featured Joy's valve gear. They were not a great success, due to their small boilers, and all were rebuilt from 1896-1901, and yet again from 1912-14. Thereafter, they lasted into BR ownership.

the MR and LNWR in, say, 1890. On the Premier Line, while speeds were modest, the engines were built, and expected, to work hard to earn their corn. So, one might easily find a small 'Jumbo' 2-4-0 — diminutive even alongside its MR cousin, at the head of an express that ran at similar speeds to the MR rival, yet weighed far more. There is no question, you would see and hear the roaring 'Jumbo' from miles away. The MR 4-4-0 would, by way of comparison, almost purr along. The timings of some MR expresses were being improved at that time, to close on GNR standards, but should the load be a bit on the heavy side, a pilot was soon brought forth with indecent haste.

The normal driving method of a Johnson 4-4-0 was not unlike that required for a Stirling single: hauling its load up hill at speed, and then coasting down to allow the boiler to recover. The fastest recorded speed of a small Johnson 4-4-0, in the 19th century, was barely 80 mph. It was a formula that served many railways well, but few engineers perfected boiler capacity parsimony to quite the extent of Johnson. Ultimately, Johnson's numerous 4-4-0s fulfilled their intended tasks to such an exactitude, that it seemed as though the MR express services were designed round the capacity of the locomotives, and not vice versa.

Time, though, never stands still and even the MR could not ignore the trend towards faster and heavier expresses. As the

MR led the field with bogie coaches, so its train weights inevitably crept up, despite sticking with its fast, frequent and light policy. By 1900, Johnson was building ever-bigger 4-4-0s, and he then took one giant step forward. Dean and Churchward had adopted the Belpaire firebox for their 4-4-0s and Johnson did likewise, replacing the Salter safety valve with Ramsbottom's, and using a larger grate and boiler, along with piston valves. Unlike their smaller sisters, these '2606' class, or 'Belpaires', were no pretty and dainty little things. Their inside frames did not make them look quite so rustic as Dean's brutish creations, but they marked a distinct change to a more purposeful, if less elegant style — let us be polite and say purposeful.

The 'Belpaires' were intended for the arduous Settle & Carlisle, and Peak District main lines, where their power, free steaming and sure-footed climbing all combined to good effect, but they could also run along with the best. In 1904, a 'Belpaire' hauled a service train from St. Pancras-Leicester at a nett average speed of over 60 mph, while the odd sprint into the 80s mph was far from unusual. Johnson might have sacrificed a bit of grace, but gained pace and power aplenty.

If the 'Belpaires' marked something of a dramatic sea-change, Johnson's final 4-4-0 design was drastically different. Two 3-cylinder compounds were built in 1901, clearly based on W.M. Smith's NER compound, of 1898. While Smith's boss, W. Worsdell, was hardly an evangelical compound convert, Johnson was more than interested. His first two 'Compounds' had independent control for the two low-pressure and single high-pressure cylinders, but this feature yielded only marginal benefits in daily use. Only 5 'Compounds' were built by Johnson, so it was left to his successor, R.M. Deeley, to build enough to make a real impression on services. Indeed, given the later, stringent limited-load policy of the MR, it could be argued that the 'Compounds' were rather wasted on the company.

Meanwhile, on the Settle & Carlisle line, the 'Compounds' were not just a revelation, but almost a revolution. They economically hauled loads well beyond the capacity of any other engines, and reputedly topped the 90 mph mark with impunity. It was clear that the 'Compounds' were just about the equal of any locomotive running in Edwardian Britain, but they were not used widely on the southern main lines, as the typical, lightly loaded express was in more than capable hands with a small 4-4-0 at its head. Eventually, of course, the 'Compounds' became an LMS standard design, travelling farther afield than Johnson could ever have imagined. Mind you, the 'Compounds' and 'Belpaires' showed that the old dog Johnson was more than capable of learning some very impressive new tricks.

As for goods traffic, the MR was a fortunate recipient of an almost continuous procession of coal trains from the Midlands and West Riding to London. While this traffic amassed vast, ever-increasing profits for the company, it also brought operating headaches that occasionally bordered on migraine proportions. Slow, loose-coupled trains rambling along main lines are hardly compatible with the notion of railways as a rapid transport system and, in addition, there were many other types of goods trains to cater for as well.

The MR's light axle-loading placed severe restrictions on goods as well as passenger trains, and so Johnson produced a whole series of 0-6-0 designs. Over 27 years, 8 classes of these engines incorporated many modest improvements, but all were thoroughly orthodox, conventional profit-earners. As with thousands of similar engines all over Britain, once each class was successively displaced from the main lines, they found plenty of work trundling round rural branches to eke out a profitable(ish) existence, almost until the end of steam. Though Johnson's 0-6-0s were never widely lauded, all the classes put in over 60 years' hard labour.

As with his express 4-4-0s so, right at the end of his tenure, Johnson produced a much bigger animal with the '2736' class. These had a Belpaire firebox and the larger 'H' pattern boiler and, along with the 'Belpaires' and 'Compounds', showed the hand of Deeley, working behind the scenes. These larger engines, though still relative light-weights, formed the basis of designs by Deeley and Fowler, both of whom rebuilt many of Johnson's engines. Despite Johnson's numerous, modestly different goods designs, the MR was amply provided for, including a number of American 'moguls' purchased at the turn of the century. As with his 4-4-0s, Johnson's 0-6-0s formed the basis of the locomotive fleet into the early years of the LMS.

It was no different with Johnson's branch and suburban passenger, and shunting tank-engines: as with the 4-4-0s and 0-6-0s, he followed the same principle of modestly developing basic standard designs. From 1875-1900, he perpetuated the 0-4-4T for passenger duties: a series of designs developed from his GER work, that were as reliable as they were long-lasting. Some had condensing gear for working on London's underground lines, but although six designs were produced, each was more a case of modest progression and improvement, rather than anything approaching a change of tack.

For shunting and light goods work, Johnson settled on the 0-6-0T and five different designs were produced from 1874-1902. In fact, the differences between the first four classes were minimal in the extreme, but the final '2441' class was significantly larger. All of these designs were versatile, reliable and long-lasting, but the '2441' class was multiplied in considerable numbers by the LMS as their standard '3F' shunting tank. These eventually worked all over the vast system, including the SDJR, and Johnson's original engines soldiered on virtually until the end of steam. While goods tank engines can hardly be expected to secure a locomotive engineer's reputation, Johnson's last 0-6-0Ts were second-to-none for many years hence.

When it came to yard shunters, Johnson ploughed exactly the same furrow. The first three classes were all 0-4-0Ts having saddle-tanks and inside cylinders, with the initial '1322' class, of 1883, being particularly diminutive. Weighing only 19 tons, these engines epitomised the MR locomotive policy: the minimum size to do the job, but still with the attention to detail and presentation that graced the finest express locomotives.

Yet again, almost as a final farewell, Johnson produced a much bigger design with which to sign-off. The '1528' class was not only bigger, it was quite different to its smaller brothers. Side-tanks replaced the saddle-tanks, while they had outside cylinders worked by Walschaert's valve-gear. As a result, these were quite unique and though none were especially long-lasting, in comparison with most of Johnson's designs, they were all still thoroughly efficient engines.

In a sense, such a standardised fleet of locomotives would have suited most British railways yet, with few exceptions, it was almost out of date by 1910. That Johnson's designs were able to survive so much longer was due to the later MR running policy, with strictly enforced loads for each type of engine. Thanks to the MR management being able to impose these standards on the LMS, Johnson's engines, rebuilt or not, enjoyed an enhanced life-span when, in truth, they were really beyond the requirements for a modern railway.

Thus, the small 4-4-0s were still acting as main line pilots to LMS 'Compounds', on trains the latter were perfectly capable of handling by themselves. It was pretty much the same for the 2-4-0s — even Kirtley's — though to a lesser extent while, as heavy goods engines did not work on the MR lines, the diminutive 0-6-0s enjoyed themselves for years after they warranted pensioning off. Then again, few MR engines really knew what hard work was.

So, Johnson's engines, though ideally suited to MR requirements, had been little more than par for the course. Only the 'Compounds' would have been able to look their contemporaries squarely in the buffer-beams, and not felt a tinge of inferiority. However, the best has been saved until last. By the time Johnson designed his first single-driver locomotive, in 1887, astute observers of railways were realising that their grand era was, if not drawing to a close, approaching its zenith. Adhesion factors alone limited these dashing princes of the road, and with the increasing use of bogie coaches, train weights were unlikely to be reduced.

Yet, a combination of circumstances enabled Johnson to build his single-drivers long after others had given up the ghost. There are various stories connected with their introduction: some involving a shed foreman running one of Kirtley's singles after Johnson had ordered them to be laid-up; another concerning the use of Westinghouse air-brake pumps to force sand onto the rails, thus improving the singles' adhesion. As with Chinese Whispers, these stories have evolved over the years but, whatever recalcitrant employees were up to, Johnson had also been carefully considering the use of singles as MR axle limits were steadily raised.

Once the Derby Works Manager, F.C. Holt, devised steam-sanding, after the abortive trials using air-forced sanding, it was inevitable that Johnson would try his hand at designing a single-driver. The first engines of the '25' class emerged in 1887, with 7 ft. 4 in. driving wheels, 18 in. cylinders and cart springs beneath the driving wheel bearings; the majority had 7ft. 6 in. driving wheels, 18½ in. cylinders and twin coil-springs. Steel boilers were used with double-frames: a seemingly retrograde move aimed at taking care of the more concentrated stresses. As usual, an Adams bogie controlled the front end. Naturally enough, sand pipes were fitted fore and, later, aft of the big driving wheel and very soon these 'Spinners' were creating a name and reputation for themselves and their designer, with some decidedly fine running.

Despite the rising train weights, the MR policy of fast, frequent and light was eminently suited to these superb engines, as they demonstrated their prowess on the southern

Undoubtedly, Johnson's finest tank engine was the '2441' class, that enjoyed a lengthy life, and successfully traversed the gap between 19th and 20th century designs. The LMS went and built a further 422 of these '3Fs' and they just about saw out the end of steam on the Midland Region of BR. Rather earlier, No. 2444 shunts the yard at Childs Hill during its first years.

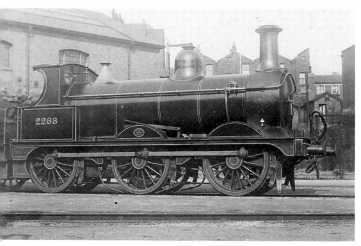

This is how it all was. Even goods engines were fully lined-out and brightly burnished. A typical Johnson 0-6-0, No. 2268 built in 1897, stands at Kentish Town, in London. This was one of the unlucky ones, being withdrawn in 1947, as the majority saw service on BR. Not especially outstanding locomotives, they still earned good profits from their hard work over many decades.

---

and south-western main lines. By the 1890s, there was a renaissance for single-drivers for, almost flying in the face of reality, the GWR, GER, NER and, of course, GNR built many new engines, and Johnson confirmed his conversion to the cause by building in greater numbers than them all. His '179' class emerged in 1893, having slightly larger cylinders operated by piston valves and, three years later, the outstanding '115' class took its bow. Not only did these feature a new boiler but, as with the 4-4-0s, they had a reduced heating surface and a larger firebox. These fine engines were probably the fastest of Johnson's singles, combining power, speed and grace to enable the MR to all-but match the pace of the GNR expresses.

The main thesis behind the single-driver locomotive was that the large driving wheel would allow higher speeds to be reached than with coupled wheels, whether smaller or not. P. Stirling designed his singles to run up hill at a fair old lick, and for their diminutive boilers to recover on the downhill stretches: just when high speeds could be expected to be reached. It was rare for Stirling's singles to go much faster than 70 mph in everyday service, despite hauling the fastest passenger train service in the world. The same was generally true for Johnson's singles, though speeds of 80+ mph were not entirely infrequent. This apparent contradiction had its benefits though, as the singles were seldom driven hard and so were light on fuel, while should the need for high speeds arise, the singles were more than up for it.

Then, just as the era of the single-driver was seemingly doomed, Johnson brought out the '2601' class, in 1900. These were not quite the last singles to be built in Britain as,

strangely enough, the last year of the century saw the GNR and GCR also producing new designs. The 'Princess of Wales' class hauled substantial double-bogie tenders and, perhaps, lost a little in the elegance stakes, but they were still pretty and impressive. That, of course, is purely a matter of opinion and not especially relevant to an engine's daily work, but the class possibly came along too late to be fully appreciated, unlike the '115s'.

Thanks to the MR's fast, frequent and light policy, Johnson's singles enjoyed longer active lives than their counterparts elsewhere. Despite giving way to Deeley's 'Compounds' on the expresses, the singles were regularly used as pilots. They were also put to good use on local trains, especially in the Midlands, while it was not unknown — but surely a waste of resources — to find one as pilot on a goods train during the First World War. The last of Johnson's singles was withdrawn in 1928.

It is clear that Johnson built a great many fine locomotives. They were exquisitely styled and finished right until the turn of the century, when his hand was forced and even the MR found a need for larger, more powerful engines. None of them was a truly great design though; equally, none was a failure, and the 'Compounds' did much to counter the poor reputation for this type of engine. On the other hand, Johnson only built 5, and while Deeley and Fowler multiplied them, they too fell short of being really great engines.

Johnson retired at the end of 1903. Webb and Dean also stood down at about the same time, and Britain's railways lost some outstanding engineers. Of the many, great late-19th century Locomotive Superintendents, it was Johnson who had, perhaps surprisingly, the longest-lasting effect. This was not because his locomotives were the best, simply because the MR senior management seized control of the LMS and 'Compounds', 4-4-0s and other basically Johnson designs were multiplied. Ultimately, in the long-run — but also seen by some at the time, this small engine policy was a mistake: one that, had Stanier not arrived to effectively reverse it, could have been disastrous for the company. That was not Johnson's fault though, any more than it was the fault of Karl Marx that so-called socialism failed in Eastern Europe. If principles are poorly applied at the wrong time, what else can one expect?

There is almost a contradiction in our title Stars of Steam, in that hardly any of the featured locomotive engineers were stars in the accepted sense, and nor — on the whole — did they seek the limelight. Professional recognition by their peers was another matter though, and all of our 'stars' would appreciate any such honour bestowed upon them. While Johnson's locomotives were perhaps the foremost example of 19th century railway mechanical art, that by itself would not gain him wide respect. It was more the suitability of his designs to their allotted and intended tasks that made them special.

Although this is not a Johnson engine, R.M. Deeley's 'Compounds' differed to his predecessor's only in detail. With these, the transition from mid-Victorian to Edwardian design was complete and the MR had some of the finest passenger engines of their day. Working mostly over the Settle-Carlisle and Peak District lines, No. 1037 — one of the batch built in 1908/9 — is seen in its earliest days, at Manchester.

There were exceptions, but generally it was the immediate compatibility of the locomotive to its intended work, often enabling improvements in timings to be made, that was such a feature of each successive Johnson design.

Unlike Webb, Johnson did not mastermind a nigh-revolution, only to fall way short of the target. Each of Johnson's successive designs was a carefully measured, modest step forward, though such a circumspect approach did not preclude innovation, as demonstrated by his early use of steel boilers and piston valves. Such progress, coupled with a finish that was bettered by no other railway — at a time when such things really counted, ensured that Johnson's work was highly regarded by all in his profession.

Thus, he became a council member of the IME in 1884, a Vice-President 11 years later, and received the ultimate honour of being elected President in 1898. Similarly, he was the first Chairman of the ARLE, in 1890, and became President of that body in 1895. These honours are an accurate indication of the esteem that his fellow engineers held both Johnson and his work, and should not be taken lightly given that few steam locomotive engineers ever became President of the IME.

As with most Stars of Steam, Johnson's career and family dominated his life. His only son, John, had been the Locomotive Superintendent of the GNSR from 1890-94, not with any lasting success, while he also had five daughters. Just as it is today, though often with a not inconsiderable remuneration on quango's, so people in Johnson's position either sought, or were sought-after, for civic duties. Johnson became a JP in his adopted city of Nottingham and also an Income Tax Commissioner. These were no more than par for the course at the time; such positions rarely being granted to working people, who were usually too busy making a basic living to indulge in flights of fancy. Nowadays, of course, it is all jobs, money, influence and connections for the boys: the idea of duty — as in Johnson's time — being long-gone.

Once he retired, Johnson lived an anonymous life in Nottingham for a further 9 years. It seems strange that so many of our Stars of Steam devoted all their lives to their profession yet, when the time came to stand down, most seem to have severed all links, if not with the railway industry as a whole, with their former employers. No doubt, each had many reasons for so doing, but the departure of such talented men must have been a loss not easily replaced. Go Johnson did though, while he did not undertake still further civic duties. At least he never saw his life's work eliminated or heavily modified by his successor, Deeley. Indeed, it must have given him pride to see first Deeley and then Fowler seemingly follow and develop his path, in everything except the styling of his earlier designs.

Johnson was not a great railway locomotive engineer, but either through new designs or the rebuilding of his predecessor's — or even his own earlier ones, he totally transformed the locomotive fleet of one of Britain's major railways. In addition, the 'Compounds' were the most successful of their kind then produced and, even though they were by no means Johnson's own work, it was he who instigated their building and use. That any of his locomotives looked magnificent at the head of their trains, especially once the Crimson Lake livery had been adopted was, as with Sir William Lyons, the real mark of his genius. No other 19th century British steam locomotive engineer produced so many outstandingly styled designs, whether for passenger, goods or shunting.

JOHNSON's PRESERVED LOCOMOTIVES

YEAR	CLASS	RUNNING NUMBERS	TOTAL
1887	115	673	1
1878	1377	B.R. 41708	1
1902	Compound	1000	1

JOHNSON IN BRIEF

BORN:	14th October 1831, Bramley, Yorks.
EDUCATED:	Leeds Grammar School.
TRAINED:	E.B. Wilson & Co. App. under James Fenton.
EMPLOYED:	Great Northern Railway. Works Manager, Peterborough.
SENIOR POSITIONS:	1859 Works Manager, Gorton. Also acting Loco. Supt. M.S.L.R.
	1864, Loco. Supt. Edinburgh and Glasgow Railway
	1865, Loco. Supt. of Western Division, N.B.R.
	1866, Loco. Supt. G.E.R.
	1873, Loco. Supt. M.R.
RETIRED:	31st December 1903.
HONOURS:	1884, Council Member, I.M.E.
	1895, Vice President, I.M.E.
	1898, President, I.M.E.
	1890, Chairman, A.R.L.E.
	1895, President, A.R.L.E.
	1895, Magistrate, Nottingham.
DIED:	14th January 1912, Nottingham.

Johnson's Locomotive Designs

YEAR	CLASS	WHEEL ARRANG'T	CYLINDERS (INCHES)	BOILER PRESSURE	DRIVING-WHEEL DIAMETER	WEIGHT	No. IN CLASS
Edinburgh and Glasgow Railway							
1864		0-4-2	16 x 22	120 psi	5 ft.		
Great Eastern Railway							
1867	No. 1	2-4-0	16 x 22	140 psi	5' 7"	29 tons	40
1867	417	0-6-0	16½ x 24	140 psi	5' 3"	30¾ tons	60
1871	477	0-6-0	17 x 24	140 psi	5' 1"	32¾ tons	50
1871	T7	0-4-2T	15 x 22	140 psi	5' 3"		15
1872	133	0-4-4T	17 x 24	140 psi	5' 3"	42¾ tons	45
1874	C8	4-4-0	17 x 24	140 psi	6' 6"	39½ tons	2

YEAR	CLASS	WHEEL ARRANG'T	CYLINDERS (INCHES)	BOILER PRESSURE	DRIVING-WHEEL DIAMETER	WEIGHT	No. IN CLASS
Midland Railway							
1876	1312	4-4-0	17½ x 26	140 psi	6' 6"	41 tons	10
1877	1327	4-4-0	17½ x 26	140 psi	7 ft.	43 tons	20
1882	1562	4-4-0	18 x 26	140 psi	6' 9"	43 tons	30
1884	1667	4-4-0	18 x 26	140 psi	7 ft.	43 tons	10
1885	1740	4-4-0	18 x 26	160 psi	7 ft.	43 tons	20
1888	1808	4-4-0	18 x 26	160 psi	6' 6"	48 tons	35
1892	2183	4-4-0	18½ x 26	160 psi	7 ft.	48 tons	25
1893	2203	4-4-0	18½ x 26	160 psi	6' 6"	48 tons	45
1897	150	4-4-0	18½ x 26	160 psi	7 ft.	51 tons	30
1898	60	4-4-0	19½ x 26	170 psi	7 ft.	52 tons	15
1899	2591	4-4-0	19 x 26	175 psi	7 ft.	52 tons	25
1900	Belpaire	4-4-0	19½ x 26	180 psi	6' 9"	53 tons	80
1901	Compound	4-4-0	L.P.21 x 26 (2) H.P.19 x 26 (1)	195 psi	7 ft.	59 tons	5
1876	No. 1	2-4-0	17½ x 26	140 psi	6' 2½"	40 tons	10
1876	1282	2-4-0	17½ x 26	140 psi	6' 6"	41 tons	40
1877	101	2-4-0	18 x 26	140 psi	7 ft.	41 tons	20
1879	1400	2-4-0	18 x 26	140 psi	6' 9"	41 tons	65
1887	25	4-2-2	18 x 26	160 psi	7' 4"	44 tons	60
1893	179	4-2-2	19 x 26	160 psi	7' 6"	44½ tons	10
1896	115	4-2-2	19½ x 26	170 psi	7' 9"	47 tons	15
1900	2601	4-2-2	19½ x 26	180 psi	7' 9½"	50 tons	10
1878	1357	0-6-0	17½ x 26	140 psi	5' 2½"	34½ tons	30
1885	1698	0-6-0	18 x 26	140 psi	4' 10"	34½ tons	60
1888	1798	0-6-0	18 x 26	140 psi	5' 2½"	35 tons	10
1890	1873	0-6-0	18 x 26	150 psi	5' 2½"	35¼ tons	100
1891	J & J2	0-6-0	18 x 26	150 psi	5' 2½"	36 tons	120
1892	M	0-6-0	18 x 26	150 psi	5' 2½"	36 tons	250
1901	2641	0-6-0	18 x 26	160 psi	5' 2½"	36¼ tons	95
1903	2736	0-6-0	18½ x 26	175 psi	5' 3"	39½ tons	40
1875	6 or C	0-4-4T	17 x 24	140 psi	5' 3"	39½ tons	10
1875	1252	0-4-4T	17 x 24	140 psi	5' 6½"	40 tons	30
1881	1532	0-4-4T	18 x 24	140 psi	5' 3½"	40½ tons	65
1889	1823	0-4-4T	18 x 24	140 psi	5' 3½"	40½ tons	10
1893	1833	0-4-4T	18 x 24	140 psi	5' 3½"	40½ tons	30
1895	2228	0-4-4T	18 x 24	140 psi	5' 3½"	41¾ tons	50
1874	A or 1102	0-6-0T	17 x 24	140 psi	4' 6½"	35½ tons	40
1878	1377	0-6-0T	17 x 24	140 psi	4' 6½"	35 tons	185
1882	1552	0-6-0T	17 x 24	140 psi	4' 6½"	35 tons	20
1895	1121	0-6-0T	17 x 24	140 psi	4' 6½"	35 tons	40
1899	2441	0-6-0T	18 x 26	160 psi	4' 6½"	40 tons	60
1883	1322	0-4-0T	13 x 20	140 psi	3' 9½"	19 tons	10
1893	1116A	0-4-0T	13 x 20	140 psi	3' 9½"	19 tons	10
1897	1134A	0-4-0T	15 x 20	140 psi	3' 9½"	26½ tons	10
1902	1528	0-4-0T	(o)15 x 22	160 psi	3' 9½"	32¾ tons	

DAVID JONES
The English Highland Chieftain

Some years ago, when still a student, I attended an interview in Whitehaven. There were only two other candidates and, to be perfectly honest, I undoubtedly had the best interview in my life. It was a little out of the ordinary insofar as there were about a dozen people sitting round a large table and I had to stand for about an hour. Now, I am a musician in a rock group and am not unused to performing in front of an audience, and I was quite aware that many of those present were very impressed. It seemed that I could hardly put a foot wrong, and if the interviewers had stood up en masse and applauded at the end, well, it would not be the done thing, but I would not have been too surprised.

The short wait while the final candidate was interviewed was a worrying time. We candidates stayed in the same hotel and came to know each other pretty well. This final candidate was hardly a shining academic and, shall we say, lacked knowledge and intellect. The first candidate said that his interview was mediocre, and had indifferent qualifications in any case. 'Surely,' I thought, 'the job is mine, but...did I really want it?'

Over the years, my bicycle peregrinations have taken me round 30-odd countries yet, despite visiting various far-flung corners of the world, Whitehaven felt a bit off the beaten track. Was I too young to work in a sleepy backwater, miles from friends, family and, most important, the sport and music activities on which I thrived? There were many things to weigh up: not least a damned good excuse for not accepting the job for, if one refused, interview expenses would not be paid. With the long journey, the hotel and dinner bills, these soon mounted up.

Engrossed in my thoughts, the door opened and in walked the last candidate. 'What, already', I thought. I could not make a decision, or think of a good excuse. Then the door opened again, and the spokesman said her kind words of consolation about how close it had been...difficult choice and all that flannel, but would — at which point I began to rise — Miss ? please follow her to the... Talk about mixed emotions — sheer relief and yet I was flabbergasted. A decent job in a nice town, but oh so remote. Mind you, the spokesman later explained that I had indeed had an outstanding interview. I had impressed everyone: all — that is — except the one who really counted, the Chairman of Governors.

Of course, that took place in the late-20th century, but just imagine the thoughts of a young Mancunian, who had travelled little, as he set out for a job in remote Inverness, in 1855. If the musician Sting could write about the minor alienation of an 'Englishman in New York', I wonder what the 19th century version would be of an Englishman deposited in the far north. For that is where the young David Jones was heading.

Born in the town at the heart of the Industrial Revolution, that became the catalyst for the revolutionary theories of Frederick Engels and Karl Marx, Jones was apprenticed to the LNWR, at Longsight Works. He was briefly tutored by J. Ramsbottom and made a good impression. Jones also spent some time at Crewe and, one might surmise, was ideally placed and situated to further his chosen career either with that rapidly expanding railway, or one of the many engineering firms thereabouts, when he completed his apprenticeship in October 1855. Just three weeks later though, Jones began not only a new job but, in effect, a whole new life at Inverness, as part engineer/part driver on the Inverness and Nairn Railway, a mere 10 days after it opened for business.

Then, as now, Inverness was the unofficial capital of the Highlands. Despite the Caledonian Canal, it was a remote small town, especially in winter. The area had undergone considerable turmoil in the previous 100 years or so. The rising of 1745 had been crushed and the army exacted a massive revenge on the Highlands and the Jacobites, none more so than the serving Scottish troops. Before long, roads and other improvements were underway, but then came the infamous Highland Clearances.

As young Jones stepped off the coach in Inverness, the Clearances were ongoing, and no man was more reviled than one of his employer's patrons, the Duke of Sutherland. Even today, tempers rise at the mention of the ducal family whose ancestors put sheep before man, over thousands of acres of land they, and other chieftains, robbed from their clansmen and kinsfolk. Did Jones realise what he had let himself in for?

Quite unlikely, but he buckled down to make the most of his opportunities under William Barclay, the company's Locomotive Superintendent. Barclay was no remote boss, aloof and out of touch with ordinary staff. With a fleet of just 2 locomotives and 6 coaches, there were no delusions of grandeur. While Jones was nominally concerned with maintaining the rolling-stock, he also had to roll up his sleeves and fire and drive the engines as well. The contrast with the LNWR, even in those formative railway days, must have been, at least, quite stark.

The line from Inverness-Nairn was unlikely to make anybody a fortune, but it was only precursor for a number of schemes. By 1858, the grandly titled Inverness and Aberdeen Jctn. Rly. extended onwards to Keith, thereby connecting with the GNSR and creating a through line to Aberdeen. This was a year of some note for Jones, who was not only promoted to become Barclay's Principal Assistant, but tied the knot in more personal matters, to a local lass at that. Thus, if not exactly shackling himself to the Highlands forever, at barely 24 years of age, Jones had indicated where his future loyalties would lie.

Barclay was a nephew of the renown Alexander Allan who, though never in overall charge at Crewe, was the instigator of what became known as the Crewe-type locomotive. These were distinctive and, for the time, highly effective, having extended smokebox wings enveloping the outside cylinders — as seen on the preserved 1837 'Columbine' and 1847 'Cornwall'

This picture of 2-4-0 No. 35 betrays its Allan/Barclay/Stroudley heritage, but is typically Jones in its entirety. Not surprising really as, starting life as a 6 ft. 2-2-2, built in 1864, it was rebuilt by Jones as a 2-4-0, along with its soulmates. Even so, scrapping began in the 1890s, but No. 35 was reboilered and given 6 ft. 3 in. wheels, and was a lone survivor, as No. 35A, until Grouping. Here, it rolls into Luncarty, between Perth and Stanley Junction, presumably with a local train to Dunkeld. *(NRM)*

locomotives, and also Allan's straight-link valve-gear. In 1853, Allan was appointed Locomotive Superintendent of the Scottish Central Railway, based at Perth, and Barclay was more than happy for Jones, who undertook most of the detail work, to do little more than copy his uncle's designs.

So emerged the 'Raigmore' class passenger 2-2-2s, in 1855, followed three years later by the 'Seafield' class 2-4-0 goods engines. These engines were more than adequate for trundling along the easily graded line to Nairn, even if the section on to Keith had the odd sting in its tail — neither did the intended push north to Invergordon hold any perils for them. However, the Inverness and Aberdeen Jctn. Rly. was anything but happy at being shoe-horned into its sparsely populated corner of Scotland, sharing the somewhat less than lucrative Inverness-Aberdeen traffic with its distinctly awkward and inefficient partner, the GNSR. It was soon to hatch some ambitious and distinctly grandiose plans.

In 1861, it was decided to push a line south from Forres to connect with the Perth and Dunkeld Railway, thus creating a direct through route to the south. It took only two years, to carve out and sculpt this magnificent line onto, the most fearsome landscape traversed by any railway in Britain. To greet this new, in many ways company-saving, line Barclay again turned to Allan for advice. Jones was set-to adding the details to the '14' class development of the 'Seafields', the 'Small Goods' class 2-4-0s and, certainly in hindsight if not at the time, the quite astonishing 'Glenbarry' class.

Now the diminutive 'Glenbarry' 2-2-2s were expected to undertake all passenger services on the new line. Fine, except that with two very long, stiff climbs to summits at Druimuachdar and Dava, with other short but fierce hills and no steam-sanding remember, these poor little mites were completely overwhelmed by even the lightest of trains. Ten slightly beefier 2-4-0s of the 'Medium Goods' appeared in

1864, which helped out in the summer months, but the locomotive situation was decidedly precarious. Then, in 1865, the HR was formed by an amalgamation of the Inverness and Aberdeen Jctn. Rly. and the Inverness and Perth Jctn. Rly., and Barclay was on his way...out.

For fully three weeks, Jones was acting-Locomotive Superintendent, but then W. Stroudley arrived from the Edinburgh and Glasgow Rly.; Jones became the Loco. Running Supt. Apart from his latent potential, Stroudley brought three assets with him. First, he introduced a livery known as Stroudley's improved engine green, or a sort of mustard yellow to those who are not colour blind: if nothing else, this was highly distinctive. Of more importance was his organisation skills, and the Inverness Lochgorm Works soon felt a chill wind sweeping through — one even stiffer than those off the mountains. This task was accomplished by the third asset, the arrival of none other than Dugald Drummond as Works Manager. Has so small a railway works ever had three such distinguished and ultimately legendary locomotive engineers working in harness together, almost as equals?

All these new routes and vital stock purchases would have been a severe strain on any railway, but for the fledgling HR, it was crippling. Yet, they had to expand further to achieve anything like their full potential. More locomotives could not be bought, and costs needed reining in. This is where Stroudley and Drummond — with almost exquisite engineering preparation, and Jones — by fully utilising the company's inadequate locomotive and rolling-stock, came into their own.

By 1868, the northern HR line, to Invergordon, had been linked by the Sutherland Rly. to Golspie, but the money had run out. It took the infamous Duke of Sutherland to start the ball rolling again, by building the line to Helmsdale, by 1871: the only private main line in Britain. In the meantime, further change was in the air. Stroudley had only built one locomotive — the first 'Lochgorm Tank', and rebuilt the first two 'Raigmores' as rigid 2-4-0s, before he was enticed away by the LBSCR, at the end of 1869. Briefly, Drummond held the reins before he followed Stroudley south. So, the HR board did perhaps the most obvious thing: out of 30-odd candidates, they chose the known, tried, trusted, urbane and fiercely loyal Jones as their next Locomotive Superintendent.

It was by no means a pushover though. Jones was still only 35 years old and, while he had undertaken much of the detail design for Barclay, those engines were clearly inadequate, at least over the hills. You could hardly expect the board to understand the engineering minutiae of why this was the case. Still, it proved to be an appointment as canny as any, in the best Scottish tradition.

This was an exciting time for the development of railways in north Scotland, yet nerve-wrenching if one was involved with their financing. The Inverness and Skye Rly. — worked by the HR, opened from Dingwall to Strome Ferry in 1870: one still had to travel 'over the sea to Skye', but the land journey was a darned sight quicker. The push to the far north was completed to Wick and Thurso, by 1874. This northern line was owned by three separate concerns, but worked by the HR, and that meant more money was needed for rolling-stock and locomotives.

At least Jones had a firm base. Stroudley and Drummond had transformed Lochgorm Works and inculcated a regime that paid a painstaking application to detail. Locomotives were thoroughly prepared, and while Stroudley and Drummond stuck their noses in everywhere, Jones soon established his own standards with a slightly more aloof approach. As was usual for Victorian times, Jones was a stern disciplinarian with his men and hated carelessness, but he was not wholly and unreasonably rigid. He was a gentleman and soon earned the full respect of his men, no less than Stroudley and Drummond had with their slightly less refined approach. It was a base from which the HR was to benefit greatly over the next quarter century.

It was clearly obvious that the tortuous curves and stiff banks of the Skye line required something a little more flexible in the wheelbase, than the 'Seafield' class that first worked the route — a bit more in the way of oomph would not go amiss either. In 1873, Jones rebuilt No. 10 with an Adams leading bogie, 17 in. x 24 in. cylinders, a Stroudley-esque cab, and his own unique and distinctive feature, a louvred chimney. This comprised an outer sleeve round an inner chimney, with louvres at the front to admit air and increase the draught, thus lifting the exhaust clear of the driver's view when running without steam, as was often the case on the long descents. Well, that is but one of several reasons given for the louvres, none of which came from the horse's mouth, but is as plausible as any.

The reincarnated No. 10 also served as a test-bed for a new passenger design, while it performed adequately enough on the Skye line to warrant sister engine, No. 7, to be likewise converted two years later. These two, after overcoming initial problems with the Adams bogie, soon settled down to working the Skye line for the next 20 years or so. They were still a bit skittish in the adhesion department when faced with a train of any weight, but were undoubtedly a vast improvement over their fellow 2-4-0's.

Then, in 1874, the first of Jones' own designs emerged: not just one, but ten 4-4-0 locomotives of the 'Duke' class, in fact. Superficially, these bore a very close resemblance to the rebuilt No. 10, having double-frames — with the outer frame dividing round the valve-gear to join the smokebox extensions that encompassed the cylinders, Allan's valve-gear, an Adams bogie, a Stroudley-like cab, a similar boiler and the louvred chimney. There were many differences though, such as the Thomas Adams transverse safety valve, a dome and, not least, the 6 ft. 3½ in. driving wheels. The 'Dukes' were intended for the Perth line, thus releasing older locomotives to work the new line to Wick.

The first engines were built by Dübs and Co., and represented not just a large investment by the HR, but considerable faith in Jones by a distinctly cash-conscious board. They need have had no fears. No other British Star of Steam has produced such a finely proportioned and reliable locomotive, so ideally matched to its intended, arduous tasks, that was so advanced and was the most powerful passenger engine in Britain, as his first design. Neither Gresley, Stanier nor even Churchward could manage that.

The 'Dukes' remained the principal express engines on the Inverness-Perth line for over 15 years, the free-steaming capacity of the boiler ideally matched to the demands of the cylinders. These distinctively handsome machines were exquisitely turned out in their Stroudley green, and were the perfect company flagship, however impoverished. Every now and again, from 1876-88, Lochgorm Works would build another — the works first new tender engines — with a slightly reduced heating surface, and the last having a 150 psi boiler pressure. All 17 engines contributed to the fine reputation, of one of the outstanding designs of the 19th century. Towards the end of the century, they worked the far north and even the Skye lines and, although demoted to secondary duties in the Edwardian years, the 'Dukes' still acted as regular main line pilots.

The 'Dukes' were but the first of a long line of similar locomotives. Before the next version appeared though, Jones designed the distinguished 'Skye Bogie' class 4-4-0s, in 1882. Only one engine was built at first, followed by four more from 1892-5, and finally four more by Jones' successor, P. Drummond, down to 1901. As the name implies, they were intended for the Skye line, wore a new livery of pea green and were, to all intents and purposes, a goods version of the 'Duke' class, with a slightly shorter boiler.

Seldom can a class of locomotives have been so popularly associated with a single route although, as is quite apparent, until the mid-1890s they were not the sole engines working the Skye line. From the opening of the Kyle of Lochalsh extension, in 1897, until the First World War, and again from 1918 until the mid-1920s, these outstanding engines made that remote outpost of British railways their own personal demesne. The sharp curves deterred them not and, while hills are always a challenge for steam engines, these sure-footed little troopers were excellent climbers that could dish it out with the best. So good, in fact, that when the LMS sent 6-coupled engines to replace them in the 1920s, the crews regularly left the newer engines sitting on the shed.

Mind you, the 'Skye Bogies' — hard though they might have worked when actually pulling a train, were not exactly heavily utilised. In 1897, only four trains a day plied the extended Skye line: two passenger, one mixed and one for goods. This less than comprehensive service — yet one that is better than today's, required fully 7 locomotives to work it. We might not like our characterless Sprinters, but they are a darned sight more cost efficient than our beloved steam engines.

In 1886, Jones then produced a mildly enlarged version of the 'Dukes': the 'Clyde Bogie' 4-4-0s. I say larger, but the boiler was almost a foot shorter. Having only two rings rather than the 'Dukes' three, the total heating surface was a little less, though the boiler was pressed to 160 psi, and the firebox was modestly enlarged. External differences were few and far between, but the dome sat farther back and, most obviously of all, they featured the new pea-green livery, lined in black, white and red with olive green borders. The frames were crimson while, as before, even the wheel spokes were lined. No. 76 was displayed at the 1886 Edinburgh Exhibition and, not surprisingly — given such ornate, yet entirely standard, paintwork — it won a gold medal.

The 'Clyde Bogies' went straight into service on the demanding southern main line, all 8 being built by the Clyde

The 'Clyde Bogies' were an updated version of Jones' 'Duke' class. The outside frames and the combined housing of the cylinders with the smokebox leave one in no doubt of the identity of the designer. No. 76 'Bruce', looks every inch the premier express passenger engine that it most certainly was.

Loco. Co. Ltd. They remained front-rank engines until the new century, and then were gradually dispersed to undertake secondary duties, such as pilots on the southern line and working to the far north. They were every bit as fine and successful locomotives as were the 'Dukes', but were never quite the bees-knees — nationally — as had been the older engines.

Six years later, in 1892, Jones produced his final passenger 4-4-0 that traced its lineage from the Raigmore' class 2-2-2s and, more specifically, the 'Dukes'. The 12 'Straths' were modestly developed 'Clydes'. The boiler was enlarged to 4 ft. 6 in. diameter, the heating surface increased, and they were the first Scottish engines to be fitted with combination injectors. It has been said that the bigger boiler was less than beneficial to the appearance, but such comments are merely hair-splitting, purely personal and quite irrelevant.

The 'Straths' undertook much the same duties as the 'Clyde' and 'Duke' classes, except that their time as front-rank express engines was shorter still. True, they continued to work as pilot and banking engines on the southern main line, and double-heading became the norm once the shorter route via Carr Bridge was opened, in 1898, bringing still more traffic. They later worked the Wick line and even the trains to Keith. As was usual, locals from Inverness, the occasional branch line working and work on the Skye line helped the 'Straths' to eke out a living until Grouping in 1923. Then, as with all bar the 'Skye Bogies' the axe fell pretty quickly indeed.

One might be thinking that, by 1892, Jones was losing his touch. Okay, perhaps he could not second-guess the considerable increases in train weights and speeds that were to occur over the next decade or so, but to perpetuate a virtual 20 year-old design, when even the HR owned some corridor coaches, was hardly forward thinking. Jones was nearly 60 years old and his employer had little need of engines at the cutting edge of steam locomotive development, in any case. Had he lost his touch, traded youthful zest, innovation and brio for solid respectability? After all, his empire had expanded and he was highly regarded: an Englishman who had won over the hardened Scots. That, by itself, was no mean achievement.

Going back to 1877, Jones already had a history of designing locomotives that would have been more at home in the past. A need for engines to work the Inverness-Tain locals saw him produce the 'Raigmore II' class. Rather like the plethora of films where the second in the series gives that awful feeling of oh no, not more of the same — and am I being ripped-off, 'Raigmore II' looked little more than a copy of Stroudley's 1869 2-4-0 rebuild of the original 'Raigmore' 2-2-2. Yes, the new ones had a larger boiler — pressed to a higher pressure, and the engine was undoubtedly heavier but,

I ask you, it was all a bit behind the times. I suspect Jones thought likewise, as he wanted to build a 4-4-0, but the cost-conscious directors decided otherwise.

Naturally, the Sons of Raigmore spent their entire lives on mundane duties. That did not stop Lochgorm Works building and maintaining them to their highest standards though, but once older 4-4-0s gravitated to the north, so they were soon displaced. Trundling along branches off the Keith line, pushing snow-ploughs on the Inverness-Perth line and working the Thurso branch, one wonders just how cost-efficient they were, compared with a 4-4-0. Oh yes, they out-lasted the first 'Dukes', but worked rather less in the meantime.

Though the HR had several branch lines — no doubt some larger railways considered it one long branch, such was the lack of traffic that there was no pressing need for specialist tank engines. As a result, Jones only designed three such classes, encompassing all of five locomotives, while five more 'Yankee Tank' 4-4-0Ts were purchased from Dubs and Co., on Jones' advice These served the company astoundingly well, considering they were built for the penurious Uruguay Eastern Railway, proving to be quite useful on the various branches and were not averse to a bit of shunting about Inverness. Jones was able to tailor the last three to his liking and they became a very shrewd purchase in the long-term.

Jones' 2-4-0T design was based on the redoubtable 'Raigmore II', and soon all three were employed on branch lines. Not for long though, as the rigid wheelbase chaffed on the tight curves of the lightly built lines and all were rebuilt as 4-4-0Ts, from 1885 to 1887. This was a master-stroke for, drastic though it was, little else was altered and each survived at least 50 years, retaining their original boilers. Now, that was economy.

Then, in 1890, Jones produced a singleton 0-4-4T for the Strathpeffer branch, to serve the very town that forced the Skye line to take an arduous, avoiding detour. This was quite a different animal to anything Jones had previously designed, with inside frames and cylinders — to the same pattern as Stroudley's 'Lochgorm Tanks', and a non-louvred chimney. It wasn't half an unusual looking engine as well, with its short saddle tank looking very much an after-thought.

For 12 years, this weird contraption trundled up and down the 5 mile branch until, in 1901, P. Drummond rebuilt it with side tanks. Thereafter, from 1903, it worked the Wick-Lybster branch and occasionally the Dornoch branch, both of which ran mixed trains on their lightly laid track. Right at the end of its humdrum life, as if to say a last farewell, LMS No. 15050 returned to Dingwall for a final few months, to relive its childhood.

Jones' final tank engine design was for the Duke of

Sutherland's personal use: an 0-4-4T. Jones had always immersed himself in all aspects of locomotive design, as had Stroudley, and it was no different with this engine. His nibs even drove the engine on occasions, as was his right, so Jones fitted a full-width leather seat and cushions for the honoured guests to enjoy a comfortable cab ride. Jones also authorised the rebuilding of the Kitson's 2-4-0T, purchased by the HR from the duke that same year. This was not really of much use to the HR in either the short or long-term, and was a poor economic decision.

So, by the early 1890s, it appeared that Jones was winding down and, like other once-great locomotive engineers — such as P. Stirling, was harking back to the designs with which he made his name, to meet the needs of a rapidly changing age. However, in 1893, a former HR apprentice returned as Jones' Chief Draughtsman after a period with Sharp, Stewart & Co., and Dubs. David Hendrie was experienced in designs for overseas railways, as was Jones as an independent consultant engineer, and may have acted as a catalyst for Jones' last designs that, once again, brought him to national prominence.

The HR had never been a large freight carrier, although considerable loads were taken at particular times of the year. It still relied solely on Barclay's two goods designs, that were then 30 years old, and these little pip-squeaks were hopelessly out-classed on the Inverness-Perth line, even when double-heading trains. As a result, the HR board really took the bull by the horns and made a massive investment, ordering 15 locomotives to a completely new design by Jones, for delivery in 1894. This was a touching act of faith in their long-serving Locomotive Superintendent, and one from which the company was to benefit for the rest of its existence.

There is a majesty about the engine, and sheer pride in the men. No wonder, for Jones' 'Big Goods' marked a complete revision of his design principals, was clearly the biggest engine on the HR, was far ahead of any similar engine in Scotland and was Britain's first 4-6-0. For 40 years, these great engines trod the Highland rails, whether on passenger or goods trains. No. 113 seemingly bursts with pride, as well she might.
(NRM)

As far as the HR was concerned, Jones' 'Big Goods' was a revolutionary design: even on a national level, it advanced the steam locomotive more than a notch or two. This was Britain's first 4-6-0 engine, at least for home service. For that reason alone it gained considerable public recognition, but there was more to it than that. Out went the old Crewe-style double-frames and the Allan front-end, although the straight-link motion was retained. This was to be no existing design with a mere addition of an extra pair of driving wheels.

The boiler diameter was 4 ft. 9 in., was fully 13 ft. 9 in. long and was pressed to 170 psi, and soon to 175 psi: its heating surface was a third greater than that of the 'Straths'. Similarly, the cylinders were larger while, also uniquely for the HR, it had a part-sloping grate. In other respects, such as the dome, cab, transverse Adams' safety valve and, of course, the louvred chimney, it bore an obvious family resemblance: more that of a cousin than, say, a brother. Jones had produced his undoubted masterpiece.

Built by Sharp, Stewart and Co., the first engines were delivered in July 1894, but were not accepted due to dismally poor steaming. The builders soon sorted out a problem with the blast-pipe and all 15 duly arrived in just three months. To celebrate the splendour of his new engine, the first three were painted in Stroudley's unique green. Here was an outpouring of faith in a return to the 1870s, when the little HR briefly led the way, for the 'Big Goods' was Britain's most powerful engine when it first took to the rails.

As with all of Jones' main line designs, the 'Big Goods' class was an immediate success. Once accepted, they suffered no teething troubles and simply got down to the business of earning their corn on the Inverness-Perth line. These were powerful and reliable engines bereft of idiosyncrasies, yet were easy to maintain. As such, both crews and maintenance staff loved them, while they were a godsend to the HR. Fitted with vacuum brakes, but not steam-heating, they were also invaluable on heavy passenger trains in the busy summer season, and dominated goods traffic on the southern main line for fully 30 years.

Towards their latter years, and from 1904 onwards, the big engines found work on the far north line, and once they turned 40 years of age, some were sent to work the Skye line — an unusual sort of pensioning-off. No engines had their frames replaced, or were modified to any extent, while reliability and an instant willingness to undertake hard work merely enhanced the reputation of this outstanding design.

The introduction of the 'Big Goods' did not quite go so well for Jones, though. He was badly scalded during some early trials and his left leg became increasingly incapacitated. Despite having much time off work, he still had one more outstanding design in him though, in retrospect, it might have been better to have simply built a passenger version of the 'Big Goods'. Instead, Jones provided the HR with a thoroughly modern 4-4-0: to all intents and purposes, a smaller 'Big Goods'. The new 'Lochs' had a slightly larger boiler than the 'Straths', bigger cylinders, were the first Scottish locomotives to be fitted with piston valves (to the design of W.M. Smith of the NER, and soon replaced by slide valves) and were a great initial success.

Fifteen were built in just three months during 1896, but a further 3 — almost identical except for minor boiler alterations — were added in 1917, when there was an acute HR locomotive shortage due to Grand Fleet being based at Scapa Flow. Not un-naturally, and just like their predecessors, the 'Lochs' worked the Inverness-Perth line, though their tenure on front-line expresses was relatively short-lived. This was little to do with any failings in their design, but with the shortened route south from Inverness, via Carr Bridge, opening in 1898, and ever-increasing loads, they were never really big enough to cope with the increased traffic.

Jones was, indeed, well into designing a passenger version of his 'Big Goods' when, due to failing health, he retired in the autumn of 1896. His successor, P. Drummond, finished off the design — with much work being undertaken by Hendrie, to bring out the excellent 'Castle' class 4-6-0s in 1900. From then on, the 4-4-0s were gradually side-lined to double-heading and piloting heavy main line expresses, or worked secondary duties. The 'Lochs', however, were not dispersed all over the system until much later, well into LMS days, and they remained prestige engines for the rest of the HR's existence. Although the first withdrawals began in 1930, 7 of the original 15 were still in service as the Second World War began, and 3 survived that conflict. The last 'Loch' locomotive was withdrawn in 1950.

So, the 'Lochs' brought down the curtain on the career of a splendid locomotive engineer. Jones enjoyed the outstanding distinction of never having designed a main line locomotive that was anything other than nigh-perfect, from the moment the first one turned a wheel. Furthermore, he had produced two ground-breaking designs in British steam locomotive history: these being fully 20 years apart. In so doing, Jones was one of the few engineers who successfully crossed the divide by successfully building locomotives for mid-19th century conditions, and also for the radically different conditions pertaining at the end of the century. Stirling failed, Webb tried valiantly with something less than unequivocal success, Dean never fully crossed the Rubicon, and even Stroudley cannot have failed to be impressed by what his former subordinate had achieved. Jones had built carefully on Stroudley's bequest, in particular with his involvement in all aspects of design and works control, and with the standard of work undertaken by his department. This was clearly manifested in the presentation of the engines, that could hardly have been bettered in contemporary Britain.

As for coaches, more often than not, the reverse applied. True, there were exceptions, and Jones designed Britain's first non-Pullman bogie sleepers in the late-1870s, while there were also some pleasant first class carriages and an observation

The 'Loch' class was Jones last and changes can be seen. Gone are the outside frames and the extravagant smokebox wing-plates, and the engine looks every inch a late-19th century design. On the other hand, No. 131 'Loch Shin' is in less than pristine condition, while the engine behind shows that this picture was taken after Jones had retired; probably well after. The unique louvred chimney remains though.

coupe. On the other hand, the general run-of-mill HR coach was a 4 or 6 wheeled affair, often — if not usually — as appallingly shabby as was the locomotive gloriously grand. Of course, better coaches ran between Inverness and Perth, but these mostly belonged to other railways.

Jones was also responsible for rebuilding most of Barclay's goods engines, all of which saw in the new century, with two surviving to Grouping. Nearly all the 'Glenbarry' 2-2-2s were rebuilt as 2-4-0s and while P. Drummond soon swung his axe at these, one still — somehow — managed to survive until 1923. This something-for-nothing work was vital to a penurious concern like the HR, especially in its early decades, and consumed as much of Jones' time and effort, if not more, than new designs. There is no doubt about it, the HR could hardly afford any minor disasters in the locomotive design field. With Jones at the helm, quite possibly no contemporary British railway company had a Locomotive Superintendent so in harmony with its needs. Certainly, none could have been a more cost effective engineer to his employers.

Jones' decision to retire on his 62nd birthday was not taken in the happiest of circumstances. The HR board was less than pleased with Jones' absence through illness, for 5 months of

1895, and went so far as to demand the same level of commitment that he had given in the previous 40 years. This Jones was unable to give and so he went. In the end, the hard-nosed directors granted him a pension and allowances amounting to £500 p.a., or ten times that of a manual worker, for the rest of his life.

Whether it was because of such treatment, or because of continuing his consulting work with overseas railways — particularly in India, Jones upped sticks and moved to Hampstead in London. There he lived in semi-retirement for a full decade before, somewhat ironically, a car accident deprived him of the use of his right leg, leaving him incapacitated. He died at the end of 1906.

In fact, after Stroudley had died in 1889, the LBSCR board offered Jones the position of Locomotive Superintendent. It is worth considering just what he might have achieved at a far wealthier railway, one that really was in the public eye: there would have been no need for an equivalent to the 'Big Goods' though. Then again, perhaps, after nearly 35 years in Inverness, Brighton seemed an awfully long way off his beaten track, just as once Inverness had been, or even Whitehaven.

DAVID JONES IN BRIEF

BORN:	25th October 1834, Manchester.
TRAINED:	Longsight, Manchester and Crewe Works, LNWR Apprentice 1847-55.
EMPLOYED:	Inverness and Nairn Railway, 1855.
SENIOR POSITIONS:	1858-65, Principal Assistant to Locomotive Superintendent W. Barclay.
	1865, Acting Locomotive Superintendent HR.
	1865-70, Loco. Running Supt., HR.
	1870-96, Locomotive Superintendent, HR.
RETIRED:	October 1896, to Hampstead, London.
DIED:	2nd December 1906, Hampstead.

Jones' Locomotive Designs

YEAR	CLASS	WHEEL ARRANGEMENT	CYLINDERS (INCHES)	BOILER PRESSURE	DRIVING-WHEEL DIAMETER	WEIGHT	No. in CLASS
1874	Duke	4-4-0	18 x 24	40 psi	6' 3½"	41 tons	17
1877	Raigmore 2	2-4-0	16 x 22	140 psi	6' 3"	35 tons	2
1878	Jones' Tank	2-4-0T	16 x 24	140 psi	4' 7½"	36 tons	3
	Rebuilds	4-4-0T			4' 9½"	37T 12 cwt	
1882	Skye Bogies	4-4-0	18 x 24	150 psi	5' 3½"	43 tons	9
1886	Clyde Bogies	4-4-0	18 x 24	160 psi	6' 3½"	43 tons	8
1890	Strathpeffer	0-4-4T	(i)14 x 20	100 psi	4' 3"	32 tons	1
1892	Strath	4-4-0	18 x 24	160 psi	6' 3½"	45 tons	12
1894	Big Goods	4-6-0	20 x 26	170 psi	5' 3½"	56 tons	15
1895	Duke of Suth.	0-4-4T	(I)13 x 18		4' 6"		1
1896	Loch	4-4-0	19 x 24	175 psi	6' 3½"	49 tons	18

Locomotives Purchased by H.R. on Jones' advice

YEAR	CLASS	WHEEL ARRANGEMENT	CYLINDERS (INCHES)	BOILER PRESSURE	DRIVING-WHEEL DIAMETER	WEIGHT	No. in CLASS
1891	Yankee Tank	4-4-0T	16 x 22	160 psi	5' 3"	42½ tons	5

JONES' PRESERVED LOCOMOTIVES

YEAR	CLASS	RUNNING NUMBERS	TOTAL
1894	Big Goods	103	1
1895	Duke of Suth.	'Dunrobin'	1

JOHN FARQUHARSON McINTOSH
Lifting the Drummond Tradition to its Zenith

Let's have a bit of fun with social stereotyping: you know, fitting the square pegs of our preconceived ideas into the round holes of reality. Close your eyes and think of the typical American rock star. What do we have? A showy extrovert of limited talent, hyped-up as the greatest musical happening since, well, his predecessor, and who has a predilection for throwing televisions out of hotel windows. Do we all agree?

Right, what about a typical English aristocrat? A tall, lean chap of whom the term 'chinless wonder' is but a mild exaggeration, with a brain the size of a pea, a character as developed and unique as a potato, and an imagination as bright as a mushroom-growing shed. Yes?

Okay, one last go. How about a successful Scotsman? Well, he has probably left his homeland, maybe has a dour and serious personality — aside from when imbibing the national drink or reminiscing about home, has a character as hard as the native granite, and perhaps works as a government officer or an engineer. So, do you agree with these hypothetical examples? Of course, these are broad sweeping, faintly ridiculous generalisations, but in railway engineering terms the latter case is not without its merits. I suppose this scenario is influenced by the likes of Dugald Drummond and Patrick Stirling, but despite J.F. McIntosh being, if not quite a disciple, a keen adherent of Drummond, our caricature is some way off the mark.

In McIntosh's case, the portents of his rise to the top were not good. For a start, he was born into a family of no great railway or, indeed, engineering tradition. Nonetheless, he was apprenticed to the Scottish North Eastern Railway, at Arbroath, and this company was absorbed into the CR in 1866. By that time, McIntosh was a fireman, and a year later passed-out as a driver and moved to Montrose for the next decade.

By 1876, McIntosh had risen to the airy heights of Northern Division Loco. Inspector, but he was out on a limb and well away from where the action really was. Then, not long after taking up the appointment, his world almost fell in on him. A footplate accident at Montrose cost him his right hand and part of the arm. For a man working on the railways, that would seem to be that, a promising career nipped decisively and conclusively in the bud, especially as he was right-handed.

Well, McIntosh may not have shared the personality of our hypothetical Scotsman, but he certainly had the characteristics. Loss of hand or not, he overcame the physical difficulties and, no doubt, prejudice to be appointed District Locomotive Foreman at Aberdeen, in 1882. Two years later, Drummond arrived from the NBR, and McIntosh was transported from the CR's north-east wilderness, to the hub of the system at Carstairs. Such was the mark he made, and — let's face it — a one-handed Locomotive Foreman could hardly be ignored if he was successful, that in 1886 he was appointed District Locomotive Foreman at Polmadie shed, the most important on the whole railway.

With the Drummond revolution in full-swing, McIntosh was able to assimilate its vicissitudes, and was close enough to St. Rollox Works to get himself noticed. Still, it was a pretty unlikely scenario to expect even a highly rated, one-handed District Locomotive Foreman, with precious little design experience, to become the Locomotive Superintendent. Sitting in the chair occupied by Drummond, and kept more than warm by his successor J. Lambie, must have seemed little more than a pipe-dream until, that is, he became Lambie's assistant.

While one admires the trust of the CR board in appointing a loyal and increasingly distinguished servant to the top locomotive post, McIntosh was put on 6 months' probation. Furthermore, his salary of £700 p.a. — well over £100,000 today — was less than half that of Lambie and not even a third of Drummond's. Oh yes, the praiseworthy display of loyalty was tempered by the Scottish reputation for parsimony. Even so, the saving of money apart, the appointment of McIntosh was at least unusual in the climate of the times. The CR's prestige had risen inexorably since Drummond's days: by 1895 it was not just the foremost railway in Scotland, but well respected throughout Britain. Not only could McIntosh have been deemed something of a risk but, when considered alongside his counterparts on other leading railways — such as Webb, P. Stirling, Johnson, Dean, Adams and, of course, Drummond himself, he was a mere engineering novice.

McIntosh's works experience was limited to the five years he spent as Lambie's deputy. He would certainly have been a risky appointment except that he fully understood what was required from a locomotive in the field: the capacity to work as expected. As an out-and-out running man, he knew that simplicity was best: new fangled ideas were fine in theory, a great headache in practice. Drummond had revolutionised the CR's locomotive stock, St. Rollox Works and the maintenance, reliability and performance of the engines. Lambie had, mild tinkering apart, added to the whole with a seeming reverential zeal.

At first, it appeared that McIntosh would also follow Drummond's path in exactly the prescribed manner. After all, Drummond and Lambie had given the CR just what it wanted, fast and powerful engines that worked hard, but appreciated a light rein. Drummond had tried to impose a wide-regulator/short cut-offs method of working. His engines could work all day and more, but did not take kindly to rough and ready driving, nor a lack of respect for their capacities.

There were times, admittedly few and far between, when a Drummond engine was required to go beyond the bounds of reason and sweat even more, but had no more to give. In this, Drummond was in good company: Stirling, and Johnson both followed the same route and did not want to see their majestic engines thrashed mercilessly. On the other hand, a Webb locomotive was, if not born to be wild, built to be driven

The '709' class was McIntosh's first new design and, although seemingly quite typical 0-6-0s, they were regarded as virtual mixed-traffic engines, being painted Prussian blue. No. 574 approaches Wemyss Bay with a train full of animated passengers.

---

mercilessly — though some needed just that to get moving. McIntosh had his own ideas. Yes, Drummond's instinctive, stylish and efficient route was just right, although a bit more in the guts and heart department was not only required, but was what his men — the drivers — wanted. Whereas Drummond's engines combined the skill and speed of the Scottish football inside forward, with the grit of the ball-winning midfielder, McIntosh's locomotives also had the never-say-die, up-and-at-'em spirit of the old fashioned centre half. The new mixture was compelling, occasionally raw and, at times, awesome.

Of course, McIntosh did not sit down and plot out all the dimensions and details of his new locomotives. No, he read the board's collective mind and, with his vast running experience, knew exactly where further improvements could be made. In the chapter on Bulleid, an analogy was drawn between his locomotives and the Lotus cars of Colin Chapman: brilliant performers one day, exasperating the next. McIntosh's locomotives had more in common with the great Bentley cars of the 1920s — 'the fastest lorries in the world'. Fast? Oh most definitely so. Stylish? To some, but certainly distinctive. Reliable? As Big Ben. Rugged? As an anvil. Unbreakable? Without a doubt: the drivers wilted before either a Bentley car or a McIntosh steam engine. Each could be driven to the limits and beyond, and then come back for more.

Within a year of succeeding Lambie, McIntosh had introduced a class of each main type of locomotive used by the CR. It was not as though there was any desperate need for them, but if the railway were to continue forging ahead, it needed sufficient motive power. The '709' class 0-6-0s were, to all intents and purposes, a Drummond 'Jumbo' with minor boiler modifications. These engines had the Westinghouse brake, were painted blue and worked mixed-traffic and goods trains mainly on the central and southern lines. Five were fitted with condensing apparatus to work on Glasgow's underground lines, and they were a useful addition to an already sufficient fleet.

Shortly after, ten condensing 0-4-4Ts of the '19' class were built to work suburban trains through Glasgow's underground. These were also developed from a Drummond standard, being ideally suited to their intended work. Then, nine '29' class condensing 0-6-0Ts, initially begun by Lambie and modified

by McIntosh, were built for shunting in and round Glasgow's underground lines. Yet again, these were straight out of Drummond's mould. From these promising and orthodox beginnings...well, McIntosh was certainly not going to let the side down.

Having sailed through his probation, McIntosh crowned his first year at the helm with a design that out-shone Drummond's finest, yet was a mere precursor of even greater things: the 'Dunalastair' express 4-4-0s. Drummond desired an efficient performance from his locomotives, but here, McIntosh was to differ. As with the previous designs, McIntosh took the basic CR express 4-4-0, tweaked the odd bits here and there, and placed a much larger boiler onto the, essentially, Drummond chassis. This simple formula, giving the drivers an engine that would burn coal and produce steam in ample quantities, at once created a true thoroughbred classic. As fast as any of Drummond's engines — yet with still greater power, plus being able to be worked long and hard, a 'Dunalastair' was, without any doubt, a driver's engine, just like a vintage Bentley.

Within months of building, the 'Dunalastairs' were producing some of the finest and most consistent running in Britain. Swooping round the curves of Clydesdale, raising the sky as they pounded up Beattock bank, racing along historic Strathmore — with Glamis Castle and Dunsinane resounding to their rhythmic beat, the 'Dunalastairs' were peerless performers. Yet, when the Scottish weather took one of its many turns for the worst, they had ample power and a capacity to be flogged head-on into the fiercest of gales. Precocious thoroughbreds they were not: they were more akin to a mighty cavalry charger. And yet, in the true Drummond tradition, they looked every inch the distinctive and distinguished legendary performers they became. A 'Dunalastair' in full-flight was a truly majestic sight.

For McIntosh, though, there was to be no resting on his laurels. Over the next decade the board was to demand, and McIntosh to instigate, a locomotive policy that took the CR to the forefront of Britain's railways. It was, in many respects, a path similar to Gresley's 'big engine policy' of later years. Engines were designed with ample power reserves to undertake their expected duties for not just the then-and-now, but well into the future. Oh yes, they were renown as coal-eaters but, by goodness, there was never any doubting the

The Cathcart Circle, in Glasgow, and Edinburgh's Balerno branch were not the easiest lines to work, having a multitude of short, steep gradients, close-spaced stations and tight curves. McIntosh built the relatively small '104' class 0-4-4Ts specifically for these routes, and the crew of No. 111 poses with their pristine engine in Edinburgh.

(L. Lord)

Twenty engines of the ostensibly goods '812' class were painted blue and fitted with the Westinghouse brake. These helped out with the excursion traffic, but also regularly hauled the prestigious and competitive Clyde Coast services and were, in effect, mixed-traffic engines. No. 824 is being cleaned ready for its next duty; these were most definitely not lowly goods engines.

capacity and ability of a McIntosh engine to do the work for which it was designed.

Of course, McIntosh could never have been responsible for four new designs within a year of taking over, had it not been for the high class drawing and manufacturing staff and facilities that were built up over the previous decade. After such a heady and assured start, new designs emerged more slowly — although engine building continued unabated.

In 1897, came the '92' class 0-4-4Ts. These were virtually identical to the '19' class, but had a greater water and coal capacity, and were also intended for suburban work. Ten similar engines were built in 1899/1900, the '879' class. These were finished in black, though retained the Westinghouse brake, and had very minor boiler differences. Such an improvement of an existing design was to be a feature of the McIntosh era.

Time never stood still and, in 1897, a new express design emerged: the '766' or 'Dunalastair II' class. This had a substantially larger boiler — pressed still further, bigger cylinders and so forth. The 'Dunalastairs' had been an outstanding success, but train weights were increasing rapidly and McIntosh had found his feet. Not only did he personally select the express drivers, but he furnished them with the engines they required and desired. There is no doubt about it, the 'Dunalastair IIs' caused almost as great a stir as did their elder brothers. Yet this was only the start of a second, less forthright, revolution at St. Rollox.

It is often claimed that the last British CME to gain widespread influence overseas was W. Adams. That may be correct, but in 1898 Neilson & Co. built five 'Dunalastair IIs' for the Belgian State Railways. These so impressed that a further 225 were built. Thus began a love affair with McIntosh's designs that resulted in the BSR building nearly 800 of his locomotives: the '812' class 0-6-0s being particularly numerous and long-lasting. McIntosh might not have had the widespread influence of Adams, but he was to Belgian railways what Hercule Poirot became to fictional British private detectives.

As far as express locomotives went, the CR advanced remorselessly under McIntosh's guidance. Just as, 20 years later, W.O. Bentley steadily improved his basic car by fitting ever-bigger engines, so McIntosh placed still larger boilers onto the 'Dunalastair' chassis. In 1899, came the '900' class; the 'Dunalastair IIIs'. Featuring a larger grate and boiler, they were a still further advance on the 'Dunalastair IIs'. Unlike Bentley's cars, they were no faster than their predecessors, but were even more powerful.

The CR were not unique though. The late-Victorian/Edwardian era is regarded as the 'Golden Age' of cricket, ocean liners and even hats, and surely it must be so for the express locomotive. Churchward and Dean, on the GWR, and Drummond on the LSWR were forging onwards, while Ivatt had built Britain's first Atlantic. Soon, the MR had its first 'Compound', and the LNWR's 'George the Fifths' later tore about with an almost messianic zeal: on almost every major railway, ever-larger express locomotives of many differing types were being conceived. Twenty-five years ago, the HST was the blazing standard-bearer of British expresses. It is not leading the pace nowadays but, at a pinch, could still just about do the job. So great were the advances a century ago, that an express locomotive of 1895 would be totally out-classed on the eve of the First World War, on any railway you care to mention. McIntosh was determined that the CR was not just going to keep its head above water but, in this rapidly changing world, was to positively lead the way.

In 1902, McIntosh designed the CR's first 4-6-0. The '55' class mixed-traffic engines were intended for the Oban line, but a year later came an express 4-6-0. The '49' class only comprised two locomotives, and almost immediately No. 49 was deputed to haul the most prestigious train of the day, the 2 p.m. 'Corridor' from Glasgow-London and its north-bound return from Carlisle.

These new engines clearly depict McIntosh in the Bentley mould: enlarging a well-tried concept rather than following the Chapman/Bulleid path of starting with a completely clean sheet. The new engines kept faith with the inside cylinder format, although things were getting a bit tight between the frames and the slide valves were placed above the cylinders. The 4 ft. 10¾ in. diameter boiler, though not the largest in Britain, had a considerably greater heating surface than anything north of the border, and was pressed to 200 psi. As you can see, it looks every inch a purposeful and powerful, yet elegant, leviathan: an impression aided by the massive 55 ton tender. Unlike Churchward, who gave his 'Stars' a puny, almost under-nourished tender, McIntosh ensured that his were man enough for the job and fully matched the locomotive in question.

The '49s' were not an initial success, unlike the various 'Dunalastairs'. Despite being the most powerful express locomotives in Britain — with a turn of speed to match, they were found to be shy steamers if really pressed. Certainly, No. 49 could take 400 tons south over Beattock unaided, but if the weather was a bit nasty, as it often is in Clydesdale, it could be left gasping like an asthmatic fell-runner. Big though the boiler was, the large cylinders had an enormous appetite. As with a person of obese proportions, the remedy was plenty of exercise and slimming, so the cylinders were re-designed and slightly reduced the following year. Thereafter, no more steaming problems occurred, while they could still out-haul and run with the very best.

The sheer length of the '49s', and an absence of accommodating turntables, ensured that they remained a small family and McIntosh returned to his tried-and-tested formula in 1904, with the '140' class 4-4-0s or, you've guessed it, the 'Dunalastair IVs'. These had a 5 ft. diameter boiler — with a still greater heating surface, and a few other modifications. This latest version of a 20 year-old theme was just about the ultimate in non-superheated locomotive development. Certainly they were more powerful than their predecessors, though considerably short of the '49s', but had lost their fast legs in the process. The highest recorded speed of a 'Dunalastair' was 85 mph, whereas that of the '140' class was almost 10 mph slower. Train loads had risen considerably, though they were no faster and the youthful, lithe 'Dunalastair' had filled-out as it had grown up, sacrificing speed for essential strength.

Finally, in 1906, McIntosh produced what was to become his, and St. Rollox's, masterpiece; the '903' or 'Cardean' class 4-6-0s. These great engines were the ultimate in Scottish express design — Drummond's work on the LSWR notwithstanding. Fast and powerful, graceful and practical, reasonably economical and yet capable of immense work, 'Cardean' was the perfect company flagship. The former rich Prussian Blue had, by this time, been lightened to the renown Caledonian Blue, and wearing this proud livery — set off with delicate lining, purple frames and blue wheels — 'Cardean' hauled 'The Corridor' daily for nigh on a decade. No company can have been prouder of, or better represented by, such an ensemble. As superheated, from 1911 onwards, they were even quite economical.

In reality, the 'The Corridors' 2¼ hour schedule — a mere 45 mph average speed — was symptomatic more of leisurely Victorian times than the racy Edwardian era. Though the weather could turn nasty, 'Cardean' made sure that punctuality was rarely affected. Indeed, the whole reputation of the class rests solely on the metronomic consistency of 'Cardean's' performance with 'The Corridor'. A mere 205 revenue-earning miles was her daily lot, a bit of a doddle even then. Seldom can such a great locomotive have been so feted for so easy a life.

Mind you, that was hardly McIntosh's fault. He produced an engine capable of undertaking anything thrown at it for the next 20 years or more. The class worked the CR main line from Carlisle to Aberdeen until well after the CR had ceased to exist. Perhaps, if a proposed Scottish railway had come to fruition at the 1923 Grouping, they might have been a blueprint for an all-purpose Scottish express design, but England dictated otherwise.

Hauling 'The Corridor' apart, the most impressive performance of a '903' class engine came in the 1909 exchange with the LNWR. 'Cardean' visited its West Coast ally's metals for a month to undertake a daily Crewe-Carlisle and return roster. Nothing too exceptional was required, although the round-trip of 282 miles was a bit more like it from a working point of view. However, the train was illogically scheduled to cover the 13½ miles from the Penrith stop to passing Shap Summit in 18 minutes, with about 400 tons behind the massive 57 ton tender. 'Cardean's' timed performance in getting within 30 seconds of the tight, nigh-impossible, schedule — and maintaining speeds in the high 40s up the 1 in 125 grades — was one of the great feats of pre-Grouping railways. Add to that the exceptionally fine effort in reaching Penrith from Carlisle in 23½ minutes, and for a brief ¾ hour 'Cardean' showed just what was possible, had the spirit of 1895 been revived.

For those readers who hanker after something a little different, though, McIntosh might not feature too highly in their ratings. A visit by D. Drummond brought a bit of a shock when the old grandee thought his protege's '49' class 4-6-0s too big and cumbersome. So, before 'Cardean' emerged McIntosh had drawings made for a 4-cylinder compound atlantic: Churchward was not the only engineer aware of overseas practices. As many soccer managers have found — after a brief love-affair with foreign players, McIntosh could see that, when the British weather enters the equation, a bit of good old native grit, effort and sheer simplicity often produce better results than a few fancy-dan tricks that will save a few pounds of coal here and there.

While McIntosh was clearly no great innovator, he just about took the traditional, British inside-cylinder format to its physical limit. On the other hand, he kept a look out for practical new ideas. Three 'Dunalastair IVs' were built in 1910, and were followed by his final express design. The '139' or superheated 'Dunalastair IV' class was a Scottish first, and the initial five featured a Schmidt superheater, 8 in. piston valves and a lower boiler pressure. In other words, McIntosh — perhaps stung by directors' questions about the healthy appetite of his engines — was looking to superheating as a means of economy and reducing boiler maintenance costs, rather than to enhance the more than adequate performance. The other '139s' had a 170 psi boiler pressure, 20¼ in. cylinders and Robinson superheaters.

Tests of the superheated 'Dunalastair IVs' alongside a saturated 'Dunalastair IV' showed savings in coal and water of about 25% — even with the mines of Lanark on their doorstep, that was attractive to thrifty directors. Money was available to superheat the express 4-6-0s and a start was made on the other 'Dunalastairs', though not the original engines. This practical application of new technology, with a still-born compound atlantic and 4-cylinder pacific, shows that although McIntosh organised his department to think primarily in terms of simplicity and performance, it was clearly aware of other developments and innovations.

Clearly then, McIntosh's express locomotives left the CR in awe of no other British railway by 1906, but he was also responsible for several fine 4-6-0 mixed-traffic designs as well. These began with the '55' class of 1902, designed specifically for the Callander and Oban road. Their 5 ft. driving wheels and short wheelbase were ideal for the tight curves, while the boiler and firebox — based on that of the '766' class — were suited to the short-sharp-shock, switch-back nature of the line. A real dose of power could be delivered for the steep grades, while the short firebox did not eat coal while meandering downhill, often round curves that were not conducive to speed. These fine engines worked the line for over 25 years, on trains of all description.

An altogether different proposition emerged in 1906 with the '918' class 4-6-0, also with 5 ft. driving wheels. These had a shortened 'Cardean' boiler, of 5 ft. 2¼ in. diameter, and were intended to haul fast goods on the southern main lines. However, they were fitted with the Westinghouse brake, were finished in passenger blue and were not irregular performers on excursions and other passenger trains, while in 1914 some were sent to assist on the Oban line. A little treat that the war soon put to an end.

A sister class also emerged in 1906. The '908' class was superficially similar, but had many detail differences. With 5 ft. 9 in. driving wheels, these were true mixed-traffic engines, and spent many years working semi-fast and express trains over the Aberdeen route, and also the best Clyde Coast services. So successful were they, that McIntosh produced a superheated version a few years later. The '179' class was intended to work fast goods trains, but was still finished in passenger blue and fitted with the Westinghouse brake. These had a Robinson superheater, 9 in. piston valves, a steam reverser — as did the other mixed-traffic 4-6-0s, and featured a cab with side windows. None of McIntosh's superheated locomotives showed any marked improvement in performance over the saturated variants — they were never meant to, but were certainly cheaper to run. All the mixed-traffic 4-6-0s performed well for 30 years, but once Stanier's 'Black Fives' arrived, their demise was like good communication: brief, clear and most decidedly to the point.

McIntosh always thought big when it came to his engines, and so it was with the more traditional goods/mixed-traffic designs. Several of the '812' class 0-6-0s — though not the later '652' version, and the four engines of the superheated '30' class, were painted blue and fitted with the Westinghouse brake. These were all modelled on Drummond's famed 'Jumbos', but were not simply goods engines. While many of the '812' and all the '652' classes worked goods trains throughout the CR system, the blue engines not only hauled the occasional excursion, but even the prestigious Clyde Coast trains. These indefatigable engines survived to into BR's ownership, and were as valuable in their own work as were any of the express locomotives introduced during McIntosh's reign.

In fact, the superheater made the '30' class a bit nose-heavy and so, ever alert to problems — and giving the lie to suggestions that he was blinkered in his simplistic designs, McIntosh produced Scotland's first Mogul. If the '34' class looked little more than a '30' with a leading pair of wheels, well, that is just what it was. This simple expedient solved the problem of the additional weight, although it looked a slightly odd machine with the smokebox being set so far back — an aristocratic chinless wonder? The LMS was not impressed though, and the last was withdrawn by 1937, outlived by nearly all of the '30' class.

Another first for McIntosh came in 1901 when he introduced the 0-8-0 to Scotland, with his '600' class. Although heavy goods engines, these were fitted with the Westinghouse brake to haul specially built 30 ton double-bogie mineral wagons, in trains of 30 wagons a time. These powerful engines were more than capable of hauling such loads, and considerable savings on such operations in southern Scotland looked to be on offer. Unfortunately, the left hand of McIntosh's department did not inform the right hand of the operating authorities, and refuge sidings for such long trains were few and far between. In the end, trains of just 15 double-bogie wagons were the norm — no longer than loose-coupled ones: the only advantage was the use of the Westinghouse brake.

The '600' class was, thus, never fully utilised, but the locomotives were certainly distinctive with their most unusual wheel spacing. The gap between the centres of the middle pair of wheels was 5 ft. 4 in., while it was fully 8 ft. 6 in. between these and the outer wheels, but at least symmetry was maintained. The reasoning behind this was to gain flexibility — with specially jointed coupling-rods — to allow for working over the steep curves of the many mineral lines. They were mainly found on the southern main line, but once subsumed into the LMS — with many similar engines, these non-standard locomotives became the first McIntosh class to become extinct, by 1929.

The Drummond 0-4-4T was perpetuated throughout the McIntosh era. The various developments proved most valuable machines and those with the 5 ft. 9 in. driving wheels all survived into BR ownership, the last being withdrawn in 1962. Then, in 1899, McIntosh produced the diminutive '104' class specifically for Glasgow's Cathcart Circle, and Edinburgh's Balerno branch. These routes had tight curves, sharp inclines, closely spaced stations and, most relevant, a low axle loading. The '104s' worked these almost exclusively, until the numerous bridges were strengthened. Then, their time was up and the lot had gone by 1938.

If McIntosh's passenger tanks were a conspicuous, long-lasting success, so too were his goods tanks — odd ones apart. The 0-6-0T predominated and was perpetuated with the '782' class that became, numerically, McIntosh's largest. In 1903, the '492' class 0-8-0T version of the '600' class emerged. Like their big brothers, these were also fitted with the Westinghouse brake to shunt the 30 ton wagons, and also shared an odd wheel-spacing: the leading wheel-centre was 7 ft. 9 in. from the second set, the rest being 5 ft. 7½ in. apart. These were also deemed non-standard in the Stanier revolution and were swept aside by 1939.

In 1911, McIntosh designed his only outside cylinder locomotive. Only 2 were built before he retired, although his successor, W. Pickersgill, built more. These 'Beetle-crusher' '498' class 0-6-0Ts were designed to work tightly curved dock lines. Though quite mundane engines, they were far superior to the older little 0-4-0STs, and some worked into the 1960s; Money for Nothing all right.

So, adaptations of four Drummond standards, a number of variations on the 4-6-0 theme — amounting to only 42 locomotives, and a few odds-and-ends of goods and shunting engines. Is McIntosh — a man with little works or design experience, really entitled to be called a Star of Steam? His reputation lay mainly in the construction of elegant, sturdy, powerful and reliable engines, usually with a good turn of speed, and no peccadilloes that warranted a kid-gloves approach. In their day, and this is more important than making judgements in the fullness of time, McIntosh's locomotives saw the CR climb from the higher slopes of British locomotive design to join the elite few at the very summit.

In some respects, the CR appeared over-engined, but supposing the truce following the 1895 races had not lasted for nearly 40 years? Of all the railways likely to compete for traffic to Glasgow, Edinburgh, Aberdeen or any other important Scottish destination, McIntosh saw to it that the CR was the best equipped of the lot. Whether it was fast and light, fast and heavy, or even slow and luxurious, the CR had just the engine for the job — in all weathers. During the second half of his reign, the MR was building its 'Compounds', the GNR had Ivatt's large atlantics, the LNWR the 'George the Fifths', and the NER both atlantics and 4-6-0s. Some of these certainly had greater potential than 'Cardean', for example, but few realised it on a daily basis. Others were technically more

'Dunalastair IV' No. 146, is in pristine condition, amid the hills on the main line to the south, as shown by the bow-tie position of the train indicator in front of the chimney. Despite their magnificently elegant appearance, these were no foppish dandies, but very willing and powerful engines. The appearance also draws one's eyes away from the motley bunch of carriages it has in tow.

advanced, but on the road — all year round — a 'Cardean' or a later 'Dunalastair' would give anything a run for its money.

It is certainly true that the McIntosh 4-6-0s that remained were swept aside once the 'Black Fives' arrived, but then the LMS seemed to delight in Scottish ethnic cleansing. The last superheated 'Dunalastair IV' was scrapped in 1959, while several 0-6-0s and tank engines survived even later. In many respects, the survival of a locomotive is not just a reflection of how good it was, but whether suitable replacements had been built. Nevertheless, the costly to run and maintain, and the unreliable seldom survived the LMS cull and BR purges: a McIntosh locomotive was certainly reliable and easy to maintain.

The CR locomotive stock under McIntosh was both admired and envied. True, the foundations laid by Drummond and Lambie did not need any under-pinning but, as most aristocratic families — and many pre-Grouping railways — have found, it is easy to squander an inheritance. It takes considerable foresight, planning and not a little attention to small details to build successfully for the future. For McIntosh, without a vast drawing and design experience, and without his right hand, his achievements were even greater: at least Churchward, who equipped the GWR with a locomotive fleet every bit the equal of the CR, had many years design experience behind him. No, the CR wanted consistent, reliable work, whether on the fastest express passenger or the meanest shunting duties. McIntosh gave it just that, with the potential to add copious amounts of spice if ever it was required.

Once again harking back to Edwardian times, to those who knew, McIntosh was held in the highest esteem. There were no learned papers — read by the very few; no mass applications for patents — that nobody used; no pretence of engineering greatness — when others did most of the real work. All McIntosh did was to provide engines that reliably undertook all that was ever asked of them, and much more besides. He was elected President of the ARLE, in 1911, but in 1913 received his highest honour, one almost unique in the railway industry. King George V personally made McIntosh a Member of the Royal Victorian Order, an honour usually bestowed for services to the sovereign: it seems that the king was more than aware whose locomotives put up the best performances on visits to and from Balmoral.

McIntosh was not a CME like, say, Drummond who was almost feared. Neither was he as worldly wise, with wide-ranging interests as W. Adams — few railway people ever were. He fell somewhere between the two, but was no compromise. McIntosh was the thorough, practical Scotsman, with little

McIntosh was undoubtedly a big-engine man and when No. 49 was built, in 1903, they did not come much bigger, in Britain at least. It had quite massive proportions for its day, to say nothing of its gargantuan tender and, once a few teething problems had been sorted out this, and its sister engine, soon got to work and put themselves about on the main lines to the south, and also to Aberdeen.

time for grandeur and other small-minded status nonsense. Yet he was far from being a stern, humourless martinet so often associated with those of his standing.

There is no doubt that it was McIntosh, and not the great man himself, who took the very best of Dugald Drummond's — and Scotland's — engineering tenets to their very limit. Like the original, practical engineer that he was, Drummond tried to incorporate many advanced developments into his designs, or to evolve his own variations. Not so McIntosh. He might not have had the background many of his peers enjoyed, but he put his vast practical experience to the greatest use. Having first improved the basic Drummond formula by adding a big free-steaming boiler, he enlarged the concept to just about its practical limits. Drummond might have seen the limitations and tried to forge new paths; for McIntosh, such limits lay well into the future.

No, in terms of practical applied steam locomotive design, McIntosh was the finest Scotland produced, possibly the best of his time and among the very best from Britain. After all, he never designed a poor locomotive, and if CR enginemen treated all with contempt — whether Scottish rivals or West Coast ally, well, McIntosh gave them the engines to justify their aloof attitude. As any sportsman will tell you, one can only be up there with the best of your era; it is little use claiming to be better than any predecessors. McIntosh could more than just claim to be up there among the Stars, and if he did so it would be with a smile, certainly not the dour Scottish scowl.

MCINTOSH IN BRIEF

BORN:	1846, Forfarshire.
TRAINING:	1862-7, Arbroath Works of Scottish North Eastern Railway, Apprentice.
EMPLOYED;	1867, CR at Montrose
SENIOR POSITIONS:	1876, Loco. Inspector of Northern Division, CR.
	1882, District Loco. Foreman, at Aberdeen.
	1884, District Loco. Foreman, Carstairs.
	1886, District Loco. Foreman, Polmadie.
	1891, Ass. Locomotive Superintendent to J. Lambie.
	1895, Locomotive Superintendent CR.
RETIRED:	May 1914, Glasgow.
HONOURS:	1912, President, ARLE.
	1913, Member Royal Victorian Order.
DIED:	6th February 1918, Glasgow.

McIntosh's Locomotive Designs

YEAR	CLASS	WHEEL ARRANGEMENT	CYLINDERS (INCHES)	BOILER PRESSURE	DRIVING-WHEEL DIAMETER	WEIGHT	No. IN CLASS
1895	709	0-6-0	18 x 26	150 psi	5 ft.	41¼ tons	83
1895	19	0-4-4T	18 x 26	150 psi	5' 9"	53¾ tons	10
1895	29	0-6-0T	18 x 26	150 psi	4' 6"	49¾ tons	9
	Dunalastair I						
1895	721	4-4-0	18¼ x 26	160 psi	6' 6"	47 tons	15
1897	92 + 879	0-4-4T	17 x 24	160 psi	5' 9"	55¾ tons	22
	Dunalastair II						
1897	766	4-4-0	19 x 26	175 psi	6' 6"	49 tons	15
1898	782	0-6-0T	18 x 26	150 psi	4' 6"	47¾ tons	138
1899	104	0-4-4T	17 x 24	150 psi	4' 6"	51T 2 cwt	12
1899	812 + 652	0-6-0	18 x 28	160 psi	5 ft.	45¾ tons	96
	Dunalastair III						
1899	900	4-4-0	19 x 26	180 psi	6' 6"	51¾ tons	16
1900	439	0-4-4T	18 x 26	160 psi	5' 9"	57½ tons	68
1901	600	0-8-0	21 x 26	175 psi	4' 6"	60½ tons	8
1902	55	4-6-0	19 x 26	175 psi	5 ft.	57½ tons	9
1903	49	4-6-0	21 x 26	200 psi	6' 6"	70 tons	2
1903	492	0-8-0T	19 x 26	175 psi	4' 6"	62¾ tons	6
	Dunalastair IV						
1904	140	4-4-0	19 x 26	180 psi	6' 6"	56½ tons	19
1906	903	4-6-0	20 x 26	200 psi	6' 6"	73 tons	5
1906	908	4-6-0	19 x 26	180 psi	5' 9"	64 tons	10
1906	918	4-6-0	19 x 26	175 psi	5 ft.	60T 8 cwt	5
	Dunalastair IV (superheated)						
1910	139	4-4-0	20 x 26	165 psi	6' 6"	59 tons	22
1911	498	0-6-0T	(o)17 x 22	160 psi	4 ft.	47¾ tons	23
1912	30	0-6-0	19½ x 26	160 psi	5 ft.	51T 2 cwt	4
1912	34	2-6-0	19½ x 26	160 psi	5 ft.	54¼ tons	5
1913	179	4-6-0	19½ x 26	170 psi	5' 9"	68½ tons	11

Engines designed by Drummond

1895	611	0-4-0ST	(o)14 x 20	140 psi	3' 8"	27½ tons	14

McINTOSH'S PRESERVED LOCOMOTIVES

YEAR	CLASS	RUNNING NUMBERS	TOTAL
1897	92	(B.R.) 55189	1
1899	812	(B.R.) 57566	1

FRANCIS WILLIAM WEBB
The King of Crewe

I approached the oak-darkened corridor not simply in trepidation, but with an increasing sense of fear. There was no way out, I had to face the music and, quite literally, was on a hiding to nothing. Distraught with my predicament, I hovered outside the heavy wooden door attempting to compose myself: clever-clogs Willie was about to get his cum-uppance. Like it or not, and I most assuredly wouldn't, this was an episode one just had to grin and bear with traditional English stoicism and fortitude.

Quietly, I knocked the door...nothing. Gathering myself together, I tried again, only with a firm knock, knock, KNOCK. An apparent age later a firm voice from within called, "Come". Turning the knob and giving the door a hefty push, I entered, closed the door and stood to attention before the large writing table.

The man sitting in his gown presently looked up. The black mortar board hung ominously on its stand.

"Ah, it's Williams isn't it?"

"Yes sir." I think he sensed my anguish.

"I always enjoy our little meetings, boy. So, for what do I have the pleasure today?" The Headmaster asked, with a twinkle in his eyes, while ostentatiously flexing his fingers.

"Sir, I am afraid that Mr. Rawson has sent me", I said handing over a note. This was it. For the last 10 minutes, or was it hours, my mind was enwrapped in the note's contents. Although I had not read it, I knew exactly the message it conveyed. Six strokes of the best, three on each hand. The moment of truth had arrived.

The prospect of writing about F.W. Webb reminds me of my first introduction to bamboo, as a 13 year old: it was not pleasant. It is situation one cannot win. Omit Webb from a book about the Stars of Steam — the easy way out and, no doubt, many readers would nod in knowing agreement, while an equal number would equate that to an act of blasphemy and cowardice. Include Webb and one is just asking to be ridiculed, either for giving support or criticism. Just like a visit to the headmaster, this is going to hurt.

You see, few people with an interest in railways fail to hold an opinion on the man: good or bad. If one offers the slightest support to Webb, the accusations of 'apologist' will ring out very loud and clear. Criticise and one will be castigated as simply jumping on the anti-Webb bandwagon. With Webb, as with Baroness Thatcher of Kesteven, there is no such thing as taking the middle ground. You either love him, hate him or know nothing about him. You never ignore him.

Yet, on the whole, so little is known of the man. He was an autocrat, though with occasional benevolent tendencies, and ruled his vast demesne at Crewe Works like a monarch claiming divine right. Nobody, but nobody dare interfere with his authority and, as the years rolled by, any criticism of Webb or his deeds was unlikely to enhance one's future prospects, inside the LNWR, or out. He was obstinate, firmly backed his own views and principles, was highly inventive — always being prepared to try something new, and ran a fiendishly tight ship,

to which he devoted his whole life. That is all we know with any real certainty. To his many critics, all this is damning evidence with which to lambaste Webb, while his supporters offer an entirely contrary view. Undoubtedly though, today's senior mis-managers would positively drool over the prospect of such power, control and authority.

However, the evidence against Webb being a Star of Steam is both wide-ranging and diverse, but before considering the charges against the defendant, we need some background details. Webb was born in Staffordshire in 1836, another engineering recruit saved from a clerical calling. In 1851, the year of the Great Exhibition, Webb was apprenticed to Francis Trevithick, at Crewe Works, finishing his training five years later and entering the Drawing Office. Webb was clearly one of the most talented young men in Crewe at that time, for he was appointed Chief Draughtsman in 1859, and became Works Manager and Chief Assistant to the Locomotive Superintendent, J. Ramsbottom, only two years later. That was most definitely fast-track promotion and, especially under Ramsbottom, must have most assuredly been fully deserved.

For five years Webb was a faithful, devoted No. 2, heavily involved with detail locomotive design. Then, without warning, he jumped ship to become the manager and a partner in the Bolton Iron and Steel Co. This might be seen as a backward step, but Ramsbottom was only 52 years old and could easily have had a couple of decades' work ahead of him. Webb had enjoyed a meteoric rise until he was 30, a potential stalemate until he was 50 was unlikely to be too appealing. After all, he clearly had ambition — of that there is no shred of doubt.

Before long, Webb was imbued, impressed and immersed in the new steel-making processes. This was a time, remember, when British engineering ruled the world. Though there were numerous spokes radiating in all directions, the hub of world engineering was firmly planted in the north-west of England: it was the 19th century equivalent to the silicon valley of computers. Though living conditions were dire for most of the populace, many men went on to make considerable fortunes and reputations. Webb was no different and was prepared to chance his arm, but the allure of Crewe was just too strong. When Ramsbottom supposedly retired, in 1870, the call went out to the prodigal son. In 1871, Webb returned to take over the at Crewe's helm and, before long, held the enhanced title CME.

Webb's appointment was due entirely to the LNWR's Chairman, Sir Richard Moon. He was a forthright man, expecting and demanding good, thorough and economic management, and strong leadership. Webb was all that, plus an original thinker and had an un-erring determination to get his way. Moon was no shrinking violet either and put all his energies into running and shaping the LNWR. Webb and Moon were probably too alike to work closely together, their respective egos would be entwined in permanent conflict. Still, if Moon was akin to a Roman Emperor, Webb was the ruler of a province: his word went unquestioned within his demesne, yet he was devoted to the greater good of the Empire. Moon never interfered with events at, or emanating from, Crewe and Crewe, under Webb, was as faithful to the LNWR as was any dog to his master.

If you think that this portrays Webb as something of a yes-man, do not be fooled. Webb was devoted to the LNWR, to Crewe Works and to his men, in that order. Anything or anyone who tried to distract Webb from that path or, worse still, poked his nose where it was not required, was likely to come a cropper or, at the very least, have it bloodied. With Moon in charge, everything ran seamlessly, but when he retired, Frederick Harrison was appointed General Manager. As so often happens, new brooms have a tendency to do a bit of sweeping and Webb's way was not that of Harrison. Webb had always been directly responsible to the board, but Harrison tried to block that route and attempted to make Webb a direct subordinate. That did not work, but increasingly Webb was an outcast from, and a thorn in the side of, the new Euston-based regime. As such, Webb and Crewe found themselves shunted to a far-off siding, never to be quite at the centre of power again.

Throughout the 1890s, until Webb retired in 1903, the CME's department, like those of rival companies, was having to cope with the massively changing requirements for its products — as trains became heavier and faster, and also its altered position within the company. If some way short of being under constant attack, policies and actions were no longer simply accepted. Webb was under increasing pressure, and remember, he was then over 60 years old — though not too old to learn new tricks, but with age came obstinacy. No doubt, with every perceived attack or new demand on his beloved department, Webb was ever-more inclined to dig in his heels and turn inwards. An understandable reaction, one might think, or was it the last stand of an insane dictator?

It all began so much earlier though. LNWR train services had never been dynamic, at least while Moon ruled the roost. On the east side of the country the GNR was sending forth expresses at speeds that left the world agog. By the time Webb became CME, Stirling's 8 ft. singles were soon hauling the fastest passenger trains in the world. To the west, the GWR still sent its broad gauge expresses thundering along its superbly engineered line to Bristol. And what of the LNWR? Well, according to Moon, 40 mph was quite fast enough for a gentleman thank you very much, and that was that.

Such a statement which, to us, might be seen as conservatism gone raving mad, had its basis in simple economy. The hallowed cry of businessmen is that they are competitive people, thriving on the cut-and-thrust of commercial life. Some even claim to be the modern-day equivalent of jousting medieval knights. Not on your life, except that they live off the backs of what others produce. What they really seek is a monopoly, or at least a niche in a market where competitors are not met head-on.

During Moon's tenure as chairman, the LNWR enjoyed if not a monopoly, at least the shortest route from London to most of its important destinations. By running trains from London at a pedestrian 40 mph average speed, not only did the LNWR still offer the fastest services to places such as Liverpool, Manchester and Glasgow, but it ran with great economy. After all, there is little point in running a costly fast train to, say, Liverpool, when the opposition cannot get within an hour of the company's time in any case.

In any case, as the LNWR's permanent-way was easily the finest in the country — it was, after all, the Premier Line — Ramsbottom and Webb were able to build light, inside-frame locomotives, making further savings over the sturdier locomotives required elsewhere. For most of Moon's reign, Britain was in the throes of the Great Depression. This was not so deep as the depressions of Thatcher's years, whereby millions of jobs were lost and real unemployment reached over 8 million, but the effects were not dissimilar. If one was in work, real wages probably rose: many were not. A stagnant economy restricts opportunities for growth and so to maintain profits a company must cut costs. This was Moon's philosophy, and Webb was in full agreement.

So, while not being totally unique, Webb's locomotives were designed to be worked very hard, with little in reserve. If, for 4 days a week, a given train was within the capacity of an allocated class of engine, only to be increased in weight on a Friday beyond that engine's ability, then surely it would be more economical to use a pilot on the Friday rather than have a larger, more costly locomotive with much un-used potential running for 4 out of 5 days, yes? Well, many engineers, in Webb's time, and later, said no, but Webb was his own man.

Thus, Webb's first express design was the 'Precursor' 2-4-0s, of 1874. These were a development of Ramsbottom's similar 'Samson' class, with even smaller driving wheels, that were intended to work expresses from Crewe-Carlisle. It was expected that the 'Precursors' would run up the hills at a decent lick, and thus obviate the need for frantic dashes downhill: economy ever to the fore. This was possibly an idea Webb picked up when visiting America soon after his appointment — or had it anything to do with the arrival back at Crewe of the Worsdell brothers? Something was amiss though, because the 'Precursors' were soon removed from main line duties and were demoted to hauling Leeds-Manchester trains and other lowly tasks while, later, many were rebuilt as '910' 2-4-2Ts — surely, the final insult?

The 'Precursors' used the same boiler as Webb's 'Coal Engines' of 1873, a possible reason why they did not exactly sparkle over the arduous Westmorland and Cumberland fells. It was an entirely different matter for Webb's simultaneous express design for the London-Crewe line: the 'Precedent' class. These equally diminutive locomotives were a development of Ramsbottom's 'Newton' class which, with the 'Samsons', Webb had part-designed in the first place. Though visually similar to the 'Precursors', there were, nevertheless, a couple of crucial differences: the 'Precedents' driving wheels were a foot taller and the firebox was 10% larger. Both had Allan's valve-gear, short and direct steam passages, and large bearing surfaces, but it was the large steam chest that enabled the 'Precedents' to become fast runners and gain their legendary reputation.

That did not happen overnight though, for crews still preferred McConnell's 'Bloomers'. Webb had no easy ride and the 'Precedents' initial performances, and the 'Precursors' failure, fuelled his critics. Eventually, following modest timetable improvements during the mid-1880s, the 'Precedents' came into their own. Then, after being rebuilt in the 1890s, they wrote themselves firmly into the record books with their running in the 1895 'races': the brilliant exploits of 'Hardwick' were a fitting climax, and produced one of the greatest steam engine runs in history. Strangely enough, if the 'Precedents' were reputedly working nigh flat-out on the reasonably light and easily timed pre-1885 expresses, their anaerobic capacities must have been enormous given the work they were undertaking a decade and more later, and on into the 20th century. Still, even Webb's critics acknowledge that the 'Precedents' were fine locomotives: it was their intended successors that really caused all the fuss.

If Webb's mighty flyweights have come in for some

criticism, that is as nothing to that meeted out to his compounds. The general gist of the venom spat at these engines is that they were incapable of meeting even the modest standards set for them. Some critics have gone further and have written the whole lot off as poorly thought out and bad designs, the work of a man who had lost all touch with reality. Some of this invective is certainly not untrue, but remember that anyone who has actually done something, successful or otherwise, is ten times the person of the mealy-mouthed critics who have done bugger-all.

There is no doubt that his compounds gave Webb much scope for thought and improvement. For a start, he viewed compounding from the standpoint of economy — no doubt, had Webb survived another decade, he would have enthused over superheating for much the same reasons. Compounding seemed to offer a something-for-nothing potential that is attractive to both engineers and businessmen alike. Inspired by the Swiss engineer J.T.A. Mallet, Webb devised his own unique system, using 2 outside high-pressure cylinders and an inside low-pressure cylinder. Compounding was to dominate Webb's thinking for the rest of his days.

After conducting a singular, and not overly successful experiment, Webb took another step forward by building what was little more than a 3-cylinder compound 'Precedent', appropriately called 'Experiment'. Sharing the same boiler, firebox, wheels and a similar chassis to a 'Precedent', the engine had 11½ in. H.P. cylinders and Joy's new valve-gear, that Webb came to favour over the ensuing years. Most peculiar of all though, and still incredulous to some, Webb omitted coupling-rods from the two pairs of driving wheels, so the engine was, in effect, a double-single. Joy's gear did not allow space for the coupling rods!

The large inside cylinder drove the leading axle, and the two outside cylinders the rear axle. The small H.P. cylinders were, unfortunately, left to move a train off the starting-blocks and then, when underway, did the lion's-share of the work — a bit like riding a tandem with an idle companion. In a sense, the arrangement was similar to a 4-WD car, with the rear wheels frantically spinning to get a grip, and the front ones not giving a damn and letting them get on with it. Coupling the wheels would at least have spread the work more evenly.

Obvious though coupled wheels may seem now, it was not quite so clear-cut in the 1880s. This was, after all, the decade when the single-drivers enjoyed a big revival. Apart from singles being widely used for high-speed trains, coupling-rods were still regarded as somewhat unreliable, though with Crewe's steel-making experience — not forgetting its long use of 2-4-0 locomotives — this was hardly applicable. So, while Webb has been roundly criticised for his use of un-coupled driving wheels on his new 3-cylinder compounds, he had acceptable reasons. Remember also that, right at the end of the century, D. Drummond built double-singles, and while one swallow does not make a summer, neither does one error make a bad engineer.

'Experiment' was tested extensively and ran over 100,000 economical miles in its first year. Of course, it was cosseted and only consumed high quality fuel, but that was still an outstanding achievement. A second locomotive was built with 13 in. H.P. cylinders, effecting an undoubted improvement, and Webb got permission to build a further 28 locomotives. Now, though they were poor starters and performed some way short of 'Precedent' standards, the 'Experiments' were, to all intents and purposes, fully up to the standards required of them. It did not last and they were undone by the modest speeding-up of trains in the mid-1880s. It is easy to say, but Webb should have developed the design a bit more before going in for quantity production.

Still, the 'Experiments' have provided good ammunition for Webb's critics and before long he gave still more. Webb developed his 3-cylinder compound theme into the 'Dreadnought' class, incorporating a larger boiler — pressed to 175 psi, separate adjustment for the high and low-pressure cylinders, and an increased port area to improve the exhaust flow. Though crews were then better able to apportion the work between the cylinders, at starting and at speed, the 'Dreadnoughts' were still unreliable and indifferent runners: little better than the 'Experiments', in fact.

Webb was not one to be defeated though. He tried still more developments to gain the economies he sought, and the ensuing 'Teutonics' were to be his finest 3-cylinder compounds. Though the boiler and cylinders were essentially those of the 'Dreadnoughts', increased valve travel, and especially the use of a slip-eccentric on the inside cylinder — instead of Joy's valve-gear, produced all-round improvements. On the road, the 'Teutonics' were similar performers to the 'Improved Precedents' then coming on tap and, so far as running costs were concerned, they were claimed to be so economical as to off-set the additional capital costs of compounding.

Of course, being little better than a mere development of a 20-odd year old design is not too proud a boast, but it showed that Webb was making progress. Webb's next compound design, the 'Greater Britain' raised all sorts of doubts once again. One could but marvel at the large boiler and its peculiar, yet distinctive elegance. Alternatively, one might shake one's head in disbelief that Webb persisted with uncoupled driving wheels, despite having plenty of room for coupling rods and, more pertinently, query his very thinking behind the boiler design.

About halfway along the boiler, Webb placed a combustion chamber between the two sets of tubes. He reasoned that the gasses passing through the first set of tubes would ignite in the combustion chamber and raise the heat in the second set of tubes. Was Webb out of his mind? One might also question his relationship with his Drawing Office, as nobody came forward to proclaim such an idea as being, politely, unbelievable. Just the one engine ran before being 9 more were built, but surely it was discovered that the combustion chamber did not work? Perhaps so but, even then, not before a smaller wheeled locomotive was built: the first of the 'John Hick' class. Despite this singleton being identical to the 'Greater Britains' in all respects except its smaller driving wheels, it was an indifferent performer. Even more surprising is that 9 more were built in 1898, just as a pair of 4-cylinder 4-4-0s was undergoing trials. The 'John Hick' class, rather like the earlier 'Precursors', were soon ousted off their intended Crewe-Carlisle route, and were demoted to mundane secondary work.

The whole episode of Webb's final 3-cylinder compound designs surely suggests that, if he was not entirely off his rocker, his engineering and intellectual capacities were being severely stretched. Had he ever fully understood all the requirements of compounding? Of course, Webb had made definite progress over a decade or so, but then simple expansion locomotive design had not exactly been standing still either.

From 1897, Webb changed tack with his compounds and opted to use four cylinders. As these all drove onto the leading axle, so coupling rods were essential for the ensuing 4-4-0s. With a boiler of 'Teutonic' dimensions, and with the mid-combustion chamber quietly forgotten, Webb followed his independent path in providing a leading bogie. Not for him the simple remedy of, say, adopting the popular Adams bogie. Oh no, having already produced his own highly successful radial truck, he designed a double-wheel version which, incidentally,

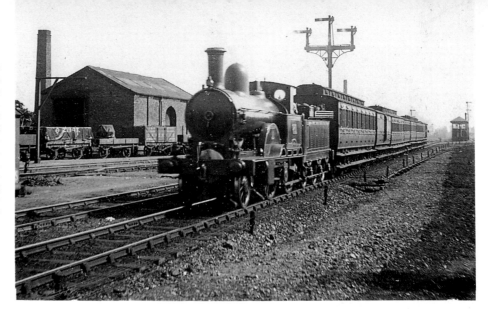

Despite Webb's expectations that his first 3-cylinder compounds, the 'Experiments', would soon push the 'Precedents' off the main expresses, this did not happen. Very soon, it was the sluggish and slow-starting compounds that found themselves demoted to secondary services. 'Experiment' No. 323 'Britannic', hauls one such train, at Hooton in Cheshire, but is still in outstanding condition with its giant inside cylinder clearly visible beneath the smokebox door.

assisted all four cylinders driving onto the same axle, called the double radial truck. Ingenious!

One of the 'Jubilee' class was built as a simple-expansion engine, with 4 cylinders of 14 in. x 24 in., and ran with alongside a 4-cylinder compound version for evaluation purposes. It was not exactly a fair test, as the simple engine's boiler was only pressed to 175 psi, and not the 200 psi of the compound! Despite not demonstrating a conclusive superiority, the compound, not unnaturally, won the day and another 38 such engines were constructed.

Webb has been criticised as these so-called tests clearly were biased in favour of the compound. Well, so what? Everyone has their favourite approach and Webb genuinely thought compounding would yield benefits. As a hockey captain, I expect a high level of fitness and commitment from my players. If a player cannot display those attributes, he will not get in the team, no matter how skilful. Yes, his trial is also loaded.

Mind you, the 'Jubilees' were some way short of being an outstanding success as well. Though better starters than the 3-cylinder compounds, they were still sluggish runners because the L.P. cylinder valves were not big enough. Webb had made the same mistake with the 'Dreadnoughts', but it is easy to be critical with all the knowledge of the many 20th century valve improvements. These were common mistakes made right into the 1920s and, Churchward apart, if an engineer got the valve sizes right before then, it was often more by luck than judgement and, as with G. Hughes, he was probably unaware of exactly what he had done in any case.

Then, to greet the new century, Webb introduced an enlarged version of the 'Jubilees': the 'Alfred the Great' class. These were very little better, but in 1903, almost as a final act of defiance, Webb provided independent control for the outside valve-gear. If hardly transforming the engines, they performed rather better than before, but the 'Jubilees' were not converted. And with that, the reign of the compound on the LNWR disappeared abruptly on Webb's retirement.

On the whole, Webb's passenger designs performed satisfactorily, although the 'Precedents', 'Whitworths' — a sort of improved 'Samson', and the 'Teutonics' could justly claim to being particularly good, if simple designs. While Webb's many detractors have roundly lambasted his compounds, his supporters seem only capable of saying they were not really as bad as all that — almost as an apology. Well, though the compounds' performance did not exactly stir the blood, contemporary reports suggest they were not a let-down either:

For lesser passenger duties during Webb's reign, 2-4-2Ts played a very full part in the life of the company. They found themselves working all over the system, as this picture of No. 2128, at Cambridge, shows. On odd occasions, thanks to various operating restrictions imposed early this century, a few even found themselves acting as pilots on expresses. Somehow, one cannot see the GNR, or even the MR, stooping to such levels.

competent and just about on top of the job allocated to them, is probably a fair epitaph.

G. Whale, Webb's successor, thought otherwise though. He was in charge of the LNWR Running Dept. during the latter part of Webb's reign, and was responsible for providing locomotives to run the services. Though the compounds were in a distinct minority, Whale had to face up to their defects and problems, day-in, day-out. Not unexpectedly, such people prefer simplicity and reliability, while an engine that can do a job, in all conditions, is preferable to having to find another to assist every now and again. Whale did not just dislike the compounds, he positively hated them.

Almost before Webb had vacated his chair, Whale instituted an engineering ethnic-cleansing of his predecessor's beloved compounds. Within a decade it was all-but complete. Never before, or since has there been such a wholesale slaughter, or conversion, of a predecessor's pet locomotive

The front end of 'A' class 3-cylinder compound No. 1850, with its combined smokebox and cylinders, would not have been out of place 50 years earlier, and was copied by D. Jones on the HR. Despite all the criticism of Webb's compounds, these 0-8-0s were fine engines, ideal for heavy goods work and contributed massively to the regular handsome dividends paid by the LNWR.

---

designs, except perhaps for those of Bowen Cook, Whale's successor. This is often cited as an accurate contemporary reflection of the true worth of Webb's work. After all, did not Webb suppress all criticism of him?

Such charges do not show Webb in a good light, but he was actually in quite good company. On the NER, T.W. Worsdell's compounds were axed and converted to simples by his younger brother, W. Worsdell, no less. On the GWR, Dean designed some delightful singles and double-framed 4-4-0s in the 1890s. His brilliant successor, Churchward, soon put these in their place, and the singles onto the scrap-lines. P. Stirling is another Star of Steam who persevered with singles for too long. His successor, H.A. Ivatt, also had a shot at them before realising their limitations and then put Stirling's masterpieces to the sword. Finally, had the Second World War not been in full-swing, would not E. Thompson have cut great swaths into the ranks of his illustrious predecessor's locomotives or, failing that, at least removed Gresley's favourite conjugated motion from them? Oh yes, Webb is certainly not alone.

One cannot deny though that Webb's passenger compounds hardly took the railway world by storm, though they never passed unnoticed. Occasionally, as with his central combustion chamber, one might question whether Webb knew what he was doing. However, Churchward — and later Collett and even Stanier, for a while — never seemed to appreciate the benefits of high-degree superheat. Then it took the GWR/LNER locomotive exchanges, of 1925, for Gresley to understand the advantages of long-travel, long-lap valves. Yes, there are several Stars of Steam who occasionally failed to see the wood for the trees, so Webb is in good company. In any case, Webb was the one doing the work, rather than talking

about it, and he was directly involved in detail design. Perhaps that was the problem?

As for Webb's non-passenger designs, he enjoyed rather more, acclaimed, success. His 'Coal Engines' were thoroughly orthodox 0-6-0s, but right up to the minute in chassis design. The immortal 'Cauliflowers' were an enlarged version, for fast and general goods work, and they were the first British engines to be fitted with Joy's valve-gear. It is impossible to realistically compare their abilities with the multitude of similar engines, contemporary or otherwise, but they remained firm favourites of all who came into contact with them: professional railwaymen, railwayacs and enthusiasts alike.

In 1892, a singleton 2-cylinder 0-8-0 was built and tested against a similar 3-cylinder compound. To nobody's great surprise, it was the compound that won the day and entered series production. From 1901, the 'B' class 4-cylinder compound 0-8-0 was built in even greater numbers. The very fact that goods engines did not have to go at any great speed eliminated their passenger-brothers' occasional reluctance to run with a sense of brio. Yet, despite being sure-footed and powerful, and some of the best goods engines in Britain, once Webb had gone, they also took their turn in the lengthy queue for rebuilding. Finally, Webb produced a mixed-traffic 4-6-0 class, the '1400s', that did not endear themselves to anyone. The idea was fine, ahead of its time, but poorly executed. An engine equally at home on semi-fast passenger or express goods? The 'Bill Baileys' found domestic bliss on neither.

Webb also produced a doughty range of tank engines. Two classes of 2-4-2Ts were classics of their time, and roamed the LNWR network with consummate dexterity. His 0-6-2T 'Coal Tanks' and '18 in. Tanks' were also fine and successful designs in their own right. To no great surprise, Webb tried his hand at compound tanks and, indeed, spent quite some time in the mid-1880s tinkering away: four singleton designs finally emerged. All suffered fatally from the surging motion of the uncoupled driving wheels and divided drive, this being far more exaggerated than on the tender engines, and all experiments finally dried-up. As with his passenger designs, conformity won the day, but Webb certainly gave compounding a good trial.

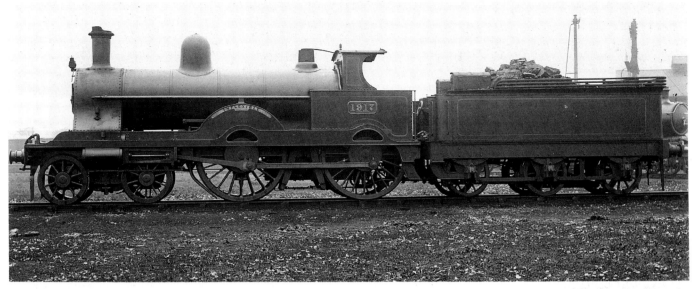

By the time Webb had produced the 'Jubilee' class 4-cylinder compounds, it seemed as though he might be getting onto the right track. Even so, despite these being a distinct improvement over the earlier 3-cylinder compounds, they were some way short of being truly fine locomotives. No. 1917 'Inflexible' was probably not named after Webb's approach towards his beloved compounds.

Of his contemporaries, a period when Dean, Johnson, D. Drummond, Jones, P. Stirling, W. Adams, Stroudley and the Worsdell brothers were in power — surely as glittering a Golden Age as any, Webb produced more than his fair share of indifferent performing locomotives. He certainly designed a few duds, but several outstanding classes as well. On the other hand, Webb was not a slave to orthodoxy. Not for him the conservative approach, continually enlarging what had done the business before. The main difference between Webb and other locomotive engineers who pursued alternative paths to the promised land of increased performance and economy, is that they usually, if finally, produced one outstanding design. So, Bulleid's 'Merchant Navys' eventually came good; Churchward and Gresley had many advanced successes; even Drummond's 'T14s' had their moments. Webb never really cracked it with his compounds, but his simple-expansion designs, and the many rebuilds he undertook, ensure that he is more than a worthy Star of Steam.

There is rather more to being a CME than designing locomotives though. Webb was not responsible for carriage and wagon production, but there is little doubt that all his professional pride was manifested in Crewe Works. Initially working with Ramsbottom to develop such activities as steel manufacture even, eventually, making their own rails, Webb turned Crewe into one of the finest engineering establishments in the country, and about the foremost of its type in the world. It was a massive undertaking and, quite unlike most railway works that, even then, were noted more for their engineering conservatism, led the way in several fields.

Webb ruled Crewe firmly, but fairly: even the emperor — Moon — did not interfere. When others tried after Moon retired in 1891, they received a very short-shrift, whoever they were. Out of all British CME's, none enjoyed quite the autonomy and authority of Webb. When asked to provide exhibits for the 1890 Edinburgh International Exhibition,

Webb was the only CME who did not need to seek any approval: his word was law and, once given, that was that. Considering the august list of British CME's then holding office, that gives a clear idea of how powerful Webb really was.

All things engineering interested Webb. Thus, he took to electricity and its use in Crewe Works, just as some people became bewitched by computers in the 1970s/80s. Crewe used electric machine tools decades before some factories ceased using water power. Other detail designs were of interest to Webb, and he instituted over 80 patents. Not all of these were of any use, but as he left a will of over £200,000 — with wages barely in excess of £3,000 p.a., he must have done well from the royalties — none of which came from the LNWR.

As with all people, there were other aspects to Webb's life but, above all, he was a devoted railway man. He held office on local councils, as did many in his position, but these were of secondary interest. His work was his life, and if he took an arrogant 'I know what's best for them' attitude to his thousands of employees, at least he had their interests at heart, so long as that did not adversely affect his beloved LNWR.

Webb was a true giant among steam locomotive engineers. If some of his designs and ideas were found wanting, in particular the precarious Clark and Webb train brake, he more than made up for that with his development of Crewe Works. After his retirement, the LNWR lived off this great legacy, and the country benefited immensely from it during the Great War. If the early regimes of the LMS did much to squander Crewe's vast resources, H.P.M. Beames oversaw its thorough rehabilitation that enabled Stanier to fully realise its potential.

Of course, there were aspects of Webb that were less than appetising. He ruled almost as a totalitarian dictator and, had he co-operated a bit more, then perhaps not only would he have made better progress with his compounds, but Crewe might have been an even more outstanding works. That was not Webb's way though, and few others would have had quite the inspiration, devotion, strength of character and will to meet his exacting standards. Perhaps what Webb really needed was a supremely gifted assistant — as Dean had with Churchward — whom he could have tutored, if not fathered, to follow in his footsteps, yet who had the talent for Webb to respect his opinion. Heaven knows, enough men of outstanding ability began their training at Crewe, and subsequently left to reach the highest of heights elsewhere.

WILLIAM ARTHUR STANIER
The Most Honourable

On the 1st January 1963 Alf Ramsey was appointed Manager of the England football team. His mandate was quite clear: after 13 years and four indifferent World Cup campaigns, England's standing in world football had fallen to its lowest ebb, it had to be revived. Ramsey's appointment seemed a rather innocuous event at the time, but three and a half years later, and for the following five or so years, he succeeded quite brilliantly at keeping England at the very forefront of world football.

Thirty one years earlier, the LMS appointed its fourth CME in just seven turbulent years. Like Ramsey — the footballers' choice, the new incumbent W.A. Stanier was hardly the populist man, but was the engineers' CME. The similarities between these two men, the unlikely mating of these quite different professions notwithstanding, went much further than that. Both had to undertake something of a mission, both had their own methods of working — with neither caring too much for tradition for its own sake, both were taking over the helm of ships of great potential, but ones that had drifted rudderless for some time, and both courted disaster en route to their eventual triumph. Ultimately, despite the apparent Ramsey Revolution in football tactics, and the Stanier Revolution with the LMS locomotive fleet, both of these men relied to a surprising degree on their respective inheritances.

Ramsey's appointment ended years of England mis-management by committee. In the main, he retained the existing coaches, then moulded them to his own requirements. Considering the short careers of footballers, almost half of his 1966 World Cup squad of 22 players had represented England under the old regime. His revolution did not require a wholesale slaughter of the innocents. Ramsey was a brilliant manager who knew his aim, analysed how to achieve it, and set about it with a clear and concise mind. He selected the right players and then moulded them all into an harmonious unit, dedicated to achieving their collective target.

Stanier strode a very similar path. Knowing that the current and future needs of the LMS would require a radical approach, he too appraised his staff and saw both a rare quality and an unenviable riches of resources. Stanier made some relatively minor personnel and methodological adjustments, then led his re-shuffled team forward to achieve their common goal. The various, seemingly warring-tribes of engineers at Derby, Crewe, Horwich and St. Rollox, whose shifting alliances and back-stabbing tendencies would not have been out of place in high-politics, were melded into the single outstanding team in British locomotive history. Long after both Stanier and the LMS had left the scene, Stanier's men led BR through the myriad uncertainties of the post-war world. I bet the Football Association wished it had pursued a similar policy of continuity after Ramsey.

Here the analogies end though. Stanier spent most of his professional life obscured from public view by two domineering shadows. Hailing from the GWR, Churchward's giant reputation masked the achievements of everyone else within his department. Even after Stanier escaped, he initially stood in the shadow of, if anything, a still brighter star who, far from waning, went on to ever-greater achievements: H.N. Gresley. As is so often the case, any assumed rivalry between Stanier and Gresley was more imagined than real. Both were outstanding locomotive engineers who were not exactly unfamiliar with each other, but they each enjoyed taking an opportunity to put one over the other, in the nicest possible way, of course.

As Stanier gradually emerged from the CME stage's dark shadows, Gresley was already the established star of the show. Stanier remained in Gresley's shadow for the rest of the LNER man's days, but then — quite ironically, as he did not produce any new locomotive designs — he was virtually thrust into the spotlight. It was almost a case of, 'the King is Dead, Long Live the Emperor'.

In the end, despite having spent most of his professional life either in the wings or as support to the main star, Stanier had more honours — professional or otherwise — bestowed upon him than any other CME. In reality, as with many in their 60s whose best years are certainly not ahead of them, Stanier was offered advisory or director-type positions on government bodies as a result of his status, and possibly experience, rather than for his drive or initiative. That is, of course, no fault of Stanier's and reflects more the peculiar British system that places tired and worn has-been's, and especially never-was types, into positions of privilege: jobs for the boys and conservatism. I wonder what Stanier really thought of his colleagues on these committees? There is something typically British in having a steam locomotive engineer as a director of Power Jets Ltd., or sitting on the Aeronautical Research Council. No wonder Britain has been overtaken in so many fields!

Such governmental work was to steal Stanier away from his beloved railways just as he emerged into the public limelight. There was, naturally, precious little afterglow in the midst of the Second World War, but Stanier's path was to be followed almost slavishly by his successors, C.E. Fairburn and H.G. Ivatt. However, in view of Stanier's proposals for a 4-6-4 express locomotive, among others, before leaving the LMS in 1944, his very best years were certainly not behind him, but were snatched from his grasp. He was, of course, far from being the only one to suffer likewise at that time, but it is worth pondering just how BR's locomotive policy might have evolved, had Stanier still been at the helm in 1948.

By the early 1940s, it seemed that Stanier was an LMS man through and through, but that was not quite the case. As with seaside rock, where the name of the resort appears wherever it is cut — Cleethorpes for instance, peel away Stanier's LMS wrapping and cut through him at any point you choose — arm, leg, neck — and there would be revealed his true love: the GWR. As with so many who worked for that great capitalist concern, Stanier would have gladly toiled away almost for the privilege. There were, seemingly, more evangelical ex-GWR

The epitome of GWR express design? Well, Stanier's 'Princess Royal' class Pacifics are to some. Although not entirely faultless performers at first, by the time No. 6204 'Princess Louise' was caught passing Harrow with the West Coast Postal, just prior to the Second World War, they were doing very nicely. Very powerful, fast and economical, these fine engines were a great asset to the LMS after years of turmoil and struggling with small engines. *(R. Cockcroft)*

men than ever there have been Christians. In Stanier's case, this was not surprising.

Having joined the company as a 15 year-old office boy, Stanier had risen dramatically to become the loyal and highly effective second-in-command to C.B. Collett, the CME, and was his assumed successor. However, his hopes of succeeding to the throne — for that is what some would have you believe it was — foundered when the directors told Collett that they expected him to carry on until he was 70 years old. By then, Stanier would be 65 and, so it seemed, was destined never to inherit the earth.

That was a mortal blow to one who, by then, had devoted 40 years to the GWR rising to sit by Collett's right hand had taken, indeed demanded, all that Stanier could give, and finding he was not the anointed son was just like having his birthright snatched away. Stanier's father had served the company well, working with both J. Armstrong and Dean. Stanier himself came to Dean's attention while working through the ranks, first as an apprentice, then in the Drawing Office and, finally, gaining valuable running experience in London and Swindon.

None other personage than Churchward came to value Stanier's opinions regarding locomotives in service and, at Swindon, Stanier was there on the footplate as each successive Churchward masterpiece first took to the rails. During these years of plenty, 1906-12, Stanier was directly involved with the early running of the 'Stars' and the 'Great Bear' pacific, and conducted trials with the Schmidt, Cole and Churchward's own superheaters. Such a practical grounding — though, as Divisional Locomotive Superintendent, he would hardly be expected to undertake the physical work himself — was invaluable in seeing just how theories worked in practice.

Stanier then became the Swindon Assistant Works Manager, and immersed himself in all aspects of production, organisation and repair work, to complete the cycle of design, running, building and repair of locomotives. Much effort was expended organising production for the war, but when he succeeded Collett as Works Manager in 1920, Stanier must have thought that the ultimate prize was coming within his grasp. Had that been the case, I wonder what plans, if any, he had for a post-Churchward locomotive policy?

One thing was certain, the world was changing rapidly. The TUC might have spurned the chance to run the country and overthrow the establishment status quo, but even Churchward had felt the cool blast of air from below — the shop floor, while the heat from above — the boardroom — was not going to allow anyone such autonomous authority again. Churchward's position was increasingly likely to be compromised, and so he departed with his good health and his sanity. This was just a bit too soon for Stanier. Another five years and he could have been in the running to succeed Churchward. As it was, in 1922, he was not even a contender. Though not entirely unopposed, Collett was the obvious choice: clearly the right man to follow Churchward.

Under Collett, the GWR led the way in the all-important matter of express locomotives, as first the 'Castle', and then the 'King' 4-6-0s improved impressively on Churchward's 'Stars'. Stanier, along with Chief Draughtsman F.W. Hawksworth, proposed a pacific design, but the time schedule was against them. In any case, Collett considered it far more prudent to further develop a tried, trusted and very successful, formula and was engrossed in producing a comprehensive locomotive fleet of which Churchward would have been proud. The 'Kings', of course, were an absolute triumph, and if there was any doubt as to which British railway had the best locomotives, all that was washed away in one fell-swoop. Over on the LNER though, Gresley was showing that he was as adept as Churchward in learning from overseas practices, and was soon to move the goal-posts dramatically. Within a few short years, even the majestic 'Kings' would appear decidedly old-hat.

There is no question about it, Stanier was a most able, loyal and supportive No. 2 to Collett, and was a regular stand-in on public occasions. He was an ideal ambassador when accompanying 'King George V' to the Baltimore and Ohio Railroad Centenary celebrations, in 1927, and never seriously thought of leaving the GWR. No doubt, Stanier hoped that, if Collett retired at 65, he would have at least five years at the helm and, of course, he had his own ideas on developing the locomotive fleet. All he wanted was the call. As events turned out, when it arrived, the call came not quite from the direction he had been expecting.

The 1920s was not one of Britain's most memorable decades. Many of the promises that duped people into continuing an imperialist war — such as Homes for Heroes — had long since been broken, and the old-guard returned to rule the roost. Social and political change had come but slowly and, as in recent years, even the first Labour government was little different from its predecessors. On a world-scale, unsteady political situations caused trade to stutter along, yet the British government still pursued draconian economic policies to enable a return to the Gold Standard, at pre-war parity. When that was finally achieved, not only was Britain at a serious disadvantage, but the infamous Wall Street Crash was soon to knock a massive hole in world trade.

On a practical level, this policy stifled investment and made British exports uncompetitive which, in turn, caused unemployment on a massive scale. This, coupled with increased competition from road transport, did not help the railways one jot, and almost half the goods traffic lost during the strikes of 1926/7 never returned. These were not favourable trading conditions for even the most efficient companies, but for those reliant on heavy industry for much of their trade, and especially one seemingly in the throes of self-destruction, any form of order was welcome.

The LMS was Britain's largest railway. It had been formed out of a government-forced amalgamation of several proud, powerful and fiercely independent railways, and a few of lesser economic standing: many had been non-too-friendly rivals. In the 1920s, the LMS was a virtual maelstrom of internecine war. Managers were often more concerned with defending their little empires, rather than integrating to the greater good of the company. This was not entirely surprising, given the apparent lack of decisive leadership or, indeed, a clearly defined aim: common failures of British industry for 200 years.

In such a seemingly catastrophic situation, many overseas companies would bring in experts to sort out the mess and to give a clear, cohesive direction. In Britain, we had — indeed have — our own unique approach: bring in an outsider who knows nothing about the industry! So, in 1925, Josiah Stamp became the first LMS President, becoming Chairman as well two years later. He proceeded to turn a much-troubled giant into a company that nearly fulfilled the great economic role seemingly pre-destined for it. Stamp led from the front and was a manager for whom cost-control is the be-all, and end-all, of commerce — he would, no doubt, be a great success in today's mish-mash of a railway industry. Credit where it is due though, his ordered mind was just what the LMS needed and, after several false-dawns, Stamp took a more active interest in 'those smoky machines that pull our revenue earners. What are they called? Oh yes, steam locomotives.'

Now, H. Fowler had begun solving some of the problems that beset the LMS locomotive fleet. In six years as CME, he reduced the locomotive stock by about 1,000 and began a basic form of standardisation. Unfortunately for the LMS, he was a former MR man thoroughly imbued with that company's small-engine policy. Thus, the engines that he introduced in not inconsiderable numbers were fine in themselves, but were hardly what was required for a new order of faster and heavier express trains and heavier freight trains. Time was running out.

Apart from the capabilities of Fowler's locomotives, little was being done to integrate and harness the vast potential and resources of the company's locomotive works. For example, H.P.M. Beames thoroughly overhauled working practices and equipment at Crewe Works, restoring it to being the most advanced railway works in Britain. Yet, as Fowler was an ex-MR man, Crewe played a secondary role to Derby. Such a poor use of resources was anathema to the likes of Stamp, and it was a matter he intended to resolve.

E.J.H. Lemmon was temporarily appointed CME for a year, while Stamp sought a long-term solution. It seemed to him that the only way to pull the CME's department round was to bring in an outsider. Gresley would have been an obvious choice, but he ruled from Kings Cross, if not quite absolutely, with rather more power than Stamp envisaged for the new incumbent. Collett, well, he was anointed in any case, but he had a useful Principal Assistant. Stamp approached Stanier informally and, after some deliberation, he took up the reins in 1932. Stamp was happy that he had chosen the right man, but even he did not realise just how successful and influential that choice would be in the coming years.

Stanier's task was not one for the faint hearted. It soon became apparent that he had some weeding-out of personnel to do, but he also realised that there were many highly polished round pegs sitting uneasily in some odd-shaped holes. Put the pegs in the right places and he too might inherit the earth. Perhaps the various factions of Crewe and Derby, in particular, but also Horwich and St. Rollox, had grown weary after almost a decade of total, barely concealed war. It may also have been that Stanier's prestige and persona won them over. Whatever the cause, Stanier chose his senior assistants from within his new empire with care, tweaked things here and there, and then fused these engineers into an homogeneous team that was, ultimately, to out-Swindon the GWR. The new CME's team, with Stanier firmly at its head was also, for the first time on the LMS, in harmony with, but not slaves to, the demands of senior management. Within a short time it was soon clear that the LMS was no longer treading a road to recovery in locomotive matters, but pursuing a path to triumph.

All was not hunky-dory right from the start, though. For example, Stanier did not immediately appreciate just what an invaluable ally he had in Beames: he soon saw the light. On the other hand, many other aspects of his department were in fine shape, with Crewe Works being able to build and repair locomotives quicker and cheaper than any other works, Swindon included. And neither were the engineers stuck in some Dark Ages time-warp. For example, various modern design features had been used, and their value understood, for several years, such as large, long-travel piston valves and the Belpaire firebox. What, on the surface, appeared to be something of a jumbled inheritance, was better than Stanier might have expected.

The greatest endowment that Stanier brought with him though, apart from a great chest of drawings, was 40 years of Swindon know-how. The truth was, though the LMS locomotive fleet was just about holding its own in 1932, the company intended to speed-up the Anglo-Scottish trains, and improve the London-Liverpool/Manchester and some Midland line services. In addition, increasing motor car ownership, buses and lorries were all eating voraciously into a diminishing market. The LMS needed to act rapidly in the not-too-distant future just to maintain its market share.

Stanier was a bit too dogmatic in his application of Churchward's strictures in his early years on the LMS. His first two pacifics suffered steaming problems, but those were as nothing compared with the strangulated 3-cylindered 'Jubilees'. Nothing appears to be amiss with No. 5587 'Baroda' as it heads north past Kilburn when new, but it has been said that their problems brought Stanier close to being shown the door. Good sense prevailed and Stanier soon learned from his mistakes, although the 'Jubilees' never quite lived up to their promise.

Stamp fixed Stanier's mandate soon after he arrived: he would need to provide a new standardised locomotive fleet to enable uneconomic older designs to be withdrawn en masse. Stamp's costings showed that new engines could recover their initial cost through lower maintenance, greater working capacities and enhanced reliability, within a relatively short time. This was almost a golden chalice for any self-respecting locomotive engineer, with one proviso: get it wrong and it would not only be poison that the chalice contained.

Once Stanier had reviewed his new demesne, he set his staff to producing the new goods. In particular, there was an urgent need for mixed-traffic engines, a heavy express locomotive and passenger tanks. A heavy freight design was also essential, along with an ordinary express design, but these were less pressing. Stanier indicated the broad outlines for the new designs and then left his men to get on with it. Radical changes were afoot, and included a GWR-type tapered domeless boiler, a vastly improved smokebox arrangement — with a jumper-top blastpipe, axle-boxes and a de Glehn leading bogie. However, alongside these went other features already current on LMS designs, with the exception of high-degree superheat. Stanier was in business.

Stanier's first two designs emerged in 1933 and they soon showed all the benefits of the new-broom. Outstanding orders for the Horwich 'Crab', mixed-traffic 2-6-0, were turned into a batch of 40 moguls from the Stanier-school — well, almost. They were a curious mix of Swindon, Derby and Horwich design: a marriage of Swindon boiler and cylinders, and an LMS chassis. It was a fair old start, and the first ten also had a GWR boiler-mounted safety-valve. Stanier soon realised that arrangement would prove restrictive on larger boilers, and so the rest reverted to the standard LMS firebox mounted, pop safety-valves. These later engines also had a slightly larger superheater, but this was something Stanier had not then come to terms with. Walschaert's valve-gear operated the horizontal outside cylinders, a significant departure from both GWR practice and the 'Crabs', and its half-way house image was completed with a 'Crab' cab and a Fowler 6 wheel tender.

Stanier's moguls were never intended to hit the headlines. No, their's was a life of the hum-drum, mundane and ordinary, except perhaps for the occasional glamour of seaside excursions, alongside the 'Crabs'. Initially, they found themselves working all over the LMS on passenger and fast freight trains, but as the years rolled by they were increasingly concentrated on the northern former LNWR lines. Naturally, as Stanier's team really got going, these moguls were pushed still further aside, but though bettered, they were never entirely surplus to requirements and lasted for over 30 years.

Mixed-traffic locomotives, no matter how good, were hardly a yardstick by which to measure the new regime: even Stamp realised that. A large, prestigious express locomotive was the favoured rule-of-thumb. Manfully though the 'Royal Scots' were working the Anglo-Scottish expresses, the flagship of the LMS, they were always going to be second-class citizens alongside Gresley's 'A3' pacifics. There was no chance of them competing with impressive non-stop runs, and the LNER was simply running away in the publicity stakes. Stanier had the mandate to produce a real winner, he also had the resources; all he had to do was deliver.

The first requirement was for a firebox big enough not to be clogged up on a 400 mile journey. As for the rest, well, something based on a GWR 'King' would do very nicely, and so two 4-6-2s were built that, in many respects, were virtual pacific 'Kings'. Of course, there were numerous detail differences, including four sets of Walschaert's valve-gear and a wide Belpaire firebox, but the ensuing 'Princess Royals' were probably just what Stanier had in mind when he proposed a pacific express engine to Collett, in 1926.

The first two pacifics certainly had their moments, but something was clearly not quite right. Stanier was no slave to Swindon practice, merely to good design, but what was good for the Swindon goose was not necessarily so for the LMS gander. In particular, Churchward's low-degree superheat did not translate happily to the quite different operating conditions on the LMS. It took two years of running and testing before the superheater was doubled in size to 32 elements. Almost overnight the pacifics' performance was dramatically improved. Actually, it was just in the nick of time, for the first of the 10 production engines were under construction and were then fitted with 24 or 32 element

On the other hand, Stanier's 'Black 5s' were the finest mixed-traffic steam locomotives ever to run in Britain. Of course, some engine crews favoured the LNER 'B1s', others the GWR 'Halls' but, partisanship aside, the 'Black 5s' were universally admired; by all, that is, except enthusiasts who would, occasionally, rather see something different. No. 5042 is making a good fist of the 4.20 p.m. St. Pancras-Manchester express, as it leaves Elstree tunnel.

superheaters, and a firebox combustion chamber.

Well, the rest of the 'Princess Royal' story is well known and they settled down to 25 years of solid, sometimes outstanding and, occasionally quite brilliant running on WCML expresses. Combining power and speed, they were the perfect riposte to Gresley's 'A3s', although as only 12 were built they could never quite match the apparent LNER Anglo-Scottish hegemony.

One imaginative and unique derivative was the 'Turbomotive': a turbine driven 'Princess Royal'. The idea of a turbine driven steam engine emanated in Sweden and Stanier, aware of the potential benefits in fuel economy with more power, gained the board's blessing to have a go: as far as Stamp was concerned, it was a gamble that might pay considerable operating dividends. Unfortunately, the higher initial cost was never likely to be overcome, while maintenance was also far from cheap. Eventually, 'Turbomotive' was rebuilt as a hybrid 'Princess Royal', with a 'Duchess' front end, only to be destroyed in the Harrow accident, in 1952. However,

with the 'Turbomotive' saga, and by accepting that small superheaters were not suited to LMS needs, Stanier demonstrated that he was hardly a dogmatic Churchward clone, and was prepared to test, listen and learn.

If the first two years of the 'Princess Royals' gave Stanier the occasional sleepless night and not a little concern, his intermediate express engine, between the 'Royal Scot' and the 'Patriot' classes — intended for the Midland lines — raised still more eyebrows in the corridors of power. In late-1934, Stanier's stock was not at its highest and he was, reputedly, not far from staring down Stamp's twin-barrels. The truth was, that the 'Jubilees' had gone straight into production and, far from being the expected next-big-thing, were proving to be something of a very damp-squib.

As with the 'Princess Royals', a small superheater was cited the source of trouble, but it went far deeper than that. The 'Jubilees' just would not steam, and lost time on trains that even 'Compounds' hauled with little difficulty. Several years of seemingly fruitless testing eventually led to Churchward's jumper-top blastpipe being called into question. This arrangement was an essential adjunct of the Swindon success story, but it did not translate to the 'Jubilees' because they had three cylinders, not two or four. Various blastpipe profiles were then tried and by the late-1930s the steaming problems seemed to be over. The 'Jubilees' carried a mixture of domeless and domed boilers, as did most Stanier designs, but never quite delivered the performance they promised. Though hardly failures, they certainly fell short of the top echelon of

express engines, but played their part in the all-round improvement of LMS passenger services immediately prior to the war.

Stanier was not the only locomotive engineer to get off to a stuttering start, but his mixed-traffic 'Class 5' 4-6-0s, following hard on the heels of the 'Jubilees', were nigh-perfect right from the off. Almost immediately, they wound their way into the hearts of railway staff and enthusiasts alike. If ever there really were doubts about Stanier's appointment within the LMS board, the 'Black 5s' soon quashed them in no uncertain manner. These became the ultimate go everywhere/do anything steam engine, from fast passenger to slow goods, working the length and breadth of Britain.

Even these began life with a traditional GWR domeless boiler, short firebox and small, 14 element, superheater. Unlike their larger 3-cylinder sisters though, the 2-cylinder 'Black 5s' were quite happy with a Swindon front end. By 1937, the first engines had been given 21 element superheaters, and new engines were built with still larger ones, a domeless boiler and bigger firebox. With the standard Walschaert's valve-gear, fully 472 locomotives were built in only five years, and if any engine was synonymous with the transformation of LMS services, on the eve of the Second World War, this was it.

Eventually, the 'Black 5s' became Stanier's second most numerous design, though many were built after he had resigned. More of these great all-rounders, of Botham-esque stature, ran in Britain than any other 20th century design. These outstanding engines were soon welcomed wherever they worked and, once BR came into being, they could be found even further afield. As might be expected, partisan tendencies — or sheer unfamiliarity — occasionally led non-LMS engine crews to prefer their own locomotives, but Stanier's team first got all their sums right, and produced one of Britain's greatest steam locomotives, with the 'Black 5s'.

Once Stanier's men had found their range, like true expert marksmen they hit the target bang-on every time. In 1935, the '8F' 2-8-0 heavy freight engine took its bow, although it never quite became the all-encompassing standard like the 'Black 5s': there was not quite the pressing need. Only the first dozen had domeless boilers, with the rest having an enlarged boiler

with a decent amount of superheating. The ultimate accolade for these unsung heroes came when they were adopted for quantity production by the War Department, ahead of the GWR '2800', and the more complex LNER 'O2' classes.

Eventually, each of Britain's four main railways built '8Fs', and they ran all over the country, as well as in Turkey and the Middle and Near East. Known as 'Churchills', they ran in Turkey until fairly recently, which says much for the quality of design, plus a great deal for their robust build. As it happens, only 126 ran on the LMS before the Second World War, but it was clear that Stanier had, once again, produced a design that would, in time, supersede the huge, disparate fleet of ageing 0-8-0s.

Looking to the future, Stanier had the disgraced experimental locomotive 'Fury' rebuilt as an improved 'Royal Scot', complete with all the Stanier trimmings, in 1935. Despite having 3 cylinders, this engine was an immediate success and formed the basis for Stanier's last major locomotive contribution to the LMS. He approved a similar conversion for the 'Royal Scots', but utilised the 2A boiler first tried on two 'Rebuilt Jubilees', in 1942. The ensuing 'Converted Scots', were rebuilt as their boilers were renewed — in no particular hurry, and came close to challenging Collett's two masterpieces as the ultimate British 4-6-0. They were given unusual, curved smoke deflectors, from 1947, adding distinction to their distinguished looks, and both 'Rebuilt Jubilees' were kitted-out likewise.

While it can be something of a trawl reviewing an engineer's locomotive designs, in Stanier's case these formed part of an all-encompassing plan. Each successive design was, like Churchward's, intended to fill a need and each, in turn, was an eventual success. This was not quite the case when it came to tank engines, principally for suburban or light passenger duties. The passenger tanks that first appeared in 1934 were, in many ways, a 3-cylinder version of Fowler's highly successful 2-cylinder design. It was intended that these would have rapid acceleration to go with their other attributes of economical and fast running, and so they did.

Whatever the initial intentions, the class soon gravitated onto the former LTSR lines, where they were openly welcomed

Another great design? Quite probably. Stanier's '8Fs' were outstanding heavy goods engines, some of the finest to have run in Britain. In some respects, as No. 8031 shows, they were the most elegant of the lot and yet, when the chips were down, would work in the filthiest of conditions. They were equally happy on long-distance excursions, or very heavy freight trains.

(R. Cockcroft)

Right —
Going somewhat against the grain, Stanier's 3-cylinder 2-6-4Ts were very good engines, but hardly warranted the added complication of the extra cylinder, in comparison with Fowler's 2-cylinder engines. So, in 1935, Stanier produced a 2-cylinder version, and very successful they were too, if not — reputedly — quite so fast as Fowler's. No. 2629 shows just what fine engines they were, when brand spanking new. *(NRM)*

and lasted until the long-promised electrification finally came about. These could have been a new standard design, except they were little better than Fowler's 2-cylinder cousins and not worth the bother and cost of an additional cylinder. So, when it came to series production, 1935, Stanier also introduced a 2-cylinder 2-6-4T. These were cheaper to build and maintain, weighed less and, eventually, worked all over the LMS system. Once again, another thoroughbred.

Quite what encouraged Stanier to produce a 2-6-2T though, is not entirely clear. Without a shadow of doubt, Stanier came to the LMS full of GWR ideas and ideals, seemingly intent on implanting Churchwardian principles on his new employees. It took a while for him to learn that there really was an alternative to the Swindon way, so was this 2-6-2T a last, not entirely successful fling? As with the larger '4P Tank', this 2-6-2T was Stanier's version of a Fowler standard. They were not as successful as the 2-6-4Ts, just as Fowler's 2-6-2Ts had singularly failed to distinguish themselves. Oh yes, even the greatest can make mistakes. Mind you, despite gaining a reputation as indifferent steamers, and having a somewhat indeterminate role, well over a hundred were built. They were, though, the first Stanier class to be completely withdrawn.

Somewhat ironically, Stanier's undoubted masterpiece was virtually penned and built while he was on secondment in India. T. Coleman, his unsung Chief Draughtsman, was responsible for translating Stanier's broad aims into engineering reality. As with the 'Black 5s', these graceful, streamlined, yet immensely powerful locomotives were immediately nigh-perfect. They are, of course, Britain's most powerful express steam locomotives, and there is no doubt that they also had a fair old turn of speed.

Unlike Gresley, who was enthusiastic about streamlining his 'A4s', Stanier had to be cajoled by senior management to so endow his 'Duchesses'. Whatever people say about the benefits, or otherwise, of locomotive streamlining, one only has to ride a bicycle to realise that, as speed rises, so does the air resistance, markedly. It was found that Gresley's 'A4' pacifics gained not inconsiderable improvements in overcoming head-on air resistance, over his orthodox 'A3s'. These were substantial at the 60-90 mph bracket at which express trains usually ran so, it worked where it really mattered. Indeed, given all the brouhaha and favourable publicity generated by Gresley's 'A4s' in 1935, Stanier really had little option but to streamline the 'Duchess' class.

For some, the greatest steam locomotive design ever to run in Britain. There is no doubt about it, the 'Duchess' class in their original blue streamlining was one of steam's truly great sights. Coupled with the 'Coronation Scot' train, as this picture of No. 6221 'Queen Elizabeth' shows, surely nobody could fail to be impressed. Of course, some utter stick-in-the-muds abhorred the streamlining and made snide comments at the time, but one really ought to feel sorry for such people, as sights such as this was their very great loss.

(L. Lord)

The 'Duchesses' were to be Stanier's crowning glory, as plans for still larger express engines were quashed by the onset of war. Styling is purely a personal matter, but interesting though the 'Duchesses' were, the dynamically painted streamlining sat rather uneasily on the engines: an obvious addition rather than an obvious part of the whole. Beneath the metal shroud though, lay one of the most distinguished British steam locomotives. If the 'A4s' epitomise speed, and the 'A3s' and 'Kings' elegance, then the 'Duchess' class exuded sheer, graceful power. Until 1937, Gresley had the field to himself for brilliance of innovative design, from then on he knew he had a serious rival. The Second World War turned the world upside down, but quite what designs these two great locomotive engineers would have introduced to counter the aims of each other's boards, was something anyone interested in railways must have pondered at some time or another. Oh what we missed.

Stanier returned to India, in 1938, but by then his best work for the LMS was behind him. As the war clouds loomed, the LMS had built nearly as many of Stanier's locomotives, in just 7½ years, as the GNR and LNER had built to Gresley's designs in 27½ years. That was the impact of Stanier and it was to continue to grow for years afterwards. As Churchward had been influenced by foreign designs and integrated these with his own ideas, to transform the GWR locomotive fleet, so Stanier had carried the flame onward, fanned by yet more

overseas influences — and current LMS practices, and thoroughly revitalised the motive power of an apparent lame duck. His principles were then carried onward to BR and the last fling of British steam. It might not have been Stanier's engines that were to bow out in a final blaze of glory, but it was his men who rebuilt Bulleid's unreliable pacifics that took the final curtain call. By that time, Stanier's influence had crossed all boundaries.

There is no doubt about it, Stanier was a great locomotive engineer in his own right. He and his team might have lacked the innovative brilliance of Gresley and Bulleid — the LMS under Stamp wanted economical orthodoxy not expensive failures, but it was Stanier who had the greatest long-term influence. Even pre-war, it was the LMS that ran the fastest express services in Britain; the LNER ran the fastest trains, but these were one-off's amid the general daily grind. Stanier's engines allowed the LMS to make substantial timing improvements on all its main traffic routes from the mid-1930s, while the locomotive fleet had shrunk by 1,500 engines, or about 15% in just 7½ years. Stanier's impact was enormous.

After 1942, Stanier effectively had little to do with the LMS, and resigned in 1944. He took an active role on all the bodies to which he was subsequently invited to serve but, not surprisingly, nothing matched his work for the LMS. The honours continued to roll in and he became the deserved, grand old man of British steam, enjoying a retirement every bit as active as had been his career.

On the other hand, one cannot but wonder what might have happened had Stanier succeeded Collett at Swindon, which was by no means a certainty. Had Collett seen out his time, Stanier would only have five years to carry forth the torch first held high by Gooch. Even if the GWR had the will, it did not have the need for the sheer number of new designs that Stanier produced in his first half-decade at the LMS, and he would probably never have had the chance to be considered one of Britain's great locomotive engineers. Fortune indeed favours the brave — sometimes.

The sloping smokebox top of 'Duchess' No. 46244 'King George VI' shows that this was a former streamlined engine, until 1947. I find this to be quite attractive, but this is certainly not a universal opinion. It is wearing the experimental BR blue livery that it carried until 1953. This engine was originally named 'City of Leeds'.   *(R. Cockcroft)*

As it happens, Stanier almost slavishly introduced Swindon principles to the LMS without necessarily understanding their suitability to the new operating or financial conditions. This is not to be condemned outright, for most people pursue a path with which they are comfortable and familiar and, in any case, his vast Swindon experience was undoubtedly one of the attractions to the LMS board. What Stanier did, to his everlasting credit, was to adapt, evolve and change his ideas to benefit the LMS, mainly in the fields of superheating and the later use of domed boilers and streamlined internal steam passages. It was this amalgamation of GWR, LMS and overseas practices that enabled Stanier to produce the finest group of steam engine designs, in terms of performance, economy and maintenance, ever to run in Britain.

Let us not beat about the bush. Churchward was able to take the GWR from a locomotive position some way down the national ladder, to the very top and to keep it there for two decades. Not only were some of his designs the finest of their type in the country, but the GWR built an almost unassailable lead in British steam locomotive technology. Its fleet of standard locomotives really did make every other railway seem like second class citizens. The Churchwardian revolution took British steam design into the modern age, but he was not wholly an outright innovator.

Gresley pursued a different path; one forced by the penurious economic circumstances and policies of his employers. Like Churchward, he too advanced British steam locomotive design by a considerable margin, though the Gresley revolution was never so widespread. Stanier's impact on the LMS matched that of Churchward's on the GWR, and

he too bequeathed a tradition that went beyond locomotive design, to the building and repair of steam engines more economically than ever before. As Churchward equipped the GWR to take it dramatically onwards, so Stanier did likewise to take the LMS right through the middle decades of the century and beyond, had circumstances allowed. Unlike the 19th century Stars of Steam, who mostly built for the present and immediate future, Stanier, Churchward and Gresley all designed with an eye to likely circumstances in 20 to 30 years' time. That was the measure of their greatness.

As with the system so successfully devised by Sir Alf Ramsey, in the hands of lesser managers and coaches it was abused, mis-used and, frankly, badly mis-understood. So it is with the subsequent application of Stanier's tenets by his disciples; primarily with BR's Standards. The jury is still out. Certainly the Bulleid school of thought is that Stanier's men, on the whole, emasculated and stifled steam's last chance. Just as many football managers copied Ramsey's system, without having the players or appreciating its nuances, so members of Stanier's former team hamstrung BR with a whole series of unnecessary and hum-drum designs. Many critics contend that these were little better than those already in existence, and were certainly no better than Stanier's. Still, whatever one's opinion, BR's 'Standards' could have been working today, had not circumstances changed so dramatically 50-odd years ago.

That is, though, all by-the-by. If Churchward initially led the way, and Gresley produced the most innovative and outstanding locomotives, it was Stanier who, ultimately, had the greatest influence of all. Only his designs were widely used throughout Britain, and then formed the basis for BR's 'Standards'. In the matter of the all-round equation of performance, economy, reliability, and cost effectiveness of build and maintenance, then Stanier's locomotives — as a group — had a clear edge over those of any other Star of Steam. As far as the steam locomotive went, Stanier's engines were the finest, most efficient fluid capital equipment that belonged to any British railway.

The 'Royal Scot' class finally became the great engines they always threatened to be, once Stanier initiated their rebuilding, from 1942. The unusual and distinctive smoke deflectors can be seen to good effect as BR No. 46116 'Irish Guardsman' pulls into Llandudno Junction.

(B.G. Williams)

Stanier's Locomotive Designs

YEAR	CLASS	WHEEL ARRANGEMENT	CYLINDERS (INCHES)	BOILER PRESSURE	DRIVING-WHEEL DIAMETER	WEIGHT	No. IN CLASS
1933	5F MT	2-6-0	18 x 28	225 psi	5 ft. 6 in.	69 tons	40
1933	Princess Ryl	4-6-2	(4)16½ x 28	250 psi	6 ft. 6 in.	104½ tons	12
1934	4P Tanks	2-6-4T	(3)17 x 26	200 psi	5 ft. 9 in.	92¼ tons	37
1934	Jubilee's	4-6-0	(3)17 x 26	225 psi	6 ft. 9 in.	79½ tons	191
1934	Black 5's	4-6-0	18½ x 28	225 psi	6 ft.	70T 12 cwt	842
1935	Turbomotive	4-6-2		250 psi	6 ft. 6 in.	110½ tons	1
	Rebuilt 1952		(4)16½ x 28			105 tons	
1935	8F	2-8-0	18½ x 28	225 psi	4 ft. 8½ in.	70½ tons	852
1935	4P Tank	2-6-4T	19¾ x 26	200 psi	5 ft. 9 in.	87T 17 cwt	206
1935	3P Tanks	2-6-2T	17¼ x 26	200 psi	5 ft. 3 in.	71¼ tons	139
1935	Brit. Leg.	4-6-0	(3)18 x 26	250 psi	6 ft. 9 in.	84 tons	1
1937	Duchess	4-6-2	(4)16½ x 28	250 psi	6 ft. 9 in.	105¼ tons	38
1942	Reb. Jubilee	4-6-0	(3)17 x 26	250 psi	6 ft. 9 in.	82 tons	2
1943	Conv. Ryl. Scot	4-6-0	(3)18 x 26	250 psi	6 ft. 9 in.	83 tons	70

STANIER IN BRIEF

BORN:	27th May 1876, Swindon.
EDUCATED:	Wycliffe College.
TRAINED:	G.W.R. Swindon. Apprentice 1892-97.
SENIOR POSITIONS:	1904, Ass. to Divisional Loco. Supt., London.
	1906, Ass. to Swindon Works Manager.
	1912, Ass. Works Manager, Swindon.
	1920, Swindon Works Manager.
	1922, Principal Assistant to C.M.E.
	1932-44, C.M.E. of L.M.S.
	1942, Scientific Adviser to Min. of Production.
	1943, Director of Power-Jets Ltd. Also, other appointments.
HONOURS:	1936 and 1938, President, I.L.E.
	1941, President, I.M.E.
	1943, Knighted.
	1944, Fellow of Royal Society.
	1945, Honorary Member of I.M.E.
	1957, I.L.E. Gold Medal.
	1963, I.M.E. James Watt International Medal.
DIED:	27th September 1965, Rickmansworth.

STANIER's PRESERVED LOCOMOTIVES

YEAR	CLASS	RUNNING NUMBERS	TOTAL
1933	Princess Royal	46201/3	2
1933	5F (MT)	42968	1
1934	Jubilee's	45593/6, 45690/9	4
1934	Black Five's	44767/806/871/901/932	18
		45000/25/110/163/212/231	
		45293/305/337/379/407/428	
		45491.	
1934	4P Tank 3 cyl.	42500	1
1935	8F	48151/173/274/305/431	8
		48518/624/773.	
1937	Duchess	46229/33/35	3
1943	Conv. Ryl Scot	46100/15	2

JAMES HOLDEN
The GER's Knight in Very Shining Armour

Continuity is usually regarded as an essential prerequisite for success with any type of venture, whether cultural, sporting, individual or business. Constant chopping and changing of personnel, equipment, policy or leaders is seldom a blueprint for progress; more likely a recipe for disaster. A sense of order and method creates conditions where people can grow, understand, develop and evolve, and with these come efficiency, steadfastness and familiarity. With the latter, though, there is always a danger of contempt and stagnation.

Change also has its benefits and burdens. Without effective change, life can become too comfortable — too easy. Where progress towards a target was once rapid and continually evolving, the same old people, the same old policies, the same old rhetoric can eventually have the opposite effect. Times change, peoples' aims alter, but life carries on regardless.

Does one change with the times, go with the flow, follow one's instinct, or settle down and find a niche? Innovative and rapid progress, or empire building? Any organisation that does not evolve will wither and die. On the other hand, if one is constantly in the throes of change, almost permanent revolution, then aims and objectives become blurred, perhaps even forgotten. It is a fine line between knowing when to change and when to consolidate: a delicate balancing act that is the keystone of good management.

Of course, not every organisation is fortunate enough to pick and choose when it will, or will not change, particularly with regards personnel. In its first 23 years' existence, from 1862, the GER had six Locomotive Superintendents. While change can be a catalyst for innovation, in railway engineering — where the products are expected to last for a generation or more — many opportunities are likely to be lost. Some of these engineers were no slouches either: in particular Adams, Johnson and T.W. Worsdell each undertook invaluable work for the company. Adams updated Stratford Works, Worsdell produced the invaluable 'Y14' class 0-6-0s and Johnson, though serving when company finances were at their very lowest ebb, contributed several distinctly useful designs. Unfortunately for the GER, each engineer had different ideas on how to fulfil their allotted task, so there was a great deal of chopping and changing, and not much in the way of continuity and progress.

It was not as though the GER was some twopenny-ha'penny railway either. True, it was not in the big league alongside the likes of the LNWR or GWR, but it had a greater route mileage than, say, the GNR, and its passenger traffic expanded remorselessly, despite the Great Depression. By the end of the 19th century, the GER carried more passengers per year than any other British railway. Just dwell upon that quite fantastic fact. If not quite a slumbering giant, the GER probably had a right to expect a little more from its successive Locomotive Superintendents and, at long last, the board finally found the man seemingly tailor-made for the job.

James Holden had a good engineering pedigree, but was not exactly steeped in locomotive design experience. After serving an apprenticeship under Edward Fletcher — his uncle and the well-respected Locomotive Superintendent of the York, Newcastle and Berwick Railway, and the succeeding NER, he worked through the ranks to become the GWR's C & W Manager — with Churchward, no less, as his assistant — and Chief Assistant to Dean. As was the squire's son in asking for the hand of the farmer's daughter, Holden was a good catch for the GER, though he was more a specialist in rolling-stock than locomotives. But Stratford held great promise and potential and it was an opportunity Holden could not miss.

Dean was having trouble with two prototype compound locomotives on the GWR and, not surprisingly, his former assistant was equally wary of them. Holden had barely got his feet under the Locomotive Superintendents table before he ordered Worsdell's 4-4-0s to be rebuilt as simples, despite their being more economical than the other passenger engines. On the other hand, Holden recognised the value of Worsdell's versatile 'Y14' 0-6-0s, and many more were built, to become the largest GER class of all on the. Soon, Holden was initiating the rebuilding of other older designs.

So, Holden's arrival almost immediately led to yet more changes on the GER. It was fortunate that he stayed for fully 22 years, as the consequences of another short-term appointment were unthinkable, especially as the GER was ambitious and did not intend playing second-fiddle to anyone: especially in East Anglia. In particular, its London suburban traffic grew enormously throughout the rest of the century, though as 90% of passengers arriving at Liverpool St. had travelled less than 12 miles, by 1901, much of this traffic was barely profitable. On the other hand, long-distance express patronage, excursion and continental passengers also increased — albeit somewhat less spectacularly, from which there was most certainly good money to be earned.

There was also considerable scope for freight development, as much agricultural traffic originated in East Anglia, while coal and minerals had to be brought in. East Anglia was almost the GER's private fiefdom and competition was restricted to the passive MGNJR in Norfolk, and the combative LTSR down by the Thames. The GNR ran to Cambridge and later to Cromer, via the MGNJR, but the GER pushed a joint-line with the GNR to Doncaster — with running-powers on to York, via Spalding and Lincoln. So, the GER was not solely content to be master in its own back yard, but intended to compete for other lucrative traffic.

All these ambitions were fine but, of course, the GER was short on the required mechanical wherewithal. The advantages of continuity in locomotive design and design policy could be seen throughout Britain, at the time of Holden's appointment. On the LNWR the work of Ramsbottom and Webb had yielded magnificent dividends for that great company. On the GWR, the transition from Gooch to Armstrong to Dean ran as seamlessly as did their locomotives. Even on the rival GNR, though Sturrock and P. Stirling may have been personally

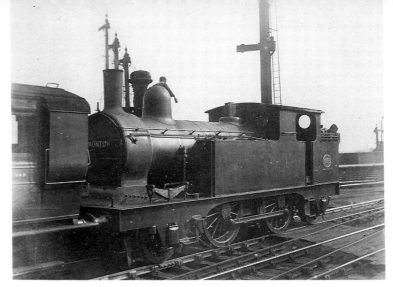

Holden's 'C32' class was the tank-engine equivalent of his 'T26' Intermediates 2-4-0s. They shared many components, and both went on to enjoy equally long lives. In much earlier times, No. 1039 is at Stratford, when still a front-line engine on the very busy suburban services out of Liverpool St.

Below —
For the inner suburban services, and especially those running on the underground, Holden produced the 'S44' class 0-4-4Ts. Not surprisingly, these ran equally well in either direction, perhaps even better bunker first and, like all Holden's tank engines, they enjoyed long lives. As this picture of No. 1123 shows, they were hardly pretty little things. Simple and straight forward, these were no-frills profit earners.

incompatible, there were no sweeping engineering changes to negotiate. On the GER, it seemed as though each Locomotive Superintendent had his own ideas and was keen to pursue them irrespective of what had gone before. Holden was no different, but out of nigh-anarchy came stability and then standardisation. From these grew constant and consistent improvement, until the locomotives of the GER were as distinctively Holden's, as were those of the LNWR Webb's, and the MR Johnson's.

By the time Holden handed over the reins to his son, S.D. Holden in 1908, nearly 80% of GER locomotives were his designs. Moreover, many had interchangeable components, from boilers down to the smallest nuts and bolts. Back in 1885, it was all so very different. Not only were there numerous unique locomotive classes, but shared components, let alone broad design principles, were as rare as moon-dust.

Holden's long reign did not begin with a dramatic revolution, and he never produced a single design that made the locomotive engineering world gasp in astonishment; at least in series production. Without drama or any great flourish, almost imperceptibly, the GER locomotive stock was transformed from being a diverse bunch of spasmodic and irregular performers, to a uniform, efficient, yet highly individual modern fleet. Nevertheless, the true measure of Holden's work was found not so much with his principal express engines, but with his little 0-6-0Ts. Just before Grouping, the GER inaugurated a new, intensive London suburban service, and Holden's then 30 years-old little warriors were again called to the colours to bear the brunt: the

'Jazz' was the most concentrated steam-hauled suburban service in the world. Although long retired, Holden lived to see this in successful operation, and what pride he must have felt.

That is rather jumping the gun, though. Given Holden's limited locomotive experience, he was heavily dependent on his design team, guiding them to his requirements and then letting them get on with the job. In particular, he relied on his Chief Draughtsman, F.V. Russell, for the detail work, rather as a sports team manager expects the captain to implement the tactics and strategy for a particular game. Holden had his mind on the performance over a season, not simply who was going to take a particular free hit.

That does not mean to say Holden abdicated control. On the contrary, he established quite definite trends. For example, small-wheeled 0-6-0Ts hauled the busy inner-London suburban services, while those that ran further afield, not unnaturally, were left to the larger 0-4-4Ts or 2-4-2Ts. Holden's way was quite the opposite to that of Stroudley on the LBSCR, but he achieved outstanding results just the same.

Indeed, not unlike the LBSCR, Holden was pre-occupied by the problems of hauling London's ever-growing suburban traffic throughout his term of office. Lines such as those to Epping, Enfield and Chingford were not particularly well built and there were numerous stations: stop-start, stop-start, stop-start. The work was not easy either, as peak-trains were heavily loaded: passengers were crammed in — as today — until a train could take no more. So, not only did Holden's little 0-6-0Ts have to slave away for their living, but woe betide any failures. Trains were tightly timed with a very short head-way between them. Any hiccoughs could result in all sorts of problems; ones with which commuters are still all-too familiar.

During the late-19th century, Britain's 0-6-0Ts were mostly used for shunting or goods work. Holden was one of the first to use them widely on suburban services, and with good reason. Firstly, that was the way of the GWR — Holden's main source of inspiration and experience, while all their weight was available for adhesion. This latter was essential for the intensive and arduous work on the inner-suburban routes.

Holden's first 0-6-0T emerged barely a year after taking office. The 'T18' class was immediately sent to work the inner-suburban lines, but also undertook shunting duties throughout the GER. Before too long, shunting became their main activity, especially the work that was too dirty, too demeaning for engines with grander aspirations. Mundane it might have been, but they were kept at it for many long years, usually working well beyond the public gaze, in London's less salubrious areas. One just survived into the 1960s.

Other similar engines soon followed. The 'E22' class was Holden's smallest 0-6-0Ts, built to work the Blackwall line and, rather later, various rustic branches deep in rural East Anglia. These were also ideal shunting locomotives, capable of negotiating tight curves, and some had their leading coupling rods removed — turning them into 2-4-0Ts — to work the lightly built Kelveden-Tollesbury line. These powerful, yet lightweight engines again served the railway well, some surviving to BR ownership.

Of more long-term significance though, were the very similar 'R24' and 'S56' classes of 0-6-0T. The former was closely related to the 'T18s', while the latter had only detail differences. These two classes soon formed the backbone of the London suburban services and, whether rebuilt or not, became the mainstay of the 'Jazz' service, when introduced fully 30 years after the first locomotives took to the rails.

Cheekily distinctive, with their dome and stovepipe chimney almost holding hands above side-tanks of a disproportionate length, and with their Westinghouse pumps busily chattering away, these powerful little engines were an essential component of the Liverpool St. atmosphere for over 50 years. Familiarity breeds contempt and, despite their noisy and fussy demeanour, they were often ignored when going about their metronomic work. In the long-term though, these small 0-6-0Ts were probably the most successful 19th century engines that worked London's busy inner suburban services.

Not that such work was all they got up to, oh no. As newer and bigger designs came to join-in the 'Jazz' jamming-sessions, so these 'R24' and 'S56s' were seconded to shunting and pilot work. The LNER even sent some to work in Scotland, Lancashire and at various other locations far away from home. Such versatile locomotives: 19th century in design, 20th century in spirit, yet outstanding in every way. They were just what the GER needed, and not before time.

For the outer London suburban services, not nearly so intense in the late-19th century as they are today, Holden already had 30 of T.W. Worsdell's 2-4-2T 'Gobblers' in service, and he built the final 10 with Stephenson's motion, reduced $17\frac{1}{2}$ in. cylinders and a raised boiler pressure of 160 psi. Worsdell had been close to creating a very successful locomotive, but not close enough. Holden's modifications rendered their nickname redundant. Eventually, the original 30 'Gobblers' were rebuilt to Holden's specifications.

The 'Gobblers' coped with the outer suburban services for a while, but soon something bigger was needed: if a new design could help on the developing coastal branches, so much the better. Holden's solution was the comparatively massive, 'C32' class 2-4-2Ts. To all intents and purposes, this was a tank version of his 'T26' 2-4-0s of 1891 — for secondary main line work, and shared many common components, such as boiler, cylinders and wheels. Several 'C32s' were fitted with condensing apparatus for working London's dark and dingy tunnels, but later ones went straight to the breezy seaside branches, such as Clacton and Felixstowe.

Once again, these were versatile machines, working everything from fast and heavy outer suburban trains, to leisurely passenger trains, and then taking their turn on the branch goods. There was nothing spectacular about them, and they looked rather ancient alongside an 0-6-0T. Nevertheless, although their reign on the outer suburban trains was short, they were an ever-present on the coastal branches until the last was withdrawn in 1953: curiously, some five years before the final 'T26'.

Tank engines were clearly Holden's speciality and a third distinct type emerged near the end of the century: the 'S44' class 0-4-4Ts. This arrangement was nothing new to the GER

though, for Johnson had introduced a similar design. The 'S44s' were intermediate between the small 0-6-0Ts and the altogether larger 2-4-2Ts and, being fitted with condensing apparatus, soon found themselves working the busy branches of north-east London. They were, of course, slower accelerating than the nimble 0-6-0Ts, but were fine runners once on the move. Yet again, these were very capable engines, but Holden turned away from this wheel arrangement when further suburban locomotives were required. The last 'S44' was withdrawn in 1939.

With a sense of irony, Holden returned to his development of Worsdell's 'Gobblers' when it came to building his final suburban tank engines; just about the first class to feel the effect of Holden's new broom as it began its sweep of Stratford. The 'M15s' were almost identical to the rebuilt 'Gobblers', combining the 'C32' boiler with the 'Gobbler' chassis, and adding Stephenson's link-motion. Standard parts were used extensively, without any of the fuss and fanfare that greeted such changes on other railways.

Eventually, 128 'M15s' were built, including Worsdell's 40 'Gobblers'. Working mainly on the outer-suburban services, they combined solidity, reliability, power, speed and acceleration over several decades working front-line duties. There was nothing striking about these or any of Holden's passenger tanks, but their intensive work gave them a unique distinction. There is absolutely no evidence to suggest that Holden's tank engines were better, or worse, than those of any other railway, but no others worked so hard with so little fuss. Whatever their size or shape, Holden's tank engines epitomised Victorian Britain: getting the job done, however difficult, without flourish or notions of grandeur, if not necessarily in the most efficient method.

Holden's approach to the GER's London suburban network, his solid and unpretentious tank engines, was that of the 19th century: electricity was the power for the new century. The call for electrification was understandable, but it was expensive and a rival scheme was hatched. The new century had barely dawned when the old monarch died and with her went the restrained and sober way of life. Electrification's problem, then and now, is its prohibitive capital costs and not only was the GER far from wealthy, but the very services that would benefit from its installation were, quite paradoxically, barely profitable. The stuffing could have been comprehensively knocked the out of the GER's fragile finances had it pursued the electrification path.

Holden set his department to work on a conventional alternative; a scenario paralleled over 30 years later when the LNER introduced its streamlined steam trains. A remarkable 0-10-0T emerged from Stratford, with three cylinders, a massive boiler and an American-inspired wide firebox. 'Decapod' was designed to accelerate a fully laden suburban train from a station to 30 mph in just 30 seconds. Perhaps the biggest surprise of all, was that this lithe leviathan was more than capable of so doing and, joy of joys, the electrification scheme was quietly forgotten.

When built, 'Decapod' was the most powerful locomotive in the world. It was suitably heavy, yet had an axle loading of only 16 tons, theoretically light enough even for the GER's featherbed branches. If the future looked bright and rosy, 'Decapod' had a badly exposed Achilles Heel: its five closely spaced axles compressed its gargantuan 80 tons into an abnormally short length of track. There was not a hope in hell that the Civil Engineer would give his approval, and yet another potentially ground-breaking design fell victim to conservatism.

'Decapod' re-emerged as an 0-8-0 tender engine in 1906,

A bit late in the day really, Holden's 'P43' class 7 ft. singles were, nevertheless, visually quite magnificent locomotives. As with Dean's great singles, there was a rugged elegance about them, with a copper-rimmed chimney, but they only enjoyed short lives. No. 18 has already been converted to coal burning, and is not in the most pristine condition; one might assume its express hauling days are behind it. The last single was withdrawn in 1910.   (P. McGuire)

with two outside 18½ x 24 inch cylinders, a much smaller boiler pressed to 180 psi and a Belpaire firebox; the whole weighed a mere 54¼ tons. The reborn 'Decapod' worked heavy goods trains to and from the joint-line north of March, but was no better than an 0-6-0 and was withdrawn in 1913. The experiment was at an end and any electrification scheme remained still-born for five long decades. 'Decapod' was quite unlike any other design of the Holden years, but demonstrated that his department could, if necessary, produce a locomotive as imaginative as any in Britain.

Back in the last two decades of the 19th century, the GER was not renown for its long-distance passenger services, let alone expresses. Speeds were distinctly modest, with Norwich trains running via Cambridge rather than Ipswich, and other destinations had what would only be described as, at best, a semi-fast service on many other railways. Even before 1890 though, there were direct trains to York, and while these could not compete with the GNR expresses, better engines were needed. Worsdell's economical compound 4-4-0s were not the answer for a railway that had pretensions of grandeur.

Holden was not a unique Locomotive Superintendent in looking backwards when trying to go forwards. His 'T19' express passenger 2-4-0s were in good company: Johnson built this type of locomotive for MR expresses, albeit a decade before. Still, by aiming at the uncomplicated — going back to basics, as we might say — Holden produced a robust, if unspectacular, design that would at least hold the fort for the time being.

In fact, the 'T19s' became the GER's intermediate passenger engines for the rest of the century, and well beyond. Old-fashioned and quaint looking, spectacular runners they were not, even with the GER's leisurely schedules, but they were solid and stolid, bread and butter, go anywhere engines. Once the first 'Claud Hamiltons' entered service, 21 were rebuilt with a Belpaire firebox, while 60 more were transformed into Belpaire 4-4-0s. Even then, they were sluggardly performers, and mostly worked secondary main line services. While none of the 2-4-0s lasted into LNER ownership, the final 4-4-0 was not withdrawn until 1944. The various versions of the 'T19s' would hardly enhance Holden's long-term reputation, but they were essential when first built and proved versatile enough to cope in an altogether harder world.

A sort of mixed-traffic version of the 'T19s' was produced in 1891, for main line semi-fasts, branch line work and to haul the growing number of fish trains. The 'T26' class 2-4-0s looked very similar to their bigger brothers, indeed they shared the same boilers, and became known as 'Intermediates'. Once again, they were durable and versatile engines, the very thing the GER needed and, having smaller driving wheels, were able to work successfully down the ranks over the passing years. They were the last 2-4-0s in service on BR, with the final one was not being withdrawn until 1958,

and gained more recognition than ever before.

Holden was fortunate in that Worsdell left behind one truly outstanding design. The 'Y14' small 0-6-0s were deservedly regarded as Maids of All Work, for they could undertake most duties should the need arise and Holden built his own version, the 'N31' class. These were virtually identical to Holden's improved 'Y14s', that continued to be built long after Holden had stopped building his own. The 'N31s' were hardly out and out flops, but the ironic nickname bestowed on them, 'Swifts', accurately conveyed their major deficiency. Though they shared many common parts with the 'Intermediates' and Worsdell's 'Y14s', they were the poor performers of the triumvirate.

Holden built a solitary 'N31' as a Worsdell/von Borries compound: the only compound goods engine on the GER. Holden made bold claims for the economy of Worsdell's compound 4-4-0s, but he still rebuilt them. The same fate befell No. 127, by 1890, bringing the curtain down on such experiments.

The first decade or so of Holden's reign was clearly very much a case of bolstering the fort. Dynamics never really entered the GER psyche but, with a steady ship, Holden tried to create an opportunity to improve express services by designing a 2-2-2: the 'D27' class. This was some way short of being state-of-the-art, and the first engine was really a rebuilt 'T19', betraying the ancestry and influences of the design. As with other single-drivers, the 'D27s' were intended for the fastest expresses — not that the GER had many of those.

They found work on Norwich trains, and especially on the line to York, but were almost out of date before leaving the works. Still, they were capable of hauling trains of about 200 tons, and were surprisingly good at climbing hills, reputedly being better than the 'T19s'. Rather perversely, the latter engines were faster than the singles at going down them! Engine design was hardly a science in the 19th century.

The 'D27s' came into their element with the introduction of a fast train to Cromer, from 1897. For two seasons, six dedicated locomotives ran the 139 miles to the Norfolk resort, from Liverpool St., in only 160 minutes -a fair old task with a decent load. Unfortunately, Holden provided corridor coaches for this prestigious train and soon their time was up; their cameo of an innings was over by 1907. They were, though, the first GER locomotives to remotely approach the standards of express performance taken for granted elsewhere.

These were superseded by even larger single-drivers, the 'P43' class 4-2-2s: another graduate of the part-engineering/part-work-of-art school. Holden appears to have been influenced by the success of Johnson's MR 'Spinners', and Dean's majestic singles, and his 'P43s' were handsome and finely proportioned engines. Unfortunately, they caused their own downfall. As elsewhere, the 'P43s' hauled fast trains of corridor coaches that attracted more passengers. Soon, these

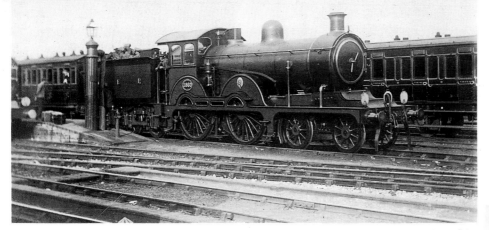

Undoubtedly, Holden's finest design. The 'Claud Hamiltons' would have graced any British railway during the Edwardian years, and were more than just a quantum leap forward for the GER No. 1860, an original round firebox engine, stands at Cambridge with an express. Their rich blue livery, made these the most exquisite of engines, even having driven some admirers to poetic verse.

trains were becoming too long and heavy; the paradox being that the very success of the last generation of single-driver locomotives sounded their own death-knell.

For a further two seasons, Holden's new flag-bearers hauled the prestige trains to Cromer, often with over 250 tons behind their tenders. They ran north to York, where they were a marvellous, grand advertisement for the railway, but within a year or two of the new century, they looked positively archaic alongside the great new Atlantics of the GNR and NER that epitomised the forward-thrusting Edwardian age.

Most unusually though, Holden had been experimentally running locomotives on waste oil from the company's gas works. The 'P43s' were all converted to oil-firing: a long-lasting and successful experiment that would draw much praise in today's climate. Once again though, it was killed off by its very success, for to make it commercially viable more engines had to use the fuel, and oil had to imported to supplement that provided by the gas works. This was in the days when King Coal ruled, and British coal was cheaper than imported oil. The experiment ended early in the 20th century, and by the end of the decade, the 4-2-2s had all gone. A brief, but spectacular interlude in GER locomotive history. But only a precursor for a design worthy of the new century.

As it happens the first of Holden's new express passenger locomotives, the 'Claud Hamiltons', took to the rails at the end of the 19th century. Almost immediately, it was obvious that these were to be Holden's masterpiece; the finest pre-Grouping engine to run the rails of East Anglia, and by quite some margin. They were big and strong engines, finely engineered in the bold Victorian fashion, yet with a care that made them virtual works of art. They were powerful starters, quite important for a railway with few non-stop runs of any length, though were never noted for particularly high speeds. The ability to haul 400 tons at a steady 60 mph, after a good start, was what really mattered on the mildly claustrophobic main lines of East Anglia. The 'Claud Hamiltons' fitted that particular bill perfectly.

The first 40 locomotives were built with a round-topped firebox, but the rest had a Belpaire type: the earlier engines were eventually so rebuilt, and weighed almost two tons more. All the engines had a Worsdell-profile cab, but they were no technical ground-breakers. Several locomotives were fitted for oil burning, and as the class emerged in considerable numbers, so they allowed for something of a revelation in GER main line passenger services, if not a revolution. For example, whereas a 'P43' could take about 250 tons on the premier trains to Cromer, a 'Claud' could take over 400 tons. Norwich services were re-routed via Ipswich and were vastly improved, and at long, long last the GER had the locomotives to match and achieve its aspirations. It too could now look towards joining the ranks of the very top railways in Edwardian Britain.

When the mighty 'Decapod' was first built, in 1902, there was no more powerful steam engine in the world. Holden's masterpiece it was not, but it was soon able to demonstrate its ability to accelerate a train of over 300 tons to 30 mph, in 30 seconds. Had the will been there at the time, this prototype could possibly have been developed to the point where it really would have made electrification superfluous, at least as far as Edwardian technology allowed. It was, though, a missed opportunity. (N.R.M.)

If this marked a turning point, the start of a new era, Holden aimed to do likewise for the burgeoning goods traffic. The earlier 0-6-0s were fine engines, but bigger and better freight locomotives were desperately needed. Holden's 'F48' class 0-6-0s were nothing less than a goods version of the 'Clauds', with all their many attributes. They soon gained a Belpaire firebox and were built in relatively large numbers. With these two classes, Holden not only gave his employers the means to begin a considerable transformation of their services, but also vastly enhanced his reputation as one of the finest locomotive engineers in contemporary Britain.

These two classes, when built in numbers, brought to completion Holden's transformation of the GER locomotive stock. His final new design was the 'C53' outside cylinder tram engines, intended for the dock estates at Yarmouth, Lowestoft and Ipswich and, of course, the infamous Wisbech and Upwell Tramway. They were the first GER locomotives fitted with Walschaert's valve gear and were the ultimate version of this unique type of tram engine.

By the time Holden stood down in favour of his son, his impact on the GER locomotive stock was as great as was that of Churchward on the GWR. Of course, nobody in their right mind would suggest that Holden was ever as remotely innovative as his former Swindon subordinate, but while he might not have advanced steam locomotive design, he thoroughly transformed the GER locomotive fleet: in other words did what he was paid to do. By 1910, over 1,100 out of 1,350 GER locomotives had been built during Holden's reign, the vast majority to designs for which he was responsible. Even Churchward could not match that.

Prior to his arrival, the GER had more different classes than there were train services: some pretty fair, a few good, but the majority of quite indifferent performance, at least if timetables are anything to go by. When he retired, most of these had been pensioned-off and the reliance on his good, solid and thoroughly workman-like engines was pretty-nigh total, certainly on the main traffic lines.

If his locomotive design work was invaluable to the GER, he was also instrumental in organising Stratford Works to the point were its potential could, at long last, be realised. No doubt, the continuity of his years in charge contributed greatly towards this: no more upheavals for a start, but by the time the 'Claud Hamilton' class began to emerge, the quality of build and finish bore comparison with the best in the country.

In particular, repairs were undertaken far quicker than had hitherto been the case, aided by the use of a wide range of standard parts, while the work was undertaken to a far higher standard. This, and a happy workforce, is a sure sign of good engineering leadership. Holden might not have been an innovative locomotive designer, but he knew what his employer required, and ensured his department was more than capable of delivering the goods. Would it be that all locomotive engineers could achieve such success. Without the slightest doubt, Holden's years of assured stability were instrumental in assisting the pronounced development of the GER from that of a provincial railway, into one that could stand four-square on the national stage.

Out of darkness came light. The portents upon Holden's appointment were not exactly promising. Was he yet another engineer using the GER to further his own career? That might have been a passing thought for both Holden's staff and the GER board. They could, though, hardly have made a better choice: the right man at long last. Holden's tenure gave stability, while measured change was never ignored. This subtle amalgam eventually allowed the GER to realise its ambitions and to attain the stature it had craved for so long.

JAMES HOLDEN IN BRIEF

BORN:	26th July 1837, Whistable, Kent.
TRAINED:	Gateshead Works, York, Newcastle and Berwick Rly. Apprentice.
EMPLOYED:	Engineering works in Sunderland. 1865, G.W.R. Carriage and Wagon Dept.
SENIOR POSITIONS:	Superintendent of works at Shrewsbury and Chester. Carriage & Wagon Works Manager, Swindon. Chief Ass. to W. Dean. 1885, Loco. Supt. G.E.R.
RETIRED:	31st, December 1907.
HONOURS:	J.P. in Essex.
DIED:	29th May 1925, Bath.

Holden's Locomotive Designs

YEAR	CLASS	WHEEL ARRANG'T	CYLINDERS (INCHES)	BOILER PRESSURE	DRIVING-WHEEL DIAMETER	WEIGHT	No. in CLASS
1886	T18	0-6-0T	16½ x 22	140 psi	4 ft.	40¼ tons	50
1886	T19	2-4-0	18 x 24	140 psi	7 ft.	39 tons	110
1888	N31 comp.	0-6-0	H.P.18 x 24 L.P.26 x 24	160 psi	4 ft. 11 in.		1
1888	N31	0-6-0	17½ x 24	160 psi	4 ft. 11 in.	39 tons	81
1889	D27	2-2-2	18 x 24	140 psi	7 ft.	40 tons	21
1889	E22	0-6-0T	14 x 20	140 psi	4 ft.	36½ tons	20
1890	R24	0-6-0T	16½ x 22	140 psi	4 ft.	40 tons	51
1890	S56	0-6-0T	16½ x 22	140 psi	4 ft.	42½ tons	109
1891	T26	2-4-0	17½ x 24	160 psi	5 ft. 8 in.	40¼ tons	100
1893	C32	2-4-2T	17½ x 24	160 psi	5 ft. 8 in.	58½ tons	50
1898	S44	0-4-4T	17 x 24	160 psi	4 ft. 11 in.	53½ tons	40
1898	P43	4-2-2	18 x 24	160 psi	7 ft.	50 tons	10
1900	Claud Ham.	4-4-0	19 x 26	180 psi	7 ft.	50¼ tons	111
1900	F48	0-6-0	19 x 26	180 psi	4 ft. 11 in.	44½ tons	90
1902	Decapod	0-10-0	(3)18½ x 24	200 psi	4 ft. 6 in.	80 tons	1
1903	C53	0-6-0T	(o)12 x 15	180 psi	3 ft. 1 in.	27 tons	12
1903	M15	2-4-2T	17½ x 24	160 psi	5 ft. 4 in.	54 tons	88
1905	T19 reb.	4-4-0	18 x 24	180 psi	7 ft.	48¼ tons	60

HOLDEN's PRESERVED LOCOMOTIVES

YEAR	CLASS	RUNNING NUMBERS	TOTAL
1891	T26	B.R. 62785	1
1900	F48	B.R. 65567	1
1904	S56	B.R. 68633	1

THOMAS WILLIAM WORSDELL
and
WILSON WORSDELL
Two Paths, One Goal

Being born with a silver spoon in one's mouth is often a passport to a prosperous, if not easy, life. As the saying suggests, anyone with a million pounds can make another million: it is getting the first million that is the difficult bit. I can only confirm the second part to be true, but if one starts out in life with financial assistance from the family then, not surprisingly, it is easier than beginning right at the bottom of the pile.

On the other hand, following in the footsteps of a successful parent is never the easiest of tasks. If one succeeds, it is a case of, 'well, what do you expect with all their advantages'; while if one does not live up to expectations a more likely response is, 'oh yes, he's okay, but not a patch on his old man. Now if I had the advantage of his up-bringing...' We are all probably familiar with such comments.

It is no different within railway circles. Until recent years, it was almost the done thing for a son to follow in his father's footsteps, whatever the old-boy's position. There are many examples when both scaled considerable heights. In railway engineering one immediately thinks of such eminent families as the Brunels, Trevithicks, Reids, Cubitts, Spooners, and, of course, the Stephensons. There are many other father/son relationships where one, the other, or both have gone on to become a Loco. Supt. while, apart from those already mentioned, three of our Stars of Steam can be included in their exalted ranks.

It is rather less common for brothers to be a striking success in a similar field though. There are some notable exceptions, such as the Kray twins, while Bobby and Jack Charlton and, in the present day, Philip and Gary Neville, are outstanding footballers. In railway engineering the Cudworth, Gooch and Stirling families each sired brothers who became British Loco. Supts., but only the Worsdell brothers each reached the level of success to be, arbitrarily, classed as a Star of Steam in their own right.

It was not unexpected that both Thomas William Worsdell (T.W.) and Wilson Worsdell (W.W.) would work in railway engineering. With a grandfather, father and uncle all holding relatively senior positions within the early railway companies, it was almost a racing certainty they would. Born into a Quaker family, both T.W. and W.W. were educated at a Quaker boarding school. A strict adherence to the Protestant work-ethic was inculcated from an early age and not forgotten. Although the brothers were born 12 years apart, their respective careers followed a similar path that crossed and re-crossed during their working lives. Now, while this smacks of nepotism running wild, and there certainly was a time when W.W. was carried along on the shirt-tails of T.W., that was not the case in later years. W.W. soon showed that he was very much his own man.

There is no question, having a father and grandfather who both knew, and worked extensively with the Stephensons on various pioneering railways, did the Worsdell brothers no harm at all. T.W. all but walked into a job at Crewe Works, before undertaking an engineering apprenticeship with an uncle in Birmingham. On completing this, he returned to the Crewe Drawing Office: his father — Nathaniel — was in charge of the Carriage and Wagon dept. T.W. could have been set-up for life, but he was ambitious and soon left to become manager of an engineering works — one up to him.

Then, in 1865, T.W. accepted a position at the Pennsylvania R.R's Altoona Works. Though the American Civil War had only just finished, it seemed likely that there would be many opportunities forthcoming: after all, Altoona was something of a New World equivalent to Crewe. T.W. soon became a Master Mechanic and settled down to six years' work that was to shape his future plans and ideas.

In the meantime, W.W. had completed his education and had taken a junior post in Crewe's Drawing Office — the family connection at work again? Then, in 1867, he went and joined T.W. at the Altoona Works, undertaking an apprenticeship under the Locomotive Superintendent, Dr. E. Williams. For four years the brothers' worked in tandem, though at a distance, but in 1871 they decided to return to Old Blighty; not un-naturally to their old stamping-ground at Crewe Works. This was due, in the main, to F.W. Webb succeeding J. Ramsbottom as Locomotive Superintendent and wanting T.W. as his Works Manager. This was a major coup for T.W. and he soon accepted. W.W. was found a position, first in the erecting shop and then the Drawing Office and, with their father still holding a senior position, the Worsdell family seemed to be making Crewe their dynastic home.

At that time, Crewe Works was expanding very rapidly. Ramsbottom had built on the initial work of F. Trevithick and set Crewe on the path to becoming one of the finest railway works in the country. Under Webb's far-reaching plans, Crewe became not only the best railway works, but probably the finest engineering establishment in all Britain: the workshop of the world, no less! Although the general plans and much of the detail layout for Crewe's transformation were the responsibility and work of Webb, it was T.W. who oversaw the day-to-day management, and ensured that routine work was carried out both efficiently and by adhering to the great Crewe tradition of economy.

Although heavily influenced by Webb, T.W. was able to sift and select the experiences he thought would be most useful, and moulded them to formulate his own ideas, as he had done in America. Perhaps it was just as well that T.W. departed Crewe when Webb was having his first stab at production compound locomotives, but the idea of compounding, and much else, was soon to surface in his own work.

The Worsdell brothers and their father spent just a single year in harness together at Crewe Works, before W.W. moved away to take the first of several increasingly senior positions at locomotive sheds, over the next decade. No doubt, the Worsdell name carried some weight, but W.W. was out by

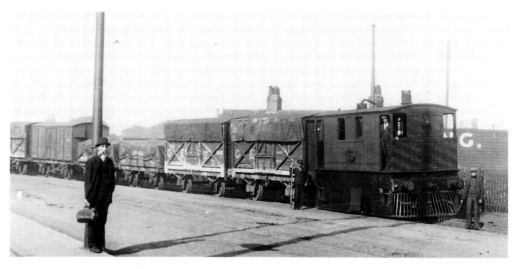

The 'G15' tram engines for the Wisbech and Upwell Tramway were quite unique. They were equally at home on the docks of East Anglia and, judging by the attire of the man holding the basket, Gt. Yarmouth might be the location for this picture. No. 129 was built in 1885, became an LNER 'Y6' class and was withdrawn in 1933. The last steam tram engines were withdrawn in 1952. *(G. Askham)*

himself, rising or falling by his own efforts. Clearly he was good at his job, for there were no obvious backward steps, and the Worsdell brothers' career paths began to diverge. Then, when T.W. was appointed Locomotive Superintendent of the GER in 1882 — and W.W. did not follow, it appeared that all working links might be severed forever.

At that time, the GER appeared to be something of a finishing school for Locomotive Superintendents: T.W. was its sixth in its first 20 years. It seemed as though ambitious engineers gained much-needed experience and then, just when beginning to benefit the company, were snatched away and went on to make their name and reputation elsewhere. Well, that is what happened to Johnson and Adams, and T.W. was the third Star of Steam who promised Stratford the earth, but delivered the goods to another address.

Despite Adams' successful re-organisation of Stratford Works, it had lapsed into a less than model manufactory by the time T.W. took up his appointment. Was it his experience and success at Crewe Works that clinched the position for T.W., as he had little to do with locomotive design? He did have ideas though, and compounding was foremost among them. The compound locomotives' potential for improved performance and enhanced economy seemed limitless at that time (Webb had not yet begun to put people off), and T.W. was convinced he had a system that would work.

The GER always had a need for up-to-date engines, as the comings and goings of its previous Locomotive Superintendents inevitably left shortfalls somewhere in the locomotive fleet. T.W. did not get off to a promising start, at least with regards locomotive design for, right from the outset, his 'G14' class express 2-4-0s were not noted for their speed, even taking into account the distinctly leisured nature of contemporary GER expresses. Possibly inspired by Webb's 'Precedents', and definitely showing his LNWR bent by using Joy's valve-gear, these poor engines were nobody's favourite and were soon demoted to less demanding work.

If T.W. was a bit wide of the mark with his initial design, the first fruits of his appointment were soon apparent as Stratford Works began to build locomotives in quantity. Prior to the arrival of T.W., Stratford had built relatively few locomotives and the GER was a regular customer of the specialist building companies. That was all about to change, and if T.W. did nothing else for the railway, his work allowed his successors to begin providing the locomotives the company deserved.

Fortunately, T.W. soon got the department working his way and, in 1883, produced what may well lay claim to be the most

useful design in the railway's history. The 'Y14' class was not the sort to have railway enthusiasts salivating at the prospect of one appearing round the bend, for the diminutive 0-6-0s were more stage-hands than even second-string actors. That might be unjustly putting them down a bit, for they were front-line goods engines for many, many years, yet easy to ignore: just as one does a 'Sprinter' today.

When travelling on East Anglia's railways a 'Y14', or an LNER 'J15', was a common sight right into B.R.'s days. By then, of course, they no longer worked the main line, but were still trundling local pick-up goods on branches up and down the region. Forty-two served abroad in the First World War and, with 289 engines being built, you did not usually have to look too hard to find one. Though never a locomotive to make an engineer's reputation, the ubiquitous and eager 'Y14' was a steady dividend earner for the company.

That same year T.W. also introduced some of the most unusual locomotives ever to run in Britain: the first of the renown Tram engines, principally for the opening of the Wisbech and Upwell Tramway. The 'G15' class 0-4-0T, was a unique solution to the problem of working a railway that ran through villages and along a public highway. It also spurned later designs that found work on East Anglia's docks and harbours, as did the 'G15s' themselves. The name 'Toby' was most appropriate for the tram engine that ran on the Rev. W. Audrey's railway, and encapsulates their unique individual persona.

There was no way a 'G15' could be mistaken for anything else, except possibly a guard's van. With side-plates covering the wheels, and cow-catchers front and rear, these distinctive and original locomotives also had dual-controls, condensing apparatus and a spark arrester. They were a highly original solution to the tramway's unique requirements: a design that was to be subsequently copied and enlarged in the future.

Without a doubt though, T.W's most important technical advance came with his 'G16' class express 4-4-0s, the intended flagship of the GER. Outwardly, these were fine, but unexceptional looking engines, apart from wearing the new, rich royal blue livery, and gave no obvious clue to their innovative character. Neither were they the fastest of engines on the line, but appearances were deceptive. The 'G16' class was the first Worsdell/Von Borries 2-cylinder compound: T.W's development of A. Von Borries' designs for the Prussian State Railways. The intention was simple: to gain the potential performance and economy of compounding, without the extra expense and complication of multiple cylinders. Webb, of course, was busy pursuing the 3-cylinder compound path with rather mixed success and, while at Crewe, T.W. had briefly been able to assess their potential, but sought a somewhat easier route.

The Von Borries' system seemed to offer decent performance at reasonable cost. It became widely used in both Germany and Russia, but was not really suited to high speeds: unfortunately, just what T.W. had in mind for it! The main difference between the Von Borries and Worsdell/Von Borries' compounds was the latter's use of inside cylinders. These did nothing to aid daily maintenance, but were the accepted norm in Britain and, in any case, showed a degree of initiative on T.W's part.

The 'G16s', though, did not live up to T.W's expectations. Using Joy's valve-gear, they were distinctly sluggish runners even by the GER's low standards. On occasions, it was not unknown for one to be unable to start, as steam intended for the low pressure cylinder entered the high pressure cylinder and, effectively, prevented that piston moving. A valve was soon fitted to prevent this, but still they were not man-enough for the job. By 1892, J. Holden had converted them to simples, with 18 in. cylinders, yet still they were far from ideal. All were gone by 1901, although Holden used the bogies to convert some 'T14' 2-4-0s into 4-4-0s. The 'G16s' were a brave, innovative design by T.W., but were not really the stuff of a Star of Steam.

Webb's influence was also apparent in T.W's last GER design. The 'M15' 2-4-2Ts were inspired by the LNWR's established favourite and, once again, used Joy's valve-gear and radial axle-boxes. These became a mainstay of the GER's outer suburban services well into the new century, with a modified version being produced by J. Holden until 1911. Even the 'M15s' were not an initial success, at least so far as economy went, and they soon earned the nickname 'Gobblers' for their voracious appetite for coal. Their performance could not be denied though, and when Holden replaced Joy's valve-gear with Stephenson's link-motion and reduced the cylinders to $17\frac{1}{2}$ in., along with other minor alterations, these finally rose to earn their place in the small passenger tank Hall of Fame.

While T.W. had been raising hopes and establishing order on the GER, and creating a name for himself, young W.W. had not been idle either. It is extremely doubtful that he intended to follow T.W. to Stratford, as he had to America. In any case, W.W. was forging his own successful career. He probably expected to stay with the LNWR, but in 1883 was appointed Assistant Mechanical Engineer to A. McDonnell on the NER, at Gateshead. It seemed then, that the brothers' careers had finally diverged to opposite ends of the country.

A year later, with the NER locomotive department in turmoil following the forced resignation of McDonnell, an interim express locomotive was designed as an urgent measure under the temporary aegis of General Manager H. Tennant. The ensuing 'Tennant' class 2-4-0s were to prove just the right engine in the NER's darkest hour of need. Not surprisingly, the General Manager, though temporarily in charge of locomotive affairs, had little to do with the design, a task most likely to have been the responsibility of W.W.

Quite obviously, the situation whereby a major department of the NER did not have its own amply qualified head could not last and, one might assume, W.W. probably thought that his good work would place him in pole position when it came to considering a new appointment. No such luck, but the new incumbent might at least have been a little more acceptable to him than most: his brother T.W. was called north to take the helm. Once again, W.W. had to follow in his brother's tracks: the pill might have been relatively sweetened, but there remained just a hint of bitterness.

In the long-run, the decision was probably the right one as the NER locomotive department had just passed through a very stormy sea, and an experienced captain was needed to guide it to calmer waters. However, of the two, it was W.W. who had produced the most successful express locomotives by that time, for T.W's had been less than outstanding on the GER. Then as now, experience — whether good or bad — counts for everything and T.W. seemed to be much less of a gamble: just what the railway did not need.

In no time at all, T.W. set off at a cracking pace with seven new types of locomotive, to five different basic designs, emerging during his first year or so in charge. Such a burst of activity had not been seen on a British railway before. The NER locomotive department might recently have suffered at the top, but there can not have been too much inherently wrong for so much to be achieved so soon. Not all of these new designs went straight into quantity production, and four of them were Worsdell/Von Borries' compounds: hardly the easiest of designs to undertake without any previous experience.

Quite appropriately, T.W. started a new locomotive classification scheme, at least for his own designs, and the first to emerge was, not un-naturally, the 'A' class 2-4-2T. In essence, this was a modified version of his GER 'Gobblers', complete with Joy's valve-gear and radial trucks. These were soon put to work on the heavy suburban traffic in the north-east and proved to be very successful, long-lasting, economical and versatile. A real asset to the NER and, ultimately, the LNER.

The 'B1' class 0-6-2T was used primarily for short-distance goods work and were, to all intents and purposes, simple orthodox locomotives. That was not the case with the similar 'B' class: similar in all respects, that is, except for being compounds. They were T.W's first compounds for the NER, and were rather a strange choice given the starting difficulties previously encountered with 2-cylinder compounds. That did not stop T.W. though and for every simple 0-6-2T, he built five compounds. W.W., as we shall see, did not share his brother's predilection for this complex mode of propulsion and soon rebuilt the 'Bs' as 'B1s'. Later, many were rebuilt with 19 in. x 26 in. cylinders and had their Joy's valve-gear replaced by Stephenson's link-motion, and both simple versions survived to see service on BR.

T.W. repeated the tactic of building simple and compound versions of the same design for, respectively, the 'C1' and 'C' class heavy goods engines. As usual, Joy's valve-gear was used and, over a period, both classes underwent cost comparisons. The 'C' class compounds were claimed to be the more economical and it was these were sent forth to multiply. Quite how accurate these tests were is not known but, once again, W.W. soon began to rebuild them as simples when he succeeded his brother.

The 'C' class was Britain's first mass-production compound goods design, and was a substantial engine for its time. They were also the first locomotives to feature T.W's large, generous cab, probably inspired by those he saw in America. This was not the first large cab used in England, nor even the north-east, but they were a vast improvement over the traditional skimpy cabs of the era and were certainly appreciated by the footplate crews. As such, the NER certainly led the way and T.W. had made an incisive mark.

These goods and tank designs were all of undoubted value to the NER, but T.W. had still to produce a successful express passenger design. The NER not only conveyed its share of the lucrative Anglo-Scottish traffic, but was also responsible for hauling expresses over NBR metals, from Berwick-Edinburgh.

On the GNR, these trains were hauled by P. Stirling's great 8 ft. singles, but the NER was saddled with game 2-4-0s of increasingly doubtful capacity. Action to remedy this situation was needed sooner rather than later.

T.W's initial response seems somewhat baffling, with hindsight. The 'D' class, compound 2-4-0 was hardly a long-term prospect, as T.W. had already built compound 4-4-0s for the GER. The first one, No. 1324, was an orthodox Worsdell/Von Borries' compound, but two years later came No. 340. This was almost identical except for having a single 7½ in. piston valve for the H.P. cylinder, and two 5½ in. piston valves for the L.P. cylinder. One might assume that neither of these engines were entirely successful, for they remained the sole members of the 'D' class, but they pioneered the use of W.M. Smith's segmental piston valves.

Finally though, in 1887 T.W. achieved his major breakthrough. He produced ten simple and ten compound express 4-4-0s: effectively a 'D' class with a leading bogie. The fuel consumption and performance of these 'F' class compounds and 'F1' class simples were measured against each other in some rather spurious tests. The 'F1s' were handicapped with a low boiler pressure, a trick that Webb used to ensure his beloved compounds always came out well on top. T.W. was still influenced by the master!

On the other hand, the 'F1s' were not noted for any speed-worthiness while the 'Fs', though hardly greyhounds, were at least very capable runners on the expresses. Occasionally, an 'F' performed in the 1888 races, performing well above the norm of everyday running, yet without raising too many eyebrows. T.W. arranged Joy's valve-gear so that the L.P. cylinder had a longer cut-off than did the H.P. at any particular setting, thus enabling the cylinders to do a similar amount of work. This was the main difference from his GER 'G16s', and was probably the reason the 'F' class ran so much better. These compounds were clearly pretty good, but were far from being great. Even so, once T.W. had retired, W.W. converted them to simples.

The 'D' and 'F' classes were important as being the first reasonably successful Worsdell/Von Borries' compound express locomotives; they were also the first to bear the new styling that distinguished NER locomotives for the rest of its existence. The large cab had, of course, already made its appearance, but it was the continuous splasher over the coupled wheels and the brass encased Ramsbottom safety valve, that rounded-off a most distinctive design. Something of which the NER could justifiably be proud.

An intermediate passenger 2-4-0, the 'G' class, and the 'H' class dock tanks followed, with the even smaller 'K' class 0-4-0Ts specifically built for Hull docks in 1890. However, possibly influenced by S.W. Johnson of the MR, T.W. then turned his attention towards the potential of single-driver locomotives. Thanks to Johnson's introduction of steam-sanding gear, the era of the single-drivers, having seemed to be drawing to a close, was given a shot in the arm that ushered in a long and glorious finale. For the next decade, many British locomotive engineers seemed blinded by the speed potential of a great whirling driving wheel, almost overlooking the advent of the bogie coach and the remorseless increase in train weights. It was these latter changes that brusquely and finally killed-off the reborn single-driver, not anything to do with their suitability for working high-speed trains.

Typically, each locomotive engineer who turned to single-drivers did so on their own terms. Thus P. Stirling's favourites had outside cylinders, Dean's had double-frames and Johnson's had inside cylinders. It was therefore no surprise that T.W. built his 'I' class 4-2-2s as compounds. As with his other compounds, this was not readily apparent from a casual glance, but there was no mistaking T.W's lines. Unlike the other single-driver locomotives of the era though, the 'I' class was not intended for front-line expresses, but was principally used for secondary work over the level lines at the south of the NER system. They worked Leeds-York-Scarborough trains on which they were an undoubted success, but a year later T.W. joined the swelling ranks of British locomotive engineers who followed the single-driver path for the principal express locomotives.

The 'J' class 4-2-2s were visually almost identical to the 'I' class locomotives, except for having larger driving wheels: underneath the skin, though, this was far from being the case. Having to accommodate 44 in. of cylinder between the wheels was a tight squeeze in the 'I' class; the 'J' class had 48 in. of cylinder and there was just not enough room for a conventional parallel layout. T.W's remedy was to raise the massive L.P. cylinder above the driving wheel axle line, and to lower the H.P. below it. With Joy's valve-gear, there was no room at all for the steam chests, so these were placed outside the frames and worked by a complex, and not entirely foolproof, system of levers. The result was a design not dissimilar to the 'F' class 4-4-0s: an express engine of much potential, but one that was not entirely convincing.

So it proved. Claims were made of one 'J' class engine touching 90 mph downhill, while another was supposed to have reached 86 mph on the level, hauling 224 tons. These claims were not universally accepted at the time, 1889/90, and were subsequently treated with scorn. Two short trials were also held with Stirling's 4-2-2 and 2-2-2 locomotives and, in both performance and economy, Stirling's engines came out comfortably on top: the 'J' class, though, was far from disgraced. The Worsdell/Von Borries' experiment was clearly making considerable progress, especially over such a short time but, once again, T.W. had failed to turn out a really successful express passenger design.

Once W.W. got his hands on the 'J' class though, they were rebuilt as simples by 1896 and became respected performers on main line expresses for several years, including doing well — but not outstandingly so — in the 1895 races. The 'I' class engines were also rebuilt as simples, by 1902, and both classes then undertook useful secondary work for two further decades, primarily in the south of the NER system. Neither class, however, survived to join the LNER ranks.

By 1890, the pace and pressure had begun to tell on T.W's health and he resigned in the September. He was not an unqualified success on the GER, but had laid solid foundations on which J. Holden was, at long last, able to give the company a locomotive fleet it really needed and justly deserved. Progress had been much more rapid and successful at Gateshead, and necessarily so. When T.W. retired, his locomotives were making improvements in all spheres of NER operations, from expresses, through suburban passenger to heavy goods and shunting duties. True, the compounds were unconvincing, yet were far from being failures, unlike the GER's 'G16s'. Ironically, T.W. was enjoying rather more success with his compounds than his former mentor at Crewe, F.W. Webb — the 'Teutonics' apart, but who would have dared to say so at the time?

As far as Victorian passengers were concerned, T.W's engines bore a stately appearance; an assumed grandeur. For giving engine crews decent protection from the elements, they were decades ahead of most British railways. Perhaps most important of all though, T.W. laid a very firm bedrock from which the NER could only benefit. His freight, tank and secondary locomotives were all good, thoroughly reliable

According to T.W.W's successor, J. Holden, the 'G16' compound 4-4-0s were economical express engines. That did not stop Holden converting them to simple expansion locomotives at the earliest possible moment, after which they soon began to be replaced as express passenger engines. Not exactly an exciting picture, but No. 230 is in its original condition. *(NRM)*

designs, while another five or 10 years' work with the compounds might have realised all their potential.

These days, people from all walks of life claim to suffer the effects of stress. Are we becoming a society of wimps? Work is often cited as a major cause of this inability to organise oneself, yet several 19th century locomotive engineers were adversely affected by such pressures. Of our Stars of Steam, Webb and P. Stirling seem to have endured mental problems — though these came in old age: Gooch and Johnson both either retired prematurely or had time off work with bad health, while Stroudley died quite young. To this list can be added T.W. and, whether it was the pressures of the work or simply the less than hygienic conditions in railway workshops, that is a high proportion of senior engineers who came out of their working lives materially wealthy, yet poverty-stricken in health.

That was not quite the end of T.W. for he remained a Consultant Engineer for three years, before finally retiring to the Lake District, where he died fully 23 years later — at least he lived to enjoy the not inconsiderable fruits of his labours. His years as a consultant was more of a safeguard for the NER, as T.W. was succeeded by none other than W.W., then still only 40 years old. While continuity was seemingly guaranteed, W.W. never had much time for compound locomotives and, although T.W's compounds continued to be built, once T.W. had finally departed, their mass conversion to simples was the order of the day.

Despite having been a Locomotive Superintendent for only eight years, T.W. had produced 20 new designs — for two railways, to which over 900 engines were eventually built. Historically, of course, it was his adaptation of the Von Borries 2-cylinder compound that marks him out as an original thinker. These demonstrated considerable improvements since first built in 1884, with potentially much more to come. On the other hand, his GER 'Y14' and 'Y6' classes and NER 'A', 'B', 'C' and 'E' classes were all built in considerable numbers, were long-lasting and even formed a basis for future designs. It was a measure of his value to the northern giant that, upon

T.W's arrival, new engines of all types were required. When T.W. retired, there was no urgency for W.W. to produce anything new. Job done!

W.W's career had begun to diverge away from his brother a few years after they returned from America. Soon after T.W. moved to Stratford, W.W. took up a senior position at Gateshead, and one might have assumed that would have been the end of their brotherly partnership. Circumstances were to dictate otherwise though. They were back in harness, at Gateshead, in 1885, and W.W. might have been expecting another long spell in his brother's shadow. Once T.W. stood down though, W.W. was the natural successor, having proved himself with the 'Tennant' 2-4-0s while clearly being an able and circumspect lieutenant. Furthermore, he had his own ideas, in which the Worsdell/Von Borries' compounds did not feature too strongly, yet he would leave detail work to others while improving the efficiency of his department as a whole. In short, though revolution was not in the air, a new and distinct era was about to begin at Gateshead.

W.W. spent 20 years as first Locomotive Superintendent and then CME of the NER. It was a time of enormous change, both for society and its railways. In 1890, single-driver or diminutive 4-4-0 locomotives hauled express trains that often comprised 6-wheeled coaches; twenty years later, heavy, bogie corridor coaches were pretty much the standard fare. In 1910, most of the major British railways were using either Atlantic or 4-6-0 locomotives, and even a solitary Pacific, on their expresses: all these were of far greater capacity than anything running in 1890. Whereas T.W's 'C' class goods 0-6-0s were considered fairly big engines in 1890, twenty years later 0-8-0s and 2-8-0s were rampant. The trains they hauled might not have been any quicker, but they were a darned sight heavier. In any case, not a few railways had introduced 4-6-0s or similar locomotives to haul fast goods trains as well, and the NER was prominent among them. There was to be no going back.

Apart from larger locomotives there were other, more far-reaching advances. While compounding never really gained general acceptance in Britain — except on the MR, superheating, Belpaire and wide fireboxes, larger and vastly improved boilers, multiple-cylinders with better steam passages, and long-travel piston valves were all embraced to some extent. True, no single locomotive in 1910 encompassed all of these advances, but any Locomotive Superintendent of 1890 had to radically adapt their thinking to survive 20 years later. Although the Stars of Steam who served as Locomotive Superintendents from the mid-1890s to 1910 — Drummond,

T.W. Worsdell's first NER express locomotives, the 'F' class 4-4-0 2-cylinder compounds, were more sprightly runners than his GER counterparts. Though some way short of being outstanding they were, nevertheless, good for the time, though their simple counterparts, the 'F1' class, were quite undistinguished. Despite this, W. Worsdell soon rebuilt the compounds as simples. That is the condition of No. 1542 at Leeds Central as it waits for its train to take forward to Newcastle.

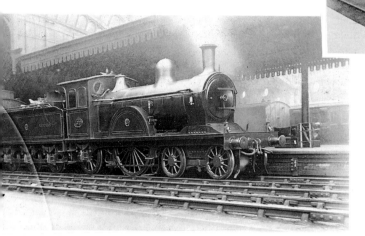

The 'I' class 7 ft. singles may have been influenced by T.W. Worsdell's friendship with S.W. Johnson of the MR, who had begun to build them in 1887. Worsdell went one further and built his as 2-cylinder compounds. These were not intended as front-line express engines, but were intended to haul fast trains over the level Leeds-Scarborough line No. 1329 is at York on one such train, having been rebuilt as a simple in 1894, with 19 in. x 24 in. cylinders.

McIntosh, Robinson, W.W. and, almost, Holden — each managed to successfully enlarge their basically Victorian locomotives and incorporate some new improvements, but none demonstrated a thorough understanding of these innovations. Churchward undoubtedly led the late-Edwardian pack, but it was not exactly a dynamic field.

W.W. was very much a Victorian locomotive engineer. His tenure of office fell into three unequal phases, throughout which the NER advanced remorselessly. Initially, and for almost a decade, W.W. by and large followed the path pursued by T.W. The compounds were converted to simples, Stephenson's link-motion replaced Joy's valve-gear and, thanks to the work of his Chief Draughtsman — the deservedly renowned W.M. Smith, he brought piston valves into widespread use. The second phase began in 1899 when the his large engines began to emerge: the 'S' class was Britain's first passenger 4-6-0. These were followed by Atlantics, 0-8-0s and other designs, each of gargantuan construction. Finally, in his last few years before retirement, he began to dabble with some newer ideas, such as multiple-cylinders and superheating. NER locomotive design under W.W. did anything but stagnate.

The most enduring effect of W.W's term of office is that many of his goods and tank engine designs worked right until the last years of steam in their home region. Of course, they had been rebuilt and modified, but that is a true measure of W.W's work. Conversely, and quite unlike his brother, W.W. produced several good, and even very good express passenger designs. There is no doubt that W.M. Smith's hand played a major part in W.W's success, while W.W. allowed his Chief Draughtsman a degree of autonomy to follow his nose seldom encountered within the rigidly hierarchical structures that were Britain's railways.

In 1892, a Worsdell/Von Borries 'M' class compound 4-4-0 took to the rails, complete with Smith's piston valves. The following year came the first 'M1' class simple equivalent. This was more than just an enlarged 'F1', as the valve chests were moved outside, Joy's valve-gear was discarded and an extended smokebox was fitted. For once, it was the simples that were built in quantity, these being the heaviest British passenger engines of their day — they certainly looked it. They could run a bit too, for No. 1620 ran from Newcastle-Edinburgh at a record average of 66 mph, in the 1895 races. This was, of course, the exception rather than the rule, but the 'M1s' were very successful locomotives that worked for over 50 years. No. 1639 was the odd-man-out, having piston valves, and was reputedly more economical than its slide valve sisters. So, with his first real effort, W.W. had managed to do what, in reality, had always eluded T.W.

Then, following the 1895 races, W.W. produced two further express 4-4-0 designs. The 'Q' class looked almost identical to the 'M1s', except for the clerestory cab roof: a somewhat expensive measure to provide adequate ventilation. They had slightly larger cylinders but, following the lead of P. Stirling and Johnson, a reduced heating surface. These were, again, fine express locomotives and demonstrated a capable mastery of current schedules, despite not having piston valves.

The second design, although it was the first built, was an out and out racing version: the 'Q1' class. These two engines had larger driving wheels, grate and cylinders and were intended to haul the lightweight expresses that would run should racing with the West Coast rivals break out once again. Though there was to be no repeat of the racing heroics, W.W. was not going to be caught with his pants down.

Clearly W.W. had a penchant for the 4-4-0 wheel arrangement on express locomotives, and he turned to this twice more before the end of the century. Judging by the haste with which he began to convert his brother's compounds, it might seem strange that W.W. allowed Smith to transform the singleton

All the grace and elegance of British locomotive design is shown to good effect in this striking picture of W. Worsdell's 'Q' class, No. 1928, at York. These were little different to the earlier 'M' class and were fine express locomotives for their day. They were soon demoted from the front-line expresses, due to increasing train weights, but saw lengthy service on secondary work. The clerestory cab roof, an expensive and not repeated means of providing ventilation, is seen to good effect.

'M' class Worsdell/Von Borries' compound into a 3-cylinder compound. This featured piston valves for the inside H.P. cylinder and slide valves for the outside L.P. cylinders — the reverse of Webb's layout. A larger boiler was fitted, but the longer grate was difficult to fire and had water tubes across the firebox, as later used by D. Drummond. Visually, apart from the obvious outside cylinders, the long splasher over the driving wheels was given a brass beading that aligned with the wheels. This distinction was shared by the 'R' class 4-4-0s and was a half-way house towards the eventual substitution of individual splashers for each wheel. This '3CC' locomotive remained a unique singleton, which might give some indication of W.W's estimation of its worth.

This was certainly not the case for his final express 4-4-0 of the 19th century. The 'R' class was larger than its predecessors and its boiler worked at a higher pressure but, crucially, it had $8\frac{3}{4}$ in. piston valves. Deservedly so, these became the most numerous of the NER's 4-4-0s and continued to haul the company's expresses for the rest of its existence. Perhaps not quite the equal of later GWR and LNWR locomotives for speed, these were undoubtedly one of the best designs of their era and were very highly regarded.

Although somewhat out of chronological sequence, a still larger 4-4-0, the 'R1' class, appeared in 1908. These carried a 5 ft. 6 in. diameter, 'V' class Atlantic boiler, 10 in. piston valves, a saddle-mounted smokebox, an adjustable blastpipe and a GWR-inspired part-sloping grate: W.W. was pally with Churchward. Being quite capable of hauling 400+ ton expresses, they were not far short of being great locomotives, but they emerged a bit too late: Atlantics and 4-6-0s were the motive power of the 20th century. No matter how good an express 4-4-0 might be, it was rather old-hat, even if it incorporated several of the latest design features.

There is no doubt that the 'R1s' were the NER's finest 4-4-0s, and among the very best in Britain. Had they emerged five years earlier, they could have ranked alongside Churchward's 'Cities'. With a bit more speed and stamina, they might have matched Bowen Cooke's 'George the Fifths'. The 'R1s' were undoubtedly very good engines, but were built too late to be great. After all, I am sure that Stanier or Gresley could have designed Britain's finest single-driver locomotive, in the 1930s, but it might have struggled to find enough work to do. That was not quite the case with the 'R1s', for they still gave 40 years' service, but as front-line express locomotives they were more of a backward glance than a thrust into the future.

Now, with the help of Smith, W.W. had begun to guide the NER locomotive department towards meeting the expected needs for express trains in the new century. The 'Rs' were joined on the main line by a type of locomotive that was something of a breakthrough for British railways, signalled a turning point for the NER towards much bigger locomotives, and yet still harked back to good old Victorian traditions. The 'S' class certainly looked mighty engines for their time and, breaking with NER tradition, had outside cylinders. However, they still used slide valves, while the seemingly commodious cab was deceptive as, on the first two engines, it was reduced by two feet in length to accommodate the locomotive on turntables. Fortunately, subsequent engines were not so encumbered.

The 'S' class was the first of W.W's new breed of large engines. So impressive did they appear that No. 2006 won a Gold Medal at the 1900 Paris Exhibition, aptly bidding farewell to the old century while heralding in new standards. They were not, though, a great success in traffic. Intended to haul the heavy expresses from Newcastle-Edinburgh, doubts were soon raised about their suitability for such work. In the latter years of the Grouping era, it was quite apparent that engines with driving wheels of about 6 ft. diameter were more than capable of running at express speeds. Forty years earlier, this was not so. The combination of modestly sized, short-travel slide valves and small wheels made the 'S' class more sloggers than sprinters, and their tenure on the best expresses was short.

All was not lost though, for the 'S' class was deployed to work a variety of duties and became, in effect, Britain's first mixed-traffic locomotives: an un-intended forerunner of, among others, Stanier's 'Black Fives'. More engines were built a few years into the new century with 8¾ in. piston valves, and these were much better suited to their new role. Eventually, the original 'S' class engines had their slide valves so replaced.

It did not take W.W. long to realise that the 'S' class was not going to fulfil expectations, and so he soon attempted to put matters right. The 'S1' class looked the same, seemed the same and even hauled the same services, only somewhat better. These had piston valves, a longer boiler and larger wheels. This combination worked and the 'S1s' were immediately superior to the 'S' class on expresses. Unfortunately, they were still no better than the 'R' class and yet cost more to build and to run. As with other 4-6-0s of the early 20th century, they suffered draughting problems, probably caused by having a too small grate of an inappropriate profile. W.W. was in good company, as even Churchward had struggled to sort out this problem. Though no more 'S1s' were built, W.W. had made the transition to larger locomotives with a moderate degree of success.

Three years later, W.W. tried his hand at the alternative approach for express locomotives then gaining favour in Britain. The 'V' class Atlantics were huge and heavy, but they looked powerful and fast. Powerful they certainly were, but fast they were not, though they coped with the moderately timed services of the day. Despite having piston valves, a large 5 ft. 6 in. diameter boiler and a pair of outside cylinders, the 'V' class was a bit of an agricultural machine. Had it been a rugby player, there would have been no pretensions of a darting, weaving sprint through the defence for the line. No, it would have been a case of head down and simply charge through: more a case of stop that...if you can. Nothing much did. Solid and reliable — if costly in fuel, a 'V' Atlantic typified its age: bigger and therefore better, whether battleship, motor car or steam engine.

W.M. Smith was absent while the 'V' class was designed and kept his distance from it. His way was not exactly that of W.W. Had they been motor car designers, W.W. would probably have replaced a 4-cylinder engine with, say, one of 6-cylinders for more power. Smith would have sought more ingenious ways to improve matters, perhaps by trying double overhead camshafts. W.W. would have produced a Bentley; Smith a Lotus.

Right at the end of his reign, W.W. produced the 'V1' class, an improved Atlantic. This still belonged to the bigger is better mould, despite having smaller cylinders. Just before this, W.W. had produced a 3-cylinder shunting tank, but overlooked this arrangement for his final express design. Not his successor though, for V. Raven used three cylinders, and other improvements, to create the 'Z' class Atlantics. These were what the 'V1s' should have been and they soon gained preference over W.W's engines in the pecking-order. The rustic yeoman strength of the 'V1s' was that of the old century, rather than the finely tuned finesse of the sprinter from the new age.

So, unlike his brother, W.W. produced several successful express passenger locomotives. The hand of W.M. Smith was well to the fore, but it was W.W. who held the ultimate responsibility. The NER tradition of having big, rugged, solid and stolid express locomotives was really that of W.W.: mid-Victorian engineering, with a dash of innovation, extended to its physical limits. W.W. did not lead a revolutionary regime and neither did he build many express locomotives, but from 4-4-0, to 4-6-0 and finally 4-4-2, all did good and reliable work for the railway. He was anything but behind the times for contemporary designs.

Neither was W.W. an autocratic leader who ruled by fear, as were many Locomotive Superintendents, nor was he constantly poking his nose into every aspect of his department's work. He delegated effectively and Smith was certainly tethered to a particularly slack chain. Smith was far from enamoured with his boss's 'V' class Atlantics and set about showing him what could, or should, be done. Two 4-cylinder compound Atlantics emerged, each having a smaller boiler with a Belpaire firebox. The first engine used two sets of Stephenson's link-motion, the second two sets of Walschaert's gear to operate the in-line cylinders. A series of tests confirmed the '4CCs' potential, though at a high cost. A new class might have been in the offing, but Smith died and W.W. took the matter no further.

For all his success in building fine, occasionally outstanding express locomotives, it was his freight and tank locomotives that really mark W.W. out as a Star of Steam. T.W. bequeathed some particularly useful goods designs, that W.W. continued to build, but soon W.W. had produced his 'P', and almost identical 'P1', class 0-6-0s. These were smaller than T.W's 'C' class, but were pretty much go-anywhere goods engines, and though the Durham coalfields were their usual haunts, passenger trains were not entirely unknown to them.

Such engines are not the stuff of legendary reputations, but 190 of these diminutive sloggers — more mule than cart-horse — were valuable dividend earners for the NER. Cheap to build, maintain and operate, versatile and vital, no railway could ask for more and though their numbers were eventually thinned-out, the NER, LNER and finally BR were each in turn grateful recipients of these un-glamorous foot-soldiers.

Likewise the 'P2' and 'P3' classes. This pair of nigh-identical designs differed only in details, though they were altogether bigger beasts than their forebears. Having a 5 ft. 6 in. diameter boiler, the 'P2s' were the biggest 0-6-0s in Britain but, like the 'P3s', were pure goods engines. In later years one might be found wandering aimlessly about with a passenger train in tow, but they earned their corn drawing the heavy coal trains on which the north-east economy thrived. With these various 0-6-0s, W.W. provided the NER with just the right locomotive for the mundane jobs that made this the wealthiest provincial railway in the land.

Even before these large 0-6-0s emerged though, W.W. had been requested to build something even bigger to haul the coal from the mines down to the coast. The turn of the century was clearly a time of change for British locomotive design and, for many, size was everything. The LNWR, under Webb, had long been using compound 0-8-0s for heavy goods work — with great success, and other engineers were beginning to think likewise, though without the complication of compounding. W.W. was no exception, but he also considered a 2-8-0 as an alternative. The real matter for debate was the location and number of cylinders, and while W.W. finally opted for the 0-8-0 path, he also plumped for outside cylinders.

The result was a large, somewhat ungainly locomotive which, for all that, must have been the most welcoming of goods engines, so far as the crews were concerned. The 'T' class, and their fellow 'T1s', were not engines to be trifled with. They might have been a bit top-heavy, unsteady and even rolled about at speed, but who cared? For the work on which they were to be employed, such things did not matter. Sure-footedness, high slogging power and an ability to work in less than salubrious conditions were more important than theoretical niceties, such as saving the odd pound of coal here and there.

One acknowledgement in the direction of technical progress was the inclusion of piston valves in the 'T' class but, howsoever caused, tests in 1906 showed that these were 10% less economical than an engine with good old slide valves. Sure enough, the 'T1s' — of which 50 were built — eschewed the modern for the ancient and reverted to slide valves. All of the 'T' classes were sent abroad in the First World War and then returned to resume their metronomic duties, day in and day out, until BR withdrew the lot well before the end of steam was in sight. Despite that rather unkind reward for their years of unremitting toil, these were outstanding locomotives, so typical of W.W's regime in every way, and invaluable to the NER and its successors.

Unlike many locomotive engineers, W.W. seems to have been less than driven by a desire to build locomotives using as many standard parts as possible. Horses for courses was very much a W.W. trait. Not only did he use a wide variety of locomotive types, but major and minor design variations were an almost constant theme. This is clearly demonstrated with his passenger and mixed-traffic designs, and also his tank engines. Most British railways used these as work-horses and W.W. favoured the good old 0-6-0T, so much so that he designed four classes: add two designs of 0-6-2T and you have quite a variety of similar locomotives. These mostly worked goods, shunting or pilot duties, with only the '290' class finding regular passenger work.

One reason for this lack of passenger work was the outstandingly successful and popular 'O' class 0-4-4Ts. These were used throughout the NER, from sleepy branch to thriving suburbia; hacking over the Pennines or sauntering down to the coast. While they seemed to do a good bit of pottering about, not unlike a fussy maiden aunt in her garden, they could also lift their skirts and really fly, as would Aunt Alice would when young William was about to pluck her favourite rose. True, there is no objective method to show that these were any better than their contemporaries, but NER men swore by them, and not at them.

Indeed, it was to give the 'O' class some relief from the tortures of the Saltburn-Whitby-Scarborough line that W.W. designed the massive 'W' class 4-6-0Ts. The first engines' coal bunker and side tanks were too small to satisfy their voracious appetites, and when this was remedied they became the first NER locomotives fitted with a variable blastpipe. On paper they were more powerful, sure-footed and had a greater capacity for hard work than the diminutive 'O' class but, as we all know, it is when the talking has stopped and the action begins that performances can be measured: that is when they fell down. For a start, the 'W' class never ousted the 'O' class from their sole intended route, while Raven soon rebuilt them as 4-6-2Ts. Even so, they only ever enjoyed a measure of, highly qualified, success.

Finally, as a swansong, and an example of W.W's general horses-for-courses approach to engine design, he built a heavy, 3-cylinder 4-8-0T shunter for the new Erimus Yard on Teeside: the 'X' class. W.W. seems to have been inspired by Robinson's 0-8-4Ts for the GCR, and reached his own conclusion. With all three cylinders in a single casting, divided-drive and piston valves, these locomotives incorporated some modern ideas and signalled the dawn of W.W's brief, final design phase though, as usual, they still looked part of the NER family. W.W. had got the design mixture right once again: nothing far-reaching, just solidly engineered, honest-to-goodness locomotives that earned their living year after year, decade after decade.

Not everyone will consider the Worsdell brothers worthy Stars of Steam. After all, every other engineer in this book has been responsible for at least one truly outstanding locomotive design. Even Webb, for all the disappointments of his compounds, produced two great designs in the 'Precedents' and 'Cauliflowers'. The Worsdells' never quite reached such heights. T.W. was an undoubted innovator and his 'Y14s' and 'C' class designs were invaluable to the GER and NER respectively. He made several other good contributions to both companies' locomotive fleets, in particular to the NER and, one might think, that had he been able to spend longer with the compounds, well...who knows. On the other hand, as with Webb's 3-cylinder compounds, might they not have been seriously flawed in basic design, having only two cylinders?

For all T.W's many good designs, there was to be no jewel in the crown: in other words, no outstanding express passenger locomotive to his credit. Such locomotives seldom contributed massively to profit margins, but his work at Stratford and Gateshead, and particularly his rapid laying down of a good range of basic designs for the NER, marks out his star quality. His work with compounding almost certainly influenced W.M. Smith who, in turn, encouraged S.W. Johnson to design what became Britain's most successful compound locomotives. So, while his employers directly benefited from his work, his influence, by something of a circuitous route, was far-reaching. In more favourable circumstances, so much more might have been achieved as well.

In some respects W.W. had it easy. After all, had not his brother removed all urgent design pressures from Gateshead? Quite possibly, but times changed particularly rapidly during W.W's tenure, and though the NER was never at the cutting-edge of British steam technology, it was right at the front in other respects. Outside cylinders, piston valves, cab design, compounds, sloping firegrates, variable blastpipes, firebox cross water-tubes and so forth, W.W tried all of these — in various combinations, quite apart from building some of the largest locomotives of his day.

Then, right at the end, W.W. began to experiment with superheating and multiple-cylinders. He seems to have been quite undecided, or convinced, about the merits of either, but he had a go before many other engineers did. Though not a rival to Churchward in the ranks of contemporary British locomotive engineers, W.W. was right up there with the best of the rest. But W.W. never quite managed to design a truly great locomotive Yet, he went close — at times very close, and his express engines did all that was required of them: in particular, the magnificent 'R' class excelled in no uncertain terms.

When push comes to shove though, it is the value to the railway that counts most. W.W. gave the NER the modern locomotives it required to remain a highly profitable business, and V. Raven was able to develop further important designs from these. Locomotive building was transferred from Gateshead to Darlington, and W.W. ran a tight, yet happy ship. He also worked extensively on the Tyneside electrification project, that opened in 1904. This was groundbreaking stuff and there were plans afoot to extend the electrification to the ECML. That this took nearly nine decades to come to fruition is no reflection on the extensive and pioneering work undertaken by W.W. and his department.

Revered W.W. was not, highly respected he most certainly was. During his reign as first Locomotive Superintendent and then CME, the NER pioneered a progressive management structure. W.W. ran his department on less stringent lines than was the norm on Britain's railways, and was rather more of a 20th century delegating manager than some of our more renown, autocratic Stars of Steam. And if quality of locomotive output is to be his judgement, then W.W. was not found to be wanting.

The front overhang of W.W's 'T' class 0-8-0s rather gives the impression that light fingers have been at work, and that the front bogie has been removed. If it is a case of handsome is as handsome does though, then W.W. could not be faulted, for these rough-riders were yeoman engines. On the other hand, even the cherished Worsdell cab sits uncomfortably on No. 2122, while its short wheelbase gives it the top-heavy look of those old Hornby clockwork engines. *(NRM)*

It is a matter of opinion as to whether the combined efforts of Daniel and John Viret Gooch, and Patrick and James Stirling, matched those of the Worsdell brothers. In the former two cases, D. Gooch and P. Stirling were undoubted Stars of Steam. Their influence was widespread as a result of their outstanding work and each added by far the greater share to their respective brotherly reputations. The Worsdells were more equal parties. T.W. was an innovator and driving force, W.W. probably the one who had the greatest long-lasting effect: certainly for the NER.

In the final count, the Worsdell brothers had over 1,800 locomotives built to their designs, with some 1,500 of these for the NER: a large proportion of the company's fleet. The NER was also one of the most profitable of Britain's large railways prior to the First World War. As such, the work of its locomotives was shown in the brightest of lights in the balance sheets, right where it really matters. Standardisation for its own sake was not the be-all-and-end-all for the Worsdell brothers, they adopted more of a horses-for-courses approach. For those who revel in the many claims for the standardisation path, Worsdells' locomotives showed that each method had its merits. There was more than one route to success.

As with all of our Stars of Steam, the locomotives of each Worsdell brother, could be instantly recognised. True, a T.W. 'F' class was almost visually identical to W.W's 'M' class, and there were other designs of striking similarity, but W.W. eventually produced much larger, yet equally distinctive locomotives. They were both men of their time and both played a leading role in British steam locomotive engineering. Neither T.W. nor W.W. was a ground-breaking engineer like Churchward, but their combined efforts to produce a thoroughly modern, all-encompassing locomotive stud for the NER was probably more effective than any other British Locomotive Superintendent during their era. About 75% of NER locomotives were of Worsdells' design in 1910.

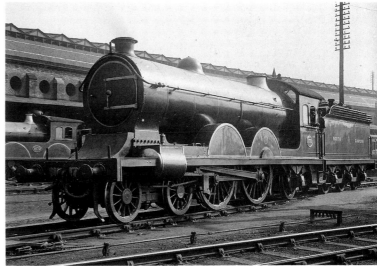

As this picture of 'V' class Atlantic No. 1792 shows, W. Worsdell's later engines were hardly dainty little things. Quite the opposite in fact, and though they were big and powerful steamers, they were certainly not the swiftest of express engines, nor the most economical. Still, built only two years after H.A. Ivatt's last singles, they looked to be of a completely different era and, to all intents and purposes, could pull the pants off anything else on the ECML at the time.

Thirty years later, a visit to the North-East of England would have seen changes. Raven's and then Gresley's locomotives undertook many of the major passenger and goods duties, but there were large geographical areas that still relied exclusively upon Worsdells' locomotives. Almost unbelievably, a decade later, the nascent BR built yet more 'E1' class, or LNER 'J72', tank engines. This really was the ultimate compliment paid to a traditional Worsdell design. Initiated by T.W., as an 'E' class, developed by W.W. and built by BR. Like nearly everything the Worsdell brothers did, they might not have been ultimately great, but they were ideally suited to their intended tasks. No railway could ever ask for more.

T.W. Worsdell's Locomotive Designs

YEAR	CLASS	WHEEL ARRANG'T	CYLINDERS (INCHES)	BOILER PRESSURE	DRIVING-WHEEL DIAMETER	WEIGHT	No. in CLASS
Great Eastern Railway							
1882	G14	2-4-0	18 x 24	160 psi	7 ft.	41 tons	20
1883	Y14	0-6-0	17 x 24	140 psi	4 ft. 1 in.	37T 12 cwt	289
1883	G15	0-4-0T	11 x 15	120 psi	3 ft. 1 in.	21¼ tons	10
1884	G16	4-4-0	H.P.18 x 24 L.P.26 x 24	160 psi	7 ft.	44½ tons	11
1884	M15	2-4-2T	18 x 24	140 psi	5 ft. 4 in.	51½ tons	40
North Eastern Railway							
1886	A	2-4-2T	18 x 24	160 psi	5 ft. 7 in.	53¾ tons	60
1886	C	0-6-0	H.P.18 x 24 L.P.26 x 24	160 psi	5 ft. 1 in.	41¼ tons	171
1886	C1	0-6-0	18 x 24	140 psi	5 ft. 1 in.	42 tons	30
1886	B1	0-6-2T	18 x 24	160 psi	5 ft. 1 in	60 tons	11
1886	B	0-6-2T	H.P.18 x 24 L.P.26 x 24	160 psi	5 ft. 1 in.	58 tons	51
1886	D	2-4-0	H.P.18 x 24 L.P.26 x 24	175 psi	6 ft. 8 in	43 tons	2
1886	F	4-4-0	H.P.18 x 24 L.P.26 x 24	175 psi	6 ft. 8½ in.	46¼ tons	25
1887	E	0-6-0T	16 x 22	140 psi	4 ft. 7½ in.	37T 12 cwt	120
1887	F1	4-4-0	18 x 24	140 psi	6 ft. 8½ in.	46 tons	10
1887	G	2-4-0	17 x 24	160 psi	6 ft. 1 in.	40 tons	20
1888	H	0-4-0T	14 x 20	140 psi	3 ft. 6½ in.	22 tons	22
1888	H1 Crane	0-6-0T	14 x 20	140 psi	3 ft. ½ in.	26½ tons	2
1888	I	4-2-2	H.P.18 x 24 L.P.26 x 24	175 psi	7 ft. 1 in.	44 tons	10
1889	J	4-2-2	H.P.20 x 24 L.P.28 x 24	175 psi	7 ft. 7 in	47 tons	20
1890	K	0-4-0T	11 x 15	140 psi	3 ft.	15½ tons	5

T.W. WORSDELL's PRESERVED LOCOMOTIVES

YEAR	CLASS	RUNNING NUMBERS	TOTAL
Great Eastern Railway			
1883	Y14	BR 65462	1
North Eastern Railway			
1886	C1	BR 65033	1
1888	H	BR 68088 N.E.R. 1310	2

T.W. WORSDELL IN BRIEF

BORN:	14th January 1838, Liverpool.
EDUCATED:	1848-53, Quaker School, Ackworth, Yorks.
	1853, Queenwood College, Hants.
TRAINED:	1855-58, T. Worsdell, Birmingham.
EMPLOYED:	1854, LNWR Crewe Works.
	1858, LNWR Crewe Works.
SENIOR POSITIONS:	1860-65, Manager of engineering company, Birmingham.
	1865-71, Master Mechanic at Altoona Works, Pennsylvania RR, USA
	1871-82, Works Manager, Crewe. LNWR.
	1882-85, Locomotive Superintendent GER.
	1885-90, Locomotive Superintendent NER.
	1890-93, Consultant Engineer, NER.
RETIRED:	1893, Arnside, Westmorland.
HONOURS:	1875, Chairman of Local Board, Crewe.
DIED:	28th June 1916, Arnside.

Over a period of 30 years, the GER built 289 of T.W. Worsdell's 'Y14' class 0-6-0s. They became the LNER's 'J15' class, and about half saw service on BR. True maids-of-all-work, they started out as front line goods engines and usually ended their days on the rural branches. No. 930 runs into Ely with an Edwardian goods train.

Wilson Worsdell's Locomotive Designs

YEAR	CLASS	WHEEL ARRANG'T	CYLINDERS (INCHES)	BOILER PRESSURE	DRIVING-WHEEL DIAMETER	WEIGHT	No. in CLASS
1882	G14	2-4-0	18 x 24	160 psi	7 ft.	41 tons	20
1891	L	0-6-0T	19 x 24	160 psi	4 ft. 7½ in.	46¾ tons	10
1892	M1	4-4-0	19 x 26	180 psi	7 ft. 1 in.	51 tons	20
1893	M	4-4-0	H.P.19 x 26 L.P.28 x 26	200 psi	7 ft. 1 in.	52 tons	1
1893	N	0-6-2T	19 x 26	160 psi	5 ft. 1 in.	56½ tons	20
1894	O	0-4-4T	18 x 24	160 psi	5 ft. 1 in.	54¼ tons	110
1894	P	0-6-0	18 x 24	160 psi	4 ft. 7 in.	39 tons	70
1894	190 (reb)	2-2-4T	16 x 22	160 psi	6 ft. 6½ in.	48¼ tons	2
1896	Q	4-4-0	19½ x 26	175 psi	7 ft. 1 in.	50 tons	30
1896	Q1	4-4-0	20 x 26	175 psi	7 ft. 7 in.	51 tons	2
1897	H2	0-6-0T	14 x 20	140 psi	3 ft. 6½ in.	27 tons	3
1898	E1	0-6-0T	17 x 24	140 psi	4 ft. 1 in.	38¾ tons	75+38
1898	P1	0-6-0	18½ x 26	160 psi	4 ft. 7 in.	40 tons	120
1898	3CC	4-4-0	H.P.19 x 26 L.P.20 x 24	200 psi	7 ft. 1 in.	54 tons	1
1899	290	0-6-0T	17 x 22	140 psi	4 ft. 1 in.	42 tons	60
1899	R	4-4-0	19 x 26	200 psi	6 ft. 10 in.	55 toms	60
1899	S	4-6-0	(o)20 x 26	200 psi	6 ft. 1 in.	64¼ tons	40
1900	S1	4-6-0	(o)20 x 26	200 psi	6 ft. 8 in.	67 tons	5
1901	T + T1	0-8-0	(o)20 x 26	175 psi	4 ft. 7 in.	62 tons	90
1902	U	0-6-2T	18½ x 26	160 psi	4 ft. 7 in.	57¾ tons	20
1902	66 (reb)	2-2-4T	H.P.13 x 20 L.P.18¾ x 20	175 psi	5 ft. 8 in.	45 tons	1
1903	957	2-2-4T	17 x 22	160 psi	6 ft. 1 in.	51 tons	1
1903	V	4-4-2	(o)20 x 28	200 psi	6 ft. 10 in.	73 tons	10
1904	P2	0-6-0	18½ x 26	180 psi	4 ft. 7 in.	48 tons	50
1906	P3	0-6-0	18½ x 26	180 psi	4 ft. 7 in.	50 tons	105
1906	4CC	4-4-2	H.P.14¼ x 26 L.P.22 x 26	225 psi	7 ft. 1 in.	74 tons	2
1907	W	4-6-0T	19 x 26	170 psi	5 ft. 1 in.	69 tons	10
1908	R1	4-4-0	19 x 26	225 psi	6 ft. 10 in.	60 tons	10
1909	X	4-8-0T	(3)18 x 26	175 psi	4 ft. 7 in.	85T 8 cwt	15
1910	V1	4-4-2	(o)19½ x 26	180 psi	6 ft. 10 in.	76¼ tons	10

WILSON WORSDELL's PRESERVED LOCOMOTIVES

YEAR	CLASS	RUNNING NUMBERS	TOTAL
1902 (reb.)	66	66 'Aerolite'	1
1892	M	1621	1
1898	E1	B.R. 69023	1

WILSON WORSDELL IN BRIEF

BORN: 7th September 1850, Crewe.
EDUCATED: 1860-66, Quaker School, Ackworth, Yorks.
EMPLOYED: 1866, LNWR Crewe Works.
1871, LNWR Crewe Works.
1872-6, LNWR, Ass. Foreman, Stafford Running Sheds.
TRAINED: 1867-71, Altoona Works, Pennsylvania RR.
SENIOR
POSITIONS: 1876, Foreman, Bushbury Running Sheds, LNWR.
1877-83, Foreman Chester Running Sheds, LNWR.
1883-90, Ass. Mechanical Engineer, Gateshead Works, NER.
1890-1902, Locomotive Superintendent, NER.
1902-1910, CME, NER.
RETIRED: 31st August 1910.
HONOURS: Council member IME.
JP in Co. Durham.
DIED: 14th April 1920, Ascot.

W. Worsdell's 'P1' class was a modestly improved version of his earlier 'P' class. Although used primarily on goods trains, these engines often undertook the occasional passenger duty, especially in the summer. Some were rebuilt by V. Raven and many saw service on BR. Somewhat earlier, No. 2037 depicts not only the good, clean lines of late-19th century design.

PATRICK STIRLING
The Legend

Perhaps it is a sign of our increased leisure time that some people like nothing better than to compile a pecking-order for what are, essentially, non-competitive activities. Thus, we find Mark Knopfler or Eric Clapton described as the finest guitarists in the world. Really, how on earth can anyone know that? More likely, it is that either Knopfler or Clapton is the compiler's personal favourite — no more, no less.

Several years ago, I cycled round Spain and played with many guitarists, whose sheer ability would leave most rock guitarists looking like a young schoolboy thrust into an England football international, at Wembley. As those Spanish guitarists do not sell millions of records though, so they are unknown — Knopfler or Clapton, pah. It is so much easier if a truly competitive measurement can be made, such as holding the world record for running the mile. Break that and you put an end to all such arguments.

It is no different when judgements are made over who is the best footballer. That, again, is rather an emotive decision and is really all a matter of personal taste, and so it is with railways. As the High Speed Trains mesmerised the public in the 1970s, and Gresley's 'A4s' did likewise in the 1930s, so the great 8 ft. singles of P. Stirling gained themselves unparalleled attention in the last three decades of the 19th century: only even more so. Yet nobody in their right mind would claim Stirling's singles to be better performers than either of the other two.

Mind you, at the time those grand, galloping thoroughbreds were not only responsible for hauling the fastest train service in the world, but they were the quickest mode of propulsion then known to man, and by some not inconsiderable margin. The nearest competitors to railways were the bicycle or the horse and carriage, and while today's airliner can travel at nearly 10 times the speed of your car, you might as well be sitting in a cinema. On a late-19th century GNR express, you soon felt and knew about every single mile per hour.

Quite logically then, the designer of the engines that hauled the world's fastest trains must be about the best there is, yes?. If the engines associated almost exclusively with those expresses were themselves uniquely impressive, well, the whole matter was beyond question. Patrick Stirling was surely the finest steam locomotive engineer in Britain and, by implication, the world. The proof could be seen any day of the week. No other locomotives ran quite like his great 8 ft. singles, and certainly nothing could match them as a dynamic spectacle. The visual effect of the great, whirring driving wheel and its outside motion, has no equal in the world of railways; an 'A4' on the Silver Jubilee, or an original liveried HST might have run it close, very close indeed, but not — I fear — quite close enough.

That was the impact Stirling and the GNR made on both the general public and railway enthusiasts alike. Strange though it might now seem, but Stirling's diminutive singles were the front-runners in the field when railways were at the cutting-edge of technology. There was nothing like a Stirling 8 ft. single at speed. Take away all the imagery though, which portrayed those great engines were most definitely larger than life, and what is one left with? Was Stirling still the best? This proposition is no different to judging Churchward without his 'Stars', Stanier minus the 'Duchesses', or by deleting the 'A4s' from Gresley's locomotive portfolio. Of course, one cannot ignore these locomotives; the very idea is about as daft as considering how great an artist was de Vinci, the Mona Lisa excepted. On the other hand, this approach does rather level the playing field, and allows us to take a potentially more accurate look at just how good were these locomotive engineers at their all-round jobs.

The steam locomotive has never been subject to exact physical calculations. Each time the ideal is reached with one of its many intertwined aspects, whoops, another goes all awry. Even when the best all-round design compromise was reached, there was still the matter of maintenance, the quality of the coal and water and finally, assuming everything was in the locomotive's favour, there was the crew. If one happened to get out of bed on the wrong side, any applecart could easily be upset, and a locomotive's performance could be gutless.

Until well into the 20th century, locomotive design was based more on practical experience than anything approaching pure research. If more power was needed, then critical components were often simply enlarged. In general, a handful of engines would be built, run in service and fettled until all was well: then production would begin. P. Stirling did not produce one design that was even remotely poor, for the GNR. Yet he relied entirely on his previous experience, that of his staff and a fair bit of hit-and-miss experimenting.

In comparison with the exactitude required by, say, aeroplane and Grand Prix racing engineers today, Stirling and his like were but one up from the village blacksmith. Not only was it a wonder that the steam locomotive performed the feats it did, but practical, basic mechanics and common sense counted for rather more than engineering ingenuity. Stirling played safe and won: his one wild card was carefully evolved, and achieved rewards — if truth be told — far beyond expectations. It was hardly a gamble, but then again, railway engineering was an ultra-conservative world, not one for fly-by-nights.

That last description would be anathema to any of our Stars of Steam in any case. Stirling's rise was steady and methodical, almost as if it were planned — out and out supporters might even suggest ordained! Yet another locomotive engineer who heralded from a clerical family, there was little doubt of the direction that young Stirling was going to take in life. For three generations, members of his family made a mark in mechanical engineering, including his Presbyterian, god-fearing father. Eventually, his younger brother, James, and his son, Matthew, both became Locomotive Superintendents, of the GSWR and SER, and HBR respectively. Such a distinguished triumvirate sets the Stirling family well to the fore among locomotive engineering dynasties.

Never mind the quality, feel the width. Contemporary photographs of Stirling's GSWR engines are hardly common-place and this one lacks any information as to a location or occasion. It was taken in 1858 and shows a '2' class 2-2-2 single, No. 3, in what is clearly a posed picture. From such humble beginnings legendary greatness was to emerge. *(NRM)*

P. Stirling was apprenticed at his uncle's Dundee Foundry. There is just the merest possibility that he met the tyro D. Gooch, who worked there in 1835, and already a rising star. The possibility that two future Stars of Steam, from opposite ends of Britain, worked together at a Scottish marine engineers, emphasises the fledgling nature of the industry in those days.

Apprenticeship over, Stirling took to the road for a decade during which he worked for several well known engineering companies, as often as not involved in marine work. This included a spell as the Locomotive Superintendent of the Caledonian & Dunbartonshire Rly.: a very minor affair, despite its grandiose title. All this time, he gathered experience and ideas and, during a short spell at Hawthorn's, he found himself working on locomotives for the GSWR, who were regular customers. Stirling's work at Hawthorn's possibly helped to clinch his appointment as the GSWR Locomotive Superintendent, in 1853.

At that time, and for most of Stirling's 13 years' tenure, the GSWR was little more than a local railway that served Galloway. The main line ran from Glasgow to Ayr, via Paisley, and meandered from Kilmarnock down Annandale to Carlisle: it was certainly no rival to the CR at that stage. Locomotives were bought in, and Glasgow's Crook St. Works were soon deemed to be totally inadequate. One of Stirling's first tasks was not only to select a site for a completely new works, but to plan its layout and to oversee its completion. Within three years, Kilmarnock Works was open, and the first locomotive was constructed in 1857.

Stirling's work for the GSWR is not well documented and occasionally seems full of contradictions and changes of tack. However, compared with Ramsbottom and his 'DX' class goods engines, on the LNWR, Stirling was dealing in peanuts. As early as 1855, three separate designs had entered service: a passenger 2-2-2; a Crampton 0-4-0, for goods and mineral work — that was, by some considerable distance, far from being a roaring success; and a goods 0-6-0. All had outside cylinders.

Two years later, the first locomotives emerged from Kilmarnock: the '2' class passenger engines. These had Allan's, Crewe-type outside cylinders, a format then widely favoured,

and 12 were built by 1860. A singleton 2-4-0 goods engine soon followed — the appropriately named 'Galloway', but this type was not developed further, until he joined the GNR. In 1858, another peep into the future came with Stirling's first 0-4-2, of the '32' class, again with outside cylinders. None of these engines ever had the opportunity to really demonstrate their prowess as great designs, and none — in all probability — ever were. As each, in turn, was improved in basic design, one must assume that Stirling was still finding his feet, although at quite some speed.

Then, in 1860, Stirling introduced the inside cylinder '22' class 0-4-2: this was his first design to use the internal perforated steam-collecting pipe, in place of the dome — a renown Stirling feature. Stirling is also usually assumed to have favoured outside cylinders but, surprisingly, the opposite was true. On the GNR only his 8 ft. singles had them, so the '22' class was a fore-taste of the future, although Stirling still built non-express engines with outside cylinders for the GSWR. He was still experimenting, and while he made errors, he was not without his successes either.

During the 1860s, Stirling seems to have been unsure whether to settle on inside or outside cylinders. That was not the case for express engines though, and the '40' class 2-2-2 was, effectively, a domeless version of his successful '2' class. They remained on main line passenger work for the next 20 years while, just before he left, Stirling produced an improved version: the '45' class. Then, with the '131' class 0-4-2, he first introduced the pull-out smokebox regulator and, what became recognised as, his traditional profile cab. Initially, this had port-hole side windows, later used on his first GNR singles.

Though little is known about the performance and reliability of Stirling's GSWR locomotives, he established very definite trends that were developed and consistently improved. For express engines, outside cylinder 2-2-2s; for mixed-traffic and goods, 0-4-2s with both inside and outside cylinders; and for general goods, initially outside, but then traditional inside cylinder 0-6-0s, supplemented by 0-4-0s. The later versions of each type served the GSWR well until the latter years of the century, while all bar the 0-4-0s were to be revamped when Stirling himself moved south.

Quite apart from his locomotive designs, Stirling more than simply cut his engineering teeth at the GSWR Kilmarnock Works was established as a locomotive manufactory, while repairs, overhauls and design offices completed a comprehensive establishment. From the bottom up, this was all Stirling's responsibility. Its value to the company was enormous when, from the mid-1870s, it began to rival the hitherto dominant CR, through its connections with the MR. The energy of Stirling's formative years as a Locomotive Superintendent was to leave the little Galloway company rather better prepared for a dynamic future than it ever had a right to expect.

There is, if not a veil of mystery, at least something of a smoke-screen as to why the successful A. Sturrock and the GNR came to part company, in 1866. Being a Locomotive Superintendent, he was handsomely paid, and had struck lucky by marrying an heiress. At the relatively early age of 50, Sturrock renounced his empire and settled down to the life of the country squire: he lived a further 42 years. Or was there more to it than that?

Sturrock was Gooch's Works Manager, at Swindon, and obviously played a major role in the building and running of the finest locomotives in the world. As such he was a major coup for the fledgling GNR, when appointed in 1850, and endowed the company with many fine locomotives, and established Doncaster Works. By the 1860s, the GNR had one of the better locomotive fleets in Britain, but things then began to go awry.

First, Sturrock's innovative steam-tender 0-6-0 goods engines were costly, unreliable and not exactly popular with the crews, while his express 2-4-0s left more than a little to be desired. His star was on the wane and, despite its grandiose title, the GNR was not a wealthy railway: it could ill afford so many failures. Was Sturrock pushed, did he jump, or did he stick two fingers firmly up at the board?

Stirling was initially appointed as Sturrock's Assistant Locomotive Superintendent. Did he expect to take over in the very near future, or was it purely a career move? In the latter case, it was an odd choice, as Sturrock might have upwards of 20 years' work ahead of him, and while the GNR was undoubtedly bigger than the GSWR, his position was inferior. By October of 1866 the matter was settled in Stirling's favour: Sturrock finally departed in December. All appeared to be cut-and-dried.

Given the eventual scale of Stirling's success at the GNR, to say nothing of his earlier work, it is surprising to find that he was appointed on fully three years' probation. Images of Stirling as an old, hardened task-master — in the mould of Webb and D. Drummond — are hard to dispel, but he was only 46 when he arrived at Doncaster, though relatively experienced and successful, and in the prime of his engineering life. He was clearly a man of great drive, promise and substance, and yet here he was placed on a lengthy probation which, incidentally, was not transmuted into a permanent position in advance. Was this the board's reaction to the disappointment with Sturrock? Of course, we will never know, but it serves to remind us that Locomotive Superintendents, even those of the stature of Stirling and Sturrock, were but company servants, not policy makers.

The GNR, on the other hand — and despite its title, was some way short of being the leading railway in the land. True enough, it was one of only two companies that hauled the important and prestigious Anglo-Scottish trains out of London, but whereas the rival LNWR took them almost three-quarters of the way, the GNR did not even convey them half-distance. In fact, although its locomotives hauled the trains to York, the railway itself never reached that city, running along NER metals for the last 25 miles or so.

Thirty years later, shortly after Stirling died, the GNR's position had even deteriorated, in a direct comparison with rival railways. By then, the equally grandly titled GWR had reached Penzance, built the pioneering Severn Tunnel and was widely extending its tentacles. The GER, despite being hemmed into East Anglia, had a greater route mileage and conveyed far more passengers than did the GNR. The MR, with its Settle & Carlisle line, had joined in the Scottish jamboree, and left the GNR positively trailing in route mileage, and much else besides. No, despite appearances, Stirling had not joined a railway at the very front-rank, and it was to slide slowly backwards in the decades to come. In terms of main line services though, the GNR was soon to usurp even the Broad Gauge GWR at the top of the pile. A bold management policy of running fast trains needed an enterprising Locomotive Superintendent to produce the essential locomotives. In that respect, Stirling was to be supreme.

The GNR was also something of a sober railway. Its apple-green livery and teak coaches, though a pleasing combination, lacked the visual impact and elegance of, say, the Royal blue and teak of the GER, the crimson lake of the MR, or even the rich black locomotives and purple and white coaches of the LNWR. Whereas some railways appeared to run their services irrespective of the cost, that was never the case with the GNR nor, incidentally, with the LNWR. At no stage was Stirling ever allowed to build all the locomotives he desired or deemed necessary for the job. That he never resigned, particularly during his last years, suggests he thoroughly enjoyed his work, and also that, perhaps, his demands were a little on the high side.

For most of Stirling's time at the GNR, the country was engulfed in the so-called Great Depression. This was mild compared with the ravages and depravities of the Thatcher and Major years, especially on the areas of heavy industry, but there were similarities. For example, if one was in work, all could be very pleasant indeed, thank you. If not... Also, the population rose remorselessly, and while wages did not generally increase, prices failed to hold their own. Neither was the Great Depression a time of mass travel, though the seeds were being sown. Unfortunately for the railways, most of this new custom travelled third Class. The cost of labour, rolling stock and fuel was the same though, despite the lower revenue per passenger/mile, so cuts had to be made, and where better than in fluid capital expenditure, of which locomotives were a major item?

So, considering all the various needs of the GNR, was Stirling the right man for the job, or should the directors have looked closer to home, say to Crewe or Swindon? Considering the tight shoe-string on which Stirling worked at Kilmarnock, and in particular his expansion of a select few standard designs, it seems that his appointment was a very shrewd move. Given his lengthy period of probation, it began to look as though the GNR board really was to have its cake and to eat every last crumb.

Not surprisingly, the GNR required a greater range of locomotives than did the GSWR. For a start, the GNR ran the fastest standard gauge expresses, even in the 1860s, while it carried coal, building materials and other general provisions into the rapidly expanding capital city. It also had its fair share of branch line and cross-country traffic, plus a foothold in London's ever-growing suburban traffic. In short, the GNR was an ambitious and comprehensive railway system, with all the attendant benefits and problems.

Stirling was no miracle-maker. He faced a three-fold set of

The GNR was not all one long blaze of single-driver glory though. Greyhound No. 12, of the '103' series, built in 1887, arrives at Hitchin with the 2.30 p.m. ex Kings Cross. These fine engines were equally at home working main line semi-fast and outer suburban trains, or even goods trains. Fast and versatile, they were great favourites of the engine crews. Despite this, and being a large and very useful class of engines, none of Stirling's 0-4-2 s made it into LNER hands.

The scenery has changed as much as the train in the intervening century; beyond comprehension. This was the sight which so captivated 19th century railway enthusiasts, and no wonder. One of the final batch of Stirling's great 8 ft. singles, No. 1004, thunders north with an express; the typical plume of smoke showing that the engine was not out for a gentle afternoon's stroll. The passengers might not have been quite so enthralled by it all, in the fairly primitive 6 and 8-wheel coaches, but had the consolation of knowing that they were riding on the fastest railway in the world. No. 1004 was built in 1895 and scrapped in 1914.

problems on taking charge at Doncaster. First, there was a vital need for more locomotives. New designs were imperative, but much could be achieved by judiciously rebuilding older engines, while an urgent remedy was needed for Sturrock's steam-tender 0-6-0s. Secondly, general repairs tied up too many locomotives: improvements in maintenance would reduce the need for new engines. Finally, the GNR purchased its locomotives from specialist manufacturers, but Stirling preferred to build his own and Doncaster Works was an ideal manufactory. The all-round potential of the GNR, and solving these three problems, were to demand much of Stirling's attention for his first few years. All this with the axe still, potentially, swinging over him!

At that stage, Stirling was far from being the patriarch he eventually became. He put all his energies into the work and, not surprisingly, sought familiar solutions. Within three years, even before his probation had expired, Stirling had set out his stall that, with one outstanding exception, was to serve him until the end. Quite apart from rebuilding some of Sturrock's locomotives, Stirling produced a general goods 0-6-0, an 0-4-2 for semi-fast and stopping passenger — and fast goods services, a semi-fast passenger 2-4-0, a shunting and light goods 0-6-0ST, and an 0-4-2T for suburban passenger trains. In addition, and to no great surprise, a single-driver was designed for the important, yet relatively sparse, express services.

Not only did these designs share many common components, but the apparent indecisiveness of his GSWR days gave way to an assuredness that was never to waver. All these designs had inside cylinders, a domeless boiler, the pull-out regulator and the familiar Stirling cab. Minor changes apart, each was steadily evolved, with the 0-4-2T being displaced by the more appropriate 0-4-4T. The rate of progress was measured, yet steadfast. There were no cataclysmic mistakes, just a continued and constant improvement. Over the years, cylinders were enlarged, boiler pressures raised, and the boilers themselves very modestly increased, but each in line together.

This endless, yet seamless progress was modest, even by conservative engineering standards, but it worked. Naturally, there were exceptions, such as the '174' heavy goods engines. These were too powerful for the capacities of the main line, and their long coal trains caused mayhem when diverted via Lincoln. Then there was the diminutive '501' class specifically built for light branches, such as that from Essendine-Stamford. As for the rest of the system, from rural Lincolnshire to the hills of the West Riding and from the Midlands coalfields to suburban London, it was worked by a thoroughly uniform, standard — perhaps even bland — fleet of locomotives. And very successfully too.

Stirling had found a successful formula and honed it until it worked to perfection. Take the 2-4-0s, for example. Eventually, these worked throughout the GNR, though were most emphatically not front-line express engines: those prestige duties were ever the preserve of singles, either Stirling's or Sturrock's. Contemporary opinion was that a Webb 'Jumbo' was the faster, if not better engine. Quite so. Webb's reputation was built on those magnificent machines which, in any case, were most certainly express engines. No, Stirling's 2-4-0s were the unsung heroes for which any railway has an almost insatiable appetite and need.

So, not for them a London-Manchester flyer, or one of the Scotch expresses. No, merely a semi-fast to Peterborough, or a Grantham-Derby cross-country train. Perhaps a spot of goods work or, say, a fish train from Grimsby. Then, like a rock group that aspires to a national tour, but only ever becomes a support act, the cushioning effect of a West Riding express, on the slow part of the journey from Doncaster-Leeds. Only rarely did Stirling's 2-4-0s ever take centre stage. They were part of the chorus line — never the star of the show, but they did their work effectively and efficiently. Perhaps not loved, nor readily appreciated, they earned the profits and wherever the GNR pushed its tentacles in the coming decades, a 2-4-0 was sure to follow.

As for the various 0-4-2s, theirs was an even more mundane life, yet they did not pass unnoticed. The first locomotive built at Doncaster Works was humble No. 18, and further 0-4-2s emerged each year until 1876, when fully 58 were delivered — mostly built by outside manufacturers. The last engine to this basic design, that first appeared in 1860, arrived just two months before Stirling's death, in 1895. Oh yes, these were certainly a great success, in every way.

Modestly developed and improved, as were all Stirling's standard designs, these 0-4-2s mostly worked the wide variety of cross-country and stopping passenger services. Trundling round Lincolnshire, wending their way across the Midlands, or blasting their way over the West Riding's hills. This nondescript, hum-drum diet was enlivened with occasional excursion trains, full of excited children, to Skegness or Mablethorpe. Of even more importance, though, was their work on the fast goods trains, but in reality they seemed capable of turning a wheel to most tasks; the true all-rounders every railway needs.

However, it was their work on long-distance London suburban trains that gained the 0-4-2s their nickname 'Greyhounds', and their deserved reputation as fast and free steamers. Stirling used the same valves and ports for cylinders of all sizes, throughout his reign: this was, remember, the era of a suck-it-and-see approach to engineering. Thus, locomotives with smaller cylinders tended to be freer runners, and the 0-4-2s cylinder diameter was only 24 in. They were probably not over-stretched until the 1890s, but then, as train weights rose, so their pyrotechnics grew to ever-more dramatic displays. No Victorian engines were more flamboyant performers than the 'Greyhounds', but such fireworks only enhanced their reputation and popularity. Even the puritanical could raise a smile at a 'Greyhound' going all out.

On the whole, goods engines tend to be, well, goods engines. Their work is mundane, rarely performed in the public eye, and is seldom appreciated by the public, nor serenaded by the railway enthusiast. Yet, for many railways, the slow, occasionally arduous, and certainly unremitting work undertaken by the goods engines, earned a greater share of the profits than all the other activities put together.

Stirling, true both to his previous experience and the general practice of the time, chose the wholly orthodox, inside cylinder 0-6-0 format for goods trains. These might include long trains of loose-coupled coal wagons up to London, or perhaps general merchandise trundling round the Midlands. Most such engines had wheels of about 5 ft. diameter, but Stirling later produced a couple of classes with still smaller wheels, mostly for working the steeper grades of the West Riding. None of these became classics, like Webb's 'Cauliflowers' or Dean's renown 'Goods'. No, once again, uniformity and total reliability, almost anonymity, was Stirling's hallmark. Relatively simple efficiency, without the frills. The GNR board could not have expected more.

As for goods and shunting tanks, Stirling developed three basic types: the '392' class, initially for East Midlands work; the restricted height '396' class, built for the NLR lines to Blackwall and working in tight surroundings; and the general purpose '494' class. The latter class was divided into six separate series, each with modest differences but, as with other Stirling designs, these have been grouped in the one class. Thus, the '606' series had short frames for working in tight yards, while the '854' series had extended frames to hold an enlarged bunker, and was the first to receive a fully enclosed cab.

Whatever their minor differences, all these saddle-tanks were general shunting engines. While they occasionally met the public, when on duty as a station pilot, theirs was usually a life spent out of sight, out of mind, in yards and on docks all round the system, even acting as bankers in the West Riding. Occasionally, just very occasionally, one might do a little light passenger work, as though having an annual holiday, while the odd trip round London was not entirely unknown. Distinctive — in the Stirling mould, efficient and engines for all seasons, these were variations on another ideally suited standard design, but one still lacking that indefinable flair.

Indeed the only real change during Stirling's three decades on the GNR, came with his suburban tank engines. That, more than anything, illustrates just how successful he was. Initially, he tried the '126' class 0-4-2 well tank for London suburban services. Nearly all were fitted with condensing apparatus, and they spent about 30 years' wandering about the capital's branches before being banished to the Home Counties.

Clearly though, something with a little extra oomph was needed as traffic developed, so Stirling evolved this design into an 0-4-4T. The addition of a bogie apart, the major difference was the abandonment of the well between the frames: the water was carried in a tank beneath the coal bunker. As with their smaller brethren, engines of this design were built for nine out of ten years from 1872 — another Stirling standard?

Unusually, this proved not to be the case. In 1881, the similar, yet distinctly smaller, '629' class — all two of them — entered service on the Stamford-Essendine branch, and the following year came another small-wheeled version. The '658' class was certainly not bantam-weights, but were generally intended for more arduous work in the West Riding, with a few condenser-fitted examples for London. With these, Stirling changed tack once again, and replaced the under-bunker water tank with tanks either side of the boiler, in the more orthodox position. Even then, not all engines in the class had tanks of the same capacity. Still later, the '766' class was built primarily for London suburban duties, and their no-nonsense, rustic power earned them the nickname 'Dread-

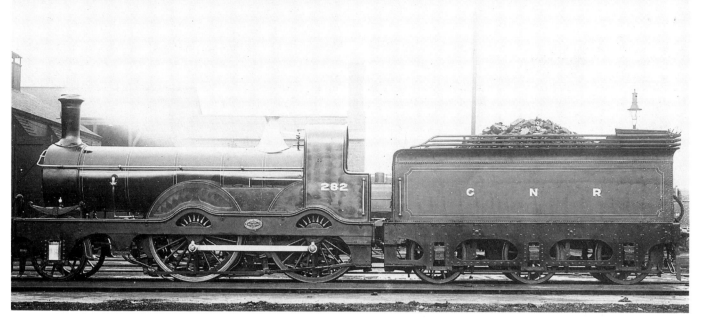

Stirling's 2-4-0s were not express engines, and seldom got an opportunity to hog the limelight. As such, they gained a sluggish reputation that might not have been entirely justified. Secondary passenger work was their lot, yet they were certainly distinguished, as No. 282 of the '280' series, built in 1867, shows to particularly good effect.

noughts'. They worked London's suburban services for less than two decades, but that was a time of much change and they later found themselves moved to the Midlands or Yorkshire.

This round-up of Stirling's locomotives, of relatively few basic types, shows just how he thought in terms of economy. Why should a design not undertake a range of tasks? Stirling's could, and quite often did while, as can be seen from the list of designs, major components were used almost across the board. Yet, while all these might just about confirm Stirling as a Star of Steam, this hardly equates with his legendary reputation.

To evaluate Stirling's work without considering his various single-drivers, is akin to having a Christmas cake without any decoration. Stirling relied on two basic types of single: the inside cylinder 2-2-2, a combination of Sturrock's and his own work at the GSWR — this was the cake's marzipan; and the great 8 ft. 4-2-2s — that were both the icing and the copious decoration.

The first engines of the '6' class had port-hole windows in the cab-side, as introduced on the GSWR. With a 4 ft. diameter domeless boiler, these were faster runners and yet better hill-climbers than the 2-4-0s. Accordingly, these 7 ft. singles bore the brunt of the increasing and improving main line passenger service out of Kings Cross, alongside Sturrock's original and rebuilt engines, for about a decade. This was a not unimpressive service for the early 1870s, with nine trains running to York and beyond, at an average of just 4 hrs. 30 mins., while seven trains went to Leeds and others to Manchester. Average running speeds were generally just below 50 mph, better than most railways at that time — except for the Broad Gauge GWR. Loads were assuredly light, but these first singles forged the path for the GNR to push to the top of the British express-speeds league.

After the 1870s, these engines were usefully employed on fast passenger services from London to Lincolnshire and Cambridge, but in the 1890s, some were given domed boilers

by Ivatt, and enjoyed a last fling on the main line, both as train engines and pilots. These were a very fine beginning for Stirling, but there was much more to come.

In 1870, Stirling built a one-off locomotive to utilise the 7 ft. 7 in. driving wheels from Sturrock's famed 4-2-2 No. 215: No. 92 was otherwise identical to the other '6' class engines. It also worked expresses in the 1870s, but was reboilered in the 1880s and, as a Peterborough-based engine, still worked turn and turn about with Stirling's later 2-2-2s and 8 ft. singles for the rest of the century. Unfortunately, as the 20th century dawned, so rising train weights forced No. 92 off into Lincolnshire and rural Leicester, and its last two years were spent on rather less exacting and exciting work.

Then, from 1870 onwards, Stirling concentrated on building new express locomotives to his 4-2-2 design. This was, of course, the age of the Great Depression and by the mid-1880s further express engines were required, though preferably at a lower initial cost than the majestic 8 ft. singles. So, in 1885, Stirling produced an updated and enlarged version of his earlier singles. The '232' class featured 7 ft. 7 in. driving wheels, a larger boiler and were otherwise generally that bit bigger and better engines than the '6' class. Their frames and boilers were made of steel, rather than wrought iron, while they had larger steam and exhaust ports than the contemporary 4-2-2s, which aided their free-running characteristics.

Only two engines were built before, a year later, a still larger version emerged. The '234' class was fitted with the longer boiler used by contemporary 4-2-2s, and soon demonstrated that they were in no way inferior to the bigger engines. Still later, the almost identical '871' series emerged, with a slightly reduced heating surface area, while the six engines built in 1894 — Britain's last 2-2-2s — reverted to 18.5 in. cylinders.

All these locomotives were, as near dammit, visually identical, and worked in the same links as the 4-2-2s. Little or no apparent distinction was made as to the type of engine used on the best expresses, while in the 1888 Races it was a new 2-2-2 that made the fastest timings on the GNR. Without a doubt, some enginemen reckoned the 2-2-2s to be the faster engines, and the highest recorded speed achieved by one, 86 mph, was 2 mph faster than the best by an 8 ft. single.

In all probability, the 2-2-2s were as economical to run as were the 8 ft. singles and, being cheaper to build, seemed a better investment. That they did not appear quite so often on the leading expresses was more to do with the numerical supremacy of the 4-2-2s, than any better performance. Early in the 20th century, the 2-2-2s were removed from the heavy expresses, but when the GNR introduced several fast and light trains, they enjoyed a further share of the action, along with the 4-2-2s of both Stirling and Ivatt. Even as late as 1910, four engines, reboilered by Ivatt, were inserted into a dedicated link to haul the 2.15 p.m. Leeds/Bradford flyer, which ran the 156 miles from Kings Cross to Doncaster in 165 minutes. This all-too-brief interlude was their final swansong, and the last of these outstanding express locomotives was scrapped at the end of 1913.

All of which brings us to Stirling's undoubted masterpiece. The 8 ft. singles were not the product of an inspired vision. They were evolved from his GSWR work, his early GNR singles and the need for stability at the front of a fast engine, given the less than billiard table smoothness of the permanent way. As ever, the attention to detail and care with the appearance created yet another design so clearly in the Stirling mould. It was, though, the outside cylinders, and the cutting away of the splasher — simply to aid inspection — that transformed a design that was exceedingly fine, into a design that was truly great — at least visually. Just look at any picture of an 8 ft. single in action, and it soon becomes clear why contemporaries waxed ever-more lyrical in their praise for these great engines. For great they most assuredly were, perhaps even being the very greatest locomotives of the 19th century.

The late-Victorian age was a time when engineering and art were ever-more intertwined, and nowhere was this more proudly displayed than with steam locomotives. Dean's 4-2-2s, with their deep frames and tall polished dome, had all the rugged beauty of snow-capped mountains: say, the Cuillins of Skye on a rare crystal-clear day. Johnson's elegant 'Spinners' embodied the symmetrical, picture-like quality redolent of a Capability Brown landscape: the almost motionless vista from a great country house, say, Castle Ashby. For Stirling's 4-2-2s though, they combined the beauty of the formal landscape with all the dynamic action of a great cascade in full flow, like that at Chatsworth House. The whirring action of the wheel and motion, and the invariable plume of smoke, undoubtedly showed these as working engines, yet they were patricians, not plebeians. Not only did they haul the fastest train service in the world but, to the archetype middle-class Victorian

standing on a suburban platform, an express hauled by a roaring 8 ft. single looked and sounded the world-beaters that they were. Mr. Pooter would believe nothing else, and it made him feel mighty proud. Stirling's 8 ft. singles would have been the modern marketing-man's dream. In 19th century Britain, they were a publicity god-send for the GNR.

Designed to haul trains of 150 tons at average speeds of 51 mph, enough 8 ft. singles had been built by the mid-1870s to have a considerable impact on the GNR's timetable. For three decades, this basic design formed the backbone of the locomotive fleet that hauled not only the world's fastest express service, but the fastest daily scheduled train in the world. By 1885, trains ran the 105 miles from Grantham-Kings Cross at 53.5 mph: loads were up towards the 175 ton mark, but there was still more to come. A decade later, the GNR worked 18 of the 55 British trains that ran more than 100 miles non-stop. Ten different trains were timed to run between Kings Cross and Grantham at an average speed of 55 mph, with loads topping the 200 ton mark. Still later, trains of over 250 tons were worked to time by these magnificent machines, albeit in fair weather only.

At no time, until the arrival of the HST's, did British express trains change more radically than during the last three decades if the 19th century. Not only were they run at speeds little bettered by ordinary services until the end of steam, but the advent of the bogie corridor coach, steam heating and vacuum brakes dramatically increased both train weights and the drain on an engine's boiler. For most of this period, the 8 ft. singles had the field to themselves. The GWR's Broad Gauge stagnated, Webb's 'Jumbos' certainly put up some outstanding work in the 1890s, and timetables show that even the MR could run, if absolutely necessary. 'Hardwick', of course, out-performed everything, while even a 'Spinner' reached 90 mph but, day-in, day-out, Stirling's 8 ft. singles set the standards nothing else approached.

In some respects, Stirling's design trends bore comparison with those of Johnson on the MR. Both preferred small boilers and enlarged the cylinders for more power. Despite the dynamic public image of their respective singles, neither were designed for fast downhill running — on the GNR main line, that might have been asking for trouble. Hard work up hill was a trait of both these engineer's singles, with the small boilers recovering their breath and poise by easy running down the other side. Experienced crews knew just what could and could

When seen from the lineside, Stirling's engines always looked to be giving their all. This '322' series goods 0-6-0, No. 847 built in 1892, appears to be having a bit of fun with this short train, near Crouch End. This might have been done for effect though, as both driver and fireman seemingly pose for the photographer.

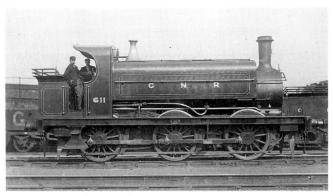

Although the list of Stirling's designs shows the '494' class of 0-6-0STs as one large class it was, in fact, made up of several series. Each of these differed in details, and the '606' series had a shorter wheelbase than the norm; ideal for shunting in yards with tight curves. No. 611 was built in 1877 and retained its original boiler until scrapped in 1928. It is seen in Hornsey yards, early this century.

not be done, and treated their mounts like their most cherished possessions.

Over the last decades of the century, Stirling steadily improved all his engines, and constantly updated the specification of older ones during heavy repairs. So, the 8 ft. singles of the 1870s received the larger boilers and cylinders of those built in the 1880s, but by the 1890s, even these were beginning to struggle as train weights climbed rapidly. By 1894, it was becoming critical. Stirling had one last throw of the dice and, as a child builds ever-bigger sand castles in a futile attempt to keep back the tide, so Stirling built the '1003' series of his masterpiece. Had more studs been fitted to the still larger cylinders, he might have succeeded, for a few years at any rate. As it was, the cylinders were knocked to bits and smaller ones were substituted, but by that time Stirling was dead. The tide of ever-heavier trains could not be turned, and brake pipes appeared at the front of his grand racehorses, a sign that even the greatest engines needed the occasional helping hand — anathema.

Still, even with their great master departed, the 8 ft. singles would not lie down. As with their junior partners, they worked expresses for a further decade, though with increased infrequency. Some drivers preferred the 8 ft. singles to Ivatt's new 4-4-0s but, then again, railwaymen were an ultra-conservative bunch. For Stirling's masterpiece though, there was to be no glamorous encore of fast, light-weight flyers, and when King George V took the throne, nearly all had gone. For those that remained there was but the odd express, as a substitute for a failed engine, the indignity of an occasional fish train from Grimsby, and then the final confirmation that the show was nearly over, the transfer to the levels of Lincolnshire. Even the latest '1003' series did not escape the cull, and No. 1006 was the final one to fall, early in 1916.

So, were the 8 ft. singles poetry in mechanical motion, or simply a great whirling mechanical anachronism? The former surely, but by the 1890s — and with all the many benefits of hindsight — it was clear that a younger Stirling would not have relied to such an extent on the tried, trusted and thoroughly tested. Perhaps he would have designed a 4-4-0 — an arrangement he rejected back in 1870 or, thinking the way he did, perhaps he would have gone straight to the 4-6-0 route. All pure conjecture, of course, but few steam engines have remained in the front rank, during a period of such dramatic change, for so long.

The great 4-2-2s were the exception to Stirling's norm. They were both the icing and the extravagant decoration on a very exceptional cake. In short, they transformed a Locomotive Superintendent from one of the very highest class, to the ranks of the greats. Without them, Stirling would still be a Star of Steam, instead of the constellation he has become: the 8 ft. singles really were the cornerstone of the Stirling Legend.

So, just how do we evaluate the work of Stirling? After nearly 43 years as a Locomotive Superintendent, it is no surprise that he transformed the locomotives of the two companies he served. Of course, by the 1890s, he no longer moved with the times, and left his successor, H.A. Ivatt, something of a shortage of modern express engines. Still, there were many others who designed single-drivers during the last decade of the 19th century, and Ivatt himself was still building them in the first year of the 20th century. Ivatt also had much to be grateful for: Doncaster Works was an outstanding asset, both for building and repair; and the standards of work at the running sheds impressed Ivatt, which was more than he thought of the permanent way.

In the late-1870s, J. Ramsbottom, formerly Locomotive Superintendent of the LNWR, was asked to conduct an in-depth inspection of the Locomotive Department, for the GNR's board. His findings showed Stirling up in the brightest of contemporary lights. GNR locomotives ran higher annual mileages, greater mileages between overhauls and earned more per year than those of any major British railway, so far as could be determined. In addition, with the exception of the LNWR, where Webb had improved massively on Ramsbottom's own foundations, Stirling's engines were as cheap to build and maintain as those of any other railway.

Then, in 1891, there were two brief trials that involved Stirling 4-2-2s and 2-2-2s, and a T.W. Worsdell 'J' class compound 4-2-2. Once again, Stirling emerged in credit as his engines not only out-performed the NER locomotive, but did so with far greater economy. Given that compounds were expected to be more economical, though more costly to build and maintain, these results were even more favourable to Stirling.

On the debit side, it was becoming clear that the GNR's board was not entirely happy with Stirling's very last efforts to provide a modern express locomotive. He was, reputedly, asked to resign, but died only 11 days later. Somewhat ironically, his successor soon received the green light to build locomotives in numbers the board constantly and consistently denied Stirling. Of course, Ivatt produced Britain's first Atlantic and, soon after, the even more massive No. 251. Despite these, he was unable to take the GNR back to the very front-rank of British express performance — Stirling's natural fiefdom.

One cannot state with any objective certainty, but the Legend of Stirling seems to be very much justified. Like, say, Knopfler and Clapton, as Stirling's engines hauled the fastest express trains in the world, he too was regarded as being the foremost locomotive engineer, in contemporary eyes. In hindsight, he might not have been the greatest British steam locomotive engineer of the 19th century, yet at a time when the likes of Webb, Drummond, Dean, Stroudley, Johnson, Holden, both Worsdell's and Jones all reigned supreme in their own demesne's, it was Stirling who was the best known both in Britain and overseas. His were the most publicly dynamic locomotives of their day and, rightly or wrongly, it was Stirling who was deemed to be the greatest of them all. Legendary indeed.

STIRLING IN BRIEF

BORN:	29th June 1820, Kilmarnock.
TRAINED:	1837-43, Dundee Foundry. Apprentice.
EMPLOYED:	Vulcan Foundry.
	Robert Napier & Co.
	1846, Neilson's & Co., Shop Foreman.
	1851, Loco. Supt. of Caledonian and Dunbartonshire Jt. Rly.
	Laurence Hill, Glasgow.
	R.W. Hawthorn, Departmental Manager.
SENIOR POSITIONS:	1853, Loco. Supt. GSWR.
	1866, Assistant Locomotive Superintendent GNR.
	1866, Locomotive Superintendent GNR.
DIED:	11th November 1895, Doncaster.

Stirling's Locomotive Designs

Glasgow and South Western Railway

YEAR	CLASS	WHEEL ARRANG'T	CYLINDERS (INCHES)	BOILER PRESSURE	DRIVING-WHEEL DIAMETER	WEIGHT	No. in CLASS
1855		2-2-2	(o)	Details unknown			
1855		0-6-0	(o)16 x 21	120 psi	4' 6"		2
1855	Crampton	0-4-0	(o)15 x 20	120 psi	5 ft.		4
1857	Galloway	2-4-0	16 x 22	130 psi	5 ft.		1
1857	2	2-2-2	(o)16 x 21	120 psi	6' 6"	23 tons	12
1858	32	0-4-2	(o)16 x 22	120 psi	5 ft.		10
1860	22	0-4-2	16 x 21	120 psi	5 ft.		20
1860	40	2-2-2	(o)16 x 21	120 psi	6' 6"	24T 10 cwt	10
1862		0-6-0	16 x 22	120 psi	4' 6"		
1864	131	0-4-2	16 x 22	120 psi	5 ft.		
1865	141	0-4-2	(o)17 x 22	120 psi	5 ft.		
1865	52	0-4-0					
1865	45	2-2-2	(o)16 x 24	125 psi	7 ft.	28T 10 cwt	11
1866	58	0-6-0	17 x 22	120 psi	4' 6"	26	

Great Northern Railway

YEAR	CLASS	WHEEL ARRANG'T	CYLINDERS (INCHES)	BOILER PRESSURE	DRIVING-WHEEL DIAMETER	WEIGHT	No. in CLASS
1867	474	0-6-0	17 x 24	130 psi	5' 2"	33 tons	35
1867	280	2-4-0	17 x 24	140 psi	6' 7"	37 tons	22
1868	18 + 218	0-4-2	17 x 24	140 psi	5' 7"	32 tons	121
1868	6	2-2-2	17 x 24	130 psi	7' 1"	34 tons	12
1868	126	0-4-2T	17 x 24	140 psi	5' 7"	42 tons	13
1868	392	0-6-0ST	17½ x 24	160 psi	5' 1"		7
1869	396	0-6-0ST	16 x 22	140 psi	4 ft.	38T 12 cwt	7
1870	92	2-2-2	17 x 24	130 psi	7' 7"	33T 10 cwt	1
1870	1	4-2-2	(o)18 x 28	140 psi	8 ft.	39 tons	37
1871	174	0-6-0	19 x 28	140 psi	5' 1"	40 tons	6
1872	120	0-4-4BT	17½ x 24	140 psi	5' 6"	41 tons	46
1873	171	0-6-0	17½ x 26	140 psi	5' 1"	36T 10 cwt	160
1874	86 + 206	2-4-0	17½ x 26	160 psi	6' 7"	39 tons	117
1874	494	0-6-0ST	17½ x 26	130 psi	4' 8"	47 tons	157
1875	605	0-6-0ST	16 x 22	140 psi	4 ft.	39 tons	2
1876	501	0-4-2ST	16 x 22	160 psi	5' 1"	39 tons	6
1880	629	0-4-4BT	16 x 22	130 psi	5' 1"	42T 10 cwt	2
1881	658	0-4-4T	17½ x 24	160 psi	5' 1"	49T 15 cwt	16
1882	103	0-4-2	17½ x 24	160 psi	5' 7"	36 tons	33
1882	684	0-6-0ST	17½ x 24	160 psi	4 ft.	42T 5 cwt	8
1883	374	0-6-0	17½ x 26	160 psi	4' 7"	36T 15 cwt	8
1884	771	4-2-2	(o)18 x 28	160 psi	8 ft.	45 tons	10
1885	232	2-2-2	18½ x 26	150 psi	7' 7"	40 tons	2
1886	234	2-2-2	18½ x 26	160 psi	7' 7"	39T 15 cwt	10
1889	766	0-4-4T	18 x 26	160 psi	5' 7"	53T 10 cwt	29
1892	871	2-2-2	18 x 26	160 psi	7' 7"	41 tons	11
1894	1003	4-2-2	(o)19½ x 28	170 psi	8 ft.	50 tons	6
1896	1021	0-6-0	7½ x 26	170 psi	4' 7"	38 tons	10

STIRLING's PRESERVED LOCOMOTIVES

YEAR	CLASS	RUNNING NUMBERS	TOTAL
1870	1	1	1

HERBERT NIGEL GRESLEY
The Man Who (Some) Would be King

Today, we live in a world of hot air. No, not just the effects of global warming, but a world where the self-publicist thrives. Thanks to the media's insatiable drive to increase sales, and thus enhance advertising revenue — in particular television, we are confronted with a never-ending procession of supposedly larger-than-life characters. Sportsmen, businessmen, politicians, actors, musicians and, especially, TV presenters: we are force-fed a diet of these hyped-up, self-gratifying people with their over-blown ego's. If only they had anything like the talent to match their publicity.

The media has become a self-perpetuating publicity machine, seemingly dedicated to justifying the fat fees of those supposed stars. Money For Nothing, sang Dire Straits, and that is certainly the case on the media circus — actually, it's more like money for old rope or, analysing many television programmes, old tripe. Though our supposed stars are portrayed as being larger than life, many are almost inane, shallow and empty — and that is in their professional life, while far too many seem to believe their own publicity. No wonder they have agents and minders, if they met real people more than a few myths would be blown asunder. It seems that, behind all the glitz, mediocrity is the norm.

Fortunately, few railway people have been so feted, at least beyond the world of the railway enthusiast. The Legend of Stirling, whose engines hauled the fastest trains in the world, gained a broad public prominence, while Webb and Gooch did not pass without notice either. However, the first railway engineer, beyond the founding-fathers, to gain an emblazoned national recognition, was none other than H.N. Gresley. Of course, there can hardly be anyone interested in British railways who has not heard of Churchward: his work was often on the lips of all contemporary enthusiasts. Gresley's name, though, went much further and he landed up on the front pages of national papers, thanks to the exploits of his locomotives. With his own fan club, the Gresley Society, and almost every aspect of his life recounted again and again in mind-numbing detail, there is little that can be written about him without tedious repetition.

Much of this was to do with the many outstanding achievements of his locomotive designs, at a time when there was precious little to crow about. Undoubtedly, Gresley and the LNER indulged in a degree of self-publicity but, unlike many today, he thoroughly deserved the attention. He remains one of the few railway engineers whose name will bring a nod of recognition from people with no interest in railways, mainly due to the exploits of his two most famous locomotives: 'Flying Scotsman' and 'Mallard'. In the 1930s though, Gresley was an occasional national hero to rank alongside the likes of Sir Malcolm Campbell.

On the other hand, not all railway professionals and enthusiasts took wholeheartedly to his work. Few could say anything critical about the appearance of his first pacifics, the 'A1s', but their performance/economy was not in the same class as the GWR's 'Castles'. By the time Gresley had evolved these into the 'A3s', all such arguments seemed, at the very least, limp. Here was the classic, yet modern British locomotive: fast, powerful, economical and probably the most elegant steam engine to have run on Britain's rails. There was a proud and mighty magnificence about them in their apple-green livery: they were most certainly aristocrats.

It was a different matter for Gresley's masterpiece though: the 'A4' pacifics. While the public seemed mesmerised by their ultra-modern streamlining, to say nothing of their almost unbelievable performance, some railway professionals and enthusiasts sneered, made puerile jokes and added pathetic nicknames at the expense of the locomotives and their designer. In their first few years, the 'A4s' magnificent performance rubbed the noses of those critics very firmly in the dirt, and demonstrated just how far ahead in thought — and bold in deed — was Gresley. The onset of the Second World War saw an end to all that. Maintenance deteriorated and failures increased and, as Gresley died in 1941, there were many with axes to grind who sought revenge; his successor, E. Thompson, was no unquestioning admirer either. The motive was already there, now came the opportunity. Gresley, his reputation and his engines were about to become the focus of a sinister, dastardly murder plot. It very, very nearly succeeded.

During BR days, Gresley enjoyed a partial rehabilitation, to which his engines contributed massively. Even so, former LMS personnel who dominated BR's locomotive design team wanted little to do with his ideals: this was a time when it was fashionable to modestly raise the standard of the majority, at the expense of excellence, in almost everything. Gresley's designs were considered extravagant: why use a Rolls Royce when a Morris Minor will do? No wonder our railways suffered so badly when they were run by men of such narrow intellect and insight, who played right into the arms of the ever-more powerful road lobby.

There is no doubt though, that Gresley's great days were the 1930s. Then, there was a bit of unofficial rivalry between the locomotives of Gresley, Stanier and Churchward/Collett. It was a return to a time of steam locomotive riches, after the paucity of the drab 1920s, as these three schools each vied to be top-dog. Similarly, in the 1980s, three great cricketers contested an unofficial title of who was the greatest all-rounder. Imran Khan, Kapil Dev and Ian Botham, were each as different in character, outlook and style as were Gresley, Stanier and Churchward. Imran was a classical batsman and bowler of great pace. There was an unhurried elegance about him, whether batting or bowling, while his speed and power could be underestimated by a seeming lack of effort: not unlike the GWR locomotives of Churchward and, later, Collett.

At the final count, the great Indian all-rounder, Kapil Dev, scored more runs and took more wickets than either of his rivals. He was never quite so elegant as Imran, not quite so dashing and exciting as Botham, but he had a rare style all of his own. Quite often, though, it was consistency and orthodoxy that brought Kapil his rewards: the same for Stanier.

Then there was Ian Botham, the most flamboyant of the three for a start. His exploits demanded the attention of the press, who then stoked his legend up still further: Gresley re-kindled. Botham was the undoubted sultan of swing-bowling, yet he adapted to become — for all too brief a period — a genuine fast bowler. For sheer power and brilliance with the bat, there was nobody to match him. A magnificent century one day, the ignominy of a duck the next. While not quite so unpredictable performers, for every flash of sheer brilliance, Gresley's locomotives could produce a surly indifference the next day. 'Mallard' majestically broke the world speed record for a steam engine, yet had to come off its train before the journey was half over.

Taking the cricket analogy still further, an 'A4' in full-flight matched the grace, poise and poetry of David Gower batting in all his majesty; yet hang 600+ tons behind its tender and it could soon dish out all the raw power associated with the most savage of Botham's innings. That a Stanier 'Duchess' could equal or, on occasions, possibly exceed such mighty work is entirely to its credit, and no de-merit to an 'A4'. Of course, all three schools' of design had much else in their respective powder-kegs, but Churchward and Stanier followed the standardisation route: Gresley, ever the individual, went solo.

For any locomotive engineer, a pupil apprenticeship under F.W. Webb must have been an experience to, if not savour, then colour one's attitude for the rest of one's days. I wonder, did Gresley, at the height of his powers in the 1930s, ever think of himself as something of a latter-day Webb? He knew he was at the pinnacle of his profession and ruled, at times, as if a patrician. Webb never quite made it to the top, but his rule was still supreme. Indeed, Gresley was born on the fringes of a minor aristocratic family, although his father was a vicar. He attended a good public school and this might have added to his ambitious, confident, even self-opinionated character, especially as a young man. He has been described as being more ponderous than talented while at Crewe, but he had ambition, of that there is no doubt, and he clearly knew his own mind.

Gresley was not one to wait for dead men's shoes. Soon after finishing his apprenticeship he moved to the LYR's Horwich Works, under J.A.F. Aspinall. After a period in the Drawing Office, followed by a spell as a shed foreman in Blackpool, he was appointed Assistant C & W Works Manager, at Newton Heath in 1901, the year he was married. There began a decade of C & W work, that saw him rise to become LYR Assistant C & W Supt. and then, on Aspinall's recommendation to his friend H.A. Ivatt, C & W Supt. of the GNR.

More than any other Star of Steam, Gresley's C & W work stands out for its innovation, occasional brilliance and total symbiosis with his locomotives. The sight of one of Gresley's apple green engines with a set of teak, often articulated, carriages in tow, or a silver or blue 'A4' with matching streamlined train is compulsive. One without the other is like Morecambe without Wise, Clough without Taylor: good, even great, but lacking the mark of genius. No sooner had he settled in at Doncaster than he set off at a truly cracking pace.

Within a year, Gresley had ousted the clerestory roof for the elliptical roof, and introduced the familiar bow-end to new carriage stock. A year later came electric lighting, the double-bolster bogie and, initially on two former 6-wheelers,

articulation. That same year, 1907, Gresley's coaches were adopted for the new East Coast Joint-Stock: his impact was already profound. There was never to be any let-up. By 1909, Gresley had settled on a general style that was to last his lifetime and, in the case of components such as bogies, way beyond. His work on wagons was similarly innovative, if less in the public eye.

Despite his work at the C & W department, Gresley was not Ivatt's assistant and there is nothing to suggest that he influenced Ivatt when it came to locomotives. Indeed, although Ivatt recommended Gresley as his successor, he was not the most obvious choice. For a start, he was decidedly young to be appointed to such a senior position at one of the country's more renown railways. Ivatt had not managed to keep the GNR at the very top of the locomotive tree, as Stirling had done, but they were up with the best. In any case, railways usually promoted on seniority and, at 35, Gresley was hardly that. Perhaps the board drew its collective breath as Gresley's appointment was announced, but Ivatt stayed until the end of 1911 to ensure a smooth transition.

They need not have worried, for whether the superheated 'J21' and 'J22' class 0-6-0s were Ivatt's last designs, Gresley's first or a bit of both, they ensured that there was a smooth hand-over of the conductor's baton. Indeed, Gresley's subsequent career seemed to unfold something along the lines of a musical symphony. The first movement, his 11 years as Loco. Eng. of the GNR, got off to a steady start, and gradually built so that it finished with a memorable flourish. The second movement, or first decade as CME of the LNER, reiterated the best moments from the earlier score, before descending into, perhaps, a tragedy followed by a gradual rebuilding. Finally, the last movement began boldly and, with increasing intensity, builds to an unforgettable crescendo and a finale that brings down the house. The classic format.

Right from the start though, Gresley was eager to learn, keen to build on the wonderful foundations laid by Ivatt and was no slave to tradition. He appointed O.V.S. Bulleid as his right-hand man, and thus began a partnership that was to reap ever-richer rewards. Ivatt had ensured that there was no need for a major building programme when he retired, unlike when he took over from Stirling. Essentially, Ivatt's advice had been to use big boilers and to keep things simple: two cylinders and low boiler pressures were just fine, thank you. Gresley's 'H2' class moguls incorporated that advice, and clearly bore American and, in particular, Churchwardian influences.

Although it is quite obvious now that Churchward was the leading locomotive engineer of his day, that was not entirely apparent at the time — not least among Locomotive Superintendents themselves. Few appreciated Churchward's work with cylinders, valves and boilers, while his engines were regarded as being expensive to build, even over-engineered. Economy, with coal being relatively cheap, was not the be-all and end-all it is today, and a few extra pounds consumed per mile hardly covered the additional hundreds of pounds Swindon locomotives cost to build. Then again, however well Churchward's engines performed, by 1912/13 it was Bowen Cooke's LNWR superheated express engines that were carrying-off all the honours. Gresley had other suspicions though.

For a few years, Gresley kept it simple and, with the onset of the First World War, there was little else he could do. A larger 2-cylinder mogul followed, the 'H3' class, along with a heavy freight design, the 'O1' class 2-8-0, both of which combined Ivatt's principles — big boilers and two cylinders — with Churchward's influences. Gresley later toyed with the idea of a 4-cylinder pacific, after he so equipped one of Ivatt's

Gresley's early years at the GNR saw some good designs emerge, but his first really outstanding one was the 'H4' class 3-cylinder mogul; later renown as the LNER 'K3s'. For 40 years, these powerful engines worked everything from the occasional express passenger and fast fish trains, to heavy goods throughout the eastern counties, and very successfully too. Back in 1920, the founder member, No. 1000, hauls an express through Wood Green, its thrusting smokebox seemingly emphasising how proud it is of its massive boiler. *(NRM)*

What could be more typical of Kings Cross suburban services for almost 40 years, than an 'N2' and two sets of quad-arts? 'Main Line' reads the headboard, to leave everyone in no doubt as to the purpose of this highly successful, all-Gresley combo. No. 4747 works with the expected degree of gusto. *(NRM)*

large atlantics. From all this work, he evolved his own ideas and, eschewing the advice of Ivatt, yet not copying Churchward, he finally brought out a 3-cylinder version of his 'O1' class.

Locomotive No. 456 featured Gresley's patent conjugated valve-gear for operating the middle cylinder, as opposed to the separate valve-gear used by Robinson or V. Raven on their 3-cylinder engines. This motion had its drawbacks though and, following meetings with the SECR engineer H. Holcroft, was modified to a Gresley/Holcroft layout in all subsequent applications. After the war, there was mounting speculation about the form of Gresley's forthcoming design (would it be a pacific, 2-6-2 or some other kind of exotic?), but the 2 to 1 layout of his infamous conjugated valve-gear first appeared on none of these, but a massive 3-cylinder mogul with 6 ft. diameter boiler. This might have been initially disappointing, but the 'K3' class was the first Gresley design to gain nation-wide attention, making the front pages for its work during the 1920 coal strike.

A 3-cylinder production version of Gresley's heavy freight engine emerged in 1921, the 'O2' class, while he demonstrated his ability to significantly develop and improve older designs, with the 'N2' suburban tank. This was little more than a modestly enlarged and improved Ivatt 'N1', with the important addition of a superheater. At a stroke, Gresley had cured the seemingly insoluble problems of the Kings Cross suburban services. This ability to modify and update in this way was not only one in which he ultimately led the field, but was to be of immense value to him and, subsequently, the LNER.

As the 1920s got underway and government relaxed its control over the railways, the future remained unclear. Nationalisation was a very real possibility, perhaps even a lost opportunity, but in the event a watered-down compromise was reached, and four large companies were formed from the hitherto quixotic multitude of smaller companies. As with BR in the last years before privatisation in the 1990s, few of these companies wanted to spend unnecessarily on new locomotives

Gresley developed the 3-cylinder 'O2' heavy goods engines from his 2-cylinder 'O1' class. Several tests demonstrated their improved performance and economy over the earlier engines, with greater power and better starting under load; they were also preferred to Robinson's ROD engines. As such, they might have been the best pre-war goods engines in Britain, but their undoubted complication ruled them out for further production in the Second World War. No. 485, a former GNR engine, bears the scars of some pretty hard work.   *(NRM)*

and rolling stock. On the other hand, prestige could be enhanced with a bit of judicious expenditure, and so the GNR board authorised Gresley to go ahead and build his proposed new express passenger locomotive.

Well, the 'A1' pacific No. 1470 'Great Northern' was, briefly, the railway star of its age. It looked the perfect locomotive and, boy, could it go. Suddenly, anything an Ivatt atlantic could do appeared distinctly second-rate, while speeds in excess of 80 mph were there for the taking. Coupled with this was Gresley's transformation of Ivatt's large atlantic, with the addition of a 32 element Robinson superheater: the future for the GNR locomotive fleet looked very rosy indeed. If the railway was to be subsumed into a new, enlarged railway company, the GNR Loco. Eng. was a favourite to be the new head of department.

Quite unbelievably, it has been claimed — by none other than Robinson himself — that the GCR man was asked to become the CME of the LNER. There was no doubt that he was the senior man, but surely, if not going outside the company, Gresley was the obvious choice for the job. Despite being only 46 years old, he was already one of the senior locomotive engineers in Britain and was clearly the man of the future, while Robinson was really no more than a safe bet. In the event, Gresley got the nod and the opening movement of his personal symphony came to a most agreeable close, with the locomotive world seemingly poised at his feet.

When considering the merits, or otherwise, of locomotive engineers, it is important to bear in mind the policy of the company they served. Whereas the LMS became a union of the constituent companies, with strict control from the centre, the LNER was more of a confederation. There was a degree of tolerance towards established practices: individuality was allowed, local responsibility encouraged. Economy, as much as anything, dictated the flow, but so long as the new corporate image was not flouted or costs were not increased, each area was held on a fairly light rein. Responsibility for locomotive running was removed from the new CME, who thus produced the locomotives required by the operating authorities. It was a system that worked, given the very tight financial situation that was to be a constant source of grief during the whole of the LNER's existence.

So, not un-naturally, it was Gresley's modern freight, mixed-traffic, tank and express engines that were built, in modest quantities, right from the start, but so too were other pre-Grouping designs. Occasionally, locomotives from one constituent were tried out in other areas, sometimes with great success — such as with GCR 4-4-0s in Scotland, and others less so — as with GCR 4-6-0s on the GNR main line. There were, of course, former loyalties that proved almost insuperable to overcome, such as NER men running tardily with their own pacifics, and positively resenting Gresley's but, in time, the quality of the new CME's designs won over even their belligerence. After all, no driver could resist being at the helm of the finest engines in the country, and Gresley's appeared to be just that.

It was the 1925 Exchange Trials with the GWR 'Castle' class locomotives that knocked any smugness out of Gresley, his department and the LNER. We will never know exactly whose idea the trials were, but there was no doubt that they were tailored entirely to GWR strengths. For a start, the LNER used the relatively easy run from Kings Cross-Doncaster: although trains did not then usually go through to Newcastle without an engine change, that might at least have taxed the GWR engines a bit more. Then, the 'A1' pacifics proceeded to squander their home advantage. Actually, thanks to a couple of failures, they fairly blotted their copy-book.

Over on the GWR, the 'A1' showed itself in a much better light, climbing stronger than the 'Castle', but generally running strictly to time. Whether there was any official compliancy or not remains unknown, but the 'Castle' was allowed to run far ahead of schedule: another seeming slaughter. There was no question, it had been a fairly comfortable points-victory for the GWR, but not a knockout. Within a couple of years, following his usual lengthy assessment period, Gresley began having his pacifics fitted with improved valve settings, and a raised boiler pressure, that turned a very good engine, the 'A1', into a great engine, the 'A3'. Thanks to his locomotives' public humiliation at the hands of the GWR, Gresley was about to hit the national front pages again as his reputation took the road to recovery.

The second movement of Gresley's time as a CME was more concerned with innovation, experiments and up-grading, than new designs. While work was in hand with the developments of the 'A1', two orthodox 0-6-0 designs were being planned while 3-cylinder 4-4-0, 2-6-2T and 4-6-0 designs also emerged from Doncaster: the latter being completed by the North British Loco. Company, who built the first engines.

Gresley's personal effort centred upon the rebuilding and updating of older locomotives, an economic necessity at that time of recession, coal strike and still deeper recession. Many pre-Grouping engines were given Gresley's boilers or otherwise modified, in an attempt to improve performance and economy at minimal cost: there was no chance of a new-build policy like that on the LMS. In particular, Ivatt's superheated atlantics were proving an outstanding success, as was high-degree superheating in general. Booster engines

A close miss, a shot well wide of the mark, or a case of the right hand of the Operating Department not knowing that the left hand of the Civil Engineer did not have siding capacity for 100 wagon trains? Take your pick. The 'P1' class 2-8-2s were magnificent engines capable of undertaking any work required of them, at a good rate of economy. No. 2394 heads an up train near Potters Bar, with the pipe to its booster engine visible beneath the cab. A sort of goods 'A1', these were the first Gresley engines to be withdrawn. *(L. Lord)*

Left —
For a small-wheeled orthodox goods engine, the 'J38' class and its larger wheeled sisters, the 'J39s', were the equal of any in the 1920s. Both were designed mainly to work short-haul goods trains, and the 'J38s' were stationed in Scotland. No. 5919 is at the head of a typical goods train, near Prestonpans. Unlike the 'J39s', these rarely found themselves promoted to occasional passenger duties.

were fitted to some locomotives, and while these had little success on the main line, they eventually found their place on new 'S1' class 0-8-4Ts of GCR parentage.

Then Gresley experimented with Lenz rotary-cam valve-gear, with or without poppet valves, later fitted to production 'D49' 4-4-0s. Gresley was clearly no stick-in-the-mud, and was always on the lookout for something that would make an engineering improvement and, hopefully, an economic one as well. The rather ungainly ACFI heated feed-water system was also tried out with some success, mostly on former GER locomotives. These, and much more, are well documented, but their long-term effect and subsequent economic benefits were strictly limited.

When Gresley became the CME of the LNER, he was responsible for 11 locomotive works and over 7,000 locomotives, while he moved his own head office to Kings Cross. This was a double-edged sword as, although it took him away from all the daily minutiae in which he might have become embroiled had he remained at, say, Doncaster Works, it also removed him from where all the action was. It is a sad fact that, as the years passed, Gresley became more remote from the very men who drove and maintained his locomotives day in, day out, but he retained their undying loyalty.

Not surprisingly, Gresley could not simply spend his time evolving new designs, at least as he had his first pacifics. There were, however, some quite fantastic exceptions in which he considerably raised British steam locomotive design horizons, even if the ultimate effect was indistinct. His first new design for the LNER did not emerge until 1925: the unique 'P1' class. These 2-8-2s were a heavy freight version of the 'A1' pacifics, incorporating a longer boiler and a booster engine. Whereas this device drained the boiler of an Ivatt large atlantic, the new Gresley design was not winded after just a short spell of booster-power.

Designed to haul 100 wagon coal trains of 1,600 tons, from Peterborough-London, the 'P1s' soon demonstrated a confident mastery of such gargantuan loads. Even the 3-cylinder 'O2s' could not cope with such work, but neither could the capacity of the main line. Refuge sidings were too short, there were too many double-track sections at which a slow-moving freight train could cause havoc and, just to cap it all, even when one of these interminable trains arrived, it brought everything to a standstill until it was divided. Great idea, but a bloody headache. Had the infra-structure been in place, these two engines could have been the forerunners of a very impressive and valuable class. In a sense, they were simply too powerful and both were withdrawn in 1945, the first Gresley engines to be condemned. They would, though, have been a godsend to the GWR and, especially, the LMS.

There was no doubt about it, Gresley admired the work of Churchward possibly more than any other locomotive engineer. However, he did not copy. Churchward and his later disciples, led by the evangelist Stanier — on the LMS and with BR, favoured a standard locomotive policy. Gresley, like many Stars of Steam before him, utilised standard components, but most emphatically not a standard catch-all locomotive. Had it been possible to design such an engine, Gresley might have been swayed, but even the greatest of the compromise engines, Stanier's 'Black 5', had its all too many limitations.

The extreme in Gresley's horses-for-courses design policy came with the advent of the 'U1' class Garratt, of 1925. Intended purely to bank the heavy coal trains up the 1 in 40 Worsborough incline, between Wath and Penistone, this was the most powerful steam engine ever to run in Britain. It was, in effect, two 'O2' class engines and pounded away at its

monotonous task for almost 25 years. When the line was electrified, in 1949, a problem reared its less than pretty head. Where else could this engine work, what else could it do? It did not find favour banking trains up the even steeper Lickey incline, near Bromsgrove, so its days were soon numbered and it was withdrawn in 1955,

By far the biggest experiment carried out by Gresley was the, once again unique, 'W1' class 4-6-4 engine. The biggest surprise of all was not it being a 4-cylinder compound — among many innovations, but its marine water-tube boiler pressed to fully 450 psi. It was the boiler that had taken so long to develop for a railway application, while it also dictated the shape of the most unusual British steam locomotive yet seen: this, again, gained Gresley exposure in the national press. Unlike the 'P1' and 'U1' classes, the 4-6-4 was to make no useful contribution towards the LNER's meagre coffers; there was no doubting its impact though, and with it Gresley's further enhanced reputation.

Over a five year period, the 'W1' put in more appearances at Darlington Works than it did on the main line. It was a failure — not an abject one admittedly, but hardly a glorious flop either, yet it showed that Gresley and especially Bulleid had their minds open to a world beyond that of standard, orthodox railway engineering. While such an experiment might not yield much by itself, it was part of a dynamic learning process. As much as anything, it was their exposure to motor car, marine and aeroplane engineering that enabled them to design such advanced and unique locomotives. The staid orthodoxy of the Churchward/Stanier/Riddles school held no real attraction to either of these innovative engineers. No. 10000 was finally withdrawn and comprehensively rebuilt as an orthodox 3-cylinder engine, emerging in 1937 to take its place among the ever-growing ranks of Gresley's thoroughbreds.

So, as Gresley's second symphonic movement drew to its natural close, in the early 1930s, he had lit the blue touch-paper, but it had fizzled and failed to ignite to the extent expected. There had been the very public nadir of the 1925 Trials, but the unique and ingenious corridor tender, and valve modifications, that enabled the 'Flying Scotsman' to run non-stop between London and Edinburgh, brought Gresley and the LNER back into the public domain. Then the new 'A3' pacifics, joined by the 'A1' conversions allowed, from 1932, the railway to begin a long overdue speeding-up of its Anglo-Scottish and other main line expresses. This process was to gather pace until the world was plunged into war once again, while Gresley's innovative coaching stock — with Tourist trains, buffet cars and new express carriages — began to make an impact: modest at first, but soon to filter down through the system.

At the dawn of the third and final movement, or phase, in Gresley's CME career, the foundations were in place for some real fire-crackers, always assuming, of course, the opportunities could be taken. Early on, Gresley had been influenced by American, German and Churchwardian developments in steam locomotive technology. He had spent much time and effort with experimental work, especially during the 1920s, while he was further influenced by lessons learned with streamlined steam passages from France, external streamlining from France and America, and smokebox and blastpipe arrangements from France and Belgium. An era of Gallic influence and joie de vivre was about to break loose.

Gresley was impressed with the work of the brilliant French engineer, A. Chapelon, and the two became friendly associates. Chapelon's work was the essential missing piece of Gresley's jigsaw and, armed with this, he was able to apply it with

One must remember that 'P2' class No. 2001 'Cock o' the North' was a prototype locomotive. That it had its failings was not surprising, given its many innovations, and later examples differed considerably; visually and otherwise. This great locomotive makes a most imposing sight in original condition, in marked contrast to the less than modern coaches it has in tow.   *(NRM)*

devastating effect. The 'A3' pacifics were, by the early 1930s, the finest engines in the land: only a GWR 'King' could possibly offer a decent challenge at that time. They were exceptionally fast, powerful and, thanks to the valve improvements, very economical. There was little they could not do, but the working arrangements of the Aberdeen line could sorely tax even these engines.

Gresley's solution was to take the 'P1' format, combine it with that of the 'A3', and spice it all up with a dash of Chapelon and a few other trinkets. The 'P2' class No. 2001 'Cock o' the North' was an Aladdin's Cave of new ideas: wedge-front cab, Lenz rotary cam valve-gear, double chimney and Kylchap exhaust, ACFI feed-water heater, internally streamlined steam pipes and, to cap it all, yet another new and distinctive external shape. It was not perfect, as one might expect, but the new engine was soon to demonstrate she was the most powerful express locomotive in Britain.

Although 'Cock o' the North' never quite lived up to its immense potential, either on test in France, or on the Aberdeen road — thanks to its inadequate infrastructure, it was soon joined in Scotland by a slightly less experimental sister. Four more engines followed, but looked quite different from the original pair, and all six then ran the heavy Aberdeen trains over that arduous route: the original engines were rebuilt to the later style. It was no more than a qualified success though, for due to flange wear and operating restrictions, engines were changed at Dundee, a mere 60 miles from Edinburgh — a woeful waste of resources. The LNER kept this up for several years, probably because it was cheaper than double-heading, but the company's policy of a few ever-heavy expresses did little to attract passengers. Fast and light — now, there was a thought.

While 'Cock o' the North' attracted more publicity to the LNER, doing Gresley's cause no harm either, it was the later events of 1934 that marked out a whole new era for him and the company. If Churchill could claim that, when he became Prime Minister during Britain's darkest hours in 1940, it was as though his whole life had been in preparation for that moment, Gresley might conceivably have done likewise. The next five years were to be the most exciting period in British steam railways, and Gresley was the central character.

The momentum had been gathering for some considerable time. Despite the ever-heavier expresses, the LNER's first 60 mph timings had been introduced and the modified 'A1' and 'A3' pacifics were coming into their own. The idea of a fast, luxury express running from London-Newcastle came to the minds of senior management, and Gresley was deputed to look into the matter. In particular, a fast diesel train called the 'Flying Hamburger' plied its trade between the German capital and Hamburg. A quotation for a similar train to run on the LNER main line was requested and, in all honesty, was a disappointment. The General Manager, Sir Ralph Wedgwood, suggested to Gresley that one of his engines with a light train could do better and the challenge was on.

In November 1934, the celebrated 'A1' pacific 'Flying Scotsman' was set-to with a light-weight train of 145 tons, from Kings Cross-Leeds, and broke all established records by a country mile. It topped Stoke Summit at fully 81 mph just for good measure. Later in the day, the 'Flying Scotsman' returned with a load of just over 200 tons, taking a few minutes more, but achieved the first fully authenticated 100 mph speed on a British railway. This was but the first of many virtuoso performances in the new railway age.

A few months later, an 'A3' pacific — the quite appropriately named 'Papyrus' — re-wrote a whole sheaf of records on a single day. Running with a six coach train, thought to be about right for a high-speed service, it comfortably kept to a four hour schedule from Kings Cross-Newcastle, and then back again. It was not simply that the engine made it with time to spare, on both runs, nor that the total high-speed mileage was without precedent in Britain, but the top speed of 108 mph was the crowning glory of the greatest day yet for British railways. There was no doubt about it, according to the daily press the LNER and Gresley not only led Britain's railway field, but had conquered the world. It was a sobering thought that, just over six months later, runs of a similar performance were to become a regular daily feature, though without the need for such a high top speed.

These were not left to the 'A3s' though, but to a design that produced the most dramatic and dynamic steam engines ever to run in Britain: the 'A4' class pacifics. Except for the streamlining and a boiler of 250 psi, Gresley relied entirely on the solid basics thoroughly developed in service with the 'A3s' and the first 'P2s'. While cynics and railway know-it-alls sneered at the streamlining, the press and public loved the first silver-grey engine. In fact, the streamlining considerably reduced the horse-power required to overcome air resistance at speeds above 80mph: the very speeds at which these finest of thoroughbreds ran, without even blinking.

Facts have occasionally been bandied about regarding the effectiveness of the 'A4s' streamlining, while suggesting that Stanier's 'Duchess' class was even more effective. Perhaps so, but I wonder. Statistics and wind tunnel experiments can show that many modern cars are more aerodynamically effective than the E-Type Jaguar. Put one alongside an E-Type though, and further discussion is worthless. The E-Type is the real thing. Incidentally, the impact on public and press alike of the 'A4' has, surely, only ever been exceeded by the launch of Britain's greatest sports car.

More than that though, Gresley's new articulated, streamlined train, the 'Silver Jubilee', was like nothing that had run Britain's rails before. Add the most sensational of launches, where a new British rail speed record of 112½ mph was reached — twice, and the package was complete. That Gresley had to go onto the footplate to tell the driver — who thought he was doing about 90 mph — to ease things up a bit as a poor old director's teeth were rattling, says all one needs to about the times, the greatest of all British express locomotives.

Two years later, Gresley even exceeded the triumph of the silver 'A4' and 'Silver Jubilee' train, with the introduction of the streamlined 'Coronation': the deciding factor was its Beaver-tail observation car. No British train, hauled by a matching garter-blue 'A4' can have had such an impact. If the 'Silver Jubilee' and its silver 'A4' brought together all Gresley's work into a whole, the 'Coronation' and its blue 'A4' took it to its mighty zenith. In full-flight, it was incomparable.

Gresley was knighted in 1936, the first British locomotive engineer to have been so honoured while in office and, of course, the World Record for steam fell decisively to 'Mallard', in 1938. In the meantime, Gresley's response for an engine capable of hauling express goods or fast passenger trains did not follow the route of the 'Black 5', but took the form of Britain's first 2-6-2: the 'V2' class. It seems as though this class, often regarded as Gresley's finest, might have been one of a pair intended to encompass such duties in a more comprehensive manner than was achieved by the 'Black 5s' and the GWR's 'Halls'. By 1938, a smaller version was planned to work similar services away from the main line, the 'V4' class, but this was slowed by the war and then halted with Gresley's death. The two locomotives that were built offered great promise, but war-torn Britain was not a place for costly developments and, as odd-bods, they enjoyed but short lives.

To recount each and every Gresley design is unnecessary and has, in any case, has been covered numerous times. It is his impact that is of greater importance. His contemporary rivals, Stanier, Collett, Riddles and Churchward were engineers who, in locomotive numbers alone, each had a far greater impact than Gresley, at least when considering his locomotives for the LNER. Indeed, looked at from the line

flowing from Churchward/Collett to Stanier to H.G. Ivatt/Riddles, Gresley was very much a side-show, not the mainstream of British steam locomotive design. Some side-show and what a glorious distraction!

Gresley's work for the GNR most definitely enhanced that of H.A. Ivatt. His combination of locomotive and carriage design could never be separated, and the bond was to grow ever-stronger with the passing years. The situation on the LNER was entirely different. Despite its great size, Gresley built nearly as many locomotives to his own designs for the GNR as the LNER: harsh economic reality over idealism. He saved the company tens of thousands of pounds by rebuilding and improving many pre-Grouping designs and engines: a situation that only Riddles of the above-mentioned engineers had to contend with. So, was it wise for him to spend so much time, effort and scarce resources in experiments that, at best, yielded marginal financial rewards? Would not a standardised policy of simple and straight-forward designs, as advocated by Ivatt, not have been of more benefit to the LNER than Gresley's sometimes complicated engines?

These are points round which many arguments have raged. Churchward utterly transformed the GWR's locomotive position and heavily influenced British steam locomotive design. Stanier took Churchward's principles and adapted them to the 1930s, as had Collett. He then added to them and these were used by BR. There was no doubt about it, Stanier's work for the LMS was every bit as valuable to that company as was Churchward's to the GWR.

Whether it was the right path for BR is a highly controversial, moot point. Received wisdom suggests that Stanier's design principles were eminently suited to the post-war austerity, but even in the darkest, filthiest days of the Second World War, Gresley's uncared-for locomotives were still undertaking gargantuan feats of haulage, and then coming back for more. Come the 1950s, Stanier's engines were seemingly running more miles per year than their Gresley counterparts, but once the former GWR engineer K.J. Cook installed cylinder optical aligning equipment at Doncaster Works, the tables were turned — decisively.

The L M S had the outstanding 'Black 5s' as a mixed-traffic locomotive, but the G W R divided the tasks between the 'Halls' and the 'Granges'. Likewise Gresley. His outstanding 'V2' class was probably the ultimate British mixed-traffic design and Gresley produced the 'V4' class for non-main line duties. Had it not been for the Second World War, and his death, this would no doubt have been multiplied as was its big brother, but Gresley's successor sought an alternative, cheaper route. The very aptly named No. 3401 'Bantam Cock' hauls a hefty train from Cambridge-London in 1941, and shows not only what a fine design the 'V4' was, but what an opportunity was passed up.   (N.R.M.)

Eventually Gresley's pacifics received Kylchap double chimneys, as had been fitted to a handful pre-war, and the transformation was complete and total. Perhaps it was significant that when Gresley's engines were replaced by those of other regions, such as the 'K4' moguls giving way to Stanier's 'Black 5s' on the West Highland line, or the wholesale replacement on the former GCR lines, the men complained, bitterly and vociferously at times. On the other hand, when Gresley's engines were sent to the former GSWR lines, the men were very pleased, even delighted with their good fortune. To nobody's great surprise, the crews fairly rejoiced when, deposed from their former stamping ground, some 'A4s' were sent to work the Glasgow-Aberdeen 3 hour trains over the former CR lines. Perhaps most surprising of all, was the welcome given to the 'A3s' by the men of Holbeck shed in Leeds, for working expresses to Carlisle. In no time at all, they claimed they were the finest engines they had ever enjoyed: 'Royal Scots' notwithstanding.

Great engineer, great engine, great picture. This has been shown many times before, yet can hardly be bettered. Gresley and his 100th pacific. *(NRM)*

It seemed, by the 1960s, just as Gresley's pacifics were going down with all guns firing in a final and entirely fitting blaze of glory, Gresley had, at last, been rehabilitated. After the 1930s, when publicity on a national scale raised his stock beyond the bounds of reason, came the counter-revolution of the Thompson years. Suddenly, everything-Gresley was bad. Then came the early BR days when, despite the results of the 1948 Interchange Trials (or was it because of them?), engineers with a narrow, un-imaginative vision ruled the roost. Orthodoxy and bureaucracy dominated in railway engineering as in society. Perhaps each deserved the other. Finally, came Gresley's rehabilitation. It was almost a farcical cameo of the fortunes of Lenin's comrades in Soviet Russia. High office while Lenin was alive, persecution and execution under Stalin, and re-habilitation under Kruschev.

The value of Gresley to the LNER was made quite apparent by the naming of his 100th pacific 'Sir Nigel Gresley', in 1937. No other locomotive engineer had a locomotive named after him while holding office. Publicity, or esteem? Possibly a bit of both, for neither missed a trick in that department. On the other hand, by then Gresley was most definitely the greatest locomotive engineer of them all, and the greatest single feat of one of his engines was still some eight months away.

Was there more to come? I'll say there was. Had there been no war, a new express locomotive was undergoing its lengthy planning process. This probable 4-8-2 could have been a real masterpiece, but might it not have been almost too big, too powerful, not unlike the 'P2s'? A 275 psi version of the 'A4' was planned, while a 3-cylinder 4-6-0 replacement for the East Anglian lines was in the pipeline. Of course, had Gresley lived, the 'V4' would undoubtedly have been multiplied as another standard. As it was, the war most certainly interrupted events and Gresley would probably have retired after 30 years' in office anyway.

Such conjecture is academic, but it shows that, even after the departure of Bulleid in 1937, Gresley never stood still, never stagnated, never looked inwards. His was an international outlook. How much more exciting and interesting would the 1950s have been, probably at no greater cost, had Bulleid got the nod — perhaps with the steadying hand of his brother-in-law, H.G. Ivatt, on his shoulder, instead of the austere regime instigated by Riddles, Bond and Cox.

It is an inappropriate question to ask as to whether Gresley was a greater locomotive engineer than either Stanier or Churchward; was Botham really better than Kapil Dev or Imran Khan? Some have suggested that the many brilliant performances of Gresley's engines in preservation confirm this to be the case, but was that not so in the 1930s when they were well maintained, and again in the late-1950s? He did not work for a railway with the finances or will-power to allow him to build on anything like the scale of the other two engineers. Both of these were followed by men who believed in all they did and stood for; Gresley was followed by Thompson who most certainly did not. Numbers answer nothing. Indeed, the question itself is a fraud and irrelevance.

Neither must we believe all we read and hear. Gresley was not a genius, certainly not the god some would have us think. He led a forward-thinking team well, even very well. He inspired, cajoled and encouraged some astounding work from his assistants. Team-work was the important maxim. It was Gresley's leadership, organisation and direction that set the pace, but he did not undertake all the work. He was, though, a great CME and one of the most original-thinking steam locomotive engineers of all time. Unlike the fraudulent, so-called stars we are presented with today, Gresley had no need of bloated media-hype. If the proof of the pudding is in the eating, then Gresley's was the richest fare possible.

Great Northern Railway

YEAR	CLASS	WHEEL ARRANG'T	CYLINDERS (INCHES)	BOILER PRESSURE	DRIVING-WHEEL DIAMETER	WEIGHT	No. in CLASS
1912	J22 (J6) *	0-6-0	19 x 26	170 psi	5' 2"	50T 10 cwt	95
1912	H2 (K1)	2-6-0	(o)20 x 26	170 psi	5' 8"	61T 15 cwt	10
1913	O1	2-8-0	(o)21 x 28	170 psi	4' 8"	76T 15 cwt	20
1913	J23 (J50)	0-6-0T	18½ x 26	175 psi	5' 8"	57 tons	132
1914	H3 (K2)	2-6-0	(o)20 x 26	170 psi	5' 8"	64 tons	65
1918	461 (O2)	2-8-0	(3)18 x 26	170 psi	4' 8"	76T 10 cwt	1
1920	H4 (K3)	2-6-0	(3)18½ x 26	180 psi	5' 8"	71T 15 cwt	193
1920	N2	0-6-2T	19 x 26	170 psi	5' 8"	70T 5 cwt	107
1921	O2	2-8-0	(3)18½ x 26	180 psi	4' 8"	75T 15 cwt	66
1922	A1	4-6-2	(3)20 x 26	180 psi	6' 8"	92T 10 cwt	52

London and North Eastern Railway

YEAR	CLASS	WHEEL ARRANG'T	CYLINDERS (INCHES)	BOILER PRESSURE	DRIVING-WHEEL DIAMETER	WEIGHT	No. in CLASS
1925	P1	2-8-2	(3)20 x 26	180 psi	5' 2"	100 tons	2
1925	U1	2-8-0+0-8-2	(6)18½ x 26	180 psi	4' 8"	178 tons	1
1926	J38	0-6-0	20 x 26	180 psi	4' 8"	59 tons	35
1926	J39	0-6-0	20 x 26	180 psi	5' 2"	57T 15 cwt	289
1927	D49	4-4-0	(3)17 x 26	180 psi	6' 8"	65T 10 cwt	76
1928	A3	4-6-2	(3)19 x 26	220 psi	6' 8"	96T 5 cwt	27 + 51 A1
1928	B17	4-6-0	(3)17½ x 26	200 psi	6' 8"	77T 5 cwt	73
1929	W1 (comp.)	4-6-4	H.P.12 x 26	450 psi	6' 8"	103T 12 cwt	1
1930	V1	2-6-2T	(3)16 x 26	180 psi	5' 8"	84 tons	82
1934	P2	2-8-2	(3)21 x 26	220 psi	6' 2"	110T 5 cwt	6
1935	A4	4-6-2	(3)18½ x 26	250 psi	6' 8"	103 tons	35
1936	V2	2-6-2	(3)18½ x 26	220 psi	6' 2"	93 tons	184
1937	W1 (reb.)	4-6-4	(3)20 x 26	250 psi	6' 8"	108 tons	1
1937	K4	2-6-0	(3)18½ x 26	180 psi	5' 2"	68T 10 cwt	5
1939	V3	2-6-2T	(3)16 x 26	200 psi	5' 8"	86T 15 cwt	10
1941	V4	2-6-2	(3)15 x 26	250 psi	5' 8"	70T 10 cwt	2

Prototype Electric Locomotive

1941 EM1 No. 6701 Bo-B0 1

* Denotes Ivatt design superheated and with other minor modifications by Gresley (536 series).

GRESLEY's PRESERVED LOCOMOTIVES

YEAR	CLASS	RUNNING NUMBERS	TOTAL
1920	N2	LNER 4744	1
1922	A3	LNER 4472 'Flying Scotsman'	1
1927	D49	LNER 246 'Morayshire'	1
1928	B12/3	BR 61572	1
1935	A4	BR 60007/8/9/10/19, 4468 'Mallard'	6
1936	V2	LNER 4771 'Green Arrow'	1
1937	K4	LNER 3442 'The Great Marquess'	1

GRESLEY IN BRIEF

BORN:	19th June 1876, Edinburgh.
EDUCATED:	1890-93, Marlborough School.
TRAINED:	1893-7, Crewe Works, LNWR App. under Webb.
EMPLOYED:	1897, LNWR.
	1898-1901, Various positions, LYR.

SENIOR
POSITIONS:
1901, Ass. Works Manager, Newton Heath C & W Works, LYR.
1902, Works Manager, Newton Heath C & W Works.
1904, Ass. C & W Supt. LYR.
1905, C & W Supt. GNR.
1911, Loco. Eng. GNR.
1923-41, CME of LNER.

HONOURS:
1920, CBE.
1922, Telford Gold Medal awarded by ICE.
Council Member, IME.
1927/8 and 1934/5, President, ILE.
1936, Knighted.
1936, President IME.
1936, Hon. D.Sc. Manchester University.

DIED:
5th April 1941, Hertford.

WILLIAM STROUDLEY
Transforming the LBSCR from Music Hall Joke to Heart of the Nation

Do you remember the television advertisements in which Jimmy Saville ('you sad man') proclaimed, "This is the age...of the train"? The star of the show was, of course, the High Speed Trains in their dramatic blue, grey and yellow livery, looking every inch 125 mph projectiles.

No matter where the HSTs were introduced, passengers flocked to them in ever-increasing numbers. For the first time since the 'A4s' ran in daily service, people with little interest in railways stood and watched as these new thoroughbreds roared past in full-flight. Suddenly, jokes about trains getting lost and stale sandwiches were old-hat, while the wrong kind of snow and leaves had yet to fall, to heap more ridicule on BR. Our beleaguered national railway had, at last, got its sums right — and how. It was the marketing coup of the age, and quite deservedly so.

At least BR delivered. Fast, frequent, if somewhat frugal services were, let us be clear on this, a vast improvement over those of the days of steam, quite apart from the absence of smoke-grimed stations, and the layer of soot that permeated everywhere and everything. Yet a hundred years before, without the aid of any so-called marketing specialists, the LBSCR pulled off a similar con-trick, and what a grand delusion it was.

By the simple expedient of changing its locomotive livery from a dowdy green to a cheeky golden ochre, displayed in a nigh-concours condition, the LBSCR came to personify all that was elegant in Victorian society, with a dash of the Bohemian thrown in. Suddenly, travelling on 'the Brighton' was not simply socially acceptable, but even a little chic. Can you imagine the parasitic droves of today's chattering-classes flocking down to Victoria station to be seen boarding one of these glamorous little trains?

This grand little image worked outstandingly well until, that is, one closed the carriage door and sat down. Suddenly, it was almost as though one had entered the underworld. You were treated to the most rickety coaches, that formed some of Britain's slowest trains. As for punctuality, well, surely the LBSCR's station clocks were always mistaken? The Brighton, to be blunt, duped its passengers. Reality was hidden behind a golden veneer to create the forerunner of our 'feel-good factor'. But best of all, it worked a treat!

The man behind this quite remarkable transformation was neither a flash Sales Director, nor a suave Marketing Manager, and not even the General Manager. It was the predilection of an austere, autocratic and somewhat dour engineer, who arrived from the HR. In the Scottish Highlands, Stroudley's 'improved engine green' had an audience of deer, sheep and only the occasional passenger, but in south-east England it was an instant hit. Of course, Stroudley needed the board's approval for such a radical livery change and, given the higher standards of presentation, an increased budget. These were the first visible signs of what became nothing less than a revolution in the LBSCR's locomotive department.

Appointed to succeed the strict, yet prolific J.C. Craven, this was a prestigious promotion for Stroudley, who had found himself almost boxed into an engineering corner, in far off Inverness. His curriculum vitae was not without its merits, but lacked direction. After several menial jobs in his native Oxfordshire, Stroudley was fully 20 years old before he secured his first railway position. He hit the jackpot though, training as a locomotive engineer at Swindon, ultimately under the legendary Daniel Gooch.

Stroudley soon moved on to the GNR at Peterborough. There, he became a Running Foreman under C. Sacre — later the Locomotive Superintendent of the MSLR and, in 1857, was seconded to drive, repair and otherwise mollycoddle the locomotives on Lord Willoughby's Edenham and Little Bytham Railway: his lordship was a friend of Gooch's. Within a year, Stroudley was back at Peterborough, but in 1861 he was appointed Manager of Cowlairs Works, on the Edinburgh and Glasgow Railway. There, Stroudley first became involved in locomotive design: nothing very grand on that penny-pinching concern, but certainly a step in the right direction. He also teamed-up with a young man who, even then, knew he was going somewhere: Dugald Drummond.

Stroudley's big chance came in 1865, when appointed Locomotive Superintendent of the impecunious HR. Poor it might have been, but its new, relatively inexperienced locomotive chief still received a salary of £500 p.a. Quite what qualifications Stroudley had over and above the acting incumbent, D. Jones, is a moot point, but luck plays its part in life and Stroudley seems to have enjoyed rather more than his share.

Inverness' Lochgorm Works was, even then, something of an engineering backwater. With an enforced policy of make-do-and-mend, antiquated Barclay 2-2-2s — hardly the most appropriate passenger locomotives for the new, steeply graded line south to Perth — were all that could be mustered. Reliability was poor but, then again, so was income and the HR operated on a badly frayed shoe-string.

Stroudley took the youthful (in age, but surely never in attitude) D. Drummond along with him, as Works Manager, while Jones became the Loco. Running Supt. Such an impoverished engineering up-bringing served Stroudley well, for he learned the value of strict cost-control, an organised works and a meticulous attention to detail: tenets that were to serve him well in the future.

Eventually, Stroudley rebuilt some of Barclay's singles as 2-4-0s, turned-out in the newly adopted improved engine green — first used at the EGR. These locomotives were never likely to make any waves in the railway world, but were a distinct improvement on anything that had hitherto ridden the Highland rails. Then, in 1869, Stroudley designed a tiny 0-6-0ST: the first locomotive built at Lochgorm Works. This was almost a forerunner of one of his most successful, later designs. Only one was built during Stroudley's reign, but two

HR No. 1 'Raigmore' was, indeed, the first locomotive of the former Inverness & Nairn Railway, being delivered to Inverness by sea, in 1855. It was then a 2-2-2, but Stroudley rebuilt it as a 2-4-0 in 1869. Its sister engine, No. 2 also received a bigger boiler and cylinders, but 'Raigmore', as can be seen, was little altered and, as a consequence, was of limited use and was soon scrapped by Jones. Stroudley stands on the tender. *(NRM)*

more emerged thereafter, and all three saw the HR subsumed into the LMS. Very good value indeed.

Considering Stroudley's limited experience, his appointment to the LBSCR was something of a surprising personal coup. One wonders if he was the first choice for the position? Quite what attributes the board thought that running the sparse services in north Scotland — and only having designed one locomotive — would bring to what was, even then, a busy railway, is mystifying. Perhaps it was the success of his locomotive rebuilding and methodical organisation of Lochgorm Works that attracted them, but they were on a minuscule level compared to the needs of his new employer. These days, I doubt he would even get an interview.

By 1870, the Brighton had just about reached its limit of linear development. Lines radiated from its joint-termini in London — London Bridge and Victoria — to Portsmouth in the west, Hastings in the east and, of course, all stations to Brighton in between. It faced stiff competition at both extremities and even its cross-Channel services, via Newhaven, were distinctly third-rate behind those from Dover and Folkestone. It was hemmed-in by the LSWR to the west, the LCDR to the east, and was finally cut-in-two and partially shared its main line with the SER. In short, while railways such as the LSWR were to expand during the next few decades, the Brighton was stymied at almost every turn.

Still, the LBSCR was very much in the public eye. Most of its trains were short-haul — its longest run being the 88 miles to Portsmouth, and about 20% of its route miles were within London. As today, these lines were both congested (sharing with the SER did not help one jot) and difficult to work. True, there was no Shap or Beattock to contend with, but anyone familiar with the North or South Downs will know that these can give a short, and distinctly sharp shock to the breathing system, for humans and steam railways. Gradients steeper than 1 in 100 were not unknown, and even if they were

relatively short, there were a few sharp curves to hinder progress, especially on the Portsmouth line.

The range of duties on the Brighton, though, were as varied as anywhere, despite the lack of long-haul expresses and heavy goods trains. Craven favoured a horses-for-courses approach and designed a different engine for each individual task: that was his idea of a standard locomotive policy. Well, that is how it must have seemed to Stroudley, for he inherited no fewer than 72 separate classes, each with few, if any, interchangeable parts. Here was a logistics and engineering nightmare — if only we had such diversity on our railways today.

Craven was certainly not a poor engineer and his locomotives, though a little un-reliable, were generally up to the work. So they should have been, but the already cramped Brighton Works was awash with unique spare parts. Thus, if an engine failed and a part could not be readily found, the locomotive was taken off the road while one was made. Capital tied-up, to say nothing of engines stored all over the show, was beyond the bounds of acceptability, even for those days.

On inspecting his new demesne, Stroudley might have had second thoughts about the wisdom of his move south; wondering where to start probably caused many sleepless nights. Like all good managers though, he chose his staff with care. Chief Engineer F. Bannister remained loyal to the cause and Drummond, once again, followed him south, as Works Manager. Realising that Craven's locomotives were, at least, holding the fort, Stroudley persuaded the board to authorise a complete re-building and expansion of Brighton Works. Bannister and Drummond were landed with that job, but it was Stroudley who did much of the general and detail planning, even to the extent of designing specific machine-tools and cranes.

Such an upheaval often arouses resentment, but Stroudley was aided by Craven — a harsh disciplinarian — being less than popular with his staff. Stroudley was no push-over either, and immersed himself in all aspects of his department's work — even to the point of being a bit of a busy-body, but he had an empathy with his men that the mercurial Craven never enjoyed. Stroudley soon imposed his will and ideals, laid a path his subordinates were more than proud to tread and gained all-round respect. The rebuilding, re-organisation and expansion of Brighton Works was a major task. Stroudley knew he had to get his operating theatre in shape before embarking on the essential, even drastic, surgery. His forward planning was a model to follow and contrasts sharply with the virtual hand-to-mouth existence of our railways today. If it was not exactly a marriage made in heaven, then Stroudley certainly created his own engineering Garden of Eden.

Another policy change entailed each driver having his own engine, with his name painted inside the cab. This, and the adoption of the golden ochre livery for passenger engines (that showed up the slightest trace of dirt), firmly placed the onus on a driver to ensure that his engine was spotless and well maintained. Stroudley expected his drivers to be loyal and to take pride in their charges, thus reducing maintenance costs. Yet another matter whereby he could teach many of today's mis-managers a thing or two.

Unlike many Locomotive Superintendents, who had their first designs for a new railway up and running within months of their appointment, Stroudley was rather slow out of the starting-blocks. He was well into his second year in charge before he produced two 0-4-2Ts that used up old boilers and other parts lying about the works.

From this rudimentary start, Stroudley soon introduced his first new design. Two 'C' class 0-6-0 goods engines — quite different from anything that had run on the Brighton before — indicated the extent of the changes brought about by Stroudley's regime. They had inside frames, an elegant copper-rimmed chimney and a generous cab. Several experimental features were tried: some successful — such as the single casting of the cylinders and heated feed-water; others less so — such as the HR-inspired Adams safety valve and domeless boiler. Most important, they were very satisfactory engines right from the start and, somewhat ironically — given the dearth of heavy goods work on the LBSCR, were briefly the most powerful engines of their type in Britain. The class was complete by 1874 and wore the dark olive green goods livery. Their modest dimensions belied their modernity, and they went on to do sterling work for 30 years. Stroudley had made an assured start.

In 1872, Stroudley rebuilt two of Craven's singles as express passenger 2-4-0s: a trick that hen had pulled-off on the HR. These, briefly, had domeless boilers and were joined by two brand new engines before the year was out: the '201' class. Their main claim to fame was purely aesthetic, being the first engines to wear the golden ochre livery, lined in a delicate red, green, black and white, with a finish that was to be an envious trademark for over three decades. Hauling a set of mahogany coaches, with their deep crimson ends, such an ensemble at least looked the part of an important express train, even if that was not the case. Image, as today, clearly counted for a great deal.

Then, Stroudley launched the first of seven major classes to appear during the next decade. This momentous building programme, when completed, thoroughly transformed the LBSCR locomotive stock into one of the most homogeneous and modern in Britain. Eventually, these various locomotives accounted for two thirds of the company's fleet.

Unlike many Stars of Steam, Stroudley was involved in all aspects of design, from conception to personally selecting the smallest and most basic components. Not for him simply drafting the main dimensions, and leaving the rest up to his subordinates. No, Stroudley wanted his engines to be his own work in all the important facets. While he must surely have taken advice, and with D. Drummond as Works Manager probably received more than he wanted, nothing went ahead without his say-so.

The first design that was to transform the locomotive stock was, arguably, the most famous: the 'A' class, or celebrated

'Terriers'. If ever there were a predecessor to Thomas the Tank Engine at his cheekiest, this was it. Quite often, nicknames bestowed on locomotives can be asinine or obscure, but in this case 'Terrier' fitted the bill perfectly. They were initially built to work the lightly constructed Thames Tunnel and South London Lines. With trains of rustic four-wheel coaches, that almost dwarfed them, they charged about in a most frenetic manner. Theirs was a life of the dull and the mundane, amidst the shabby squalor of London's less salubrious suburbs, but they brought a touch of glitz, if not glamour, to people's lives with their gaily painted colours and fussy demeanour.

As a final touch of brashness, each locomotive was initially named after the grimy suburbs in which they worked. So one had 'Shadwell', 'Wapping' and 'Deptford' to conjure with — a kind of inverse snobbery. Not that these names were concealed so that one could barely read them either, as on the LNWR. Oh no, the 'Terriers' names were brazenly emblazoned along the tank sides in such a manner that one could hardly fail to notice: they were working-class engines and clearly proud of it.

Later, 'Terriers' bore more genteel names such as 'Boxhill' and found work on many lightly laid rural branches. Wherever they went, though, they caught the public's eye: they were natural performers and would not be ignored. A simple task, say a mid-morning train on some far-flung, sleepy branch, was an ideal opportunity for a 'Terrier' to step forward and claim centre-stage. Whereas any other engine would doze away until the appointed departure time, perhaps give a gentle 'poop' on its whistle and then ease into life, a 'Terrier' had its own inimitable style.

For a start, a 'Terrier' would not simmer quietly in the bay platform, but impatiently sizzle and seethe until the appointed hour. Neither was one left in any doubt as to when it was time to depart. Just like the start of a great musical extravaganza, a loud shriek would burst forth from its whistle then, in a flurry of steam and frenzied activity, the 'Terrier' would set-off as if the end of the world was very nigh indeed. These unique characteristics masked what were, nonetheless, powerful and economical engines for their size. They certainly undertook their menial tasks displaying all the panache usually associated with the grandest, most important trains. One wonders just what performance a 'Terrier' would have put-on had one ever been allocated a Pullman train?

Despite their diminutive size, the 'Terriers' were more than capable of surprisingly purposeful work. In 1878, No. 40 'Brighton' won a Gold Medal at the Paris Exhibition. While flying the Union Jack, the LBSCR took the opportunity to drop hints to the Western Railway about speeding-up the Dieppe-Paris leg of the Newhaven Boat Train, to an eye-watering 40 mph. The French were sceptical about such a demanding schedule, and so little 'Brighton' was put-to it to give a demonstration. The 40 mph schedule was meat and drink to the diminutive pyrotechnic artist, and it shamed the Western Railway into accelerating its connecting Boat Train.

The 'Terriers' were long-lasting engines as well, and some served BR into the 1960s, each well over 80 years old. Eight were built by the New South Wales Government Railway in 1875, while several were sold when electrification began early this century. Thus, the rival SECR and LSWR each had a few, while they were popular for light railways, including two on the Weston, Cleveland and Portished Railway that ended up in GWR stock. This widespread use certainly pays tribute to these fly-weight champs and their designer.

Having got one success under his belt, Stroudley became more adventurous. He introduced the 'D' class 0-4-2 passenger tanks to work throughout the system, except for the lightest inner-London routes. They eventually became the

Engine-crews and shed staff were immensely proud of their charges during pre-Grouping days. One would imagine that, if the engines themselves had characters, none could be more proud or sure of itself than a Stroudley 'A' class, or 'Terrier'. No. 68 'Clapham' looks almost becalmed, but would soon become quite the showman once it gained an audience. The inimitable buzz and fussiness of a 'Terrier' still remains one of the finest spectacles of the days of steam.

mainstay of the line, tackling everything from branch-line trains, through outer-suburban to all but the best expresses. They were quite nippy and, like the 'Terriers', wore the golden ochre livery with their names displayed proudly for all to see. These were also named after London suburbs — though of a more genteel kind, but eventually encompassed villages from remotest Sussex.

The 'Ds' were highly efficient, versatile, extremely reliable and long-lived with several passing to BR. They replaced many of Craven's specialist locomotives, improving on their performance and, of course, saved enormously on spares. In many ways, the 'D' class locomotives was Stroudley's unsung heroes. While his 'Terrier' and 'Gladstone' classes stole the limelight, it was the 'Ds' that had the greatest impact on everyday passenger services. Had it not been for their success, the wherewithal to eventually improve the low standards of speed and punctuality would not have existed.

About a year later, came the 'E' class 0-6-0 goods tank. The majority were painted olive green, but a few wore the golden ochre for use on passenger services: versatility was certainly a Stroudley trademark. They were built in steady numbers over a decade, with the last six emerging after Stroudley's death. Despite being goods engines, all were named — mostly after foreign places whose link with the LBSCR was tenuous, to say the least — such as No. 148 'Vienna'. Their early years saw employment not only on short-haul goods trains, especially round London, but also on goods trains to the coast. Later, many were re-boilered and rebuilt to serve the S.R's West Country lines and, again, BR was to receive a fair few.

Stroudley's 'D' and 'E' classes undertook much of the routine work on the railway and, as often happens, were rather taken for granted. Not for these the adoration afforded the GWR's 0-4-0Ts, or even their fellow 'Terriers'. These two classes eventually made up almost one third of LBSCR stock, which gives a pretty good idea of their value. Add to that their longevity and sound mechanical attributes, and you have two maids-of-all-work the equal of anything produced during the 19th century.

Thus far, Stroudley's measured progress had been successful, but he had not produced a worthwhile express design, particularly one suited to the vagaries of the Portsmouth line. When he finally did, it was not exactly innovative — or even an impressive example of modern thinking, and it looked to be out-of-date almost before it turned a wheel. No. 151 'Grosvenor' was not a, then popular, 2-4-0, certainly not a 4-4-0, nor even a single-driver with a leading bogie: no, it was something of an apparent museum-piece, a 2-2-2 which,

If the 'Terriers' were the stars of the show, at least as far as tank engines were concerned, Stroudley's 'D' class 0-4-2Ts were the unsung heroes, without which the whole shebang would most definitely not go ahead. No. 633, formerly No. 33 'Mitcham', hauls an Epsom-bound train in the post-Stroudley era, but it could just as easily have been a light, fast express, or a reasonably heavy goods. No engines were more versatile on any railway in 19th century Britain.

(J. Kydd)

nevertheless, incorporated a number of innovations. Even so, was Stroudley taking a tired theme and tacking-on a few trinkets, apparently to make it appear something new?

Perhaps so, but 'Grosvenor' was both successful in traffic and an important development engine. For a start, it had the largest boiler on the railway, inside wheel bearings and utilised many standard parts. It was the LBSCR's flagship, and represented the company at the 1875 Newark Brake Trials, despite having wooden brake blocks. There, it performed commendably and was the first British engine to be fitted with the Westinghouse brake. By 1877, the LBSCR had adopted the Westinghouse brake throughout its system.

Suitably, 'Grosvenor' led a glamorous existence hauling the prestigious London Bridge-Newhaven Boat Train, until scrapped in 1907, but with a daily round-trip of little more than 100 miles, it had an easy time of it. This less-than arduous duty incorporated one of the more unusual working practices on a British railway. The driver was employed on a fixed contract, out of which he paid the running costs and staff to clean the engine and train. What was left-over was his wages: an apparent madcap scheme that, nevertheless, lasted for several years. It is just the sort of hare-brained idea that

The 'D2' class was a general purpose, or latterly mixed-traffic design. Stroudley might have been influenced by P. Stirling's successful use of such locomotives, and seems to have emulated the Scotsman. Once again, they were given foreign names, but as their duties included the continental fast goods trains, via Newhaven, this was not quite so anomalous as with the 'E' class tanks. No. 304 'Nice', fitted with an early tender, reminds us that they were equally at home on semi-fast passenger trains as well. *(J. Kydd)*

some cost-conscious, profit-motivated, modern mis-manager might come up with to take our railways into the twenty-first century. Madcap? It's brilliant...

Then, in 1877 Stroudley designed a second 2-2-2 for comparative purposes. No. 325 'Abergavenny' had a smaller boiler, cylinders and driving wheels, but still worked express services and allowed Stroudley to assess different ideas in daily use. Both of these engines were incorporated into the later 'G'-class.

After five years in office, Stroudley had achieved a great deal. Including 'Grosvenor', he had introduced five new standard classes and, more important, Brighton Works was as modern as any in the land. However, it is easy to over-state the impact felt by the general passengers, for his standard classes numbered but 55 engines between them, not even 10% of the total locomotive stock. Trains were still abysmally slow and unpunctual and, even if they looked attractive, many of Craven's engines were in less than the pink of condition. As for the coaches, primitive was the most appropriate adjective.

In 1875, Drummond returned to Scotland and Stroudley lost an important associate. Drummond almost venerated Stroudley, and paid him the ultimate compliment by incorporating many of Stroudley's ideas into his early NBR designs. Drummond's loss did not unduly hinder Stroudley's progress, though no new designs were forthcoming that year, but locomotive building gathered pace and included two more, stop-gap, express 2-4-0s. In any case, Stroudley was clearly a highly competent and occasionally innovative engineer.

While Stroudley's standard tank engines were ousting Craven's multitudinous creations, there was a need for an engine capable of undertaking a range of duties for which tank engines were not best suited: something of a mixed-traffic design. Such requirements would hardly warrant anything radical, but Stroudley's 'D2' class 0-4-2s were an unusual, novel approach, perhaps influenced by the work of P. Stirling. They made use of many standard-pattern parts: driving and trailing wheels, chimney, dome, cylinders, pistons and much else were all inter-changeable with other locomotives. Only 14 were built, but they filled a vital gap in the fleet, and performed particularly well on the fast continental goods and Sussex-London fruit trains for many years. Such was the scale of their performance that they set-off a train of thought in

Stroudley's mind that culminated in his finest and best known design.

Stroudley next addressed a need for more powerful and fleet-of-foot express engines. Building on the success of the 'D2s', an enlarged version emerged from Brighton with 'C' class cylinders. Designated the 'D3' class, No. 208 'Richmond' ran as a singleton for nine months, under Stroudley's eagle eye. Ironically, it attracted some adverse comment in the press, due to its lack of leading wheels. This was a case of practice out-doing theory, for what should not work, palpably did. Soon 'Richmond' was joined by five sister engines and they soon displaced the 2-4-0s off the fastest expresses. These premier trains of the line were nothing to get excited about as the 44 mph average speed from London Bridge-Brighton was hardly dashing, even for 1880.

So, after ten years at the helm, the Brighton had 205 of Stroudley's standard engines, numbering about one third of the total fleet. Nevertheless, they undertook the majority of main line passenger and goods, heavy goods and suburban passenger trains, and spent far less time in the works than did Craven's crocks. The line was awash with gaily painted, immaculate passenger trains: it was a pity that management did not see fit to provided better services.

One could have some sympathy regarding the Portsmouth line though. This was a difficult route to work, with numerous junctions, curves and many distinctly sharp inclines. What was more, it was considerably longer than the rival LSWR route. In short, what was needed was an engine with good adhesion, a fair turn of speed, rapid acceleration and an ability to pull: ideal requirements, one might have thought, for a 4-4-0.

Wrong! Stroudley's answer was an amalgam of 'Abergavenny', 'Grosvenor' and the 'G' class 2-2-2s. It seemed as though Stroudley had simply raided the parts store and cobbled together a new design. Apart from an inside-framed tender, the 'G' class took standardisation to new limits. At first, they worked all over the system, but were soon concentrated on the Portsmouth route. There was, however, method behind Stroudley's seeming madness, for they were sure-footed, rode well and, at under 50 ft. long, could be accommodated on the Portsmouth turntable. They were an immediate success and dominated these services for nearly 20 years.

Thereafter, though demoted to coastal stopping trains, some of the 'G' class engines led a charmed life. Although all were scrapped by 1914, three were sold to the Italian State Railways, in 1907, while No. 329 'Stephenson' was exclusively deployed on the 'Eastbourne Sunday Pullman', from 1910-12. That prestige duty was more of retirement privilege and, like so many Brighton engines, the 'G' class generally enjoyed an easy life. London-Portsmouth and back was about their most difficult duty and, given the light loads and steady speeds, there was little wonder they were reliable, very economical and easy to maintain. Still, they were another Stroudley design that was superbly matched to its intended duties: would it be that other engineers could be so successful.

While working on what was to become his masterpiece, Stroudley met a requirement for more heavy goods engines with an updated version of his earlier 0-6-0s. The 'C1' class was very similar in appearance, but featured larger cylinders and benefited from 12 years' of solid design experience. Only 12 engines were built over five years and, as with their forebears, they were also the most powerful engines of their kind in the country when new. Of course, their work was limited, but they were another great asset to the railway.

Then, at the end of 1882, Stroudley's most famous individual engine, and most renown design, No. 214 'Gladstone' took its bow. For those who followed Brighton locomotive matters closely this, Britain's largest 0-4-2, was a logical development of all that had gone before. For those not so conversant...hmm. Was there not something missing, like leading wheels? Whatever, 'Gladstone' certainly demanded attention. Only six engines of the 'B' class were built by 1887, so their impact on services was limited, but then they began to emerge in numbers, with ten built after Stroudley's death. Like all truly great engines, the 'Gladstones' were a success right from the start and endeared themselves to everyone.

Immaculately turned out, these eccentrically elegant engines were an instant hit with the travelling public; like the first HSTs, they simply could not be ignored. With an enlarged 'D3' boiler, they were powerful, economical, rode surprisingly well and were immensely popular with their regular crews. They were also long-lived, with the last one being scrapped in 1933, and the class was still working fast Portsmouth trains well into the 1920s.

Naturally, as pride of the fleet, the first 'Gladstones' were allocated to the best and most popular expresses. Their extra power and zip allowed an eventual acceleration of the fastest London-Brighton trains to 65 minutes. Though this might still seem un-inspiring, some smart running was needed given the dense traffic and the short distance involved, but it was part of a very gradual speeding-up of the best LBSCR trains. As more 'Gladstones' were built, they hauled all the fast Brighton trains, leading to improvements in both timings and punctuality. Later 4-4-0s, built by Stroudley's successor, R.J. Billinton, failed to oust them and they lasted on front-line duties for over 30 years, only bowing out when electrification finally reached the south coast.

As with all of Stroudley's locomotives, the 'Gladstones' were positively pampered. A typical day's work might entail a non-stop express from Brighton-Victoria, followed by a gentle run round to London Bridge. Then an Eastbourne express, on a less than exacting schedule, and finally a trundle back to Brighton, via the coastal route, home and bed: at less than 150 miles a day, they had it easy.

Even so, the 'Gladstones' almost became an icon for railway enthusiasts, and Stroudley was virtually deified with the Stephenson Locomotive Society as an LBSCR enclave. It was just as well, for 'Gladstone' itself was purchased for preservation in 1927, enabling us to appreciate its idiosyncratic beauty, and the outstanding livery and condition in which these engines ran in daily service. 'Gladstone' also demonstrates just how lightly Brighton locomotives were worked. Upon retirement, after 44 years' service, it had covered 1,346,918 miles, only just over 30,000 a year: this was a pretty low figure even by contemporary standards.

After completing the 'Gladstones', Stroudley had designed something for every conceivable duty. In 1884, he brought out an 0-6-0 goods-tank, developed from the 'E' class and designated the 'E1'. This featured 'Gladstone' cylinders, although No. 157 — the grandly named 'Barcelona' — remained an only child. Stroudley was also planning for the future, having a new 0-6-2T design underway when the curtain was drawn over his eventful life. The expectation was that a new standard class would surely follow, but it fell to his successor, Billinton, to modify this and to produce what was, essentially, his own design.

With that, Stroudley penned his last locomotive design, though he was working on a 2-4-2 passenger tank at the time of his death, and there has been talk of a 'super Gladstone' tank as well. And his death? That was most untimely. He was attending the Paris Exhibition, in late-1889, at which 'Gladstone' No. 189 'Edward Blount' had been awarded a Gold Medal. So entranced were the French engineers at this unusual machine, that it took part in trials from Paris-Laroche when Stroudley contracted pneumonia and died, aged only 56.

His work was far from complete. After transforming all aspects of the locomotive department, he had hardly begun to make an impact with the coaching stock, and the eventual service improvements that his engines enabled were some way off. Stroudley's efforts were not in vain, but he never lived to see just what his engines could do if pushed a little harder.

Stroudley also had several other achievements to his name. Coaches were not among them though, and his first bogie coach was only just completed when he died. Despite this, and after having tried some ex-MR Pullman cars, the LBSCR assembled a four car 'Pullman Limited', in 1881. The car 'Beatrice' was equipped with twelve electric lights, fed by batteries charged by Stroudley's own belt and pulley generator: a world first.

Eventually, in 1888, three Pullman coaches were assembled at the new Pullman Works in Brighton, with a much shorter matching car, known as the 'Pullman Pup'. The 'Pup' was specially built to carry Stroudley's generator for the whole, permanently coupled train. Thus began Brighton's long-associated tradition of Pullman trains, while a better, safer and more efficient method of lighting was introduced. By 1893, the LBSCR had over 300 electrically lit coaches in fixed-set formations.

As with many Victorian engineers, Stroudley was an innovator. He devised a locomotive speed indicator, whereby the height of water rising in a glass tube gave an approximate speed. Of more enduring use was the Stroudley and Rushbridge electric emergency communication system. This was operated by a pull-out knob on compartment partitions and lasted until the 1920s. Apart from these, Stroudley had his own design fads: so he preferred feed-pumps to injectors, and rear ashpan dampers to those at the front. Stroudley was never one to slavishly follow the pack.

So, just how complete was the transformation of the Brighton's locomotive stock at the time of Stroudley's death? By then, two thirds of the locomotives were of his design and they were fully masters of their work. They did far more than their share of allocated duties, and were a magnificent legacy to the railway for the rest of its existence. Indeed, of how many other Locomotive Superintendents can it be said, that they never penned a poor design? And remember, Stroudley really did design all major and many minor aspects of his locomotives.

For all that, in 1889, the LBSCR's services were just as unpunctual and little faster than on the day Stroudley was appointed. This was still in evidence at the time of the 1895 'Race to the North'. Following the very public, magnificent exploits of those involved in the 'races', there was a quite lengthy, occasionally virulent correspondence in The Times about 'The Crawl to the South'. This culminated in a leading article of 14th September 1895, in which the LBSCR and SER were singled out as vying to be the "...worst line in the country..." As 'Dellboy' Trotter might have said, 'come on, don't beat about the bush, give it to me straight"!

Stung by such criticism, when the Brighton finally got round to improving its services, Stroudley's immense work came into its own. He had built for the future, not simply the present. Not forgetting, of course, that by rebuilding Brighton Works and establishing all the maintenance and good house-keeping practices, he laid deep foundations on which his successors could build.

Though not without his detractors, including an exchange of views over compounding and running costs with none other than F.W. Webb, Stroudley's work was recognised by his peers. He was awarded a George Stephenson Medal and a Telford Premium for his paper, 'The Construction of Locomotive Engines' to the ICE, in 1885. In that, he advocated the higher capital expenditure on more and better-built locomotives, so that a one man/one engine policy could be adopted, thus reducing stores and maintenance costs. Needless to say, Webb returned the compliment paid to him by Stroudley, two years previously, with knobs on.

In many respects, the LBSCR was both a music hall joke and yet held dearly to the heart of the nation when Stroudley died. It was looked upon then, as we might today, view an eccentric who tries his best, but is not quite up to it: a bit like Sergeant Wilson in 'Dad's Army'. On the whole, its services were not so bad and it had charm and individuality. With those last two attributes, people can forgive most things, but there were limits. An almost complete lack of progress, when speeds and comfort were improving fast on other railways, finally did for the sloppy, inefficient ways of the Brighton and it had to act. Within a fairly short time, though, it had recovered and was back in the heart of the nation, all music hall jokes had been banished. Without Stroudley's locomotive legacy, that would surely never have happened.

Stroudley's Locomotive Designs

YEAR	CLASS	WHEEL ARRANG'T	CYLINDERS (INCHES)	BOILER PRESSURE	DRIVING-WHEEL DIAMETER	WEIGHT	No. IN CLASS
1869	HR	0-6-0ST	14 x 20	120 psi	3' 7"	23T 10 cwt	3
1871		0-4-2T	17 x 20	140 psi			2
1871	C	0-6-0	17½ x 26	140 psi	5 ft.	35T 12 cwt	20
1872	A	0-6-0T	13 x 20	140 psi	4 ft.	24T 15 cwt	50
1872	201	2-4-0	17 x 24	140 psi	6' 6"	41T 5 cwt	4
1873	D	0-4-2T	17 x 24	140 psi	5' 6"	38T 10 cwt	125
1874	E	0-6-0T	17 x 24	140 psi	4' 6"	39T 10 cwt	72
1874 *	Gros.	2-2-2	17 x 24	140 psi	6' 9"	33 tons	1
1876	D2	0-4-2	17 x 24	140 psi	5' 6"	34 tons	14
1877 *	Aber.	2-2-2,	16 x 22	140 psi	6' 6"	34T 4 cwt	1
1878	D3	0-4-2	17¼ x 26	140 psi	6' 6"	36 tons	6
1880	G	2-2-2	17 x 24	140 psi	6' 6"	33 tons	26 *
1882	C1	0-6-0	18¼ x 26	150 psi	5 ft.	40T 7 cwt	12
1882	B	0-4-2	18¼ x 26	140 psi	6' 6"	38T 15 cwt	36
1884	E1	0-6-0T	18¼ x 26	150 psi	4' 6"	50 tons	1

* includes 'Grosvenor' and 'Abergavenny'

STROUDLEY's PRESERVED LOCOMOTIVES

YEAR	CLASS	RUNNING NUMBERS	TOTAL
1872	A	Boxhill, Waddon, Fenchurch, Newport, Sutton, Stepney, Martello, Bodiam, Knowle, Freshwater	10
1874	E	2110	1
1882	B	Gladstone	1

STROUDLEY IN BRIEF

BORN:	6th March 1833, Sandford, Oxon.
TRAINED:	1853, Swindon Works, G.W.R.
EMPLOYED:	1854, G.N.R., at Peterborough.
SENIOR POSITIONS:	1861, Works Manager, Cowlairs Works, E.G.R.
	1865, Loco. Supt. H.R.
	1870, Loco. Supt. L.B.S.C.R.
HONOURS:	Telford Premium, George Stephenson Medal, I.C.E.
DIED:	20th December 1889, Paris.

DUGALD DRUMMOND
Once, Twice, Three Times a Great Steam Locomotive Engineer

Faint praise can be damning but, more often than not, it is heavily over-embellished these days. Even the most mundane acts are often described as being great: you know, the common-or-garden favour one is thanked for with the phrase, "oh, great stuff" which, though it might be pretty good, is more than a few notches short of being great. Greatness, like the confetti degrees that are now handed out willy-nilly, has been heavily down-graded.

How many footballers, for example, does one hear described as being great? Of course some — such as George Best, Pele and perhaps even Hoddle — undoubtedly were, but what about Joe Smith who played in the First Division and represented his country five times? He might have been a good player — even very good, but surely not great: that must be limited to the sublimely gifted, dedicated and lucky few.

Then again, even fewer people undertake truly great achievements in more than one field or place. Matt Busby was a truly great football manager, but only for Manchester United: a bit closer to home, O.S. Nock was a great writer, but only about railways. Of our Stars of Steam, several were clearly great engineers but, accepting the GNR and LNER as merely different scenes on the same stage, Gresley, Stanier and Churchward all designed great locomotives for just the one railway. If Stanier had taken over at Doncaster, say, on Gresley's death, he might have found undertaking great work the second time round just that bit more difficult. That is not surprising, considering the different requirements and circumstances, but one engineer managed to produce great work and locomotives, at not just one railway company, but three. For such achievements of the highest magnitude, Dugald Drummond will forever rank among the very greatest of steam locomotive engineers. And yet...

Drummond's influence was widespread and is still felt today, though not necessarily as he would have wished. There is a pub overlooking the railway from Eastleigh to Southampton, at a discreet distance, called The Drummond Arms. To my surprise, the landlord was quite aware that the Drummond in question was not Captain Bulldog: our Drummond was tee-total. On the other hand, a neighbour of mine is one of the lucky few to retain his job at Eastleigh Works, perhaps because he has no special interest in railways — he had never heard of Bulleid, for example. He was born over 40 years after Drummond died, yet still that name commands his respect. Such are the vagaries of true greatness, but for Drummond it went far wider and much deeper.

For a man whose learned contributions to steam locomotive development were few and far between, and whose modest innovations ranged from being a complete flop to barely questionable benefit, Drummond's distorted reputation is full of contradictions. From the 1870s onwards, his locomotive design principles were synonymous with those of the Scottish tradition, and his engines played a not insignificant role in three of the four post-Grouping railway companies: many lasted into the 1960s. Just look at the list of engine classes for which Drummond was responsible — few engineers managed to produce so many quite different designs.

Then again, though never a design innovator, Drummond kept abreast of practical developments, such as his early adoption of W. Adams' bogie and Vortex blastpipe. He concentrated on making steam engines go and never mind the theoretical niceties. Drummond's locomotives featured a more-than-adequate boiler, a large grate, good steam and exhaust passages, and reduced cylinder back-pressure. Hand in glove with these went an appreciation of the advantages of a high boiler pressure, and driving with a wide-open regulator and short cut-offs — even if his crews would not always play the game. Lastly, his engines were solid and rugged, with fine proportions and, especially with their smokebox wings and dome-mounted safety valve, elegantly distinctive. For most of his 33 years as a Locomotive Superintendent, Drummond produced strong, powerful, economical and free-steaming engines, of high-quality build and a style that exuded those very traits: nothing more and certainly nothing less.

Such sensible attributes are often the product of good teaching, and behind most great men stands a domineering mentor. Born (or was he hewn from the solid?) in Ardrossan, Drummond served an engineering apprenticeship, gained further experience at Thomas Brassey's, and finally met his personal guru at the Cowlairs Works of the Edinburgh and Glasgow Railway. Considering Drummond's renown pyrotechnic temper, strict and fierce demeanour, intolerance and opinionated determination to get his own way, one might assume that his sage was a not-too-distant relation of the devil. It is, then, something of a surprise to find that he was the rather mild-mannered, yet firm, W. Stroudley.

Drummond spent the best part of eleven years working under Stroudley, initially at the EGR and then as his Works Manager at both the HR and the LBSCR. Not surprisingly, Drummond was totally imbued with Stroudley's principles: good thorough — yet simple — design; and, especially, a high-class finish with fine uncluttered lines. When Drummond became a Locomotive Superintendent in his own right, at the NBR, his first three designs might almost have been taken straight from Stroudley's portfolio, in every detail and facet.

In two other respects, Drummond closely followed Stroudley's lead. First, he thoroughly re-organised his old stamping ground at Cowlairs Works — so it could undertake work to his standards, and involved himself in every aspect of locomotive design. Not for him an idea sketched-out on the back of an envelope and left to the Drawing Office to sort out. No, he stipulated the requirements, set the tightest of parameters and heaven help anyone who was foolhardy enough to transgress. Right through his career, that was Drummond's way: there was never any doubt about who was in charge.

If the young Drummond was a talented and highly skilled — yet orthodox — engineer, by the time he descended on the LSWR, with many successes behind him, so he began to tamper and experiment. Perhaps it was the passing of the era of great engineering despots, such as Webb and Stirling —

Drummond's first great design, for that it surely was, came in only 1876 for the NBR. An express engine intended for the Waverley route, the '476' class allowed a major revamp in services over that awkward line. The appropriately named No. 479 'Abbotsford' is a foretaste of the rapidly developing Scottish school of locomotive engineering; that of Drummond by any other name.   (J. Kydd)

while Dean mellowed to form a partnership with Churchward. Maybe it was the realisation that Victorian engineering tenets had to evolve or be swamped. Alternatively, Drummond may have been influenced by the fact that, despite his reputation for designing solid and dependable locomotives, and thoroughly re-organising several works, he had not materially added to the development of the steam locomotive. A new age was afoot with multiple cylinders, superheating, compounding, Belpaire fireboxes and much else. Drummond saw his chance to really make a name for himself, and he intended to have a damned good go at taking it.

Not being tempted by the something-for-nothing appeal of compounds, Drummond opted for simplicity, utilising a high boiler pressure, and efficient steam passages and cylinders — a path preferred by many British engineers. His experiments included firebox water-tubes — a worthy attempt at getting the water to the hottest part of the heating circuit; heated feed-water coils in the tender — as used by foreign engineers; then, while scornful of super-heating, Drummond used his own — ultimately ineffective — steam-drier; while his spark-arrester did that and much more, until modified. Neither did his steam-reverser gain universal admiration.

None of those gadgets was exactly successful, and most were removed by Drummond's successor and former right-hand man, Robert Urie. Then, quite typical of the man, there was Drummond's foray at improving the single-driver engine, a type he had never endorsed. At a time when it was evident that such engines lacked the adhesion for the increasingly heavy express trains, Drummond sought to counter this with his double-singles. He also seemingly tried to trump Churchward's card with multiple cylinder 4-6-0s. The word was, though nobody dared mutter it within earshot of the great man, that he was getting involved with things he did not understand. Perhaps there was some truth in that, although even Churchward had his oversights. In the end, most of

Drummond's innovations came to nought, but he tried and, he had succeeded, his standing would have been still further enhanced.

Drummond's reputation has been further tempered by his volatile character that, far from mellowing with age, became ever-more erratic. This was especially so on the LSWR where, for every tale of leniency, there were many who lived to regret ignoring a warning-fusillade across their bows. Feared and revered, loved and loathed, sated and hated. Such contrary emotions towards Drummond could be found everywhere. Some thought him an outstanding man-manager, others a sergeant-major who ruled with a fearful iron rod — a common trait among Victorian mis-managers. The difference was, Drummond — and include many other engineering greats — was widely admired, unlike the many would-be demi-gods.

That notion was not always the case though. Drummond first formulated and imposed his methods of working and designs during his years as Locomotive Superintendent of the NBR and CR. Out went the old — baby, bath-water, the lot — and in came admiration, respect and, most important, company pride. Whether in the locomotive workshops, offices or sheds, employees were driven hard and were expected to deliver the goods, but were given tools that were second to none. Opinionated and direct Drummond might have been, but he was revered in Scottish railway circles. Like Stirling, Webb and Dean, his men would have followed him unquestioningly to the end of the earth and back; that was not always the case on the LSWR.

Big in stature and anything but a shrinking violet, Drummond knew how best to achieve his targets. He expected — demanded — loyalty and obedience; if he said 'jump', you most certainly did. However, a period out of direct railway employment, from 1890-95 when, after an unsuccessful Australian venture, he founded D. Drummond & Sons — later the Glasgow Railway Eng. Co. Ltd., soured him somewhat: he was not a man used to taking orders, especially for piddling little shunting engines. He became a frustrated man. When a door finally opened at the LSWR, Drummond not only grabbed it with both hands, but intended to make up for every hour of lost-time. He forced a furious pace at Nine Elms that, within a year, saw something of a mass exodus, and left those who remained in awe, if not reverence of the man with the volcanic temperament.

Like man, like dog; like engineer, like engines. Such

Within two years of arriving at the CR, Drummond had improved on his '476' class for the NBR and designed another great express 4-4-0, the '66' class. These really shone in the 1895 Races, but in 1888 he designed a smaller wheeled version for other, none main line passenger trains; in particular, those to the Clyde Coast. These '80' class 4-4-0s were, again, outstanding engines in every way and, as No. 195 shows, looked every inch true Drummond thoroughbreds. They also worked up to Aberdeen on the overnight expresses. *(J. Kydd)*

---

analogies can be surprisingly accurate. If Drummond was a big, bold, vociferous and solid man, with an immense capacity for work, well presented with no fancy-Dan trinkets or niceties about him, so were his engines. An unprecedented 14 classes of Drummond's locomotives had working lives of over 50 years, including examples across the whole range of designs and their versatility was legendary. They all displayed their designer's personal characteristics, minus the periodic explosions, but were also extremely agile and fleet-of-foot — assets not usually associated with Drummond.

If the impact of a Drummond rage could be both considerable and long-lasting, even that pales into insignificance with his legacy to Britain's railways. Although not a founding-father of the Scottish locomotive tradition, by the late-19th and first decades of the twentieth century, to all intents and purposes, this was indistinguishable from Drummond's usual practices. His main locomotive design tenets applied not only in general but, in many cases, to specific design details on four of the five main Scottish railway companies.

Such a scenario should not be unexpected. When Drummond was the Locomotive Superintendent of the NBR, he comprehensively re-organised Cowlairs Works, which continued to design and build locomotives to his high standards for almost 50 years. His successors, M. Holmes and W.P. Reid, dined very well off his legacy.

In 1882, Drummond promptly jumped ship to the CR, receiving a vastly increased salary of £1,700 p.a. as an enticement. As with T. Wheatley before him on the NBR, there was a suggestion of irregularities in the Cowlairs accounts, so perhaps he jumped before being forced to walk the plank. Already a star in ascendancy, with one outstanding and several noteworthy designs under his well-proportioned belt, a distinctive Drummond style was ever-more evident, based on his development of Stroudley's principles.

On the CR, Drummond began by first locating all locomotive design and building at St. Rollox Works, right under his nose, and then he re-organised and shook the place

to its foundations: it soon became the finest locomotive works in Scotland. For eight years, Drummond reigned increasingly supreme. Drummond's four-coupled express engines were the best of their kind in Britain, while his other designs were the equals of their peers, and the CR was well on the way to having one of the most advanced locomotive fleets in Britain.

Drummond's sweeping revolution provided engines that virtually eliminated double-heading and made considerable running and capital economies. Out went outside cylinders and inconsistent performance, in came inside cylinders and high boiler pressures, making for free, hard-running and economical engines. Not only that, but better carriages were introduced, with steam heating and gas lighting, along with the Westinghouse air-brake: the CR was being rapidly transformed. These major improvements enabled the railway to out-do its rivals, the GSWR and NBR, over most competing routes. For compete they most surely did, especially on Clyde Coast services, and the CR proved to be the standard-setter once Drummond provided the finest engines in the land.

When Drummond departed in mid-1890, his fame had spread far beyond his country of birth. He left behind two great locomotive designs and many others only just short of the top bracket, while the locomotive fleet was completely transmogrified, and foundations were laid for still further improvements. St. Rollox could look Crewe, Swindon, Derby and Doncaster squarely in the eyes, and his successors, Lambie, McIntosh and Pickersgill barely deviated from the clearly marked Drummond path. By 1901, the CR possessed the finest locomotives in Britain.

That was not all though. If one looks at locomotives of the HR and the GSWR, they also display Drummond's influence, in both style and detail design. This was not entirely surprising for there was a little bit more than pure admiration at work. Just as Drummond had trailed Stroudley from Cowlairs to Brighton, via Inverness, and then, initially, copied his designs, so he played pied-piper to his brother. Peter Drummond followed Dugald to Brighton, Cowlairs and St. Rollox, but stayed put after Dugald departed on his Australian fiasco.

In 1896, P. Drummond was appointed Locomotive Superintendent of the HR, and in 1912 moved to the GSWR. Though a fine engineer, he lacked the abilities — and drawbacks — of his renown brother. His HR designs were almost slavish copies, including the red herrings of firebox water tubes, feed-water heating and a steam drier, though he improved Lochgorm Works. In the main though, the Drummond traditions of sturdy simplicity, efficient — though in his case not outstanding — performance, and good workshop practices were adhered to.

At the behest of the LSWR board for a single-driver express locomotive, Drummond designed a double-single (the power of two engines and only one crew) as a means of appeasement. He knew only too well that the days of the single-driver were over, but four years later the production double-singles emerged, the 'E10' class. Not surprisingly, they were successful, arriving too late in the day and lacking any subsequent development. No. 369 stands at Nine Elms, clearly a product of the Drummond school of engineering.

The younger Drummond then ploughed a similar furrow at Kilmarnock, but introduced superheating. A modified Drummond style emerged, subtly different from the quintessential paradigms of St. Rollox and Cowlairs. As an aside, one wonders just how P. Drummond's engines might have developed had he displayed a little more independence? However, P. Drummond spread the Drummond-way to the parts of Scotland the elder Drummond did not directly reach, so that Scottish locomotive design was virtually Drummond design.

After rather more than 40 days' wandering in the engineering wilderness, D. Drummond was finally summoned to replace W. Adams as Locomotive Superintendent of the LSWR. There, he was not taking over a ramshackle works with locomotives of doubtful pedigree. Adams was a virtual legend in his own lifetime and was one of the great engineers of the 19th century. He had singularly produced specific locomotive features that were widely used in Britain and abroad, had thoroughly modernised the company's locomotive stock and vastly improved Nine Elms Works. In addition, Adams ran a happy ship, and worked in partnership with his Works Manager W. Pettigrew. For nine years, these two had set standards way ahead of many other English railways.

As Adams' health deteriorated, so Pettigrew tried to hold the ship on an even keel but, with a relatively easy-going regime, complacency crept in, liberties were taken and standards came to slide. Evidence of this is only circumstantial but, Pettigrew was not chosen as Adams' successor. To replace one legend with another of almost mythological repute — for good or ill — is inspired and brave thinking, but any ideas the directors had about continuity, building on Adams' outstanding achievements and ensuring a smooth transfer of power were abruptly thrown to the wind.

Drummond's arrival at Nine Elms was of hurricane proportions, that fairly — or otherwise — swept through and made his mark in no uncertain terms. Drivers were fired for an odd tipple between duties, and any transgression meant sudden and instant demotion. Design and office staff found themselves working under an extremely hot spot-light and anybody who did not like it, well, they knew what they could do. More often than not, such a decision was taken for them. Out went the old, quite literally within a few weeks, never to come back, and in came the Scots. Drummond's men symbolically celebrated the 150th anniversary of Bonnie Prince Charlie's failed '45 rising, by arriving in London in considerable numbers — and they intended to stay.

Drummond's engineering principles, soon began to oust the established traditions of Nine Elms, as did his methods of working and organisation. Outside cylinders, right-hand drive and beautifully crafted and almost daintily styled locomotives were replaced by left-hand drive, inside cylindered locomotives of equal distinction, and a new hard-driving tradition. The regimes of Adams and Drummond were totally opposed in almost all respects, but both engineers' locomotives served the LSWR exceptionally well.

Despite the less-than-successful deviations from Drummond's norm — with the double-singles and multi-cylinder 4-6-0s, his locomotive legacy was enormous. His greatest single achievement was undoubtedly the design, layout and transfer to Eastleigh Works. Not surprisingly, when opened in 1910, it was the most advanced in Britain. All Drummond's experience of Cowlairs, St. Rollox and Nine Elms came to fruition in the fledgling Hampshire town. Eastleigh was to become the main works of the SR, and remains so for third-rail electric stock to this day.

There was still more though, for among the multitude who followed Drummond south came his former St. Rollox Works Manager, R. Urie. If ever it was possible to have a mutual working partnership with such an irascible boss as Drummond, Urie formed it. Should Urie have done nothing else in his life, he deserved credit for going a full 15 rounds with the old man.

During the master's lifetime, Urie's influence seemed little more than that of an India rubber to a piece of jagged metal, but once the old-boy had gone Urie reverted to his former master's basic principles and ditched all the experiments. Despite the Great War, Urie produced three classes of rugged, powerful, simple 2-cylinder, superheated 4-6-0s for goods, mixed-traffic and express trains. They were just what Drummond ought to have designed had he not been way-laid by multi-cylinder trickery, though they were never quite so sprightly performers as a true Drummond engine. These became the backbone of LSWR and SR main line services and ran until the last decade of steam, after further development by Maunsell. They were only finally ousted by old age and Bulleid's pacifics.

Whereas the Scottish/Drummond tradition came to an abrupt end on home soil, as first design and then building was switched to railway works in England, after Grouping, Eastleigh remained firmly wedded to Drummond's basic principles. Simplicity and strength, with a certain distinctive style, was the way of Urie, and Maunsell combined these with

Churchwardian ideals. Life at Eastleigh was lightened somewhat, the gadgets were thrown overboard and even the smokebox wing-plates disappeared. Still, much of the Drummond way survived until, that is, yet another revolution was to sweep through after Maunsell retired.

A glance at the list of Drummond's locomotive designs shows he was more than prolific: he produced great locomotives for all his employers. His first designs for the NBR were almost pure Stroudley, but when he branched out on his own, with the '476' class express 4-4-0s for the newly up-graded Waverley route, he hit the jackpot. These magnificent engines transformed the workings of that difficult line, and remained the staple express locomotive for over 20 years. From then on, Drummond was not a follower, but a leader. The '476' class was an excellent design in its own right, and was also the first of what became the archetype Drummond/Scottish 4-4-0, that were some of the finest locomotives to run on pre-Grouping British railways.

Other examples of future Drummond standards also took their bow on the NBR. Two classes of 4-4-0T appeared: one for the Clyde Coast expresses; the other for general suburban duties. These were his sole examples for, after rebuilding the '157' class 0-4-2Ts as 0-4-4Ts, in 1880 — based on another Stroudley design, he adopted that type for nearly all future passenger tanks.

One other NBR design of great merit was the '34' class 0-6-0 goods engine. This class was as good as any in its day while, as with many others, its versatility came to the fore working branch lines, local and the occasional main line goods, when well into its fifth operating decade. So, after a mere eight years and 211 locomotives, Drummond had whipped a motley bunch of press-ganged engines into a fairly homogeneous NBR crew. All classes except the '74' 2-2-2 were to out-live the railway itself, while all were of good advanced design and the '476s' were clearly outstanding. Drummond's star already shone very brightly.

If Drummond's work at the NBR gained him recognition in the Premier League of locomotive engineers, his efforts at the CR were to lift him almost to the very top. Almost, but not quite. When on the threshold of joining Webb and P. Stirling on their joint pinnacles, Drummond threw away nigh-greatness for a handful of gold: gold, moreover, of the 24 carat fool's variety. Maybe he thought that with all the senior railway engineering positions seemingly settled, the CR would offer little in the future. The CR could never join the highest league so, aged 50 years, he forsook all for an opportunity in Australia. If only he could have seen not only what disappointments lay in store for him, but also what his successors, and McIntosh in particular, were to achieve, he might never have left.

The CR locomotive position in 1882 was almost as dire as was the NBR's in 1875: there was great scope for improvement and to enhance a reputation. After rebuilding a variety of ancient relics, Drummond produced two designs better than any of their type then in Britain. The '294' class 0-6-0 goods engines eventually numbered 244 examples. Simple, sturdy, economical and unbreakable, they were everything that could be expected from such a locomotive at that time. For a few decades in the future as well, as the last was not withdrawn until the class had served fully 80 years. These 'Jumbos' were famously popular steeds and eventually worked all over Scotland in LMS days.

Just to show that Drummond really knew his stuff, his next design was the truly outstanding '66' class 4-4-0s. They were a model for Scottish express locomotives for the next generation and worked expresses for fully two decades over the whole of the CR from Aberdeen-Carlisle. These were the engines for which the drivers craved, and the CR cried-out for. Soon after taking over the Carlisle-Glasgow/Stirling services, double-heading was all-but eliminated and the number of trains needing a banker fell considerably.

The '66' class, though, really made their name in the 1895 Races. They performed magnificent feats of fast and necessarily economical haulage that, from his new post at Nine Elms, Drummond must have been delighted to see. From the templates of these tremendous locomotives, Lambie and then McIntosh went on to build still larger versions, and ultimately 4-6-0s, to give the CR a locomotive fleet unsurpassed in Britain. Drummond's legacy was most certainly not squandered.

Drummond's designs at St. Rollox encompassed the whole gamut of locomotive types, and he produced several types of saddle-tank that did much mundane work and earned good profits. His wonderful '80' class 4-4-0s gave the CR an unassailable advantage over the GSWR on the fast, remunerative and highly competitive Clyde Coast services, and who can forget the immortal 4-2-2 No. 123? This was really a Neilson & Co. engine, though Drummond had some influence in its design.

Though not a classic in their own right, the '171' class 0-4-4Ts, became forerunners of yet another great class, but that lay in the future — on another railway. In all, Drummond built 203 locomotives to his designs by the CR: including those built by his successors, the total was 372, a sizeable chunk of the locomotive fleet. Not only that, but he reduced the running cost per mile by over 15% at a time when they were often rising in England. Drummond's new designs — whether exotic, classic or plebeian — contributed immensely to such economies, while performing to standards hitherto unknown on the CR.

So, Drummond's locomotives and his overall work had placed him high in the national railway lime-light: a man of the future. Even though he resigned, so grateful was the CR board that he was given £1,000 for his efforts. In rough figures, using railway wages as a guide, that amounts to over £200,000 in today's terms. A vast amount of course, but one that pales into insignificance with some of the recent pay-offs to utter flops of imbecilic, greedy directors.

By and large, the locomotive stock on the LSWR was more than up to the mark when Drummond breezed into Nine Elms. He had a tinker with two new classes of Adams' express 4-4-0s, then nothing appeared for nearly two years. Perhaps he had over-done the executions? Despite following one of the foremost locomotive engineers, nobody would expect Drummond to be overawed, and his 'M7' 0-4-4T and 'T9' express 4-4-0 classes soon lifted him to the pinnacle of his profession. Those designs were pure classics, but there was far more powder in Drummond's dynamic keg.

The LSWR did not require a vast fleet of goods engines, but Drummond's '700' class combined 'M7' components with the best aspects of his earlier 0-6-0s. The original 'Black Motors' were one of the most distinctive goods engines ever, with a conical smokebox door that concealed an over-eager spark-arrester, though a more compact version was soon evolved. As with many things, keeping a locomotive simple and straight-forward often achieves the best results, and this was the case with the '700s': thoroughbred goods engines with a class life of 65 years. These must surely have been in the mind of the Rev. W. Audrey when he wrote about the twins 'Donald' and 'Douglas', pure Drummond engines through and through.

In between those tremendous designs of 1897-9 came Drummond's first experiment. Adams had been under pressure to build a single-driver for prestige expresses to Southampton docks. Whether the board attempted to exert such influence over Drummond is not known, but he did not favour single-drivers and, no doubt, realised that their era was drawing to a rapid close.

Drummond's response was, from a distance, another 4-4-0, but closer inspection revealed a 4-2-2-0, or a double-single: innovation followed by exasperation. Joy's outside valve-gear worked the rear driving wheels, and Stephenson's motion worked the leading axle. The four cylinders rather over-taxed the modest boiler, that was fitted with firebox water-tubes, and the 'T7' was neither a good starter, nor a particularly free-runner.

Distinctively elegant it was though, and Drummond was able to dupe the board, even if not his engine crews, by telling them that it was like having two singles in tandem, with only one crew. That is just what directors like to hear: something for nothing. Drummond was instructed to build five more — of the similar 'E10' class, but they were a let-down and he soon lost interest. He probably never believed in them anyway — they merely kept the board in order.

Thereafter, until 1904, a whole series of mixed-traffic and express 4-4-0s emerged from Eastleigh, each a little larger than the last. None was brilliant, unlike the 'T9s', but all were successful and versatile: even more so when superheated. Then, in 1905, Drummond really pushed the boat out and produced the massively proportioned 4-cylinder 4-6-0, the 'F13' class. These, and the 'E14' version were, in theory at least, the most powerful passenger engines in Britain but, like their time on such trains, that was soon eclipsed. Neither were they much use on mixed-traffic duties, but finally found their niche hauling lowly coal trains that did not over-tax their less than copious steaming capacity.

If nothing else, Drummond was not a man to be easily beaten, and by 1910 he had introduced the 'G14' and 'P14' class 4-6-0s. These retained four cylinders, though had smaller boilers, steam-driers, firebox water-tubes and, unbelievably, different types of valve-gear. This mish-mash combination firmly renounced Drummond's tenets of simplicity and also, not surprisingly, the outstanding performances of his earlier designs.

Finally, in 1911 and treading the same multi-cylindered path, Drummond produced an express 4-6-0: the 'T14' class. Although they still featured many of his gadgets, these engines showed he was, at long last, heading in the right direction. As with all his express designs, there was a distinctive magnificence about their lines, only more so. As with some earlier 4-6-0s, they climbed hills well, but could run down pretty smartly as well. Their long narrow grate caused problems for inexperienced firemen — and with only ten engines that was not unusual, and they could be difficult to handle. Still, a 'Paddleboat' at speed was a fine sight, and they were responsible for hauling the best non-stop London-Bournemouth trains that, from 1912, took just two hours.

With piston valves, four in-line cylinders and a 200 psi boiler pressure, the 'T14s' were occasional outstanding performers. Had Drummond lived longer, no doubt their numbers would have multiplied and, although never the most economical of engines, their performance would have become more consistent. As it was, neither Urie nor Maunsell could really wring the best from them, but they remained front-line express engines until Urie's 'N15s' were rebuilt into the 'King Arthur' class, in the 1920s. There is little doubt though, that a good 'T14' with an experienced crew could perform close to the highest express standards in Britain, until railway Grouping.

That was not quite the last of Drummond either. As if he

Drummond's 'L12' class 4-4-0s were given the nick-name 'Large Bulldog', as they were almost identical to his 'S11' 'Small Bulldogs', except for larger driving wheels. Built to work Bournemouth and West Country expresses, these engines were capable of over 80mph. No. 433 stands in the yard at Nine Elms. It was an 'L12' that was involved in the serious accident at Salisbury, in 1906.

had just about had enough of complex locomotives that were, at best prima donna's and, at worst, like an obese man running up hill, he went back to basics, added some of the latest touches and produced a final classic. The 'D15' class might have been Drummond's valedictory word on express locomotive design, but they were more a thoroughly outstanding late-Victorian design, that incorporated many features then coming into widespread use, than anything remotely ground-breaking. With piston valves, Walschaert's valve-gear, high boiler pressure, yet still having a few of Drummond's gadgets, the 'D15s' were fast, free-running and powerful engines. Eventually superheated, they also hauled front-line expresses until the advent of the 'King Arthurs', and then performed secondary duties until withdrawn by the mid-1950s. An apt finale for a great engineer.

Drummond also tinkered with steam railcars and, some rather diminutive engines for motor-trains. These were not a success, mainly due their inflexibility, but perhaps the ultimate demonstration of his esteem and power was the 'F9' class, or The Bug. Now, many railways had a directors' saloon, perhaps even with a dedicated engine, such as the CR's No. 123. Most Locomotive Superintendents requisitioned a locomotive to take them on an inspection, but nobody had their own personal transport, not even Webb. Such was Drummond's esteem and power, that the unique 4-2-4T single-driver had a permanently attached coach and a regular crew.

The Bug conveyed Drummond from Surbiton to Nine Elms and, later, Eastleigh. It was also used for the odd guest and, less happily for some, to take the old man round the system. Apprehension and fear often greeted the sight of the little train as it crossed over to an unwary locomotive shed. There were also occasions when an express was minding its own business only for The Bug to creep up on the slow lines, and for Drummond to deliver a verbal broadside to the driver about slack running. Airs and graces were not a Drummond trademark.

If elegance determined performance, then Drummond's 'T14' would be peerless in Edwardian Britain. They were not quite so outstanding in everyday service, but their reputation as indifferent steamers has been somewhat exaggerated. They could set very high standards of performance indeed, but with an unfamiliar crew could also get up to more than a few little tricks. Of course, they were modestly improved by superheating, but somehow never quite overcame their awkward reputation, and subsequent alterations did nothing for their appearance. No. 452 makes a quite majestic sight as it awaits the right of way, from Waterloo. *(NRM)*

Despite Drummond's many achievements of locomotive design and re-organising locomotive works, calling him a great locomotive engineer still rests uneasily, especially in southern England. Every engineer had his comparative failures, and every Star of Steam had his own distinct characteristics and style, none more than Drummond. Perhaps it was his lack of professional learned activity that makes people unhappy about considering him a great, or maybe it was just the British knack of distrusting one who thinks he knows best. There is nothing quite so satisfying, it seems, than to watch such a person have a rather sticky egg slowly dripping down his face. Drummond's 4-6-0s did nothing to glorify his otherwise outstanding reputation.

Still, Drummond's achievements on three railways are quite unique. If it was not for his few flops on the LSWR, amounting to less than 30 out of 380 engines, he would have an unblemished record. In any case, if one has never failed, one has never tried anything of consequence and if, in his 60s, Drummond seemed an old-dog to be learning new tricks, he was slowly getting the hang of things. Had he not died in 1912, well perhaps the 'T14s' might have launched the start of a new era. Could Drummond have ever out-Churchwarded Churchward?

Whatever the reluctance to consider Drummond a great

locomotive engineer though, the legend lives on. Even his death only served to enhance the reputation of a man whose character was as fearful as he was fearless. After scalding his legs badly at Eastleigh, his wounds became gangrenous, and part of a leg was amputated. He died a day later, but legend has it that he refused anaesthetic while having the limb removed, a gesture — whether true or not — entirely in keeping with the granite-hard character that he was. Oh yes, for many decades hence, enginemen gave either a respectful or a more distinctive salute as they raced past his final resting ground in Brookwood Cemetery. Even in death Drummond was never ignored.

Drummond's time at the LSWR is the most public exposition of his reputation. Yet his work for two Scottish railways was probably of greater significance. In his native land, the Drummond path became the only effective route to follow and, I suppose, such slavish adherence might have contributed towards the almost total decimation of the Scottish design teams, following the 1923 Grouping. Drummond though, had moved on and was aiming ever higher. The last thing he would do was to rest on his, or anyone else's, laurels.

Always looking to go forward, Drummond had his own way for everything. More important, it fitted into a grand plan: strict and efficient design and build standards; stylish, yet hard-working engines; a free-steaming boiler with good steam-passages and large cylinders; and economical driving. Add to that, his occasionally tyrannical demeanour and he would certainly not have been able to live an anonymous life these days. Just imagine putting the glare of the modern media onto the railways of 100 years ago: Drummond would fill the front, back and analysis pages of the daily papers.

Drummond though, was unique. He did everything his way. There was no room for compromise. Yes, he had his flops, but look at his numerous triumphs. Like Muhammed Ali, Drummond become a great, if not quite the undisputed, champion not once, but three times. That was the true measure of his ultimate greatness.

Drummond's Locomotive Designs

North British Railway

YEAR	CLASS	WHEEL ARRANGEMENT	CYLINDERS (INCHES)	BOILER PRESSURE	DRIVING-WHEEL DIAMETER	WEIGHT	No. in CLASS
1875	165	0-6-0T	15 x 22	140 psi	4' 6"	33½ tons	25
1876	100	0-6-0	18 x 26	150 psi	5 ft.	38¾ tons	32
1876	474	2-2-2	17 x 24	150 psi	7 ft.	38T 8 cwt	2
1876	476	4-4-0	18 x 26	150 psi	6' 6"	44¼ tons	12
1877	157	0-4-2/4T	17 x 24	140 psi	5' 9"	45 tons	6
1879	494	4-4-0T	17 x 26	150 psi	6 ft.	47¼ tons	3
1879	34	0-6-0	17 x 24	150 psi	5 ft.	37¾ tons	101
1880	72	4-4-0T	18 x 22	140 psi	5 ft.	35¼ tons	30

Caledonian Railway

YEAR	CLASS	WHEEL ARRANGEMENT	CYLINDERS (INCHES)	BOILER PRESSURE	DRIVING-WHEEL DIAMETER	WEIGHT	No. in CLASS
1883	294/711	0-6-0	18 x 26	150 psi	5 ft.	41¼ tons	244
1884	66	4-4-0	18 x 26	150 psi	6' 6"	46 tons	29
1884	171	0-4-4T	16 x 22	150 psi	5 ft.	37¾ tons	24
1885	264	0-4-0ST	(o)14 x 20	140 psi	3' 8"	27 tons	24
1885	262	0-4-2ST	(o)14 x 20	140 psi	3' 8"	31¼ tons	2
1886	123	4-2-2	18 x 26	150 psi	7 ft.	41T 18 cwt	1
1887	385	0-6-0ST	18 x 26	150 psi	4' 6"	43¾ tons	30
1888	80	4-4-0	18 x 26	150 psi	5' 9"	42T 7 cwt	12
1888	272	0-6-0ST	(o)14 x 20	140 psi	3' 8"	31 tons	6

London and South Western Railway

YEAR	CLASS	WHEEL ARRANGEMENT	CYLINDERS (INCHES)	BOILER PRESSURE	DRIVING-WHEEL DIAMETER	WEIGHT	No. in CLASS
1897	M7	0-4-4T	18½ x 26	175 psi	5' 7"	60¼ tons	105
1897	700	0-6-0	18½ x 26	180 psi	5' 1"	42¾ tons	30
1897	T7	4-2-2-0	(4)15 x 26	175 psi	6' 7"	54½ tons	1
1898	C8	4-4-0	18½ x 26	175 psi	6' 7"	46¾ tons	10
1899	T9	4-4-0	18½ x 26	175 psi	6' 7"	48¾ tons	66
1899	F9	4-2-4T	(o)11½ x 18	175 psi	5' 7"	37T 8 cwt	1
1901	E10	4-2-2-0	(4)14 x 26	175 psi	6' 7"	58¾ tons	5
1901	K10	4-4-0	18½ x 26	175 psi	5' 7"	46¾ tons	40
1903	L11	4-4-0	18½ x 26	175 psi	5' 7"	51 tons	40
1904	S11	4-4-0	19 x 26	175 psi	6' 1"	52 tons	10
1904	L12	4-4-0	19 x 26	175 psi	6' 7"	54 tons	20
1905	F13	4-6-0	(4)16 x 24	175 psi	6 ft.	74 tons	5
1906	E14	4-6-0	(4)16½ x 26	175 psi	6 ft.	74 tons	1
1908	G14	4-6-0	(4)15 x 26	175 psi	6 ft.	71 tons	5
1908	K14	0-4-0T	16 x 22	140 psi	3' 9¾"	32¾ tons	5
1910	P14	4-6-0	(4)15 x 26	175 psi	6 ft.	74¾ tons	5
1911	T14	4-6-0	(4)15 x 26	200 psi	6' 7"	74½ tons	10
1912	D15	4-4-0	19½ x 26	200 psi	6' 7"	59¾ tons	10

Steam Railcars and Motor Train Locomotives

YEAR	CLASS	WHEEL ARRANGEMENT	CYLINDERS (INCHES)	BOILER PRESSURE	DRIVING-WHEEL DIAMETER	WEIGHT	No. in CLASS
1903	K11	2-2-0	7 x 10	150 psi	2' 9"	23T 3 cwt	2
1904	H12	2-2-0	9 x 14	150 psi	3 ft.	31½ tons	2
1905	H13	2-2-0	10 x 14	175 psi	3 ft.	32T 6 cwt	13
1906	C14	2-2-0T	10 x 14	150 psi	3 ft.	24 tons	10
1910	S14	0-4-0T	12 x 18	175 psi	3' 8"	28T 2 cwt	2

DRUMMOND's PRESERVED LOCOMOTIVES

YEAR	CLASS	RUNNING NUMBERS	TOTAL
1886	123	(CR) 123	1
1897	M7	(BR) 30053, 30245	2
1899	T9	(BR) 30120	1

DUGALD DRUMMOND IN BRIEF

BORN: 1st January 1840, Ardrossan.
TRAINED: 1856-61, Forrest & Barr, Glasgow. Apprentice.
EMPLOYED: 1862, Peto, Brassey & Betts.
1864, Cowlairs Works, E.G.R.
1866, Lochgorm Works, H.R.

SENIOR POSITIONS: 1868, Works Manager Lochgorm Works, H.R.
1870, Works Manager, Brighton, L.B.S.C.R.
1875, Loco. Supt., N.B.R.
1882, Loco. Supt. C.R.
1890, Australasian Loco. Engine Works Ltd.
1891, Founded Glasgow Rly. Engineering Ltd.
1895-1912, Loco. Supt., L.S.W.R.
DIED: 8th November 1912 Surbiton.

RICHARD EDWARD LLOYD MAUNSELL
Making the Mediocre Magnificent

Do you know the secret of success? Many people attribute it solely to talent and sheer hard work. The reality is more a massive helping of good fortune, luck and an accident of birth, all mixed-in with those other virtues. So, Pele, a multiple World Cup winner with Brazil, is feted as the world's greatest-ever footballer. Yet because he was born in Northern Ireland, and therefore seldom had the opportunity to shine on the world stage, we shall never really know just how good was George Best, the greatest player Pele has ever seen.

The same is true for the public perception of a person's achievements. Take politics, for instance. Churchill is widely regarded as being Britain's greatest Prime Minister. He was undoubtedly a flamboyant character and did everything with a touch of panache. His moving and rousing speeches are certainly much better remembered than the somewhat more permanent achievements of Atlee, Churchill's sombre successor. Dynamism — a bit of swagger even — always catches the eye more than the thorough professional, even if one blinding success is followed by a rather less than dazzling sequel.

Thus, when it comes to great locomotive engineers, Maunsell pales in comparison with Collett, Stanier and Gresley, his contemporaries. Alongside his effervescent successor, Bulleid, Maunsell seems no more than a stoic pillar of orthodoxy, with little to commend him as an innovator either. Yet, like George Best, his stage was of humble proportions. Maunsell's engines were built in small numbers, and many were developments of older designs; his one major express locomotive performed with surly indifference; his only outstanding design was a relative minnow and his coaches were good, but thoroughly traditional. To cap it all, his many achievements were soon shunted into a far-off siding by his go-getting successor, and it seemed that, after 15 years lost in the woods, the SR's locomotive department had suddenly emerged into the bright light, or malachite green, of day.

With a bit of help from Lady Luck, it could have been so very different. Had Maunsell been CME of the GWR, he would have been half-way on the road to immortality when first he sat in the great chair. He would also have been a god-send to the LMS, in the 1920s. As it was, he was CME of the SR where steam, the ageing champion, faced a young athletic challenger, electricity. Maunsell went into the ring to defend the champion's belt with one hand firmly strapped behind his back, and a large budgetary ball and chain round each ankle. So, he relied heavily on his seconds and, though seemingly bereft of any effective output in the last few rounds, when the contest was over Maunsell just about emerged from the fray with a narrow points victory.

In any case, it was not as though Maunsell was fighting his corner in the heavyweight division. Only 311 steam locomotives were built by the SR during Maunsell's 15 years as CME, and a mere 91 after 1930. The former figure was either exceeded, or just about equalled by the LMS in six separate

years alone. In comparison, the SR was not just small-beer, it was barely the sediment.

Standardisation of locomotives and their component parts, a popular philosophy of the inter-war years, was not a roaring success either. True, Maunsell reduced the SR steam locomotive stock by nearly 450, or 19%, and the number of classes by almost 50% but, compared with Churchward's proposed standard list of six basic locomotive types, Maunsell proposed nine. To all intents and purposes, from whichever angle he is viewed, a schoolboy epithet of 'mediocre Maunsell' could just about sum him up. On the surface, compared with, say, his dramatic successor, Bulleid, it seems as though Maunsell was a mere management stooge, one who was browbeaten into permanent submission. Such conclusions could not be further from the truth.

Maunsell benefited from an orthodox and traditional upbringing. Born in Co. Dublin, in 1868, he graduated with an MA from Trinity College: a typical middle-class path. In 1888, Maunsell became a pupil of H.A. Ivatt at the Inchicore Works of the Gt.SWR, in Dublin, and three years later moved to the Horwich Works of the LYR, under the former Gt.SWR Locomotive Superintendent, J.A. Aspinall. For three years, he worked in the Drawing Office and became shedmaster at Fleetwood, before heading east — to India.

This adventurous act short-circuited the rather laborious, home railways' promotion procedure, and gave Maunsell a fair old shove up life's ladder. He became the District Locomotive Superintendent at Asansol, in Bengal, for the East Indian Railway, dividing his time between work and playing cricket. There is little doubt, that working amidst the penurious and mildly chaotic conditions of India's railways were of great future benefit to him.

Maunsell stayed in India for only two years before he returned to Dublin, in 1896, as Inchicore's Works Manager. Now Inchicore was hardly a forcing ground of revolutionary ideas, but it was the finest works in Ireland and had already sent three former chiefs to become CME's of English railways. As with all Irish railways, pennies had to be watched very carefully, but the method of working was less rigid than in England. A degree of relaxed flexibility — team-work rather than autocratic diktats — suited Maunsell's genial, yet ordered nature. There, he learnt to deal with untold daily problems and thwarted forward planning, and still left a clear desk at night. Lessons that were not forgotten.

Being reserved by nature, Maunsell made his mark as a punctilious worker and a loyal servant to his boss, R. Coey. He was no more push than shove, yet the ordered and gradual improvements in practices and output from Inchicore reflected his character and abilities. It was no surprise that Maunsell was appointed CME of the Gt.SWR in 1911, on Coey's retirement.

For some people, life is one big race, and they are constantly striving to meet a target and move on to the next

Probably inspired by the success of Churchward's '4300' class moguls, and certainly influenced by several senior GWR men who worked in Maunsell's team, the 'N' class moguls combined thoroughly modern design, with a suitable utilitarian look. They were, nonetheless, outstanding mixed-traffic engines and went on to serve the SR and BR very well indeed. No. 1414 heads a mixed goods train in the south-east. *(J. Kydd)*

challenge. Others are prepared to bide their time, see how things map out and to plan accordingly. Maunsell fitted the latter bill and, in any case, the Gt.SWR was not the sort of place where one made a big splash and moved on before the tidal backlash caught you out. Somewhat surprisingly though, Maunsell's stay as CME was short, and he only made a mere ripple rather than a tidal wave.

During his two years in charge at Inchicore, Maunsell was responsible for two locomotive designs, both developed from those of his predecessor — hardly a revolution. The first was the '341' class 4-4-0, that Coey already had on the drawing boards, to which Maunsell added a superheater and a Belpaire firebox. This was the most powerful passenger locomotive in the Emerald Isle, though was too heavy for much of the Gt.S.W.R's lightweight civil engineering. As such, it remained a singleton and was scrapped in 1928, but served to demonstrate that the new CME had kept abreast of recent developments in steam locomotive technology.

Of greater value was the '257' class 0-6-0 goods engine. These work-horses were based on Coey's '101' class, and Maunsell put his mark on the basically sound design in much the same way as before. Schmidt and Inchicore's own super-heaters were fitted to eight of these engines for evaluation, but only one was completed before Maunsell departed. These were decidedly more useful engines and the last was not scrapped until 1963.

Then, almost before he had got his feet firmly under the CME's table, Maunsell moved to the SECR. Presumably, there were few other hats cast into the ring, as Maunsell's physical credentials were thin on the ground: just two locomotives. Perhaps it was more a case of horses for courses, as the SECR locomotive department had begun to drift and fragment under H. Wainwright. Control was abdicated, Ashford Works was a sadly leaking ship and, although good locomotives were produced during the previous decade or so, increasing train loads and, just occasionally, speeds were getting beyond the company's modest locomotive stud. Britain's reputation on the

cross-Channel traffic was as much a joke then, as it is now.

Money was very tight on the SECR, so the ideal incumbent for the revised position of CME needed to have had a good workshop practice, be capable of working to a frayed shoe-string budget, had to be a clear and orderly thinker and planner, would adhere to — and enforce — company policy, and would need to produce the odd miracle to order. Given such a diverse mix of virtues, Maunsell was a wise choice — apart, perhaps, from Merlin. In time, it would prove to be positively inspired.

After a short gestation period, Maunsell discovered enough about his new department to assess his staff and its needs. He was not impressed. Essentially, the department was run by the Chief Clerk, H. McColl. Here was a gruff, tough, no-nonsense Scot in the Drummond/Stirling mould, though lacking the technical knowledge. That, though, did not prevent him ruling with a rod of iron. A mighty clash of thunder might have been expected when Maunsell began to instigate his methods, but McColl was astute enough to draw back from what little limelight there was at Ashford, and to resume the mundane duties more usually associated with his position. Indeed, the SECR owed McColl a debt of gratitude for holding the fort while Wainwright withered.

Within six months, Maunsell assembled a new team of senior officers. They deserve recognition not only for the part they played in re-vitalising the locomotive department, but for serving Maunsell virtually until his retirement from the SR — over twenty years later. Maunsell's trawl for these officers was not only wide-ranging, but displayed an open mind in not returning to his old haunts and bringing the tried and trusted along.

Having been impressed by Churchward's work on the GWR — and who could fail to be, Maunsell was able to recruit three vital members of his team from Swindon. G.H. Pearson, the Carriage Works Manager, was appointed as Maunsell's assistant and Ashford Works Manager. L. Lynes became the Carriage and Wagon Chief Draughtsman, and H. Holcroft — an engineer of originality and much behind-the-scenes work, was appointed to re-organise Ashford Works. J. Clayton, the Chief Assistant in the Drawing Office at Derby, became Maunsell's Chief Locomotive Draughtsman, and the team was completed with the arrival, from Inchicore, of C.J. Hicks as Assistant Works Manager. Once these melded into a working unit, sparks might well fly. Well, they certainly did, but not quite in the expected manner: man's greatest disaster to date was about to break forth.

Numerous people made personal capital out of the Great War, and Maunsell didn't miss out either. He was appointed as CME to the Railway Executive Committee — something of a surprise choice given the depth of talent with far greater experience; Churchward for a start. Maunsell had ordered the designs for Wainwright's un-finished 'L' class locomotives to be sent to Inchicore for checking, as his new team was not assembled. However, the recommended cylinder and valve alterations were not beneficial: a lesson was learned. Eleven of these superheated engines were built at Borsig's, in Berlin, and were delivered only months before war broke out. German fitters were even at Ashford in spring 1914, but war was not then imminent.

Much of Maunsell's war was spent organising the production of spares for a wide variety of British and foreign engines and stock, and was, of course, on top of the usual requirements of his employers. His new team had barely been assembled before it was separated and engaged on war work. All this slowed, but did not halt, the design of two locomotives Maunsell envisaged as future standards for the SECR.

First out of the hat came a mogul that combined Churchward's basic ingredients with a dash of Midland utilitarian seasoning, and was topped off with Maunsell's preference for high-degree superheat. The resulting 'N' class was, if hardly a stunner, one of Britain's first and finest true mixed-traffic engines. More important, it marked the first thorough application of Churchward's principles outside the GWR yet, with the adoption of high-degree superheat, further advanced the master's work.

Some locomotives, such as Gresley's A1/A3 pacifics, look the pure, unblemished thoroughbred racehorses that they are. The combination of wartime austerity, a drab grey colour and a need for easy maintenance might have compromised the aesthetics, but Maunsell's new mogul looked exactly what it was: a thoroughbred workhorse. That title would have suited Maunsell and his team though, they had hit their target. The 'N' class had a Belpaire firebox and taper boiler, with a unique application of top-feed within an apparent dome. Long-travel piston valves were based on Swindon principles and, in fact, the original superheater was a 2-row Swindon type, but this was soon replaced by a 3-row high-degree version. The potential was unlimited.

Hand in glove with the 'N' class was a singleton 2-6-4T, intended for main line express work: an idea borrowed from the LBSCR. The 'K' class engine was based on the 'N', but was not allowed on the former LCDR lines, because of their meagre maximum 17½ ton axle loading. These two designs were intended to form the backbone of the SECR, but as time wore on, so the government sought an end to the preponderance of smaller railway companies: wholesale amalgamation was in the air.

In advance of this idea, plans were afoot to design several standard locomotives to work throughout Britain. These ideas were hardly welcomed with open arms but, to keep Woolwich Arsenal busy, 100 'N' class engines were ordered and made available for any railway to buy. In the event, nobody wanted them and production was halted after only 50 were built. Eventually, the SR bought these at a knock-down price.

After the war, the SECR, was more run-down than ever before, having borne the brunt of the war work, yet continental traffic was about to resume with a vengeance. The ex-LCDR lines to Victoria were designated for this traffic, but even Wainwright's 'L' class 4-4-0's were prohibited from working the route. There was a desperate need for new engines, and the only immediate solution was the expensive option of double-heading by the various smaller 4-4-0s. Something bigger was needed, and time was of the essence.

From such dire situations happy conclusions can sometimes arise. Maunsell's team re-convened after the war and set to work on improving an old 'E' class 4-4-0. These lightweights were game little engines, but would have been overwhelmed by the proposed 300 ton continental trains. So, one locomotive was hastily fitted with 10 in. piston valves and generally given the 'N' treatment, and was then subjected to a crash dietary course to keep its weight down: tool boxes, wheel splashers and any non-essentials went back in the parts-bin. Suddenly, an engine that had been showing its age and Victorian ancestry, emerged from Ashford with all the zealousness and purpose of a born-again evangelist.

It was a stroke of nigh-genius. Ten further engines were rebuilt to this 'E1' specification and, almost unbelievably, went on to perform heroically on expresses for a further 40 years. Two years later, Maunsell's team undertook a similar job on the even older, non-Belpaire, 'D' class 4-4-0, transforming 10

Like their historical inspiration, Lord Nelson, these engines were unbeatable on their day. Unlike the great Admiral though, they did not have too many of those. It seemed that, whatever Maunsell might try, and — without a doubt — try he did, these fine engines worked at their own pace. As No. E859 'Lord Hood' shows, when working a continental train, they certainly had their glorious moments.

of these into virtual clone 'E1s'. More followed by 1927, until a total of 32 'D1' and 'E1s' gave the former SECR lines in Kent a game and spirited bunch of busy flyweights.

Still, 'N' class apart, Maunsell's team was less than prolific, despite the SECR's poor finances and the Great War. Holcroft had designed a conjugated motion for 3-cylinder engines, on the GWR, whereby two sets of valve-gear sufficed to work three cylinders. He had been consulted by Gresley when his similar design ran into problems and, after a single application, all future Gresley 3-cylinder engines featured the combined Holcroft/Gresley derived-motion. So, it seemed only natural to try Holcroft's conjugated motion on a 3-cylinder version of the 'N' class mogul.

The 'N1' emerged in the SECR's final year of independence, and proved superior to its 2-cylinder brothers on passenger trains. It also had a wider route availability: the smaller outside cylinders allowing its use on the restricted Hastings-Tonbridge line, for example. With this, the 'N' class in production and the 'K' 2-6-4T performing economically, Maunsell's team had laid the foundations to lift the SECR into a higher league. There was, however, the little matter of railway Grouping about to break onto a world still in turmoil.

The SECR, formed a new conglomerate with the LBSCR and the LSWR — the SR. In almost every respect, Maunsell's employers were the minnows of the trio, if not quite the laughing-stock they had once been. Their two partners had begun to electrify London suburban services — the SECR only had pipe-dreams. Their partners began to modernise and prepare for a post-war world — the SECR had very tentative plans. The SECR was rather like Cinderella, being invited to a ball where, unless a fairy godmother suddenly appeared, it would arrive in tattered rags. There was little sign of such intervention, but there was at least one asset.

When it came to appointing a CME, the SR only seriously considered the three constituents' incumbents. Urie, of the LSWR, was senior in age and had produced a group of fine, sturdy locomotives but was, at 68, a bit too ripe. At the other extreme, L.B. Billinton of the LBSCR was only 40 years old, though he had been a CME the longest. He had served overseas in the war and had some good designs under his belt at home. It was felt, however, that his experience was too limited — a bit of a gamble.

Maunsell was Mr. Middleground. Though his talented team had produced few designs, they utilised many up-to-the-minute features, were frugal and economical, and were clearly very capable. In particular, the impressive metamorphosis of two classes of OAP's into the sprightly 'D1s' and 'E1s' demonstrated an ability that would be essential to the new group. Electricity was deemed to be the power of the new, dynamic SR.

Maunsell's overhaul of Ashford Works was also a major consideration, and especially his nature as a team man. Not only was the new incumbent expected to assimilate three quite different engineering traditions, but he would be subjected to a tight, stringent rule from the General Manger's office. A Drummond or Gresley figure would have soon upset the applecart. Maunsell was able to accept his lot and to get on with the job in hand, for the overall good of the new company.

By 1923, in comparison with, say Gresley, Maunsell had produced few designs and done little in the way of innovation. This latter was not his forte, but over the next decade at least one new, or much-improved older design was produced by his team each year. None of these set the railway world alight, though some were of considerable interest, but each was designed with set tasks in mind, and not one was an abject failure.

Utility was a word that most suited Maunsell's designs, and none more so than his 3-cylinder 'Z' class shunting tanks. Equally at home shunting or on trip-workings, they were based in London and gained quite a reputation despite doing most of their work well away from the public gaze. No. 30956 appears lifeless early in BR days.
(W. Gilburt collection; K. Robertson)

Within a year, Herbert Walker became the sole General Manager. He had a vision — if not a mission — to transform the SR into the most modern in Britain. Steam was to be banished from all London suburban and medium-distance lines, as soon as possible. Maunsell had to keep things ticking-over while electrification — itself done on-the-cheap — had priority. That apart, steam was required to haul goods traffic, and 500 ton expresses to the West Country and the continent, at 55 mph average speeds. A target that was quite contra-dictory in reality.

The continental routes could not possibly cope with engines large enough for such trains, while the LSWR stations, starting with Waterloo, could not accommodate 15 coach trains. In any case, traffic requirements for the West Country were already more than taxing Urie's 'N15', 'H15' and 'S15' classes: respect-ively express passenger, semi-fast passenger/mixed-traffic, and mixed-traffic/goods locomotives. Anything more was beyond the pale. These three classes had promised much, but delivered little, mainly due to a frustrating inability to steam. By adding various 'N' class features and altering the blastpipe and chimney, Maunsell transformed these heavyweight sluggers into, if not soaring swans, more than willing, whole-hearted and reliable performers. Given the ever-increasing summer weekend traffic, the versatility of these vastly improved machines was to become a veritable god-send to both the SR and BR.

The 'N15s' evolved into the celebrated 'King Arthur' class, and never can such a relatively simple design have performed quite so admirably on expresses. They became renown for their free-steaming, no matter how inexperienced the crew. Crude, but effective, they epitomised all the sturdy, un-stinting qualities of the English yeoman, combined with just the occasional spark of brilliance. The 'King Arthurs' might have stolen the limelight, but their mixed-traffic brethren were every bit their equal on their respective duties, for over 30 years.

Such transformations, however successful, were not the same as designing afresh though. In the mid-1920s, Maunsell gave Holcroft his head to produce a 3-cylinder tank engine, the 'K1'. Now the singleton 'K' engine had its moments, but also its limitations. The West of England services were far beyond its capabilities, electrification of the former 'Brighton' lines was under-way — so it was not needed there, while its heavy-footed nature was less than suited to the feather-bed lines in Kent. The 'N1' had shown the performance advantages of 3 cylinders and was easy on the road, to boot. Perhaps the 'K1' would do likewise?

Of course, the 1920s was the decade of the Charleston, and if the 'K' class occasionally joined in the new national swing, the 'K1' was the first rock n'roller. With water surging about in the large tanks, and when hauling a fast train on poor track, the 'K' engine had a distinctive, almost jiving gait: for some reason, far from smoothing things out, three cylinders only exaggerated the rolling motion. Still, more 'Ks' were built, to become the 'River' class, and they entered service on the former SECR lines.

Now, if one 'K' and one 'K1' engines gave the permanent way staff a headache, a dancing troupe of 21 caused nightmares. De-railments were quite frequent until, in 1927, 13 people died in a disaster at Sevenoaks. It was the final straw and the lot was taken off the road. Trials were undertaken to ascertain the problem, with Gresley becoming involved for an independent view. The upshot was that, there was little wrong with the engines — on the LNER lines, but a great deal wrong with SR permanent way. The 'Rivers', though, carried the can. Despite a programme to up-grade the track, they were rebuilt as moguls — joining the 'U' class, and the 'K1' became the prototype of a 3 cylinder version, the 'U1' class.

All of which conveniently returns us to Maunsell's moguls. His 'N' class was extremely versatile and popular, however, something a little faster was needed, perhaps along the lines of a lightweight 'S15' or 'H15'. Maunsell's team, ever aware of the need for economy, based the new 'U' class on the 'Ns'. Only 30 were built initially, and were supplemented by the 20 rebuilt 'River' tanks. For a few years the class worked the Portsmouth line, while the 'U1s' saw service, with the 'N1s', at Hastings and Eastbourne, before being transferred to the West Country. The 3-cylinder versions, incidentally, had three sets of Walschaert's valve-gear, and Holcroft's conjugated motion was discarded. There's faith for you.

Maunsell's moguls eventually numbered 157 engines, and were great servants throughout their lives. Smaller than Stanier's later 'Black 5s', they were certainly game horses for all sorts of courses. These were the unsung heroes, as valuable to the SR as were the 'Black 5s' to the LMS. Maunsell and his team had, once again, come up with exactly what was required at the right, lowest, cost.

Mentioning which, Maunsell pulled another rabbit out of the hat in 1926 by improving Wainwright's 'L' class as he had earlier the 'D' and 'E' classes. The ensuing 'L1s' were, however, brand new engines. Set to work on Kent Coast and continental expresses, these further augmented the locomotive stud — that included some 'King Arthurs' by that time, and was evidence of some tentative improvement in the permanent way. While the 'L1s' looked positively antiquated alongside contemporary new engines, their appearance must have astounded foreigners who arrived at Dover, over 30 years later, to find a pair of these apparent ancient mariner's at the head of their boat train. Nobody could ever doubt their spirited abilities, or sheer guts, though.

At the height of Maunsell's prowess, he produced the 'Z' class heavy shunting tank and the 'W' class 2-6-4T. This latter utilised the discarded tanks and bogies from the 'Rivers', had the 3-cylinder arrangement of the 'U1s', and featured many parts from the 'N' and 'U' classes: no wonder Walker thought so highly of Maunsell and his team. These engines were destined for goods-transfer work round and about London: another small class perfectly matched to its intended duties at minimal cost.

And so we arrive at Maunsell's biggest moment. Plucky engines though the 'King Arthurs' were, they had no chance of hauling 500 ton trains at 55 mph day in, day out. For once, having a reasonably clean sheet, Maunsell's team set about designing the new king of the road. All sorts of options were considered and discarded, such as a compound or a pacific, but a 4-cylinder engine that combined the best Swindon principles with high-degree superheat emerged. Other features, such as cranks set at 135 degrees, that give eight exhaust beats per revolution, and a half-sloping grate demonstrated innovation and a willingness to try something new. Nothing, though, gave the new engine more distinction than its name, 'Lord Nelson'; well, that and the claim of it being Britain's most powerful passenger engine.

Publicity is one thing, reality quite another. As this was the only SR class with a part-sloping grate, few firemen had the required technique or experience. Despite the great size and expectation, the 'Nelsons', unlike the ever-willing, big-hearted and easy-to-drive 'King Arthurs', were a class of fops: all vain-glory, no heart. Oh, by heck, they could run and pull one day, but the next, just because the coal was put on in a different manner, the same engine could come over all sullen, a bit like The Rev. W. Audrey's 'Henry' who would not come out of the tunnel because it was raining. The SR needed these so desperately, and yet…

To no great surprise, Maunsell was never satisfied with the 'Nelsons', and authorised many, many alterations. One had 6 ft. 3 in. driving wheels, while other singletons had a wide firebox, longer boiler, cranks set at an orthodox 90 degrees, and a Kylchap exhaust system. Try as Maunsell might, not one of these made any real difference. If only Maunsell could put his finger on the right button, as he had done so often before, one felt that here was a great engine all ready, raring and roaring to go. As it was, like so many sportsmen with the talent — but not the temperament — to play at the highest level, so the 'Nelsons' only flattered to deceive. The lack of immediate success, coupled with the 'River' tanks fiasco even put Maunsell's job on the line. Just like George Best, Maunsell never had another opportunity to show the world what he could do.

Strangely enough, despite not really having the opportunity, Maunsell produced a world-beater in the most un-prepossessing of circumstances. A locomotive was required to work the restricted Hastings line, and if it could also haul 400 ton expresses at 55 mph, so much the better. Now, this was at a time when the GWR had its mighty 'Kings', the LNER the super-pacific 'A3s', and the LMS had the 'Royal Scots'. Another 4-4-0 from the SR was positively pre-historic. Neither were portents for the new class enhanced by its boiler being merely that of a shortened 'King Arthur' — by some distance hardly the last word on the subject, and the cylinders and motion were, effectively, three-quarters of Maunsell's recurring nightmare, the 'Nelsons'.

Rabbits out of hats were Maunsell's speciality though, and with good attention to detail and after a short settling-in period, the new 'V', or 'Schools', class began to re-write the record books. The Hastings service was modestly improved —

a line they worked for nearly 30 years; the reliability of the 80 minute Folkestone trains was transformed; and their meteoric performance on the Portsmouth line almost made electrification seem wasted. Finally, jumping into the big league, the 'Schools' mastered trains of 500 tons on the Bournemouth line with a nonchalance that bordered on arrogance, and how the men just loved their easy, free-steaming and free-running character.

Though positive minnows by contemporary express engine standards, there were no more responsive and willing performers in Britain, class for class, than the 'Schools'. Of course, some engines were faster, many were stronger, but nothing was seemingly prepared to work so hard for so long. The 'Schools' responded to all the demands their crews made of them and, by return, so the crews revelled in their high-spirited capacity. There had never been such a symbiotic relationship between engines and crews south of the Thames.

Such work continued until the 'Schools' were withdrawn, in the early 1960s. Suffice it to say, if this was Maunsell's greatest achievement, there could have been many more. The Civil Engineer, G. Ellson, ruled out several proposed designs, including a pacific, a compound 4-6-0 and a 2-6-2, as well as other sundry projects, such as a 4-8-0 and a 4-6-2 + 2-6-4 Garratt heavy freight engines. All these were drawn during the 1930s, just when output from Maunsell's team seemed to have dried up, on the surface — not a bit of it.

In fact, the Maunsell's final design was as traditional as a roast Sunday lunch. The 'Q' class goods engine appeared after he retired, in 1938, and was hardly a fitting memorial. The LBSCR Baltic tanks were rebuilt as the 'N15x' class, distinguished looking, but slightly disappointing, and that was that. Maunsell's last years may appear to have been long and drawn out, while his faithful team had begun to break up, but the combination of the depression and electrification all but halted steam engine production.

Ultimately, Maunsell's engines were reliable, economical and constantly and consistently performed above their station. Britain's other three main railways all had bigger engines, but none had a bigger heart. Only the SR would have happily handed expresses to 4-4-0s, day in day out, or run their most prestigious express to the West of England with a 4-6-0 that was almost obsolete before it was built.

Yet, for all that, Maunsell's engines were as distinctive as any — particularly after being given their unique smoke-deflectors, in the late-1920s. These hid the heavily built smokebox — a sure give-away of a bygone age and, while never graceful, left one in no doubt as to their origin. Entirely functional, these smoke-deflectors were a master-stroke, and imbued moguls, 'Schools' and 4-6-0s alike with a corporate identity as Southern Railway as were the 3-rail electrics.

Increasingly, as time went on, steam played a distant second fiddle to electricity. By 1937, most lines between Hastings and Portsmouth had been electrified, and plans for the Kent and Bournemouth lines were in hand. Maunsell and his department had to constantly give way to these developments, while re-organising and rationalising the works and staff. If money for new projects was thin on the ground, progress was still expected and old locomotives maintained. Innovation took a different form, running a really tight ship meant just that, and getting the best out of what was available became almost a science. Maunsell earned greatness not by simply doing what he did, but doing so given all the prevailing circumstances.

Maunsell's coaches epitomised his management style. They were required to suit three different loading gauges, and he was responsible for both steam and electric stock. A con-servative approach was taken — no un-necessary frills and articulated, stream-lined one-off sets here, but they were as comfortable as any in the country. Steel panels on wooden frames gave an image of modernity, while the interiors were conservative middle-England personified. Value for money, distinction and a little innovation: that phrase epitomises the coaches, the locomotives, and Maunsell and his team. That most of the electric stock was cobbled together from ex-steam stock to tight deadlines, and on a meagre budget, just about sums up the tenacity and ingenuity of the Maunsell years.

Maunsell soldiered on, ever the loyal servant, until his master, by now Sir Herbert Walker, was elevated to the company board. He suited the Walker regime down to the ground, and all his many attributes were fully utilised for the greater good of the company, its shareholders, staff and passengers. He does not come across as a great personality, like Gresley, nor a great innovator, like Bulleid, nor an inspired engineer with a long-term, revolutionary plan, like Stanier. It is that middle-England quality again, sober modesty and working within the tightest of parameters — not bad for an Irishman.

Of course, it is no more than debating matter as to whether Maunsell could have equalled the prodigious work and output of Churchward, Stanier or Gresley. By an accident of birth, George Best never had the opportunity of playing on the highest stages. Lady Luck determined that Maunsell would also be denied a similar opportunity. What he did though, was to successfully fulfil all that could be asked of him and more. That, after all, is a true measure of a man.

R.E.L. MAUNSELL IN BRIEF

BORN:	16th April 1868, Raheny, Ireland.
EDUCATED:	Armagh Royal School; Trinity College, Dublin. MA.
TRAINED:	1888-91, Inchicore Works, Gt.SWR Pupil of H.A. Ivatt.
EMPLOYED:	1891-4, LYR, Horwich Works and Drawing Office.
	Loco. Foreman, Fleetwood Shed.
SENIOR POSITIONS:	1894-6, Ass. Locomotive Superintendent, East Indian Railway.
	District Locomotive Superintendent Ansanol, Bengal.
	1896, Works Manager, Inchicore Works, Gt.SWR.
	1911, CME, Gt.SWR.
	1913, CME, SECR.
	1923, CME, SR.
RETIRED:	October 1937.
HONOURS:	1914, CME to Railway Executive Committee, of War Dept.
	President, ILE, 1916 and 1928.
Died:	7th March 1944, Ashford.

The 3-cylinder 'U1s' were most versatile engines, thoroughly in the Maunsell mould. While No. 1902 is having an easy time of it in this picture, when very nearly new, they could, and did, undertake much heavy and valuable work for over 30 years. Eventually, like all of Maunsell's moguls and 4-6-0s, they received their distinctive smoke deflectors.

(J. Kydd)

Almost universally regarded as Maunsell's finest design and, according to Bulleid, his only modern one, the 'V' or 'Schools' class was the most powerful 4-4-0 to run in Britain, perhaps even Europe. They were built with the Hastings route in mind, at a time when pacifics were either built or on the drawing boards elsewhere, yet went on to produce outstanding and truly magnificent work on all the SR's non-electrified main lines. Despite its pristine condition, it is hard to believe that No. 927 'Clifton' would be capable of some of the most exhilarating running in 1930s Britain. *(NRM)*

Maunsell's Gt.SWR Locomotive Designs

YEAR	CLASS	WHEEL ARRANG'T	CYLINDERS (INCHES)	BOILER PRESSURE	DRIVING-WHEEL DIAMETER	WEIGHT	No. in CLASS
1913	341	4-4-0	(i)20 x 26	160 psi	6 ft.	60 tons	1
1913	257	0-6-0	(i)19 x 26	160 psi	5' 2"	47¼ tons	8

Maunsell's SECR and SR Locomotive Designs

YEAR	CLASS	WHEEL ARRANGEMENT	CYLINDERS (INCHES)	BOILER PRESSURE	DRIVING-WHEEL DIAMETER	WEIGHT	No. in CLASS
1914	L +	4-4-0	(1)20½ x 26	160 psi	6' 8"	57½ tons	22
1917	N	2-6-0	19 x 28	200 psi	5' 6"	61¼ tons	80
1917	K	2-6-4T	19 x 28	200 psi	6 ft.	84 tons	20
1922	N1	2-6-0	(3)16 x 28	200 psi	5' 6"	64¼ tons	6
1924	H15 *	4-6-0	21 x 28	180 psi	6 ft.	80 tons	26
1925	K1	2-6-4T	(3)16 x 28	200 psi	6 ft.	88¾ tons	1
1925	N15 *	4-6-0	20½ x 28	200 psi	6' 7"	81 tons	74
1926	LN	4-6-0	(4)16½ x 26	220 psi	6' 7"	84 tons	16
1926	L1	4-4-0	(i)19½ x 26	180 psi	6' 8"	58 tons	15
1927	S15 *	4-6-0	20½ x 28	200 psi	5' 7"	80 tons	45
1928	U	2-6-0	19 x 28	200 psi	6 ft.	62¼ tons	50
1929	Z	0-8-0T	(3)16 x 28	180 psi	4' 8"	71¾ tons	8
1930	V	4-4-0	(3)16½ x 26	220 psi	6' 7"	67 tons	40
1931	U1	2-6-0	(3)16 x 28	200 psi	6 ft.	65¼ tons	21
1932	W	2-6-4T	(3)16½ x 28	200 psi	5' 6"	90¾ tons	15
1935	N15x á	4-6-0	22 x 28	180 psi	6' 9"	73 tons	7
1938	Q	0-6-0	(i)19 x 26	200 psi	5' 1"	49½ tons	20

+ Wainwright design with minor Maunsell modifications
* Maunsell modified Urie design; totals include Urie built engines
á Maunsell rebuild of LBSCR Baltic tanks

Maunsell's Principal Rebuilds Forming A New sub-Class

YEAR	NEW CLASS	WHEEL ARRANGEMENT	OLD CLASS	ORIGINAL YEAR	No. REBUILT IN CLASS
1919	E1	4-4-0	E	1905	11
1921	D1	4-4-0	D	1901	21

MAUNSELL's PRESERVED LOCOMOTIVES

YEAR	CLASS	RUNNING NUMBERS	TOTAL
1917	N	(BR) 31874	1
1925	N15	(BR) 30888 'Sir Lamiel'	1
1926	LN	(BR) 30850 'Lord Nelson'	1
1927	S15	(BR) 30825/28/30/41/47	5
1928	U	(BR) 31618/25/38 31806	4
1930	V	(BR) 30925 'Cheltenham' 30926 'Repton', 30928 'Stowe'	3
1938	Q	(BR) 30541	1

OLIVER V.S. BULLIED
A Man Out of His Time

Having already been a subject of books bearing the titles 'Master Builder of Steam' and 'Last Giant of Steam', Bulleid is now a Star of Steam. Yet, can one who designed a mere five steam locomotives — two of which were far-fetched experiments that were never likely to succeed, and two more that needed a thorough rebuild to get anywhere near consistently reaching their potential — be regarded as great?

For many, the answer is an un-equivocal, yes; for others, most certainly not. Yet, despite such apparent contradictions, Bulleid can be seen as the Sir Galahad of steam locomotive engineers. As a CME, he deliberately set out to innovatively prolong the life and usefulness of the steam engine, rather than to simply build locomotives that were marginally better than their predecessors. His engines were neither the most powerful, fastest, economical, cheap to build, reliable or easy to maintain, and nor did they enjoy any particular stylistic merit. He was both cursed and praised by his own staff, not inconceivably by any one person on any single day. Yet, if one wanted to stir up a hornets' nest among steam locomotive enthusiasts, one need do no more than to omit from this book, Oliver Vaughan Snell Bulleid.

With a name like that, Bulleid was clearly not going to be any old Tom, Dick or Harry. He was born in New Zealand in 1882, lost his father at the age of nine and came to Wales with his family. His was a nomadic childhood, a trait that never left him, for he eventually lived, worked and was educated in a total of nine countries. Such a domestic background was almost certain to produce a degree of unorthodoxy.

Despite becoming a premium apprentice at Doncaster under H.A. Ivatt, marrying the CME's youngest daughter and then serving under H.N. Gresley for almost 25 years — many as his Principal Assistant, the ultimate prize of becoming a CME came late in life. Bulleid was fully 55 years old when he was appointed CME of the SR, in 1937, a victim of the opportunities lost through Grouping in 1923. After a short settling-in period, he sprang into action seemingly hell-bent on making up for all those years he had spent waiting in the wings.

Once he attained his personal Arcadia, Bulleid marched at-the-double along a path to be paralleled only a few years later by Colin Chapman, the greatest racing car designer and founder of Lotus Cars. Both Chapman and Bulleid were creative original thinkers. Both planned an idea in broad terms, and often left the detail execution to subordinates while they moved on to pastures new. Both were boiling cauldrons of ideas, caring little for tradition. Each had the occasional flash of brilliance, more than the odd disaster, were open-minded enough to utilise techniques from other forms of transport — Chapman aeroplanes and Bulleid cars, and each produced epoch-making and ground-breaking designs in their own field. The main professional difference between them was that, whereas Chapman was a man clearly ahead of his time, and was a precursor of new trends, Bulleid was constantly out of step with his era and his various projects often emerged too late. Yet, both Bulleid and Chapman are, quite rightly, revered within their respective fields.

Having been the subject of one biography, a second was more prosaically entitled, 'Bulleid of the Southern'. It is for his work on that railway that he is best known, yet much of it was flawed — often seriously. Conversely, Bulleid's most successful, original work came while working under Gresley at the GNR and LNER. Still later, when CME of the Irish state railways, the Coras Iompair Eirean, far from being a Star of Steam, he oversaw its demise and master-minded its replacement by diesel locomotives. Yet Bulleid was attracted to Ireland by the challenge of building a peat-burning locomotive. Such a dramatic change-round demonstrated not so much his engineering brilliance, but the ability of a man in his seventies to alter his whole professional direction, and to use hitherto hidden talents in rational thinking. Not before time, in terms of both organisation and innovation, Bulleid had most assuredly arrived.

As with many former railway premium apprentices, Bulleid was able to gain rapid promotion. Usually, this involved moving through the lower grades of, say, the drawing office to, perhaps, become a shed foreman. For a couple of years after completing his apprenticeship, Bulleid did likewise, eventually becoming the Personal Assistant to the Works Manager at Doncaster. Then, in 1908, Bulleid obtained the position of Chief Draughtsman and Assistant Works Manager at the Frienville Works of the French Westinghouse Company.

Having married shortly after, Bulleid then embarked on three years working abroad, in France, Belgium and finally Italy, ending up as the Mechanical and Electrical Engineer of British Exhibitions Overseas, to the Board of Trade. This adventure ended in 1911, and by pulling strings and ignoring the dictum, never retrace your steps, Bulleid was appointed as a Personal Assistant to Gresley, the new CME at Doncaster.

A promising partnership was abruptly halted by the First World War and, in 1915, Bulleid was sent to the Western Front, as a Captain, on railway work. Serving in the field suited Bulleid and he was promoted to the rank of Major, but he spent the last year back in the War Department factory at Richborough. This was not a satisfactory post for him, but it first brought him into contact with electric welding, something for which he became an innovator in railway circles in the years ahead.

Returning to Doncaster in 1919, Bulleid resumed as Gresley's P.A. and was soon immersed in any number of small, but important projects, including work on the conjugated motion for the forthcoming 'K3' mogul. Then, he was appointed to succeed Edward Thompson as Manager of the Carriage and Wagon Works. It was here that Bulleid's work first came to the public eye.

Gresley's work in this field had already seen major, distinctive improvements not only on the GNR, but with coaches for the East Coast Joint Stock. Articulated coach sets were in regular use and Bulleid oversaw the introduction of a

5-car dining set, that included the world's first all-electric kitchen carriage; the whole set was mounted on just six bogies.

The first signs of Bulleid's own work came with some ECJS sleeping cars in which, rather than slavishly follow the somewhat claustrophobic Edwardian decor, he introduced a functional modern interior. A bit too functional for the time in fact for, like Chapman with his early cars, it did not exactly please all passengers and earned not a little public criticism. Even at that stage, Bulleid was not marching with the tune of the time. However, as he considered how the traditional decor might look 10-20 years hence — heavy and dated — and designed accordingly, he was just about proved right.

In 1923 came the Grouping of the multitude of smaller railways. Gresley became the CME of the new LNER and Bulleid was carried along in his wake as Principal Assistant: both moved office to Kings Cross. For the next 15 years, Bulleid made many telling contributions to the development of steam engines and other railway equipment. Some were for epoch-making machines, like the wheel valances on the 'A4s', others were on what were, ultimately, gallant failures, like poppet valves — borrowed from motor vehicle technology. Bulleid also contributed towards the magnificent decor and design of the streamlined coaches of the 'Silver Jubilee': his misconstrued work on the earlier sleeping cars coming into its own.

Innovation flowed to the fore. Bulleid pursued novel ideas from the trivial to the revolutionary. The former included a coat hanger that allowed one to hang one's upper apparel, and then the trousers — the reverse of the traditional hanger. Of greater importance was Bulleid's introduction of welded wagon and carriage underframes. This manufacturing technique saved time, weight and, ultimately, money and was eventually used on locomotive boilers. However, with all these many innovations, there was Gresley hovering in the background, with a steadying hand on the shoulder of his assistant with the tearaway ideas. It would be something that was sorely missed in later years.

Gresley's influence on Bulleid was profound, though it was not all one-way. They made an ideal team: one the innovator, organiser and, most important, the far-seeing realist with the spark of genius; the other the equivalent of the mad professor, full of ideas — many of great value, others not. Bulleid was the type of person who could solve the impossible and make improvements when nothing seemed amiss, yet who could never seemingly envisage the whole picture.

Bulleid, like Gresley, was also heavily influenced by the work of Andre Chapelon. He was directly involved on work to improve the steam and exhaust passages of Gresley's engines that, in the Kylchap 'A4s', were the finest free-steaming engines to run in Britain. The way Gresley and Chapelon worked, advanced, evolved and looked at any field of engineering that might offer scope for improvement, inspired Bulleid. Once in charge of his own department, on the SR, his initial work seemed to demonstrate a full grasp of all he had seen under Gresley, and that he had assimilated the lessons from Chapelon and others. Sadly, when it came to his own engines, they were seriously marred by flaws his former chief would never have allowed to be built, untried, into production locomotives.

The sprouting shoots of Bulleid's engineering genius began to grow at the LNER. It might have begun to flourish under his own regime somewhat earlier had he worked with a degree of orthodox engineering method: develop the idea, assess its performance and erase any flaws in isolation, and apply in prototype form before putting into production. Colin Chapman, when first making the quantum leap into Grand Prix racing, also tried to change too much, too soon.

Chapman used all the latest techniques: an aerodynamic body, fully independent suspension, a space-frame chassis and developed some of his own to concoct what should have been a potent mix. Well, potent is moat assuredly was. Lotus' cars were fast, light, agile and very brittle, earning the reputation of being thoroughly unreliable and not a little dangerous, as bits constantly fell off. Cooper won the 1959 and 1960 World Championships with their revolutionary rear-engined cars, but everything else about them was quite orthodox. Not so with Chapman. Everything was new at once, and his cars could not even win a Grand Prix. It was only when he learned to develop his ingenious ideas thoroughly, or to walk before he could run, that Lotus embarked on possibly the most thrillingly dominant era in Grand Prix racing.

Likewise with Bulleid, but boy did it take some time. In 1949, he resigned as the Southern Region's CME of BR to become, first, a Consulting Engineer to the CIE, and then its CME. Such was Ireland's economy at that time, that there was little scope for major innovation, nor for a massive scrap-and-build policy of Bulleid's beloved steam engines. Yet, he had been attracted by the prospect of designing a locomotive to run on the only effective natural fuel available in the Emerald Isle, other than hot air: peat.

This was no Bulleid pipe-dream. Previous attempts had been made, and failed dismally, but the first peat-fired power station was coming on tap so his optimism was not entirely misplaced. Peat has only about half the calorific value of coal and, if shaken about, as on a locomotive, disintegrates pretty rapidly. However, if a way could be found to carry a decent load of turf, and to sort out the draughting, it was not beyond the bounds of possibility to succeed. Bulleid was just the man to try.

It did not take Bulleid long to begin his task. First, he got the powers-that-be behind him by appealing to their patriotic vanity — using local fuel, and then began experiments by converting an ageing mogul to run on peat. This was way short of being a success, but taught some very useful lessons — mostly what not to do. Bulleid combined these with the experience gained from his last project in England, the 'Leader' class, to evolve one of the most original railway locomotives to run anywhere in the world. By not being in a hurry to change everything at once, Bulleid's peat-burning prototype showed that he had finally come of practical railway engineering age.

Somewhat unfortunately, and almost justifying the rushed excesses of his SR days, the Turf-Burner did not emerge until late-1957, just in time to celebrate the final demise of steam as regular motive power on the CIE. Unlike Chapman, who was ahead of his time and took Grand Prix racing far into the future, Bulleid had found a way forward for an outmoded form of transport. It was like evolving a faster, larger tea-clipper just as the steam-turbine came to prominence.

While the timing was, to say the least, unfortunate, the peat-burning locomotive was revolutionary. It had an 0-6-6-0 wheel arrangement, the two bogies each having two cylinders. It featured chain drive of the motion and the coupled wheels, developing a theme he introduced years earlier. Even a gearbox designed for diesels was considered: Bulleid was as aware of new developments as ever. There was a central boiler, mechanical stoker and two central cabs, giving it an undoubted visual distinction. No steam locomotive had ever looked or was anything like this, but would it run?

Unlike some of Bulleid's earlier attempts at pushing the advancement of the steam locomotive further than it appeared to want to go, the Turf-Burner was, if not a success, a prototype that showed considerable promise. The greatest pity of all was that, apart from Bulleid retiring in 1958, the Turf-Burner had conducted over 2,000 miles of trouble-free testing and could have been made to work. It had easily reached a speed of 70 mph, was reliable — though never looked like producing the 1,000 H.P. for which it was designed and, at just under 100lbs per mile, was not unduly heavy on turf consumption. It was intended to be convertible to oil-firing as well.

Here was a locomotive that, a decade earlier, could have been multiplied, perhaps even changed the course of Irish railway history. As it was, diesels had all but swept steam aside: there was to be no going back. Once Bulleid had retired, the Turf-Burner was shunted into a siding at Inchicore and never ran again. It was unwanted, unloved and, in 1965, unceremoniously scrapped. The Turf-Burner was tailor-made for the railway on which it was to operate. An ingenious answer to a question posed for over a century, and it needed a mind of vision to overcome the problem. Bulleid's reputation in the pantheon of the Stars of World Steam could have been realised. Instead the Turf-Burner became a very near miss, and is regarded by Bulleid's many critics as just another of his idiosyncratic flops.

Bulleid's tenure as CME in Ireland was, conversely, the most successful period in his professional life. Eventually, as the economic climate changed with coal prices rising and oil becoming ever-more cost effective, the Irish state adopted a policy of diesel power for their railways. In 1951, the first of 66 railcars arrived and then, in 1953, the Dail approved a major modernisation plan. This included the purchase of over one hundred diesel locomotives with, encouragingly for Bulleid, 50 coal or turf-fired steam engines, as well as carriages and wagons. The whole scenario might be considered anathema to a Star of Steam, especially one, like Bulleid, who has been seen as steam's last Champion. Immediate resignation might thus have seemed the appropriate answer for Bulleid, who was then over 70 years old.

That was not his style. Instead, Bulleid considered over thirty tenders to build the diesels and, in effect, oversaw and organised their whole introduction and take-over. Hundreds of ancient relics were swept away in a motive power change-over that ran as smoothly and sensibly as B.R's did chaotically and farcically. Effectively, just three classes of diesels worked the whole system: 60 x 1,200 H.P. Co-Co's of the 'A' class; 12 x 815 H.P. A1A-A1A's of the 'B' class; and 34 x 550 H.P. Bo-Bo's of the 'C' class. In addition, 19 'E' class shunters were built at Inchicore and 3 x 130 H.P. shunters were ordered from Germany.

Of course, there were many teething problems, not least those associated with the reduction of maintenance depots from 38 to 5, but Bulleid master-minded the operation with military precision, and ensured that steam could carry on in times of strife. The slightly dis-organised CME of the SR, who seemed to have so many innovative balls in the air that neither he nor his staff knew which to grasp next, had come full circle. Bulleid was now the supreme organiser who put all his ingenuity into setting-up the CIE for many decades hence, for which Ireland owes him considerable gratitude. Without Bulleid and his good sense, Ireland too could have ended up with BR's fiasco, whereby some of the numerous different diesel were withdrawn before the steam engines they were expected to replace. Fine for the train-spotter, but an economic and logistics nightmare.

Now if all this shows Bulleid at his best — the occasional ingenious contribution towards locomotive, carriage and wagon design on the LNER, the organisation of a traction policy change on the CIE — along with new coaches, wagons and the Turf-Burner, none of these really warrant his inclusion as a Star of Steam. It is only the design of steam engines that can earn that accolade, and here we run into trouble and controversy. An easy way to begin conversation among railway buffs, each unknown to the other, would be to ask, for example, who designed the better locomotives, Gresley or Stanier? If that would get most of those assembled at least listening, the way to hit the jackpot would be to ask something along the lines of, "...how good were Bulleid's pacifics?..." The ensuing argument would be long, heated and extremely rowdy.

Bulleid of the Southern does not attract indifference. He was invited to apply for the position of CME by none other than Herbert Walker and, in September 1937, began work alongside his predecessor, Maunsell. The two were as dissimilar as claret and champagne. One was a thorough team man, working for the good of the whole, while setting the parameters and leaving his team to get on and mature it with age. The other was an individualist who saw an opportunity both for himself and his employers; one who bubbled with ideas that could easily overflow, and who expected his subordinates to be, if not at his beck and call, then to carry out his commands without question.

Within months of taking office, along with new General Manager Gilbert Szlumper, the beginnings of a whirlpool were sweeping through the CME's department. Bulleid had spent some time assessing his inheritance and was not exactly impressed. Despite the shackles of electrification, with which Maunsell had meekly complied, the steam stock was not exactly what Bulleid had been used to. Old has-been's were still creaking their way round the system and, while yes, there were a number of decent engines about, they were viewed as products of the last generation. It was not a situation Bulleid was going to put up with, and he soon got the backing of Szlumper for a modest programme of modernisation and even a few new engines.

Bulleid's first few years on the SR showed much promise. First he took the perennial under-achievers, the 'Lord Nelsons', and made them realise the potential that had so eluded Maunsell. He devised a version of the Lemaitre multiple-jet blastpipe and chimney — arranging five 2¼ in. nozzles in a circle below the chimney, that demonstrated he had seemingly learned much from the overseas connections fostered by Gresley. With new cylinders, 10 in. piston valves, and improved steam and exhaust passages, engines that could be quite good one day, and dreadful the next, became the thoroughbreds they ought to have been in the first place.

Similar experiments were tried on the 'King Arthur' and 'Schools' classes, though without such startling results. These were more than capable performers in any case, and only about half of each class received the Lemaitre conversion. These initial alterations were not unlike Chapman's formative improvements to the Austin Seven cars when he started out: taking an old design, applying original and modern thinking, and wringing out a useful all-round improvement. It would not make an engineer's name, but was a highly promising start.

On the electric multiple-unit front, for which Bulleid was responsible for the chassis and bodies, his interior design for the Buffet cars for the new West Sussex electrification, showed an appreciation of modernity and functionalism, with a dash of elegance. The 2 HAL units for the Maidstone/Gillingham electrification of 1938/9 were little different from earlier units, but featured steel cabs — an innovation for the future.

Like Maunsell, Bulleid was asked to design a locomotive capable of taking the fast, heavy passenger expresses to both the continent and the West Country. With an axle loading of 21 tons, Bulleid also found his proposed designs foundered on the rock that was the Civil Engineer, G. Ellson. So, 4-8-0, 4-8-2 and 2-6-2 proposals all fell by the wayside, and Bulleid began work on a pacific. In the meantime, the rather nasty matter of the Second World War intervened, and with the danger of imminent invasion, followed by constant air raids, so the need for an express locomotive designed to haul 600 ton trains at 60 mph to the continent and 70 mph to the west, was some way down the list of national, let alone SR priorities.

Now, in the early months of the war, Szlumper had been replaced as General Manager by Eustace Missenden, a man who was, if not quite swept off his feet by Bulleid, perhaps bullied by Bulleid. Somehow, in those darkest of days in 1940/1, Bulleid not only passed-off his new pacific as a mixed-traffic engine, but incorporated numerous innovative, if not revolutionary, and often ill thought-out design features. Moreover, given the dire wartime conditions and the highly experimental nature of the design, Bulleid gained permission to built ten locomotives. He must have had an extreme confidence in his new design, for his old boss, Gresley, never built production engines that included so many new features.

Having been given the name of the SR's own merchant marine, 'Channel Packet', the first engine, number 21C1 — yes even that was unique to Britain, took the road as the first of the 'Merchant Navy' class. The details of this class are too numerous to list here and, in any case, there is a multitude of books devoted to them, but some of the more, shall we say, unusual features need to be considered. Electric welding of the steel Belpaire firebox, that included thermic syphons, was lighter, cheaper and capable of repair at maintenance depots. The air-smoothed casing and glass-fibre boiler-lagging not only saved weight, but was cheaper than the traditional cladding and fittings. Bulleid's own development of the USA. Boxpok wheels saved weight and were an improvement, while steam-operated firedoors and reverser, and a closer spacing of the main frames, all promised overall improvements.

It was, though, Bulleid's adoption of motor car technology to fully enclose his unique valve-gear for three cylinders, complete with chain drive, in an oil sump that was so utterly brilliant — on paper. It was also the locomotive's Achilles Heel and, because of a combination of poor seals and maintenance and, especially, the flawed idea of fixing the sump to the main frames, problems began right from the start. If one imagines the oil sump of a car being secured not to the engine block, but to the chassis, it would surprise no-one if it began to leak. This is what happened to the 'Merchant Navy' class. Quite possibly, a lack of space might have impeded the sump being secured to a sub-frame, but this would have cured the oil leaks. From these leaks, not only did the so-called maintenance-free motion need constant topping-up, but oil leaks caused wheel slipping and not a few fires in the boiler lagging.

Neither this, nor any of the other problems associated with the chains, fire-doors and steam reverser, should have proved to be insuperable, except in the early stages of a war to determine a nation's survival, and when there are ten engines to contend with. Why so many engines were built, especially when none of the above-mentioned problems — let alone others of a minor nature — had been resolved, is a major black mark against the SR's senior management, and Bulleid himself.

Not only that, but before the end of the war a smaller lighter version was under construction. These so-called lightweight pacifics, the identical 'West Country' and 'Battle of Britain' classes, eventually numbered 110 engines. Together

with a final total of 30 'Merchant Navies', these gave the SR and especially the Southern Region of BR, numerous locomotives that were more expensive to run and maintain, and more un-reliable than older designs. Though undoubtedly powerful, they were constantly under-employed and there was never enough work to justify so many locomotives, no matter how good. An image of a three coach train trundling through the West Country, hauled by an expensive green monster, was just as common as one of its fellows gloriously racing along at the head of a 15 coach express.

Today, the arguments still rage as to just how good were Bulleid's pacifics, as originally built. The 'Merchant Navies' were undoubtedly magnificent machines. Not quite so fast as an 'A4', nor as powerful as a Stanier 'Duchess', they were, nevertheless, quite probably the third finest express engines to ever run in Britain, on a good day. On a bad day — and as with a heavy drinker there were many of those, anything could happen.

The 'Merchant Navies' were never going to suffer the steam engine equivalent of anorexia, but they were more than a class above anything that had run on SR rails before. As such, engine crews loved them, even when they failed, and the class size was about right. The lightweights were also outstanding performers, so often being all but the equal of their big brothers, but why so many? Despite many crews preferring Bulleid's originals to the rebuilds of the 1950s, consistency and economy of performance dictated that something had to be done.

If Bulleid had sorted out the problems before series production began, the arguments over these engines would be irrelevant. Chapman, with his first true road car design, the Lotus Elite, produced one of the finest sports cars of its day. Like Bulleid's pacifics, it had too many innovations in one package and, though it could run like the wind, it almost brought about the demise of the company. He learned from the experience but, it seems, Bulleid was in too much of a hurry for his own good.

Bulleid designed one outstanding locomotive in 1942, the powerful 0-6-0 of the 'Q1' class. It was a relatively simple goods engine, but with modern steam passages, Bulleid's Boxpok wheels and Lemaitre exhaust arrangement, it was the most powerful engine of its kind in Britain. It was also one of the most unusual looking locomotives to ever be produced. The 'Q1s' were immensely successful though. In their field they were an outstanding and original design, but that particular field, like the countryside today, was fast diminishing.

One reason why Bulleid never solved the problems endemic in his pacifics which, incidentally, never matched their intended performance parameters, was that he was too busy with a project that promised the earth, and delivered a handful of dust: the 'Leader'. Like the Turf-Burner, this 0-6-6-0, 6-cylinder steam engine was a unique and brave attempt at taking the steam locomotive a giant leap forward. Designed to work all secondary duties, the concept was both brilliant, flawed and, like the pacifics, so far out-of-step with the time as to wonder about Bulleid's thought processes. Apart from a war of debilitating proportions, the austere post-war world demanded simplicity. Bulleid responded by producing a locomotive that would have been difficult to justify at the height of railway prosperity.

Not only that, but Bulleid craved, and almost succeeded in getting, permission to build 20 examples. In the end only five sets of frames were laid down, and only one engine was fully completed and ever ran. The financial disaster of the scheme, as it stood, could reflect nothing but ridicule on the man who initiated it: if 20 engines were built it could have been

All things considered, Bulleid's 'Merchant Navy' class engines were but a highly qualified success in their original form. Good one day, indifferent the next they might have been, nevertheless No. 21C15 'Rotterdam Lloyd' looks absolutely splendid as it cruises along the main line near Weybridge, with the down 'Devon Belle' Pullman in the summer of 1947. *(J. Kydd)*

Right —
Yes, I know this picture has been shown many times before, but there is something compelling about the combination of man and machine. Bulleid stands proudly beside his first pacific, 'Merchant Navy' class No. 21C1 'Channel Packet'. Can you blame him? *(NRM)*

Below —
Some like it hot, others... Without the maestro at the helm, the rebuilding of Bulleid's pacifics was probably the correct move. They were reputedly not quite so outstanding locomotives as when in original condition, but they were still splendid engines, and far more reliable and economical. It might not be a die-hard's cup of tea, but rebuilt 'Merchant Navy', No. 35013 'Blue Funnel', makes a fine sight when newly rebuilt, at Eastleigh. *(W. Gilburt collection K. Robertson)*

There once was a (very) ugly duckling..., but this one certainly never developed into a soaring swan. It is worth hunting out the preserved 'Q1' as it still takes the breath away. Despite that, it was the finest design of its kind in Britain and, while railway enthusiasts usually hated its half-finished look, they were great favourites of engine crews. No. 33016 stands at Reading, in 1950.

(W. Gilburt collection; K. Robertson)

catastrophic. Even if the engine had been made to work and, as with the pacifics, the arguments still resound on the matter, the 'Leader' would never, ever have reached anything like the performance or availability parameters for which it was designed. As a prototype, Bulleid deserves the utmost praise for ingenuity and brilliance; as a locomotive for production, he must have been blind to reality. Even Chapman had his un-mitigated disaster: the 4-wheel drive, gas turbine Lotus 56. Yet he did not put his company on the line, and ran the project alongside the more traditional cars. If Bulleid had his way, and nationalisation did not occur, it is possible that his locomotive building plans could have brought the SR perilously close to its knees.

Ultimately though, there was far more to Bulleid than his beloved steam locomotives. Indeed, with his all-steel 4 SUB emu, he set a standard and style of electric trains for future decades; even if a double-decker proved to be somewhat impractical. He part-introduced diesel and electric locomotives that were, to a large extent, successful. His post-war SR all-steel main line coaches were both modern and distinctive, although the infamous Tavern Cars adopted a retro-look decor, when the world at large was looking forward. A man out of step with his time — time and time again.

The multitude of brilliant ideas, followed by applications of rather modest success, show that Bulleid missed the vital quality of a right-hand man with a steadying hand. Under Gresley, when not faced with whole projects, Bulleid was in his element. Later on, at the CIE, he proved he could be as organised and restrained, yet thoroughly in tune with the political and economic climate, as any CME.

In between, when Bulleid had the virtual run-of-the-mill, he was found seriously wanting in judgement, both economically and practically. If he had a right-hand man, if he

developed a team, if he pursued all his ideas thoroughly and tested them exhaustively, then the debilitating faults in his pacifics and the 'Leader' could have — should have, been overcome. Bulleid would not have been such a controversial CME, yet for all the many professional honours heaped on him, many senior engineers regarded some of his projects, and especially his methods of working and basic engineering gaffes, with sheer disbelief: including his brother-in-law and fellow CME, H.G. Ivatt.

Undoubtedly, and quite rightly, Chapman is regarded as being a genius among racing car designers. He initiated so much that was revolutionary and, more important, made it work on the racing circuits. Yes, he certainly had his flops, but it was the ability to initiate, test and make ideas work before they were put into the racing team that really mark his brilliance. In comparison, Bulleid can best be described as a flawed genius. Even his most successful steam locomotive, the 'Q1', was given such an appearance as to cloud its many merits. The two classes of pacifics could have been just about the finest engines to run in Britain, yet they needed a fairly thorough rebuilding to achieve anything like their potential, on a regularly reliable basis.

With such a record, Bulleid falls some way short of a Colin Chapman, let alone a Gresley, Stanier or Churchward. There can be little doubt that he qualifies as a Star of Steam, but the Last Giant of Steam or a Master Builder of Steam? Those are very awkward questions. Bulleid achieved far more in life than most of us ever will, and far more than any historian and writer. Criticism is easy, doing something is not. Bulleid certainly did a lot. A little was brilliant, much was good, some a very near miss, and quite a bit downright poor or totally mis-guided.

Bulleid's locomotives are the real criteria for which he is included as a Star of Steam, but it is to his work under Gresley, and especially at the CIE, that marks the most successful periods of his life. His engines alone would leave Bulleid on the borderline as one of the better British CME's. Add the successes under Gresley and then running and organising the show in Ireland, and Bulleid runs through the finishing tape comfortably within the qualifying times, even if missing out on the main prizes. Chapman, though, would never have fallen so far short.

134

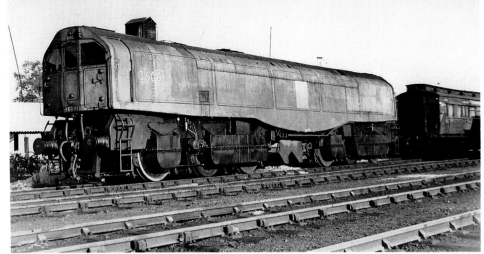

One doubts that a more contro-versial, or radical, design of steam engine ever hit the rails in Britain. Bulleid's 'Leader' class was probably a lot closer to being a success than appears to be the case. Flop it was in the end though, and the only one to run, No. 36001, is quite dead sitting in the sidings at Eastleigh.

(W. Gilburt collection; K. Robertson)

Bulleid's Locomotive Designs

YEAR	CLASS	WHEEL ARRANGEMENT	CYLINDERS (INCHES)	BOILER PRESSURE	DRIVING-WHEEL DIAMETER	WEIGHT	No. IN CLASS
1941	MN	4-6-2	(3)18 x 24	280 psi	6' 2"	96T 8 cwt	30
1942	Q1	0-6-0	(i)19 x 26	230 psi	5' 1"	51½ tons	40
1945	WC/BB	4-6-2	(3)16¾ x 24	280 psi	6' 2"	86¼ tons	110
1949	Leader	0-6-6-0	(6)12¼ x 15	280 psi	5' 1"	131 tons	1
1957	Turf	0-6-6-0	(4)12 x 14	250 psi	3' 7"	118 tons	1

Other Diesel and Electric Locomotives

YEAR	TYPE	WHEEL ARRANGEMENT	HORSE POWER	TRACTIVE EFFORT	No. WEIGHT	BUILT	OTHER
1941	Electric	Co-Co	1,470	40,000 lbs	99T 14 cwt	2	A
1949	Electric	Co-Co	1,470	45,000 lbs	104T 14 cwt	1	B
1951	Diesel	ICo-CoI	1,750	48,000 lbs	135 tons	2	B
1954	Diesel	ICo-CoI	2,000	50,000 lbs	132 tons	1	B

Notes
A = Bulleid/Raworth design
B = Bulleid/Cock design

BULLEID's PRESERVED LOCOMOTIVES

YEAR	CLASS	RUNNING NUMBERS	TOTAL
1941	MN (Rebuilt)	(B.R.) 35005/6/9/10/11/18/22/25/27/28/29	11
1942	Q1	(B.R.) 33001	1
1945	WC/BB (Unrebuilt)	(B.R.) 34007/23/51/67/70/72/73/81/92/105	10
1957	WC/BB (Rebuilt)	(B.R.) 34010/16/27/28/39/46/53/58/59/101	10

O.V.S. BULLEID IN BRIEF

BORN:	19th September 1882, Invercargill, New Zealand.
EDUCATED:	1894-99, Accrington Technical School.
TRAINED:	1901, Doncaster Works, G.N.R. Apprentice.
EMPLOYED:	1906, G.N.R.
SENIOR POSITIONS:	1908, Ch. Draughtsman & Ass. Wks. Manager, French Westinghouse Co., Paris.
	1909, Mech. & Elec. Eng. for Brit. Exhibs. to Board of Trade.
	1912, Principal Ass. to H.N. Gresley, G.N.R.
	1923, Principal Ass. to H.N. Gresley, L.N.E.R.
	1937, C.M.E., S.R.
	1948, C.M.E. of B.R. Southern Region.
	1949, Consultant Eng., C.I.E.
	1951, C.M.E., C.I.E.
RETIRED:	1958, to Devon.
HONOURS:	President, I.L.E., 1939-44. President I.M.E. 1946.
	President, Inst. of Welding.
	1949, C.B.E.
Died:	25th April 1970, Malta.

135

ROBERT ARTHUR RIDDLES
The Standards' Conundrum

When Bill Shankly first breezed into Anfield, home of Liverpool Football Club, he not so much began a revolution as brought together all that was good with the old regime, added his own unique ideas and set the club most assuredly on the road to domestic and virtual world dominance. The Shankly Legacy was developed by his successors Bob Paisley, Joe Fagan and Kenny Dalglish, and successfully exported to Blackburn Rovers by the latter, and Fulham by Kevin Keegan and more recently England.

A similar occurrence happened in rock music during the 1960s. Just as The Beatles had transformed the music scene with their distinctive brand of vocal harmonies, an American guitarist called Jimi Hendrix created a sensation with his revolutionary electric guitar playing. Many of the subsequent, so-called guitar greats, such as Page, Blackmore, Clapton and Beck were influenced by Hendrix and developed the playing of the electric guitar still further; their styles being copied and enhanced by modern musicians. The Hendrix Legacy certainly lives on.

Not unlike Shankly, Churchward took over the helm of a sleeping giant whose locomotives had consistently failed to match their initial dominating heights. His predecessor, Dean, produced some very good designs and improved Swindon Works, but there was little sense of keeping to a consistent plan. Churchward changed all that and, as we all know, realised the great potential of Swindon and gave the GWR the finest fleet of locomotives in Britain. His successor, Collett, enhanced Churchward's Legacy, but it was Collett's assistant, Stanier, who revitalised it during a memorable decade on the LMS. By 1948, as the railways were nationalised, Churchward's Legacy might have been running out of steam, but one more disciple emerged to revitalise and carry the torch onward, and to launch the last chapter of British steam on its final, glorious journey.

Only it did not quite happen for Riddles. While much of the blame for the ensuing years of torment lay elsewhere, his policy of building the Standard steam locomotives with a virtual reliance on LMS practices, caused long-term problems for the proud new national undertaking. Indeed, as the new railway's first Chief Mechanical and Electrical Engineer, Riddles' position was one of immense power, probably having a greater say in motive power matters than any former CME, with the possible exception of Webb. Apart from locomotives, Riddles was ultimately to be responsible for coaches and wagons as well. He was in an enviable position which, over the years, became quite invidious and was far from plain sailing.

The crucial question concerning motive power was fundamental to the role of BR in the brave, new post-war world. With a little less insularity of fore-thought, it was clear that the BR's future was less in its own, or the government's hands, and rather more bound up with external factors. By the late-1940s, Britain was in the throes of one of its periodic currency crises, and there was a devastating shortage of investment capital and a drive to export. As a result, there were fewer private motor vehicles than in pre-war days, and petrol rationing was rigidly enforced. Thus, a potentially relentless competitor, whose effects the railways has most certainly felt before the war, lay temporarily, and artificially, dormant.

Although air travel was hardly common-place, this too was a growing rival to the railways, especially given the dramatic technical advances brought on by the war, to say nothing of the surplus of aeroplanes. As with road vehicles, internal air transport was not considered a major threat to the railways in those drab post-war years, but such straightened circumstances could not last forever.

Riddles had immense opportunities at his disposal. There is, however, a subtle difference between a nationalised industry and a private company: the former should aim to provide the best all-round service at cost-effective rates, while the private company aims to make as much money as possible. It does this by providing the best and most appropriate service to maximise profits. Too often, the nationalised companies forgot the basic economic principles of cost-effective operating: subsidies came to govern their philosophy.

A new state-owned industry with indeterminate, ill-understood and over-ambitious aims and objectives — unlike private industry's profit motive, is likely to encourage empire-building, rather than concentrating on providing and improving its service. Using management from the former commercial industry in a monopoly situation, is even more likely to confuse matters. As far as engineering went, it was obvious that specialists had to run and plan current services, but were they the best people to plan ahead? It is fine leaving the details to the experts, but such experts — in any field — rarely take an objective view of the long-term prospects, whether we are talking about health, education, paper napkins or transport. There are, as one might expect, too many vested interests. Riddles was no different.

Electrification was Riddles' long-term goal. In reality, it was a far-off notion of which little was known, and with still less investment capital on anything like an appropriate scale, for anything other than small projects. Not surprisingly, Riddles never produced a plan and timetable that set realistic targets for the electrification of even the major main lines. Clearly, there was going to be a long, drawn-out interim period. The crux was, how best to carry on in the meantime, while protecting — if not enhancing — its custom as the competition hotted up, for that it most assuredly would? Despite its many good points, especially those emanating from the 1930s, steam power had not been capable of matching road competition: the experience of the SR electrification and its cheaper operating costs and higher revenues was a far better, though initially costly, bet.

The other matter, over which Riddles had no effective control, was the anarchic operating conditions. True, BR laboured under such ancient rules as those of common-carrier, but what enthusiasts understand as the Golden Years of BR, the 1950s, when branches and country stations were fully staffed and served by trains with a crew of three or more — the whole seemingly operated for their benefit alone, was an economic disaster. In a virtual monopoly situation, one can have staff dozing away long summer afternoons, tending their own garden patches, or shuffling through mounds of duplicate, un-necessary paperwork, but not when there is an increasingly desirable and dynamic alternative: the motor car.

Sadly, the railway management, and many workers themselves, were more concerned with traditions, old loyalties and preserving a way of life rather than facing up to new commercial challenges. I am not saying that railway workers were lazy — though many personal accounts of those years give much evidence of less than progressive minds, but the lack of innovation was immensely wasteful of scarce labour. No commercially minded business, especially a nationalised one, can operate under the conditions pursued by BR in its first two decades.

Finally, there was what became the bane of BR for the rest of its existence: government interference. The elections of 1951 saw the Conservative Party returned to power. They were far from committed to any nationalised industry, and policies soon began to change, change again...again...and yet again. This severely compromised current management and forward planning: circumstances guaranteed to severely handicap any organisation, whether a nationalised industry, private firm or the Girl Guides. For example, rightly or wrongly, from 1951-57 BR was busy building Riddles' Standard steam locomotives for cross-country, suburban, semi-fast and branch-line traffic. From 1955 onwards, large numbers of dmu's and demu's were built to replace those same services. By 1963, the Beeching Report was published and many of those very services were to be axed. Now what business, or venture of any kind, can operate successfully under such short-term about-turns.

It was no different for motive power either. Riddles retired in 1953. He must have known something was in the air and that if life was tough then, it would become even more so. In 1955, the Modernisation Plan was published and 14 types of diesel locomotive were to be purchased in small numbers, thoroughly tested for suitability and only then ordered to replace Riddles' steam engines: the Pilot Scheme was born. Okay, so this was a distinct change of policy from that pursued by Riddles, but it seemed a sensible, long-term plan.

Two years later, under pressure from locomotive manufacturers and BR's rapidly deteriorating financial situation, the government — Conservative, remember — panicked and ordered vast numbers of diesels. Not only were the tests far from complete and conclusive but, once again, there was no clear policy. Diesels were ordered that were wholly unsuitable for their tasks at the time, let alone in 20 years' time. Hence, English Electric Type 4's were never an adequate express engine for the future; Brush Type 2's soon needed expensive replacement engines; various Type 1's were obsolete while their steam predecessors were still hard at it; and the WR pursued a disastrous policy with expensive, unreliable and costly diesel-hydraulics. As enthusiasts, we might not have favoured these boxes-on-wheels over our beloved steam engines, but what variety. And what a commercial disaster and waste of public money.

This may all seem a long way from Riddles, but gives some idea of the increasingly difficult, almost impossible circumstances under which he laboured. Just imagine running your household on such idiotic, frenetic and wasteful lines; then multiply the problems to an industry with over 500,000 employees. Riddles' policy of using steam for the interim period, until electrification came to fruition was, perhaps, not

quite so muddled. However, it was flawed in essence and, in practice, was full of compromise and smacked heavily of former LMS favouritism and bias. Yet, under the circumstances, what else was he to do?

Over 40 years earlier, Riddles was a premium apprentice at the Crewe Works of the LNWR. This was far from being a passport to wealth, but offered the very best training that opened the door to untold opportunities. Indeed, six of our Stars of Steam were either former Crewe apprentices, or worked there in their all-important formative years. Just prior to the Great War, Riddles was a fitter at Rugby, and joined up for the duration in the Royal Engineers. He must have impressed the right people for, before the war ended, he was commissioned, wounded, married and began a family. In 1919, he returned to his old post, with his fitter's-mate also being a former officer in more trying times — one of many cases where a country's promised gratitude to its willing troops was not even paper-thin, and soon brought himself to management's notice.

Riddles and his mate were prepared to blackleg and drive a locomotive during a strike that did not quite materialise. Not surprisingly — in view of their lack of a combination spirit, they were ostracised by their fellow workers, so Riddles wrote to H.P.M. Beames, at Crewe Works, and asked for a position there. The two near-scabs were moved, took a wage cut, and Riddles soon found himself climbing the promotion ladder. A successful task in building pre-fabricated homes for Crewe's returning workers (homes fit for heroes?) saw Riddles promoted as Assistant to the Works Manager: he expected his career to take off.

Like many on the former LNWR, Riddles watched aggrieved as the LMS was hi-jacked by the insular and dogmatic ex-MR management. Mind you, the Ramsbottom/Webb legacy at Crewe Works, that had served country and company so well during the war, had never recovered, and Horwich and Derby were both in the ascendancy. Particularly the former, in fact, and Riddles spent some time there studying the production methods in the mid-1920s before returning to implement Beames' radical re-organisation. Beames envisaged a motor car-based production line system for locomotive repair, and Riddles spent from 1925-28 putting this into practice at Crewe. It was a great success.

He was then moved to Derby Works on a similar assignment, under H.G. Ivatt, thus beginning a relationship that was to last, on and off, for over two decades. After a highly successful time at Derby, Riddles returned to Crewe in 1931, and was there to greet Stanier as the new CME. Here, again, was the beginning of another successful professional relationship. Though shifted about during the remaining pre-war years, Riddles was heavily involved in the design, manufacture, repair and testing of Stanier's new locomotives, and was deeply impressed. He had his misgivings, such as Stanier's initial adherence to low-degree superheat and the front-end arrangements for the 3-cylinder 'Jubilees' — as did many at Crewe, but Riddles played an instrumental role in changing not only Stanier's opinions on these matters, but the designs themselves. These details, and Stanier's willingness to accept new suggestions, only served to enhance Riddles' opinion of his boss.

Then, after Riddles thought he had been shunted up the career equivalent of a dead-end siding, to St. Rollox Works, he found himself seconded to the Ministry of Supply, as Director of Transportation Equipment, at the onset of the Second World War. It was a position with great potential, and one that Riddles turned into a personal triumph. During the Phoney War, several of the Old Contemptibles that had served in the

The 'Austerity' 2-8-0s were particularly fine engines, and eminently suited to war-time production and service. Eventually, 935 were built, many of which saw service in various theatres of war, though some never made it that far, being destroyed or sunk en route. Fully 733 entered service in Britain, and No. 90085 hauls a north-bound freight on the Midland main line, in early BR years.

Great War, namely 'Dean's Goods' and Robinson's 2-8-0s were enlisted once again. These were not quite what the doctor ordered, and Stanier's '8F' went into series production for the War Department. These were neither cheap nor quick to build though, so Riddles started afresh and had the appropriately named 'Austerity' class 2-8-0s designed and brought into production during the mid-war years.

Despite his LMS background, these were more than just simplified '8Fs'. They had a round-top firebox and were designed to haul 1,000 tons at 40 mph. Once in production, from 1943-45, they were built at more than twice the rate of Stanier's engines, and were much cheaper and quicker to manufacture, thanks to savings in castings and other economy measures. The 'Austerities' found themselves employed in various theatres of war, and were later bought or used by several overseas railways. Eventually, 733 entered BR stock and — surely without any bias (?) — it is said they were preferred to the '8Fs' on the LNER.

While the 'Austerities' were most suited to their tasks, there was also a need for equally powerful engines with a lighter axle load. Riddles met this requirement by developing a 2-10-0 design, that featured a larger boiler and a wide firebox. To enable it to run on war ravaged or temporary track, it had a 13½ ton axle load and flangeless centre wheels, with the pair at either side having thin flanges to enable the locomotives to traverse tight curves. These giants of the road were an instant success, and though many worked on Britain's railways in the last years of the war, only 25 entered BR stock. The rest were warmly welcomed wherever they went, especially on the badly damaged railways of the former Nazi-occupied European countries.

His task for the Ministry of Supply finished, the LMS requested Riddles' return, to become the Chief Stores Supt. This was a senior position, and one that Riddles was keen to accept. C.E. Fairburn was acting-CME in Stanier's absence, and when the latter resigned in 1944, it was Fairburn who replaced him. Riddles was quite happy with that situation, but was less so when old boss and friend, H.G. Ivatt, was appointed Fairburn's successor, at the beginning of 1946. After all, Riddles had been responsible for the design and mass-production of two highly successful locomotives — despite there being no time for trials, and utilised sundry other locomotives for the war effort. He had something to say on this matter at the highest level, and was soon made Vice President in charge of engineering: in other words, Ivatt, as CME, now reported to Riddles.

Lady Luck, or a lack of her attention, is a major factor in the success, or otherwise, of most people. Riddles seemed to have received more than his fair share thus far, but he had put himself about and made his name in the right quarters while, when given an opportunity, he seldom spurned it. Whether Riddles would have been appointed to such exalted heights, had he not vociferously conveyed his feelings to the LMS President is not known, but once installed he was, effectively, the most senior locomotive engineer in the country. Within two years, Riddles had been appointed BR's new CM and EE, leap-frogging not only Ivatt, but Bulleid, Hawksworth and Peppercorn as well. Each of these, plus Ivatt, became the CME of their respective BR's region, while Riddles carefully worked out his department's policy within the prevailing political framework.

Like most former LNWR personnel, Riddles had witnessed many dreadful mistakes and biased decisions made by the MR dominated management, in the early years of the LMS. In particular, MR operating policies were not appropriate to the conditions on the former LNWR main line, while the small-engine locomotive policy would have been disastrous had it been pursued for much longer. Riddles was determined not to allow such nepotism again, but he still returned to the LMS to select his two senior Administrative Officers: Chief Officer (Locomotive Construction and Maintenance) R.C. Bond; and

138

Executive Officer (Design) E.S. Cox. In the event, only two of the senior officers within the three divisions of Riddles' department, namely Locomotive, Carriage and Wagon, and Electrical Engineering were non-LMS men.

Despite Riddles' best intentions, it was ex-LMS practices that came to the fore, but most people select the known, tried, tested and amply proved when choosing people to work with, not the opposite. Thus, the Churchward Legacy, via members of Stanier's team, came to prominence in a dramatically new situation: one in which the British steam locomotive might well reach its pinnacle.

Although Riddles decided that steam was the most appropriate propulsion to carry on until widespread electrification, he sought to make improvements in the operating and efficiency of the older locomotives. In 1948, the Interchange Trials took place between selected locomotives of the former companies, that threw up some decidedly interesting conclusions. The all-round stars of the show were undoubtedly Stanier's 'Converted Royal Scots', while the LMS 'Black 5s' were well to the fore in the mixed-traffic class. Of the former LMS locomotives it was, somewhat ironically, the 'Duchess' class that disappointed, showing no sparkle in performance, yet being out-done in the economy stakes.

Gresley's 'A4s', already the fastest engines in Britain and lacking little in power, proved to be the most economical express locomotives, though several failed during the tests, to confirm their fragile Achilles Heel. None of the former GWR locomotives shone and when tested again, using selected Welsh coal, this only confirmed their specialist nature: hardly much use for standard, country-wide engines. Bulleid's pacifics, of both kinds, provided some of the most sparkling performances, but the cost in terms of fuel was high, and they hardly met with Riddles' criteria of ease of maintenance and economy. If there was an ulterior motive behind the Interchange Trials to perpetuate the basic LMS design principles, then they were just about justified by the results and that, by and large, is exactly what happened.

As with all CME's, Riddles was far removed from everyday aspects of detail design for his proposed Standard locomotives, only still more so. Eventually, a list of 13 designs was drawn up that utilised common components wherever practical, and shared broad, general design principles. So, all had labour-saving devices such as a self-cleaning smokebox, rocking grate and a self-emptying ashpan. Most were general mixed-traffic engines and had two outside cylinders. All unnecessary complications were discarded, though many innovative ideas were tried that were, more often than not, a source of trouble or complaint, such as roller bearings for driving wheels or having a flat floor from tender to cab.

Soon afterwards, the list was pruned to 12 designs, while Riddles put his foot down with regards a 2-10-0 freight locomotive, rather than the 2-8-2 favoured by Cox and Bond. To refute charges of favouritism towards ex-LMS practices, Riddles made each Standard design the responsibility of a single works; a laudable aim that fooled nobody. Nevertheless, he was making an attempt to utilise the skills of the different regions, though the various orchestras still played to the LMS tune.

Indeed, compromise at the expense of excellence is one of the strongest charges laid at the feet of Riddles' Standard designs. Another was the sheer number of designs. Some of

For adherents of the former G E R , the 'Britannias' were great engines, for those of the former G W R , they were little more than a waste of time. Partisanship on both sides, I think. On the other hand, when given the attention any steam engine deserved, and needed, the 'Britannias' were excellent as crews of East Anglia, the former L N W R main line and Immingham shed would testify. Word also has it, that Cardiff Canton men — if caught off-guard — would even confirm they were better than any 'Castle' or, indeed, 'King'; heresy indeed. Still, enjoy a 'Britannia' at its very best, as no. 70012 'John of Gaunt' hauls Britain's fastest train in early 1950s, 'The East Anglian'.

Each to their own, of course, but to my eyes Riddles' 'Class 4' was the finest looking tank engine in Britain; especially in lined black livery. Combining functionalism with style, they looked precisely what they were, outstanding performers. Obviously heavily influenced by Stanier's earlier version, these engines were a great benefit wherever they were posted, although the arrival of the dreaded dmu's ensured they only enjoyed short lives. No. 80045 heads a St. Pancras-Bedford train near Mill Hill, in 1953. *(N.R.M.)*

---

these had little to choose between them, except for a lighter axle load. As much of BR's permanent-way was often in dire need of repair, might it not have been easier to have raised the weight limits while renewing the track, than to produce so many designs? Well, of course it would, but when faced with the enormity of permanent-way work required, it was not so clear cut.

During this interim period, while the Standards were being produced, yet more Grouping locomotives were built. In the event, 999 of Riddles' Standards were built, against 1,550 to older designs, by 1954. Of course, one might question whether the Standards were ever superior to these older designs in the first place. Certainly, one criticism is that by following the LMS path, an opportunity to really advance the cause of the steam locomotive was lost. Bulleid's innovative ideas were not necessarily ideal for widespread general service, but when they worked, boy did they go. By pursuing these further who knows what might have materialised. Then again, perhaps Riddles saw the writing on the wall for steam power, even before the first of his Standards was built. After all, Ivatt was more than keen on developing diesel power.

Riddles' Standards are some of the most familiar preserved steam locomotives. It would be tedious to wade through all 12 classes in detail, especially as many shared common features, but they successfully trod the fine line between traditional clean British lines, and the utilitarian approach so widely adopted abroad. Yet they were relatively easy to maintain and, in that respect alone, were a godsend in the days of full employment. Though some are little more than updated LMS designs, they bear a strong family resemblance with their high running-plate, cab, tender design, outside cylinders and Walschaert's valve-gear. Not surprisingly, they generally had a uniformity of performance fully up to Churchward and Stanier levels. Obviously, as standards of cleaning and maintenance deteriorated, their performance declined and became increasingly erratic, but they were an overall step forward for the steam locomotive, and yet, somehow, failed to deliver as promised and expected.

As such, it was a good job that the steam engine was not destined to hold the fort until the arrival of widespread electrification, or else there might not be too much of a railway system left today. Back in 1951 though, there was much to be optimistic about as the 'Britannia' class mixed-traffic pacifics were introduced: they were splendid looking engines. Despite numerous minor quibbles — mere incidentals such as the tender becoming detached at high speed, these soon showed an aptitude to perform to the very highest standards.

Over the next decade, the 'Britannias' performed outstandingly on the former GER main line, and ushered in the introduction of a much improved service. Even when diesels took over in the late-1950s, they were unreliable, and the 'Britannias' came back to show the hapless EE Type 4s how it should be done. Not unexpectedly, they did not fare so well amid the inbreeding of the former GWR. There, old loyalties died extremely hard and anything new was, at best, frowned upon. Even so, when concentrated at Cardiff Canton shed, the 'Britannias' were respected, perhaps even liked, and some crews preferred them to 'Castles' — blasphemy indeed. There were other high points for the 'Britannias' as well, such as their use on Cleethorpes-London expresses, but they could also be troublesome and, as maintenance standards fell, decidedly unreliable.

Riddles and his team seem to have become confused in their reasoning behind the medium-sized, mixed traffic tender locomotives. With three classes of mogul and two 4-6-0s, to say nothing of three classes of tank engine, there was little to choose between some of them. For sure, mogul 'Class 4' No. 76041 appears to performing well enough with its Midland outer-suburban train, but its 17 ton axle load was only 5 cwt less than the 4-6-0 version, and 15 cwt more than the 'Class 3' mogul; a bit of design extravagance in an otherwise austere world.

Riddles was also inspired by Bulleid's light-pacifics, and he authorised a smaller version of the 'Britannias': the 'Clan' class. Once again, these were fine-looking engines, but it soon became apparent that there was little work for them. Only 10 were built, further orders being cancelled, and they were concentrated in Scotland. While never being called upon to undertake any really demanding work, they were quietly competent locomotives, born almost of a whim and certainly not a well thought-out plan. Considering the menial tasks often undertaken by Bulleid's light-pacifics, the curtailing of 'Clan' production was one of Riddles' better ideas.

There were two 4-6-0 designs, the 'Class 5' based on the LMS 'Black 5s', and the 'Class 4' being a tender version of the LMS 2-6-4T. These were clearly members of Riddles' Standards family, though had something of a hunched-shoulder look, not having smoke deflectors. Both were equally fine performers, the 'Class 5s' being particularly fleet-of-foot, and often being preferred to the LMS version on its home ground. Several were built with Caprotti valve-gear, but these gained a reputation as slow starters.

Rather more anomalous were the class 2, 3 and 4 moguls. Quite what Riddles was thinking about with these very similar designs of increasing size, was never clear at the time, let alone in retrospect. There was little to choose between the latter two designs in either axle load or performance, and one might question whether the 'Class 4' was ever worth building. It was, however, the 'Class 3' that looked distinctly odd. Still having a high running-plate, yet with only 5 ft. 3 in. wheels and a small boiler, this was visually the least pleasing of the Standards. In fact, by the time they were built, most of the routes they were intended to work had been passed for higher axle loads, while the onset of dmu's soon rendered them surplus to requirements.

The 'Class 2' mogul was based on Ivatt's LMS design, but looked more rather civilised. It was the only BR Standard with a low running plate, and had something of a European look about it. These were fine locomotives and would have been a valued asset 20 years earlier. As it was, they too fell victim to the dmu revolution, the last 10 being built even as these railcars were making a rapid name for themselves and proving a big hit with the travelling public. Good though the 'Class 2' moguls were, once again one has to question the wisdom of their continued building.

To nobody's great surprise, it was a similar story for Riddles' three classes of tank engine. As a broad guide, these 'Class 4' 2-6-4Ts and 'Class 3' and 'Class 2' prairie tanks were similar to their respective tender-engine counterparts. Designed mainly for commuter, suburban and branch lines, all three performed fully up to expectations for steam locomotives: that, though, was no longer good enough. They were built at varying stages from 1951-57, the last 70 after the first dmu's entered service. To compound such insanity, the first withdrawals of the particularly outstanding 'Class 4s', began in 1962. Good though they were, these were obsolete as they were being built and, surely, older engines could have soldiered on just a little while longer?

Such ineptitude, idiocy, rank bad planning and un-intelligent use of resources, though not Riddles' fault by that time, was to blight BR for the rest of its days. No business with ambition could exist with such crass ideas: add a social duty as well, and the management of the 1950s could almost face charges of treason. It is easy to blame a lack of coherent, political direction at that time, which was probably true, but for highly paid, senior mis-managers to allow such a waste of scarce capital was the height of folly. The cost of such blundering continues to be paid to this day, to say nothing of the dreadful reputation it gained nationalisation as a whole.

The 2-6-4Ts were derived from the LMS version, while the 'Class 3' 2-6-2Ts featured a domed version of Swindon's No. 4 boiler, but were otherwise every bit a Riddles' Standard. These mostly worked former GWR lines, while the 'Class 2' was a barely altered version of Ivatt's 1946 design. If, in 1953, these engines were seen as welcome and attractive members of a new family, by the time the last were built, in 1957, one was asking the serious question, why? A good idea, far, far too late.

Quite unbelievably, an identical question can be posed of the most successful of Riddles' Standards: the '9Fs'. Thanks to the vast numbers of 'Austerities', there was not quite the pressing need for modern heavy freight locomotives and, ironically, the first '9Fs' were not built until after Riddles had retired. Once production began though, it continued until No. 92220 'Evening Star' was the last main line steam engine to be built by BR, in 1960. Just four years later, withdrawals began.

As with all the Standards, common components were widely used and these great 2-10-0s bore the strong family resemblance. The long boiler — though with a reduced diameter from that of the 'Britannias', wide firebox, large cylinders and five driving axles gave these engines enormous power, with traction to suit. They soon found themselves on the heaviest goods trains, and the image of a filthy, smoking '9F' hauling a long train of loose-coupled wagons remains an indelible picture: one so typical of the declining years of steam.

That was not all these were capable of though, for they came to still greater prominence on cross-country expresses, on the Somerset and Dorset and former GCR lines. Coupled with reports of speeds up to 90 mph, that must have been an impressive sight from the line-side — their 5 ft. wheels being a blur, the '9Fs' were the most versatile heavy freight engines ever to run in Britain. Various experiments and versions eventually emerged of this the largest Standard class, but they were all produced after Riddles had retired and so are not really part of this story. The sad fact is, that BR did its best to shed much of the traffic for which the '9Fs' were built and, once again, there was no real need for them.

Finally, after the destruction of Stanier's rebuilt 'Turbo-motive' pacific, at the 1952 Harrow disaster, Riddles managed to get a 3-cylinder express engine built. The 'Duke of Glou-cester' did not emerge until 1954, as a prototype, after Riddles had retired. Events soon overtook it, and any work to improve its indifferent steaming was stopped. As such, it was not a success and was withdrawn in 1962.

The 'Duke of Gloucester' was similar to a 'Britannia', but had a wider firebox, three cylinders with Caprotti valve-gear and a double chimney, and was otherwise something of a misfit. It was based at Crewe but, not having its faults eradi-cated, was favoured rather less than Stanier's 'Duchesses'. The 'Duke of Gloucester' finally came of age in the 1995 Shap Trials when it showed just what it could do when given a Kylchap double blastpipe and exhaust, and was in the pink of con-dition. There, it performed to the very highest standards, putting its competitors completely in the shade.

Judged by themselves, Riddles' range of BR Standard locomotives were fully the equal of those of any other Star of Steam, except for a heavy express design. They ran greater mileages, were more economical and required less main-tenance than any older designs. With their visual similarity, especially in the ex-LNWR lined black livery, they were handsome engines and would have been a valuable asset to any of the Grouping era railways — GWR included. Of course, there were many minor problems that needed to be ironed-out, just as there were for the designs of every other locomotive engineer. One might assume that, had the will been there, these Standards could have been developed much further. It is the Standards' misfortune that they ran most of their years in an increasingly filthy condition, and were poorly maintained and cared for. Such a deplorable waste of assets was seriously questioned at the time, and is beyond compre-hension in today's economic climate.

All that said, it was Riddles who was responsible for the pursuance of a steam-only policy prior to full electrification, and who then followed the safe-and-sure path of LMS designs for his Standards. In the conditions of the time, 1948, the latter choice was, shall we say, at least sensible, while the former certainly found favour given the Balance of Payments problems: oil had to be imported, coal was plentiful at home. On the other hand, he backed the wrong horse. As a result BR, rail transport's credibility and the country as a whole suffered and, one might suggest, continues to suffer the very serious consequences.

One cannot have expect Riddles to have predicted the future, but diesel technology was advancing at a greater pace than steam, especially in America, and full electrification was little more than a pipe-dream. Even if steam was to have played a role for a longer period than it did, what were basically updates of 20 years old designs, when built in the 1950s, would soon be found wanting. Any engineer knows that nothing stands still. Peppercorn's 'A1s' and 'A2s' did better work than the 'Britannias', as did Gresley's older 'A3s', while Bulleid had many ideas that would have potentially advanced the efficiency of the steam locomotive. Yet, these were virtually ignored when push came to shove. Instead, engineering conservatism came to the fore, and a great opportunity was squandered. The vision of Gresley and his high-speed stream-liners, or BR's close-to-successful APT, was beyond the ken of Stanier and his team, and Riddles was very much a product of that cabal. A policy of safe and sound over nothing ventured, nothing gained. It cost BR dear.

Hence the conundrum. No other Star of Steam was responsible for the design of a better, more comprehensive group of locomotives, and yet has been open to such criticism for doing just that. Taking a blinkered view, from the standpoint of the steam locomotive, Bulleid might have produced the more exciting designs had he become the CM and EE, but Riddles' approach and efforts were under-standable given the needs of the time. Viewed in a wider context, Riddles' policy was clearly not for the long-term. Just as many of the Standards were being built, their successors were entering service. Though the Standards could easily have enjoyed working lives of 30 years longer than they did, they were obsolete when still in the workshops. No other Star of Steam's earliest designs were so quickly superseded, although the last singles of, say, P. Stirling had similarly short lives and were soon overwhelmed by heavier trains.

Riddles was probably glad to get out of BR when he did — on the day the Railway Executive ceased to exist, just before the rot he had contributed to really set in. Despite initial intentions to enjoy a peaceful retirement, he became a senior director of a crane manufacturer, and travelled the world more than most people ever dreamed of doing. Some retirement.

Riddles' greatest work was not so much as an engineer, but as an organiser and planner, especially at the various works on the LMS. By the time BR came into being, Riddles' reputation was widespread and his range of Standards was the logical torch-bearer of Churchward's Legacy. Whether it was an apt finale for British steam is another matter. Only the recent adventures of the 'Duke of Gloucester' have finally laid the ghosts of unfulfilled promise and lost opportunity to rest.

In taking the Churchward/Stanier Legacy to its ultimate conclusion, Riddles showed that he was worthy of that tradition. He adapted it to the times, a period, I am sure, that Churchward would not have enjoyed with its restrictive practices and labour shortages. Unlike Dalglish and Keegan, the modern torch-bearers of the Shankly Legacy, that of Churchward/Stanier withered and died with Riddles. Perhaps H.G. Ivatt might have been the better man after all. Yes, he was imbued with the Legacy, but saw a definite role for diesels in the interim period. Though such a conclusion might seem harsh, and is made with all the benefits of hindsight, perhaps the ultimate Standards' conundrum is that Riddles was the wrong man.

Riddles' Locomotive Designs

YEAR	CLASS	WHEEL ARRANGEMENT	CYLINDERS (INCHES)	BOILER PRESSURE	DRIVING-WHEEL DIAMETER	WEIGHT	No. IN CLASS
1943	Austerity	2-8-0	19 x 28	225 psi	4' 8$\frac{1}{2}$"	70$\frac{1}{4}$ tons	935
1943	WD	2-10-0	19 x 28	225 psi	4' 8$\frac{1}{2}$"	78$\frac{1}{4}$ tons	150
1951	Britannia	4-6-2	20 x 28	250 psi	6' 2"	94 tons	55
1951	Clan	4-6-2	19$\frac{1}{2}$ x 28	225 psi	6' 2"	87 tons	10
1954	Duke of Glos	4-6-2	(3)18 x 28	250 psi	6' 2"	101$\frac{1}{4}$ tons	1
1951	Class 5	4-6-0	19 x 28	225 psi	6' 2"	76$\frac{1}{4}$ tons	172
1951	Class 4	4-6-0	18 x 26	225 psi	5' 8"	69 tons	80
1952	Class 4	2-6-0	17$\frac{1}{2}$ x 26	225 psi	5' 3"	59 tons	115
1954	Class 3	2-6-0	17$\frac{1}{2}$ x 26	200 psi	5' 3"	57$\frac{1}{2}$ tons	20
1952	Class 2	2-6-0	16$\frac{1}{2}$ x 24	200 psi	5 ft.	49$\frac{1}{4}$ tons	65
1951	Class 4	2-6-4T	18 x 28	225 psi	5' 8"	88$\frac{1}{2}$ tons	155
1952	Class 3	2-6-2T	17$\frac{1}{2}$ x 26	200 psi	5' 3"	73$\frac{1}{2}$ tons	45
1953	Class 2	2-6-2T	16$\frac{1}{2}$ x 24	200 psi	5 ft.	63$\frac{1}{4}$ tons	30
1954	9F	2-10-0	20 x 28	250 psi	5 ft.	86$\frac{3}{4}$ tons	251

RIDDLES' PRESERVED LOCOMOTIVES

YEAR	CLASS	RUNNING NUMBERS	TOTAL
1943	Austerity 7F	90733	1
1943	W.D. 2-10-0	600/1/3672/ 'Longmoor'	4
1951	Britannia	70000/13	2
1954	Duke of Gloucester	71000	1
1951	Class 5 4-6-0	73050/82/96/129/56	5
1951	Class 4 4-6-0	75014/27/29/69/78/79	6
1952	Class 4 2-6-0	76017/77/79/84	4
1952	Class 2 2-6-0	78018/19/22/59	4
1951	Class 4 2-6-4T	80002/64/72/78/79/80/97/98/ 100/4/5/35/36/50/51	15
1954	9F 2-10-0	92134/203/7/12/14/19/20/40/45	9

RIDDLES IN BRIEF

BORN:	23rd May 1892.
TRAINED:	1909 L.N.W.R. Crewe Works, Apprentice.
EMPLOYED:	1913 L.N.W.R.; 1914-19, Royal Engineers.
SENIOR POSITIONS:	1920, Ass. to Works Manager, Crewe.
	1925, Progress Assistant to Works Manager, Crewe.
	1928, Assistant Works Supt., Derby.
	1931, Assistant Works Supt., Crewe.
	1933, Locomotive Assistant to W.A. Stanier.
	1935, Principal Assistant to C.M.E.
	1937, Mechanical and Electrical Engineer, L.M.S. Scotland.
	1939, Director of Transportation Equip't, Ministry of Supply.
	1941, Dep. Director-General, Royal Engineer Equip't, Min. of. Supply.
	1943, Chief Stores Supt., L.M.S.
	1946, Vice President for Engineering
	1948, C.M. and E.E. for British Railways.
RETIRED:	30th September 1953.
HONOURS:	1943, awarded C.B.E.
	1950, President, I.L.E.; later awarded I.L.E. Gold Medal
DIED:	18th June 1983.

Based on H.G. Ivatt's puritanical design, Riddles' 'Class 2' mogul was the odd-man out among the Standards, with its lowered running plate. It was a throw-back to 1930s style and, to be honest, looked all the better for it. Let that not hide the fact that they were as modern as any steam engine in Britain, and performed their work efficiently and without fuss. No. 78016 makes something of a contrast with its other standard brothers. *(P. McGuire)*

Such was the depth of BR madness in the 1950s and 1960s, that quite a number of Riddles' '9F' class 2-10-0s, unquestionably Britain's finest steam freight locomotive, had barely a decade in service. For much of that time, as this picture of No. 92015 shows — on a down goods at Elstree, in 1955 — they were usually in less than pristine condition. Indeed, they performed outstandingly in levels of filth, grime and neglect seldom encountered in peace-time. The mis-managers responsible ought to have suffered the same fate as the engines. *(NRM)*